# 《金融研究》
## Journal of Financial Research

### 精编版
### 2021年（上卷）

《金融研究》编辑部◎编

中国金融出版社

责任编辑：马海敏　张翠华
责任校对：刘　明
责任印制：张也男

## 图书在版编目（CIP）数据

金融研究：精编版.2021年.上卷/《金融研究》编辑部编.—北京：中国金融出版社，2022.3
ISBN 978 – 7 – 5220 – 1548 – 4

Ⅰ.①金… Ⅱ.①金… Ⅲ.①金融学—文集 Ⅳ.①F830-53

中国版本图书馆CIP数据核字（2022）第040185号

《金融研究》（精编版）2021年（上卷）
《JINRONG YANJIU》（JINGBIANBAN）2021 NIAN（SHANGJUAN）

| | |
|---|---|
| 出版 | 中国金融出版社 |
| 发行 | |
| 社址 | 北京市丰台区益泽路2号 |
| 市场开发部 | （010）66024766，63805472，63439533（传真） |
| 网上书店 | www.cfph.cn |
| | （010）66024766，63372837（传真） |
| 读者服务部 | （010）66070833，62568380 |
| 邮编 | 100071 |
| 经销 | 新华书店 |
| 印刷 | 保利达印务有限公司 |
| 尺寸 | 169毫米×239毫米 |
| 印张 | 27.75 |
| 字数 | 360千 |
| 版次 | 2022年4月第1版 |
| 印次 | 2022年4月第1次印刷 |
| 定价 | 75.00元 |

ISBN 978 – 7 – 5220 – 1548 – 4
如出现印装错误本社负责调换　联系电话（010）63263947

## 《金融研究》
### （精编版）
## 编写人员

本 卷 主 编：王 信　匡小红

编辑部主任：王 鹏

统　　　稿：林梦瑶　李文华

# 前　言

《金融研究》是中国人民银行主管、中国金融学会主办，对国内外公开发行的正式出版物。创刊40余年来，《金融研究》已成为引领国内学术前沿的理论性、政策性、实践性兼备的权威学术期刊。2005年荣获第三届国家期刊奖。2012年入选国家社科基金资助期刊。《金融研究》编辑部设在中国人民银行金融研究所，负责期刊的组稿、审稿、编辑和出版发行等工作。

为面向国内外读者更广泛、充分地推广《金融研究》所刊载的研究成果，进一步提升期刊的学术和政策影响力，同时促进学术成果转化，更好地服务于中央决策和宏观管理部门的履职需要，《金融研究》编辑部自2019年起对已刊载论文编写精编版，每年分上、下两卷结集出版。

本书是《金融研究》2021年第1~6期共66篇论文的精编版，并结合当前经济金融热点研究领域分类编排。精编版论文为中英文对照，每篇中文内容约2 500字，充分考虑了国内外读者的阅读习惯和知识背景，对论文研究背景与意义、研究主题与思路、研究方法与理论依据、数据及来源、主要结论与政策建议、创新与贡献以及未来研究扩展方向等进行了概括和提炼，以期更完整、准确地介绍论文的精华与贡献。精编版同时兼顾现实性、政策性、学术性和可读性，注重提炼思想，阐述观点，力求用简洁生动的语言讲好中国故事，立足文章结论提出有针对性的政策建议，以供参阅。

如需论文完整版，请查阅正刊或登录《金融研究》网站（www.jryj.org.cn）下载论文 pdf 版。

欢迎扫描二维码关注《金融研究》
微信公众号（ChinaJFR）

# 目 录

## 01 宏观经济与货币政策

工业革命、金融革命与系统性风险治理……………………陈雨露（002）

庚子赔款的债务化偿付及其影响…… 王　信　张　翼　魏　磊（016）

利率市场化改革与货币政策银行利率传导…… 陆　军　黄　嘉（019）

货币政策能够兼顾稳增长与防风险吗？
　　——基于动态随机一般均衡模型的分析
　　………………………… 董兵兵　徐慧伦　谭小芬（022）

投资潮涌、双重金融摩擦与货币政策传导
　　——转型时期货币政策的结构调控功能探讨
　　………………… 战明华　李　帅　姚耀军　吴周恒（025）

混频数据信息下的时变货币政策传导机制研究
　　——基于混频 TVP-FAVAR 模型
　　………………………… 尚玉皇　赵　芮　董青马（028）

新型货币政策担保品框架的绿色效应………… 郭　晔　房　芳（031）

人口老龄化、养老保险基金缺口弥补与经济增长
　　………………………… 吕有吉　景　鹏　郑　伟（034）

老龄化、消费结构与服务业发展…… 颜　色　郭凯明　段雪琴（037）

智能化对中国劳动力市场的影响：基于就业广度和强度的分析
　　……………………………………… 周广肃　李力行　孟岭生（040）

资本回报、产权保护与区域资金集聚………… 曹廷求　张翠燕（043）

产业政策、创新行为与企业加成率
　　——基于战略性新兴产业政策的研究
　　……………………… 诸竹君　宋学印　张胜利　陈丽芳（046）

## 02　金融稳定与风险防范

中国企业杠杆：一个周期性问题？…………… 陆　婷　徐奇渊（050）

监测系统性金融风险
　　——中国金融市场压力指数构建和状态识别
　　………………………………………………… 李敏波　梁　爽（053）

资产透明度、监管套利与银行系统性风险
　　……………………… 陈国进　蒋晓宇　刘彦臻　赵向琴（056）

我国金融机构尾部风险影响因素的非线性研究
　　——来自面板平滑转换回归模型的新证据
　　……………………… 杨子晖　陈雨恬　林师涵　关子桓（059）

金融周期对房地产价格的影响
　　——基于 SV-TVP-VAR 模型的实证研究
　　………………………………… 钱宗鑫　王　芳　孙　挺（062）

基于共同冲击和异质风险叠加传导的风险传染研究
　　——来自中国上市银行网络的传染模拟
　　………………………………… 徐国祥　吴　婷　王　莹（065）

## 03 银行经营与企业融资

定向降准、贷款可得性与小微企业商业信用
　　——基于断点回归的经验证据 … 孔东民　李海洋　杨　薇（070）

银行竞争提高了企业投资水平和资源配置效率吗？
　　——基于分支机构空间分布的研究 ……… 李志生　金　凌（073）

融资租赁、银行信贷与企业投资
　　——基于2004—2016年中国上市公司的实证研究
　　………………………………… 赵　娜　王　博　张珂瑜（076）

去产能政策与融资租赁………… 史燕平　杨　汀　庞家任（079）

## 04 企业改革与创新发展

国企"混改"与企业金融资产配置…………… 叶永卫　李增福（084）

非国有股东治理与国有企业去僵尸化
　　——来自国有上市公司董事会"混合"的经验证据
　　………………………… 马新啸　汤泰劼　蔡贵龙（087）

债务结构优化与企业创新：基于企业债券融资视角的研究
　　………………………… 江轩宇　贾　婧　刘　琪（090）

股票流动性与中国企业创新策略：流水不腐还是洪水猛兽？
　　………………………… 林志帆　杜金岷　龙晓旋（093）

中国金融扩张下的本土企业创新效应
　　——基于倒"U"形关系的一个解释
　　………………………… 张　杰　吴书凤　金　岳（096）

数字金融与区域技术创新水平研究
　　　　　　　　　　　　……………………聂秀华　江　萍　郑晓佳　吴　青（098）

地方政府人才引进政策促进了区域创新？
　　——来自准自然实验的证据……钟　腾　罗吉罡　汪昌云（101）

开发区层级与域内企业创新：激励效应还是挤出效应？
　　——基于国家级和省级开发区的对比研究
　　　　　　　　　　　　…………………………蔡庆丰　陈熠辉　林海涵（104）

## 05　金融市场

央行货币政策报告文本信息、宏观经济与股票市场
　　　　　　　　　　　　……………………………姜富伟　胡逸驰　黄　楠（108）

多重信用评级与债券融资成本
　　——来自中国债券市场的经验证据
　　　　　　　　　　　　…………………………陈关亭　连立帅　朱　松（111）

私有信息、评级偏差和中国评级机构的市场声誉
　　　　　　　　　　　　……………………………………寇宗来　千茜倩（114）

资本市场开放能否提高企业信息披露质量？
　　——基于"沪港通"和年报文本挖掘的分析
　　　　　　　　　　　　……………阮　睿　孙宇辰　唐　悦　聂辉华（117）

卖空机制能够约束内部人减持吗？
　　——基于融资融券制度的经验证据
　　　　　　　　　　　　…………………………马云飙　武艳萍　石贝贝（120）

中国股市羊群效应的区制转移时变性研究……郑挺国　葛厚逸（123）

信息不对称、过度自信与股价变动………………………宫汝凯（126）

基金网络能够提高投资绩效吗？·················· 陈胜蓝 李 璟（129）

名义价格幻觉
　　——基于证券分析师目标价格预测的经验证据
　　·················· 何贵华 崔宸瑜 高 皓 屈源育（132）

## 06　国际经济与贸易

双边出口全球价值链实际有效汇率弹性理论测度及解析
　　···························· 彭红枫 刘海莹（136）

遭遇反倾销与多产品企业的出口行为：来自中国制造业的证据
　　························ 许家云 张俊美 刘竹青（139）

金融结构如何影响外资进入方式选择？········· 景光正 盛 斌（142）

汇率不确定性与企业跨境并购·········· 孟 为 姜国华 张永冀（145）

## 07　财税政策与地方政府行为

房价调控、地方政府债务与宏观经济波动
　　······················ 梅冬州 温兴春 王思卿（150）

"税费替代"：增值税减税、非税收入征管与企业投资
　　·································· 赵仁杰 范子英（153）

减税降费的价格和福利效应
　　——引入成本传导率的投入产出价格模型分析
　　································ 倪红福 闫冰倩（156）

政府间收入分成与财政收入预算偏离·········· 吕冰洋 陈志刚（159）

地方公共债务与资本回报率
　　——来自新口径债务数据和三重机制检验的经验证据
　　·················· 冀云阳　毛　捷　文雪婷（162）

财政引导金融机构支农的激励政策产生效果了吗？
　　·································· 行伟波　张思敏（165）

## 08　家庭金融、普惠金融与社会发展

住房财富对中国城镇家庭消费的影响
　　······················· 尹志超　仇　化　潘学峰（170）

住房公积金与家庭风险金融资产投资
　　——基于2013年CHFS的实证研究 ········ 陈选娟　林宏妹（172）

传统家庭观念抑制了城镇居民商业养老保险参与吗？
　　——基于金融信任与金融素养视角的实证分析
　　······································ 郑　路　徐旻霞（175）

回不去的家乡？
　　——教育公共品供给与人口回流的实证研究 ···李　明　郑礼明（178）

转入土地、农户农业信贷需求与信贷约束
　　——基于中国家庭金融调查（CHFS）数据的分析
　　······································ 路晓蒙　吴　雨（181）

义务教育能提高代际流动性吗········ 陈斌开　张淑娟　申广军（184）

企业精准扶贫行为影响企业风险？ ············ 甄红线　王三法（187）

绿色投资者发挥作用吗？
　　——来自企业参与绿色治理的经验研究
　　······················· 姜广省　卢建词　李维安（190）

## 09　公司治理与公司金融

员工薪酬竞争力与上市公司员工持股
………………………………………张会丽　赵健宇　陆正飞（194）

股权质押下的控股股东增持："价值信号"还是"行为信号"？
………………………………………………………徐龙炳　汪　斌（197）

高管团队内部治理与企业资本结构调整
——基于非 CEO 高管独立性的视角
………………………………………张　博　韩亚东　李广众（200）

商业信用与合作型客户关系的构建
——基于提供给大客户应收账款的经验证据
………………………………………江　伟　底璐璐　刘诚达（203）

独立董事返聘与公司违规："学习效应"抑或"关系效应"？
………………………………………………………杜兴强　张　颖（206）

大股东股权质押与上市公司资本运作…………陆　蓉　兰　袁（209）

避免亏损与公开增发盈余管理的识别与估计：
来自聚束设计的实证证据………………………张　红　汪小圈（212）

高管宏观认知具有管理者"烙印"吗？
——基于管理者风格效应的实证检验
………………………………………罗勇根　饶品贵　陈　灿（215）

企业家前台化影响企业价值吗？
——基于新浪微博的实证证据…孙　彤　薛　爽　崔庆慧（218）

## 01 Macroeconomics & Monetary Policy

Industrial Revolution, Financial Revolution, and Systemic Risk Governance
.................................................................... CHEN Yulu (223)

The Debt Repayment of the Boxer Indemnity and Its Impacts
.............................. WANG Xin  ZHANG Yi  WEI Lei (227)

Liberalization Reform, Interest Rates, and Monetary Policy
................................................ LU Jun  HUANG Jia (230)

Can Monetary Policy Reconcile Sustaining Steady Growth with Preventing Risks in China? An Analysis Based on Dynamic Stochastic General Equilibrium Modeling
...................... DONG Bingbing  XU Huilun  TAN Xiaofen (233)

Investment Surges, Dual Financial Frictions, and Monetary Policy Transmission: Demystifying the Structural Adjustment Function of Monetary Policy During the Economic Transition
...... ZHAN Minghua  LI Shuai  YAO Yaojun  WU Zhouheng (236)

The Time-varying Transmission Mechanism of Monetary Policy with Mixed Frequency Data: Evidence from MF- TVP-FAVAR Model
.................. SHANG Yuhuang  ZHAO Rui  DONG Qingma (239)

The Green Financing Effect of The Expanded Central Bank Collateral Framework ........................................ GUO Ye  FANG Fang (242)

Population Ageing, Pension Fund Gap Compensation and Economic Growth
.............................. LYU Youji  JING Peng  ZHENG Wei (245)

Aging, Consumption Composition and the Development of Services
.......................... YAN Se  GUO Kaiming  DUAN Xueqin (248)

The Impact of Automation and Artificial Intelligence on China's Labor
　　Market: Quantity and Intensity of Employment
　　　　……………… ZHOU Guangsu　LI Lixing　MENG Lingsheng (251)

Capital Return, Property Rights Protection and Regional Fund Agglomeration
　　………………………………………… CAO Tingqiu　ZHANG Cuiyan (254)

Industrial Policy, Innovation Behavior and Firms' Markups: Research on the
　　Policy of Strategic Emerging Industries
　　　　ZHU Zhujun　SONG Xueyin　ZHANG Shengli　CHEN Lifang (257)

## 02　Financial Stability & Risk Management

Corporate Leverage in China: Is it a Cyclical Problem?
　　………………………………………………… LU Ting　XU Qiyuan (260)

Monitoring Systemic Financial Risks: Construction and State Identification of
　　China's Financial Market Stress Index
　　　　………………………………………… LI Minbo　LIANG Shuang (263)

Asset Transparency, Regulatory Arbitrage, and Bank Systemic Risk
　　CHEN Guojin　JIANG Xiaoyu　LIU Yanzhen　ZHAO Xiangqin (266)

Nonlinear Analysis of the Determinants of Tail Risk: New Evidence from the
　　Panel Smooth Transition Regression Model
　　　　…… YANG Zihui　CHEN Yutian　LIN Shihan　GUAN Zihuan (269)

The Impact of Financial Cycle on Real Estate Prices: An Empirical Study
　　Based on a SV-TVP-VAR Model
　　　　………………………… QIAN Zongxin　WANG Fang　SUN Ting (272)

A Study of Risk Contagion Based on the Interaction Between Common Shocks and Idiosyncratic Risks: Evidence From the Simulation of Listed Banks in China ············XU Guoxiang　WU Ting　WANG Ying (275)

## 03　Banking Operation & Financing

Targeted RRR Cuts, Loan Availability, and the Trade Credit of SMEs: Evidence Based on Regression Discontinuity Design
·················· KONG Dongmin　LI Haiyang　YANG Wei (278)

Does Bank Competition Increase Firm Investment and Investment Efficiency? Evidence Based on the Geographical Distribution of Bank Branches
················································ LI Zhisheng　JIN Ling (281)

Financial Leasing, Bank Credit and Enterprise Investment
······················ ZHAO Na　WANG Bo　ZHANG Keyu (284)

De-capacity Policy and Financial Leasing
························ SHI Yanping　YANG Ting　PANG Jiaren (287)

## 04　Enterprises Reform & Innovation

Mixed Ownership Reform and Financial Asset Allocation of State-Owned Enterprises ······························ YE Yongwei　LI Zengfu (290)

Governance of Non-state Shareholders and De-zombification of SOEs: Evidence from the "Mixed" Board of Directors of listed SOEs in China
······················ MA Xinxiao　TANG Taijie　CAI Guilong (293)

Debt Structure Optimization and Corporate Innovation: A Study from the Perspective of Corporate Bond Financing
................................. JIANG Xuanyu    JIA Jing    LIU Qi (296)

Helping Hand or Punching Fist? How Stock Liquidity Affects Corporate Innovation in China
...................... LIN Zhifan    DU Jinmin    LONG Xiaoxuan (299)

Financial Expansion and Chinese Local Enterprises Innovation: An Inverted U-shaped Relationship ...... ZHANG Jie    WU Shufeng    JIN Yue (302)

Research on Digital Finance and Regional Technology Innovation
......... NIE Xiuhua    JIANG Ping    ZHENG Xiaojia    WU Qing (305)

Do Local Government Talent Introduction Policies Promote Regional Innovation? Evidence from a Quasi-Natural Experiment
.................. ZHONG Teng    LUO Jigang    WANG Changyun (308)

Development Zone and Firm Innovation: Excitation or Extrusion? Evidence from National and Provincial Development Zones
........................CAI Qingfeng    CHEN Yihui    LIN Haihan (311)

## 05　Financial Markets

Textual Information of Central Bank Monetary Policy Report Macroeconomy and Stock Market Performance
........................ JIANG Fuwei    HU Yichi    HUANG Nan (314)

Multiple Credit Rating and Bond Financing Cost: Evidence from Chinese Bond Market ...... CHEN Guanting    LIAN Lishuai    ZHU Song (317)

Private Information, Rating Distortion, and Market Reputation of Credit
Rating Agencies in China ......... KOU Zonglai　QIAN Qianqian (320)

Can Opening the Capital Market Improve the Quality of Corporate
Information Disclosure? An Analysis Based on the Shanghai-Hong Kong
Stock Connect and Annual Report Texts
............ RUAN Rui　SUN Yuchen　TANG Yue　NIE Huihua (323)

Does Short Selling Restrain Insider Selling? Evidence from Margin Trading
Mechanism ............... MA Yunbiao　WU Yanping　SHI Beibei (326)

A Study of the Time-Varying Characteristics of Herding Effects in China's
Stock Market Based on a Regime-Switching Model
............................................ ZHENG Tingguo　GE Houyi (329)

Information Asymmetry, Overconfidence, and Stock Price Changes
............................................................ GONG Rukai (332)

Can Fund Networks Improve Investment Performance?
............................................ CHEN Shenglan　LI Jing (335)

Nominal Price Illusion: Evidence from Security Analysts' Price Targets
............... HE Guihua　CUI Chenyu　GAO Hao　QU Yuanyu (338)

## 06　International Economics & International Trade

Measurement and Analysis of the Real Effective Exchange Rate Elasticity of
Global Value Chains of Bilateral Exports
............................................ PENG Hongfeng　LIU Haiying (341)

Antidumping and Multiproduct Firm Export Activity: Evidence from Chinese
Manufacturing Firms
...................... XU Jiayun   ZHANG Junmei   LIU Zhuqing (344)

How Does Financial Structure Affect the Choice of Foreign Direct Investment
Entry Mode? ....................... JING Guangzheng   SHENG Bin (347)

The Exchange Rate Uncertainty and Cross-border Mergers and Acquisitions
..................... MENG Wei   JIANG Guohua   ZHANG Yongji (350)

## 07　Fiscal, Taxation & Local Government

Housing Price Control, Local Government Debt and Macroeconomic
Fluctuations...... MEI Dongzhou   WEN Xingchun   WANG Siqing (353)

Tax-Fee Substitution: VAT Tax Reduction, Non-tax Revenue Management
and Corporate Investment .............. ZHAO Renjie   FAN Ziying (356)

The Price and Welfare Effects of Tax Cuts and Fee Reduction Policies:
An Analysis Based on an Input-Output Model with a Cost Transmission Rate
............................................ NI Hongfu   YAN Bingqian (359)

Intergovernmental Revenue Sharing and Fiscal Budget Revenue Deviation
.................................... LYU Bingyang   CHEN Zhigang (362)

Local Public Debt and Return on Capital: Evidence from New Debt Data and the
Triple Mechanism Test ......   JI Yunyang   MAO Jie   WEN Xueting (365)

Have Public Finance Policies Induced Financial Institutions to Support
Agricultural Development? An Evaluation of the Effects of the Reward
Policy On Incremental Agricultural Loans in China
.......................................... XING Weibo   ZHANG Simin (368)

## 08 Inclusive Finance, Regional Finance & Social Development

The Impact of Housing Wealth on Urban Household Consumption in China
................................ YIN Zhichao  QIU Hua  PAN Xuefeng (371)

Housing Provident Fund and Households' Investment in Risky Financial Assets: Evidence from China's Household Finance Survey of 2013
................................ CHEN Xuanjuan  LIN Hongmei (374)

Do Traditional Family Values Restrain Participation in Commercial Pension Plans Among the Urban Population? A Study Based on the Perspectives of Financial Trust and Financial Literacy
................................ ZHENG Lu  XU Minxia (377)

When can I Go Home? School Provisioning and the Decision to Immigrate
................................ LI Ming  ZHENG Liming (380)

Land-renting, Farmers' Agricultural Credit Demands and Credit Constraints: An Analysis of CHFS Data................ LU Xiaomeng  WU Yu (383)

Can Compulsory Education Law Improve Intergenerational Mobility?
................ CHEN Binkai  ZHANG Shujuan  SHEN Guangjun (386)

Does Targeted Poverty Alleviation Affect Corporate Risk?
................................ ZHEN Hongxian  WANG Sanfa (389)

Do Green Investors Play a Role? Empirical Research on Firms' Participation in Green Governance
................................ JIANG Guangsheng  LU Jianci  LI Weian (392)

## 09  Corporate Governance & Corporate Finance

Employee Salary Competitiveness and the Adoption of Employee Stock Ownership Plan ……ZHANG Huili  ZHAO Jianyu  LU Zhengfei (394)

Increased Holdings of Controlling Shareholders Under Equity Pledge: Value Signal or Behavioral Signal? … XU Longbing  WANG Bin (397)

Internal Governance and Capital Structure Adjustment: Evidence from the Perspective of Non-CEO Executives' Independence
……………………ZHANG Bo  HAN Yadong  LI Guangzhong (400)

Building a Cooperative Customer Relationship: Empirical Evidence from Credit Provision to Major Customers
…………………………… JIANG Wei  DI Lulu  LIU Chengda (402)

Rehired Independent Directors and Corporate Misconduct: Learning Effect or Relationship Effect? ………………DU Xingqiang  ZHANG Ying (405)

Large Shareholders' share Pledging and Capital Operations of Listed Companies ……………………………… LU Rong  LAN Yuan (408)

Identification and Estimation of Earnings Management to Avoid Delisting and Satisfy SPO Conditions: Evidence from a Bunching Design Study
……………………… ZHANG Hong  WANG Xiaoquan (411)

Does Managerial Macro-cognition Have "Imprinting"? Evidence from the Effect of Management Style
……………… LUO Yonggen  RAO Pingui  CHEN Can (414)

Does the Front-stage Behavior of Entrepreneurs Affect Firm Value? Evidence from Sina Microblogs… SUN Tong  XUE Shuang  CUI Qinghui (417)

# 01 宏观经济与货币政策

# 工业革命、金融革命与系统性风险治理*

陈雨露

## 一、引言

纵观人类历史，三次工业大革命极大提高了生产力，也带来了生产方式和社会关系的深刻变革。先进技术创新应用、经济结构转变和社会环境变迁，推动了金融业演进发展和升级；反过来，资本的快速积累和有效融通对科技进步转化为工业革命不可或缺，金融革命成为工业革命的重要助力。以现代商业银行为特征的第一次金融革命为第一次工业大革命提供了大资金的支持，以现代投资银行为特征的第二次金融革命为第二次工业革命重构了资本基石，以创业投资体系为特征的第三次金融革命为第三次工业革命缔造了新的推动力量。在此过程中，金融业不断通过吸纳科技创新成果并推动自我革命提升内生活力和服务实体经济的效率，极大地促进了经济社会发展。但由于相关制度规则建设和监管滞后，也频频导致金融风险累积和集中暴露，在一些情况下甚至引发严重的金融危机，使本国甚至全球经济遭受重创。金融风险和危机往往会催生重大金融体制或监管制度变革，令经济金融重拾发展动力，为下一次工业

---

\* 原文刊载于《金融研究》2021年第1期。

**作者简介：** 陈雨露，经济学博士，教授，中国人民银行。本文仅代表个人观点，不代表所在单位观点。

革命和金融革命积蓄能量。

当前，第四次工业革命赋予了金融业新的历史使命，金融科技引领的金融业集成创新有望成为第四次金融革命的突出特征。应汲取国际历史经验教训，统筹发展与安全，在金融科技带动下发挥好银行体系、资本市场、创投体系和金融科技企业服务实体经济创新发展的合力，同时做好风险防范，引导从业机构在服务实体经济和遵从审慎监管的前提下守正创新，防止资本无序扩张，牢牢守住不发生系统性风险的底线。

## 二、第一次工业革命、现代商业银行产生与中央银行制度的建立

第一次工业革命在18世纪后期率先发生在英国，并在19世纪中叶达到顶峰，主要特征是蒸汽机、机械纺织设备和焦炉冶铁技术的发明和广泛应用。第一次工业革命建立了以生产流程机械化和产业分工为主要特征的现代化大生产和经济增长模式，标志着现代工业的兴起和人类进入"机器时代"。

新发明的问世离不开英国独特的社会经济环境。一是1688年"光荣革命"推翻了英国的封建统治，国家权力由君主逐渐转至议会，英国成为世界上第一个君主立宪制国家，为资本主义发展扫清了道路。二是圈地运动合法化掀起建立大农场的热潮，农业生产率大幅提高，促进人口持续增长和城市化进程。大城市孕育了规模经济，提高了经济运行效率（Crafts and Venables，2003），18世纪英国工资水平持续上涨，是欧洲工资水平最高的国家。三是丰富的煤炭资源为城市发展提供了廉价能源。18世纪初，伦敦的煤炭价格比巴黎低40%左右，18世纪末英国煤炭产量高于其他主要国家之和（罗伯特·艾伦，2012）。四是英国对外贸易规模不断扩大，大大促进了资金流通和资本积累（布罗代尔，1993），国民财富尤其是商业财富快速增长。英国对外贸易额从1700年的5 900万美元增加至1789年的3.4亿美元（夏德炎，1991），18世纪初伦敦

25%的劳动力受雇于贸易相关行业（罗伯特·艾伦，2012）。简而言之，城市化水平提高、劳动力成本上升和能源价格低廉使各类可节约劳动力成本的新发明、新技术应运而生。同时，高工资也支持了教育发展和劳动培训，为新技术发展创造了有利条件。

工商业发展推动银行体系扩张，为第一次工业革命的全面兴起提供了大资金的支持。英国经济史学家阿什顿指出，工业革命"与人口增长相联系，与科学应用到工业中有关系，还与更加集中和广泛地使用资本相关联"。技术发明改变了生产要素配置比例，资本支出占比大幅提高。以蒸汽机为例，一台瓦特改良蒸汽机成本在2 000英镑左右，相当于1770年英国男性年收入中位数的100倍（Brunt，2006）。18世纪时，伦敦超越阿姆斯特丹和巴黎，成为欧洲金融业中心；英国已初步形成由英格兰银行、伦敦私人银行[①]和伦敦以外的乡村银行构成的三级银行网络，伦敦的私人银行代理乡村银行在伦敦的金融业务。随着工商业和海外贸易扩展，大批实业家的资金收支、贸易商在乡村银行和伦敦私人银行间的资产划拨、收入上升带来的政府税收业务扩张推动银行数量持续增加。伦敦私人银行由1750年的30家增加至1770年的50家和1800年的80家（Lipson, E., 1947）；乡村银行从1793年的400家增加至1810年的超过700家（W.H.B.考特，1992）。

银行体系的蓬勃发展促进了英国统一信贷市场的形成，缓和了工业地区的资金短缺问题，降低了地区间利率差。一方面，银行业发展提高了资金流动性。乡村银行与伦敦私人银行间的业务往来把农业区的储蓄吸收至伦敦，伦敦私人银行作为中介，以透支和支票形式向外贷款赚取利润。通过银行网络，大量资金从英国南部资金盈余地区转移至北方工业发达地区，在产业上从低经济价值项目转移至高经济价值项目。另一

---

[①] 按当时法律规定，私人银行出资者不超过6人。

方面，银行密度提高使地区间利差和资金成本明显下降。由于地区经济结构差异，1771—1820年，英国北部煤矿业发达的达勒姆郡平均年利率为18.2%，而南部的多塞特郡年利率只有3.8%，伦敦作为资金集散中心，平均年利率为4.7%。同期，乡镇银行数量从不足30家激增至1809年的755家（金德尔伯格，1991）。随着银行数量增长和银行密度上升，各地区与伦敦的利差显著下降。

工业革命和金融革命相互促进，推动英国经济增长和国民财富积累，但由于风险管理制度尚不健全，银行业快速信用扩张也为金融体系积累了大量风险。1760—1860年，英国国民生产总值从9 000万英镑增加到6.5亿英镑，国民财富从16.3亿英镑增加到46.4亿英镑（王章辉，2013）。但由于货币总量缺乏调控和货币发行权分散[①]，以信贷体系为支柱的信用和生产反复经历繁荣与萧条的交替。自1815—1850年至少经历了四次程度不等的危机（徐滨，2017），其中最为严重和最具代表性的是1825年金融危机。19世纪20年代前期，英国国内生产领域的快速扩张和对拉丁美洲的证券投资热潮使英国经济出现空前繁荣，"全英银行不节俭的金融行为"（蒂姆斯戴尔和霍特森，2017）导致信贷过度膨胀和小面额钞票超发。1825年9月起，商品相对过剩和价格下跌导致数家大型企业倒闭，并对生产和金融体系造成重创，引起金融"恐慌"、银行挤兑和风险传染，第一次现代金融危机就此爆发。6家伦敦银行，约60家地方银行倒闭（Fetter，1967）；英格兰银行的黄金储备从当年3月和4月的1 000万英镑降至12月的130万英镑以下。1825年12月下旬，英格兰银行在政府授意下，通过购买国库券、对国库券垫款等"一切可能的手段"向市场提供流动性（白芝浩，2010），危机逐步缓解。

---

①1777年，英格兰立法禁止任何银行发行5英镑以下面额的钞票，1793年前英格兰银行的钞票面额均在10英镑以上。1797年，为了应付战时需要，议会授权银行业发行5英镑以下钞票。1825年危机发生前，英国各地1英镑和2英镑的钞票发行量很大。

金融制度改革提升金融体系稳定性和抗风险能力，为银行业现代化奠定基础。1825年金融危机后，英国对金融体制进行了重大改革。一是英格兰银行逐渐从私人股份银行向兼具中央银行职能过渡。1826年《银行法》授权英格兰银行设立分支机构，以更好管控纸币流通，防止危机二次爆发；随后的《1844年银行特许法案》（又称《皮尔条例》）赋予英格兰银行更大权力，规定英格兰银行发行的银行券为全国唯一的法币，其他银行不得增发钞票，并通过分设部门使英格兰银行的商业银行业务与发行业务分开，为英格兰银行作为发行银行的垄断地位奠定了基础。此外，1825年金融危机也使英格兰银行认识到，它在银根严重短缺时期对支持金融体系负有一定责任（蒂姆斯戴尔和霍特森，2017），在危机中的救助措施也为其未来正式承担最后贷款人职能积累了有益经验；1870年后，英格兰银行公开承认其具有维护金融体系稳定的公共义务，英国金融业进入长达近百年的稳定期。二是打破了英格兰银行作为英格兰唯一股份制银行的垄断权。《1826年银行法》允许其他个人和团体设立股东人数不受限制的、"以吸收存款而不是发行银行券为业务"（蒂姆斯戴尔和霍特森，2017）的股份银行，英国银行体制由私人合伙银行向股份银行转变。1833年英国已有50家股份制银行，1841年则达到118家（金德尔伯格，1991）。股份制银行资本实力雄厚，更适合日益扩张的经济活动，成为现代银行业的发展方向。

## 三、第二次工业革命、美国资本市场和投资银行体系发展与金融监管架构的完善

19世纪70年代，第二次工业革命在美国兴起。电力的广泛应用引发了"动力革命"和"通讯革命"；内燃机的应用和汽车、航空工业的发展，重塑了美国的工业体系，并促成了燃料化工、高分子合成等新兴工业的蓬勃兴起。第二次工业革命后，美国由"蒸汽时代"跨入"电气时代""石

油时代"和"钢铁时代"。

随着经济扩张和技术进步，大规模基础设施建设及其融资需求刺激了美国资本市场和投资银行业务的发展。1783年独立战争结束后，为改善联邦政府脆弱的财政状况、偿还战争中欠下的2 700万美元债务（约翰·戈登，2005），美国财政部以政府信用为担保，统一发行新国债来偿还各种旧债，美国证券市场开始活跃，大量经纪人涌入市场从事国债承销。1811年纽约证券交易所的建立标志严格意义上的美国资本市场真正形成。19世纪上半叶，巨大的铁路融资需求使铁路证券成为华尔街的主要投资品种之一，挂牌交易的铁路证券从1835年的3只增加到1850年的38只。1861—1865年南北战争时期，联邦政府为军费融资，推动证券市场空前发展。股票发行也迅速增加，铁路股票在美国大量上市，1880年铁路股票占据美国股市总市值的60%以上（约翰·戈登，2005）。在此期间，诞生了一批兼营或专营投资银行业务的金融机构。如1850年亨利·雷曼等兄弟三人建立了以棉花贸易为主业的"雷曼兄弟公司"，逐步开启铁路债券销售等业务，并于1889年首次作为承销商发行了国际蒸汽公司（Steam Pump Company）的股票。1869年，主要从事票据交易的高盛公司成立，随后增加贷款、外汇兑换和股票包销等业务。技术进步也促进了美国资本市场的发展。1850年电报的发明使得报价信息几秒钟内就可以传递到各个角落，强化了纽约证券交易所对其他地域证券交易所的影响力。19世纪60年代中后期，大西洋海底电缆的投入使用（便利了美国市场和欧洲市场的信息传递）和股票自动报价器的推出，促使资本市场交易量稳步增长。

资本市场发展为美国第二次工业革命的科技成果向经济增长转换提供了催化剂，美国工业产值迅速扩张。一方面，资本市场为大规模工业发展提供了基础设施建设等重大项目的资本支撑。美国工业的巨大规模经济得益于高效的交通运输系统，而资本市场为工业和基础设施建设筹集了大规模资金。1825年,由证券发行为之筹资的伊利运河修建成功,直接造就了当时美国经济的繁荣,也引发了人们对运河股票的狂热追捧,启动了华尔街历史上第一轮大牛市。随着资本市场规模的扩大,美国铁路行业也得到了极大的发展。1865—1873年,铁路总长度增长一倍,铁路投资增长两倍(约翰·戈登,2005),铁路行业的迅猛发展为钢铁、机车、铜线等重工业产品创造了巨大的市场。另一方面,通过资本市场进行的并购交易优化了产业和市场结构。1887—1904年,美国共发生了2943起并购交易,3000多家中小企业被兼并(祁斌,2010),工业与金融联合形成了工业托拉斯,诞生了通用电气、通用汽车、美孚石油、杜邦等世界级企业。这些并购改变了美国产业结构,产生了规模经济效应,为美国跨国企业在全球的扩张奠定了基础。1901年,投资银行家摩根组织的辛迪加并购了钢铁大王卡内基的公司,先后吞并了50多家企业,创立了估值达14亿美元[①]的美国钢铁公司,成为当时全球最大的跨国钢铁集团。资本市场发展促进了美国经济的扩张,1859—1899年,美国企业数目增加两倍,投资总额增长近九倍,工业总产值增长了八倍。1860年美国工业产值占世界工业总产值的比重约为17%,这一比例在1890年上升到31%,超过英国近10个百分点(中国社会科学院经济研究所,1962)。

美国资本市场的发展并不是一帆风顺的,华尔街在发展的早期缺乏监管,投机盛行,股票操纵、内幕交易和欺诈行为严重,股市恐慌频繁发生。华尔街早期仅由其自身建立规则、设计运作程序。一个没有监管的自由市场在本质上是不稳定的,在压力面前很容易崩溃。例如,19世纪中期,范德比尔特和德鲁集团围绕伊利铁路控制权展开争斗,双方通

---

① 同年的联邦预算支出只有5.25亿美元,美国所有的制造业总资本是90亿美元,当时美国的国内生产总值为200亿美元,美国钢铁公司涉及的重组交易相当于美国经济总产出的7%。

过自己豢养的法官随意篡改股市规则来操纵股价，股票价格剧烈波动。在 19 世纪 90 年代之前，甚至没有法律要求上市公司公布财务报告，只有少数内部人才知道公司的真实状况，制造谣言操纵股价的现象比比皆是。20 世纪早期，美国经济在汽车工业带动下繁荣发展，低利率环境进一步激发了投机活动，华尔街很多上市公司高度杠杆化，股指上涨显著快于经济增长。1929 年 10 月 24 日，美国股市出现抛售，10 月 29 日（黑色星期二），道琼斯工业平均指数单日跌幅高达 11.7%，此后连续多日下跌。股市崩溃造成大量投资者破产，银行面临挤兑，工厂面临倒闭和产出下滑，工人大批失业。美国经济陷入长达四年之久的衰退期，引发了波及整个资本主义世界的"大萧条"。

"大萧条"后，随着金融市场监督管理架构逐步建立，美国资本市场进入规范和恢复期。一是出台多项证券业法规。"大萧条"结束后，美国在股票市场运行一百多年后出台了第一部全国性的证券业法规《1933 年证券法》，规范证券发行人信息披露，防止欺诈行为；《1934 年证券交易法》进一步对证券操纵和欺诈进行了界定，规范证券交易行为。《1938 年马洛尼法》将场外交易纳入监管范围；《1939 年信托契约法》《1940 年投资公司法》《1940 年投资顾问法》等相继颁布，基金、信托、投资公司等中介的证券买卖行为被严格监管，大大规范了证券交易行为。二是成立证券市场监管和自律机构。《1934 年证券交易法》授权设立美国证券交易委员会（SEC），负责监督证券市场和保障投资者利益。《1938 年马洛尼法》建立了全美证券交易商协会，改进行业自律。三是建立分业经营制度。1933 年通过《格拉斯—斯蒂格尔法案》，将商业银行业务和投资银行业务严格划分开，银行只能在储蓄业务（商业银行）或承销投资业务（投资银行）之中选择其一，催生了现代投资银行业。一系列改革措施对推动资本市场良性发展和恢复公众信心发挥了重要作用。

## 四、第三次工业革命、美国创业投资体系与互联网泡沫治理

第三次科技革命始于20世纪下半叶,以原子能、电子计算机、空间技术和生物工程的发明和应用为主要标志,涉及信息技术、新能源技术、新材料技术、生物技术、空间技术和海洋技术等诸多领域。

与第三次工业革命相伴相生的是以风险投资为核心的现代创业投资体系。这一体系萌芽于20世纪40年代中期。随着美国推行罗斯福"新政"以及"二战"结束,美国经济进入调整和恢复时期。依靠各国军事订单建立起庞大军火工业的美国迫切需要通过迅速发展中小企业来实现经济结构向民用工业转移,从而对创业投资资本产生了新的客观需求。但当时的美国资本市场机构早期投资动机不足,中小企业和新兴企业面临融资困难,美国许多专家、学者提出建议或方案,呼吁政府重视新企业发展并实施直接帮助。联邦储备银行波士顿分行前行长拉尔夫·弗兰德斯和哈佛商学院教授乔治斯·德瑞斯则认为,建立一个私人机构以吸引机构投资者是一个可行方案,不仅可为新企业提供充足的资金支持,还可提供管理服务,更可培育早期投资群体。二人遂于1946年在高校林立的马萨诸塞州设立美国研究与发展公司(AR&D)。1957年,AR&D以股债结合方式为数字设备公司(DEC)提供约200万美元融资(以不到7万美元持股77%,其余为贷款),1966年DEC完成首次公开发行(IPO),成为AR&D第一笔成功的风险投资。

70年代中后期,美国创投行业进入高速发展阶段。1974年颁布的《雇员退休收入保护法案》和1979年放松谨慎人规则[①]等监管规则变化,使美国养老基金可投资于风险投资基金。80年代风险投资基金行业资产管理规模飞速扩张,1982—1987年,风险投资基金行业年融资额从1亿美

---

① 谨慎人规则是指在养老金计划和养老基金的投资管理过程中,投资管理人应当在从事财产交易时达到必要的谨慎程度。

元迅速增长至45亿美元，为美国第三次工业革命提供了重要支持。

创业投资体系对科技创新企业的支持体现在两方面。一是直接融资作用。1974—2014年，全美约有1339家上市公司成立，其中556家获得风险投资的支持，占比为42%。截至2014年末，获得风投支持的上市公司总市值达4.136万亿美元，占在此期间上市的公司总市值的63%；研发投入达1150亿美元，占全部上市公司研发投入的44%（OECD，2014）。创投体系的支持不仅仅直接作用于被投资企业，企业研发创新的正外部性亦促进了社会整体经济活动。二是非金融支持，包括运营辅导、战略指引、资源支持等。学术界普遍认为，风险投资具有筛选（Screening）与督导（Monitoring）两大功能，其中筛选功能更多体现为机构挑选优秀公司的能力，督导功能则为投资机构对所投初创企业的非金融资源支持，这一功能会促进企业创新并提升投资项目成功退出的可能性（Bernstein等，2016）。

与之并行的是纳斯达克（NASDAQ）股票交易市场的设立与发展。1971年，为使投资者可通过高速、透明的电脑系统进行股票交易，美国全国证券交易商协会（NASD）设立了世界上第一家电子股票交易市场纳斯达克，此举进一步拓宽了创投基金项目退出渠道。20世纪80年代，在创投体系的助推下，一些科技公司在技术与商业上均取得成功，苹果、微软、亚马逊、思科等科技公司在纳斯达克上市直接推动了纳斯达克市场蓬勃发展，加深了创投体系与产业革新的相互交融，为美国经济发展作出了重要贡献。

在相对宽松的监管环境下，资金不断涌入创投体系，初创科技企业融资难度大大降低，但由于重发展轻风险管理，也导致美国在1995—2001年出现"非理性繁荣"及随后的"互联网泡沫"破裂。1996年12月5日，时任美联储主席格林斯潘曾发出警告，但直至2000年春季，美联储并未收紧货币政策。1997年，纳斯达克进一步放宽了上市条件，增加对公司盈利能力要求的灵活性，采用综合考虑公司规模、经营时间等因素的方式衡量公司增长潜力与上市可行性。这一修订后，大量资金涌入纳斯达克市场，互联网相关企业股价快速上升，资本市场泡沫逐渐开始累积。1999年《金融服务现代化法案》的颁布，使美国金融体系重回混业经营模式。在新概念的拉动下，大量风险投资流向互联网公司。1999年，美国457项IPO中295项与互联网公司相关，2000年第一季度互联网公司IPO达91项（Gornall和Strebulaev，2015）。然而，许多获得融资的"互联网公司"甚至仅仅是将公司名称变更为与互联网相关的名字（如在公司名称后加上".com"），而这一名称变更行为却会使公司估值应声上涨（Ljungqvist和Wilhelm，2003）。事实上，这些公司在经历野蛮生长、股价腾飞、挥霍无度和黯然消退的过程后，在科技研发及创新领域并无太多建树，也未对实体经济发展产生显著贡献。由于当时纳斯达克市场还处于发展的早期，在美国资本市场的份额并不算高，互联网泡沫并未对美国经济带来太过严重的损害。但创投体系偏好过度冒险和不透明的问题越来越突出，美国监管当局开始对有关规则进行调整，特别是2008年国际金融危机后出台的《多德—弗兰克华尔街改革与消费者保护法案》，要求私募股权基金在美国证监会（SEC）登记，披露交易信息，并接受定期检查。同时，该法案的"沃尔克规则"严格限制银行从事自营交易以及拥有对冲基金和私募股权基金的股份，防止金融机构过度冒险，威胁金融稳定。2011年，SEC又发布规则提出风险投资基金需满足若干条件，对创投体系的监管进一步收紧。

近年来，学界开始关心风险投资的投机性与顺周期投资行为引发的风险（Howell等，2020）。尽管风险投资机构更着眼于所投项目增长前景而非短期盈利能力，但其投资决策与行为同时也存在着一定的顺周期性。一方面，经济平稳运行且资金充裕时，风险投资机构可能因失于审慎而存在投资过热行为，从而引发资本市场泡沫累积，带来潜在风险；

另一方面，基于专利数据的最新实证研究结果表明，在经济衰退期，关注早期阶段创新创业的风险投资活动明显减少，获得投资的创新活动更缺乏原创性、通用性及与基础科学的关联度。可通过建立合理的激励约束机制，使风险投资机构更好地发挥其筛选与督导功能，从而更加有效地支持科技创新，推动工业革命的进程。

**五、第四次工业革命与促进金融科技健康发展**

当前第四次工业革命已在全球范围内拉开序幕。2013年9月30日十八届中央政治局第九次集体学习时，习近平总书记指出："新一轮科技革命和产业变革正在孕育兴起，一些重要科学问题和关键核心技术已经呈现出革命性突破的先兆。物质构造、意识本质、宇宙演化等基础科学领域取得重大进展，信息、生物、能源、材料和海洋、空间等应用科学领域不断发展，带动了关键技术交叉融合、群体跃进，变革突破的能量正在不断积累。"

世界主要国家均迅速反应，积极推动第四次工业革命在本国的发展。美国制订了"先进制造业国家战略计划"，成立"智能制造领导联盟"，提出"工业互联网""先进制造伙伴关系"战略等。德国依靠其强大的制造业根基，部署实施"工业4.0战略"，以期主导未来工业革命的发展。日本推出"超级智能社会战略"，大力推动其经济的自动化、智能化，试图在全球率先构筑超级智能社会。印度提出"数字印度"和"印度制造"战略，致力于充分利用人工智能、物联网和区块链等新技术，推动其向世界制造中心的转变。

第四次工业革命赋予了金融业新的历史使命。金融科技引领的金融体系集成创新将成为第四次金融革命的突出特征。金融体系能否完成支持第四次工业革命的历史使命，金融变革怎样支持实体经济创新发展，金融监管如何与时俱进、把握好金融创新与金融安全的关系、牢牢守住不发生系统性风险的底线,是需要解决的关键问题。应汲取国际历史经验教训,兼顾发展与安全,在金融科技带动下发挥好银行体系、资本市场、创投体系和金融科技企业服务实体经济创新发展的合力,同时做好风险防范,引导从业机构在服务实体经济和遵从审慎监管的前提下守正创新,防止资本无序扩张。

一方面,需要把握第四次金融革命机遇,加强问题导向,通过金融科技引领的集成创新,大力提升金融微观决策的信息对称性和金融服务的便利性、可得性,提升资源配置效率,完善对创新型企业的融资支持和综合金融服务体系。第四次工业革命存在交叉性、复合性创新等突出特征,涉及不同领域和行业。因此,在加快构建新发展格局的过程中,应挖掘金融服务与不同行业新兴技术、商业模式的结合点,完善产业链创新链融资体系,加大对高端制造业、创新企业和引领性产业集群的支持力度。完善中国特色的科创金融体系,支持金融机构按科技创新生命周期规律,为科技创新企业提供全方位金融服务,加快培育形成各具特色、充满活力、市场化运作、专业化管理的创业投资机构体系。顺应新兴技术发展趋势,支持金融科技规范发展,以重点突破带动全局,探索大数据、云计算、人工智能、分布式数据库等新兴技术在金融领域的安全应用,支持金融机构合理运用金融科技手段提升金融服务质量与效率。

另一方面,需要建立与金融科技和金融创新动态平衡的金融监管体系。近些年,许多国家金融科技发展势头迅猛、大型科技公司向金融业扩张,在提高金融服务效率和信贷可获得性的同时,也给金融稳定、金融监管和消费者保护带来较大挑战,国内外学者和机构对此已有诸多研究。例如,金融稳定论坛(FSB)在调查23个国家后指出(FSB,2020),大型金融科技公司进入金融领域可能存在五方面风险:一是存款竞争影响传统金融机构稳健经营;二是可能导致更多消费者权益纠纷和客户数据滥用,消费者权益保护面临新风险;三是大型科技公司业务壮大后可能会限制竞争，一旦倒闭或服务中断，其复杂的业务网络将对经济产生严重负面冲击；四是业务规模大、复杂程度高，可能在多国开展业务，提升监管难度；五是电信和网络设施故障或引发运营风险并影响金融稳定，一些新技术的运用还可能给基础设施运行带来新风险。FSB建议在抓好常规监管的同时，坚持"相同风险、相同监管"原则，加强风险评估、数据安全管理和消费者权益保护。欧盟2020年9月发布的一揽子数字金融计划，在支持数字金融和零售支付创新发展的同时，也特别提出建议为确保数字科技运营的稳健性立法，设置必要的保障手段和监督框架，降低潜在风险。

我国是全球金融科技发展领先的国家之一，更需要处理好金融发展、金融稳定和金融安全的关系，既要鼓励创新、弘扬企业家精神，也要加强监管，依法将金融活动全面纳入监管，有效防范风险，对同类业务、同类主体一视同仁。加强金融科技监管顶层设计和审慎监管，建立健全监管基本规则体系，针对互联网金融的地域穿透性和业态穿透性，提升穿透式监管能力，探索运用信息公开、产品公示、社会监督等柔性管理方式，努力打造包容审慎的金融科技创新的监管机制，引导从业机构在服务实体经济和遵从审慎监管的前提下守正创新，在风险可控和范围可控的前提下探索开展应用试点、产品测验、技术验证，给真正有社会经济价值的创新留有合适的空间。增强金融风险技防能力，加强网络安全风险管控和金融信息保护，做好新技术金融应用风险防范，加强金融消费者权益保护。同时，探索利用监管科技提升监测分析能力和监管有效性，为及时有效识别和化解金融风险提供支持。

# 庚子赔款的债务化偿付及其影响*

## 王 信 张 翼 魏 磊

1901年，清政府被迫与西方国家签订《辛丑条约》，赔偿白银4.5亿海关两，从1902年起，按每年4%的利率，分39年还清。这笔巨额赔款被称为庚子赔款，是中国近代史上最大的一项对外赔款，也是一笔以长期债务形式体现的对外赔款。

现有文献关于庚子赔款的研究主要包括三个方面。一是关于庚子赔款的议定过程和赔款中产生的汇兑、减免和退还等问题的研究。二是对于赔款实际支付和退还金额的考证。三是研究庚子赔款及部分退还所产生的经济、社会等诸多方面的影响。已有的研究成果相当丰富，但就经济金融方面的研究而言，仍然存在很多不足。现有的研究主要是基于传统的文献和历史学考证方法，对新史料和新方法的运用有待拓展。在研究对象上，多数研究把庚子赔款债务作为单独的事件，局限在对该事件及其影响进行论述，缺乏与同时代其他国际赔款比较，以及与全球经济金融市场相联系的综合性分析。

有鉴于此，本文从债务视角出发，研究庚子赔款债务化及其影响。基于前人的研究成果和相关资料，整理制作了庚子赔款支付流程图，相对简明清晰地阐述了庚子赔款的支付流程。进而从货币购买力和国际比较的角度，分析庚子赔款相当于经济总量和政府财政收入的占比、赔款

---

\* 原文刊载于《金融研究》2021年第2期。
**作者简介**：王信，中国人民银行研究局；张翼，中国人民银行扬州市中心支行；魏磊，中国人民银行研究局。

的价值折算和在财政、金融、货币等方面的历史影响。本文研究有以下发现。

第一，庚子赔款的本金 4.5 亿海关两，相当于清政府 1903 年财政收入的 4.33 倍。在近代历次赔款中，庚子赔款不仅在绝对量上最多，占当期政府财力的比重也最高。但通过债务化偿付的安排，每年实际支付的赔款占当年财政收入的比重逐步下降。对于列强而言，债务化偿付避免了因清政府财政破产而拿不到赔款的局面，列强利益得到维护。但对于中国而言，晚清政府的财政收入增长主要来自关税和厘金，财政收入和偿债能力的提升，实际上是以进口规模扩大和国内商品流通成本提高为代价，受损的仍然是中国经济。

第二，使用 1990 年不变价国际元和 GDP 平减指数进行折算，发现庚子赔款本金占 1900 年中国 GDP 的 2.1% 左右。此外，受国际"金贵银贱"大趋势影响，晚清时期特别是 19 世纪末到 20 世纪初，白银购买力持续下降。按白银数量计算，庚子赔款本金占近代历次赔款总量之比为 61.5%，而按照大米价格的购买力折算，庚子赔款本金占近代历次赔款比例降至 47.5%。白银贬值在客观上缓冲了庚子赔款的巨大压力。

第三，以往对庚子赔款利率本身的高低很少予以评价。一方面，与当时中国政府的内外债利率及 1900 年前后世界主要国家的长期主权债务利率相比，庚子赔款的利率并不算高。另一方面，从世界利率史看，整个 19 世纪，西方主要国家的长期利率总体呈单边下行趋势，并在 1900 年前后降至历史低点。因此庚子赔款 4% 的利率属于中等水平，既不是巨额赔款之外的额外盘剥，也不是列强对华让步或恩惠。

第四，将庚子赔款与德国在第一次世界大战（以下简称"一战"）的战争赔款进行比较，发现庚子赔款本金占中国经济总量的比重远低于德国"一战"赔款本金占其经济总量的比重，但中国每年实际支付赔款的占当年财政收入的比重高于德国赔款占当年财政收入的比重。中国政府的赔款压力并不比"一战"之后的德国轻。从赔款的金融后果看，德国为支付"一战"赔款滥发纸币，导致前所未有的恶性通货膨胀，并对此后的德国历史产生了很大影响。而签订《辛丑条约》时，中国还没有真正的中央银行和政府信用纸币，政府不具备发行纸币支付赔款的条件，自然不会出现类似德国的恶性通胀。但相对于短期冲击，庚子赔款却在更长时段上影响了中国的财政、货币和金融市场。

第五，庚子赔款对近代中国的财政金融产生深刻影响。在财政税收方面，外国人管理的海关税务司借庚子赔款的机会扩张自己的权力，垄断了中国最主要的税收来源，成为独立于中国政府的"第二财政"。在金融市场方面，外商银行通过办理庚子赔款业务，进一步强化其金融特权和市场优势，确立了在中国的"隐性中央银行"地位：包括纸币发行规模和占比不断扩大，成为20世纪初中国最主要的"发行的银行"；全面代理国库收支，成为"政府的银行"；掌控中国金融机构的流动性来源，成为"银行的银行"，尤其以汇丰银行和花旗银行的扩张最为明显。在货币方面，庚子赔款加剧了晚清币制改革的紧迫性，却没能改变币制混乱的"旧制度"。同时，又催生了货币流通的"新周期"和"新危机"，成为1910年上海"橡皮风潮"等金融危机的重要导火索。

基于上述发现，本文认为：近代史上战争赔款的债务化偿付安排不仅受政治外交形势主导，也与金融机构特别是银行跨国经营存在密切联系。战争赔款的经济影响不仅取决于偿付总量，也取决于经济治理能力和财税金融制度。国家经济治理能力和资金筹措动员能力强，则赔款对本国的冲击较小；国家财税金融制度落后，则受到的冲击较大。

# 利率市场化改革与货币政策银行利率传导*

## 陆 军 黄 嘉

2015年10月23日,中国人民银行取消商业银行等金融机构存款利率浮动上限,标志着我国完全放开利率行政管制。然而,这并不意味着利率市场化改革的最终完成,也不意味着金融体系中的价格扭曲完全消除。2020年10月29日,党的十九届五中全会通过的《中共中央关于制定国民经济和社会发展第十四个五年规划和二〇三五年远景目标的建议》明确指出,要建设现代中央银行制度,健全市场化利率形成和传导机制。经过二十多年的利率市场化改革,随着存款利率、贷款利率、市场利率、政策利率之间的联动性增强,在我国货币政策调控中形成了独特且极为重要的银行利率传导渠道,即中央银行的政策利率通过市场(基准)利率向存贷款利率等传导。在货币政策利率传导过程中,如果中央银行的政策利率能够通过市场(基准)利率向贷款利率和存款利率顺畅传导,利率市场化将有效地发挥在优化金融资源配置中的重要作用。基于此,本文从货币政策银行利率传导的角度,力图考察利率市场化改革成效。

已有研究对利率市场化改革给予了广泛关注,为如何度量利率市场化程度提供了许多颇有参考价值的思路和方法。但我国利率市场化改革

---

* 原文刊载于《金融研究》2021年第4期。

作者简介:陆军,经济学博士,教授,中山大学岭南(大学)学院;黄嘉,博士后,中山大学岭南(大学)学院。

具有渐进性和复杂性,不仅要从存款利率、贷款利率、市场利率和政策利率等方面客观地度量利率市场化程度,还应考虑货币政策银行利率传导的有效性,更加全面地评价利率市场化改革,这恰恰是当前继续深化利率市场化改革值得深思的问题。总的来看,本文研究具有以下边际贡献:(1)在马骏和王洪林(2014)的基础上,引入影响存款利率、贷款利率、市场利率和政策利率的摩擦因素,从理论上讨论了如何客观全面地评价利率市场化改革的成效。(2)进一步丰富刘明康等(2018)的研究,从宏观层面考察在渐进的利率市场化改革进程中货币政策银行利率传导的动态政策效应,从而为改革如何向更深层次推进提供参考。

具体而言,本文构造了一个多部门局部均衡模型,刻画利率市场化程度的时变特征,从理论上讨论利率市场化程度与货币政策银行利率传导之间的内生关系,两者共同决定了利率市场化改革的成效。基于1996年6月至2019年9月的季度数据,本文利用时变因子扩展向量自回归模型(TVP-FAVAR)进一步验证了理论分析的结论:首先,估计得到时变利率市场化程度,将利率市场化改革划分为不同阶段,分析不同改革阶段的特征及利率市场化程度的动态变化。其次,通过时点脉冲响应函数、提前期脉冲响应函数,分析利率市场化改革对货币政策银行利率传导的动态政策效应。最后,通过时变预测方差分解,进一步检验利率市场化改革的政策效果。

综合前述的理论与实证分析,本文发现:(1)利率市场化改革具有阶段性波动特征,利率市场化程度不是一直上升的,改革可能会曲折迂回。(2)利率市场化改革具有动态政策效应,多种改革政策共同推动渐进的利率市场化。从货币政策银行利率传导的有效性进行考察,改革仍然存在进一步推进的空间,2019年启动贷款市场报价利率(LPR)形成机制改革是拓展利率市场化深度的契机。

对于如何以完善LPR机制为抓手、进一步深化利率市场化改革,可供参考的思路如下：

第一，有序推进LPR传导机制改革，完善适应市场需求的银行内部转移定价机制（FTP）。在银行利率决定以FTP定价机制为主的条件下，逐步实现基准利率和市场利率的并轨，将LPR利率嵌入贷款FTP定价中。同时，协调推进加强存款利率自律管理、优化存款竞争结构等相关措施，逐步带动存款利率市场化。

第二，持续深化LPR形成机制和调控机制改革，理顺不同利率之间的联动关系。从完善LPR形成机制着手，进一步提高市场利率的弹性和敏感性，鼓励更多具有代表性的金融机构参与LPR报价，创新与丰富LPR衍生产品，增强LPR利率与银行间同业市场利率、债券利率等其他市场利率之间的联动性，培育更加具备基准性的LPR形成机制。同时，积极探索一个行之有效的LPR调控机制，在中央银行货币政策工具箱中选择合适的政策利率，增加较长期限的LPR报价参考利率，细化较短期限的LPR报价参考利率，形成更加完备的LPR曲线。此外，还可以在宏观审慎监管政策的配合下进一步优化LPR调控机制，实施影子银行业务差异化分类审慎监管，抑制影子银行对政策利率的消极影响，着力提高再融资工具利率的引导作用。

# 货币政策能够兼顾稳增长与防风险吗？*

## ——基于动态随机一般均衡模型的分析

### 董兵兵　徐慧伦　谭小芬

为防范系统性金融风险，我国从2015年12月起将"去杠杆"列为供给侧结构性改革的五大任务之一。随着宏观杠杆率逐步趋稳，2018年4月中央财经委员会第一次会议提出结构性去杠杆的基本思路，去杠杆政策由总量性措施转变为更加精准的结构性措施。结构性去杠杆主要从两个层面发力：一是稳定和逐步降低宏观杠杆率，即非金融部门信贷规模与GDP的比值；二是区别对待不同部门杠杆率，着重降低地方政府和国有企业杠杆率。结构性去杠杆注重通过改善微观企业信贷资源配置效率，促进经济高质量发展，防范和化解金融风险。但2018年至2019年GDP增速下行，固定资产投资和社会消费品零售总额同比增长放缓。为应对新冠肺炎疫情冲击，宏观杠杆率在2020年呈现阶段性快速上升。货币政策能否协调稳增长和稳杠杆，成为争论焦点。

在此背景下，一些观点认为在货币政策的逆周期调控下，稳增长和防风险存在矛盾，这对货币政策效果的评价是不够全面的。稳增长和以稳杠杆为代表的防风险之间的关系要基于宏观杠杆率的经济含义来探讨。单一地收紧货币政策，以通过缩减非金融企业部门的信贷规模来稳定杠

---

* 原文刊载于《金融研究》2021年第4期。
作者简介：董兵兵，经济学博士，助理教授，中央财经大学金融学院；徐慧伦，博士研究生，中央财经大学金融学院；谭小芬，经济学博士，教授，中央财经大学金融学院。

杆率，仅是从宏观杠杆率的分子角度使杠杆率增长放缓，但忽视了紧缩性货币政策可能会造成分母（即GDP）同时下降，从而使杠杆率不降反升。须从结构性去杠杆的视角出发，推行松紧适度的货币政策，优化企业部门信贷结构，使低效益企业去杠杆、高效益企业加杠杆或稳杠杆[①]，将有助于稳定宏观杠杆率和经济增长。基于此，本文主要探究以下问题：第一，货币政策能否同时实现稳增长和稳杠杆？政策基调应是宽松的还是紧缩的？第二，结构性货币政策工具应如何与现有货币政策工具相协调，以充分发挥精准滴灌的作用？第三，在货币政策与宏观审慎政策双支柱的调控框架下，货币政策应如何调整以实现这两个目标？

针对上述研究问题，本文将Jermann和Quadrini（2012）单部门模型扩展为包含国企和非国企的两部门新凯恩斯主义动态随机一般均衡（DSGE）模型。本文的稳增长是指货币政策对产出的正向促进作用，防风险是指宏观杠杆率和国企杠杆率趋稳并逐步下降，非国企杠杆率有所上升，信贷结构优化。为研究如何构建金融有效支持实体经济的体制机制，本文将在企业融资约束、成本异质性设定和宏观审慎政策框架下，考察价格型货币政策对宏微观杠杆率的调控效果。所探讨的货币政策包括利率政策和选择性货币政策工具，如窗口指导、信用控制、优惠利率等。

基于2006年第一季度至2018年第二季度中国宏观经济数据估计确定模型参数，运用脉冲响应、历史冲击分解、反事实实验等数值分析方法，研究发现：（1）稳增长和稳杠杆相互促进，央行可通过适度降低利率和增强国企抵押约束，使信贷资源由国企向非国企转移，增强货币政策精准导向和直达实体经济的效果，稳定宏观杠杆率，实现稳增长的政策目标，共同推进金融服务实体经济和防范系统性金融风险。（2）货币政策在稳增长和稳杠杆方面的效果会受到国企和非国企融资成本影响。推动

---

① 本文的企业杠杆率是指企业资产负债率。

国企贷款利率向市场水平趋近，并采取其他定向降低非国企贷款成本的结构性货币政策，可改善上述两种政策的效果，充分发挥精准滴灌的作用，增进金融服务实体经济的质量。(3)2006年第二季度到2018年第二季度，国企抵押约束对宏观杠杆率起主导作用。随着货币政策向价格型调控过渡及结构性货币政策工具的使用，2017年后利率政策对宏观杠杆率的调控作用增强。强化国企抵押约束，主动下调利率至适当水平，是下一阶段稳定宏观杠杆率的重要手段。(4)在宏观审慎政策框架下，若央行在货币政策规则中盯住宏观杠杆率，并根据不同时期的调控政策和目标灵活选择利率与杠杆率间的内生机制，有利于平衡稳增长、调结构和防风险，比如在降低政策利率和强化国企抵押约束时，应将利率与宏观杠杆率设定为同向调整的内生机制，这样在宏观杠杆率下降后央行将进一步降低利率，稳增长和防风险的效果得到增强。

本文的边际贡献如下：第一，本文的DSGE模型立足于我国经济现实，多角度刻画了企业异质性，能够反映出企业层面信贷资源配置情况及货币政策传导机制的差异性，有利于阐明货币政策在稳增长和防风险方面的政策效果；第二，通过模拟多种企业融资成本设定下货币政策效果，说明如何借助结构性货币政策工具促进金融服务实体经济，有助于进一步完善有关结构性货币政策工具效果的理论研究；第三，将理论模型与杠杆率历史数据相结合，识别出影响我国宏观杠杆率的主导因素，并借助反事实实验，说明宏观审慎政策框架下应如何继续推进稳增长和防风险。

# 投资潮涌、双重金融摩擦与货币政策传导*

## ——转型时期货币政策的结构调控功能探讨

战明华　李　帅　姚耀军　吴周恒

根据熊彼特的理论，行业的产生与消失是市场创新过程中的必然现象。然而，中国经济转型时期出现的行业非均衡现象却往往源自一些非市场化因素。宏观上，"投资潮涌"（林毅夫，2007）是行业非均衡的一大突出特征，即企业投资会系统性倾向于某一行业，并由此周期性地引起部分行业产能严重供大于求。为纠正这一长期经济失衡问题，中国货币政策在一定程度上发挥了调整行业产能的功能。例如，货币政策在20世纪90年代纺织业、2008年左右光伏业及近几年钢铁和煤炭等行业的产能调整中均发挥了强有力的作用。然而，通过货币政策调控行业产能却面临货币经济学基础理论层面上的困扰：传统上，货币政策从需求侧熨平短期经济波动，而产能调控属于长期结构调整的范畴。即便货币长期非中性，但其与产出的关系也是不稳定的。因此，我国货币政策具有行业产能调整功能的理论机制亟待探究。

行业产能特征与企业产权异质性是转型时期货币政策具有结构调整

---

\* 原文刊载于《金融研究》2021年第3期。
作者简介：战明华，管理学博士，教授，广东外语外贸大学金融学院；李帅，金融学博士研究生，广东外语外贸大学金融学院；姚耀军，管理学博士，教授，浙江工商大学金融学院；吴周恒，经济学博士，副教授，广东外语外贸大学金融学院。

功能的两个重要线索。通过将两者引入货币政策银行信贷渠道传导模型，本文基于双重金融摩擦机制构建了货币政策调控行业过剩产能的理论分析框架，尝试为上述理论谜团提供一个解释。本文理论逻辑如下：经济转型背景下的"投资潮涌"内生出行业产能过剩这一长期供给侧问题，并进一步导致过剩行业企业与其他行业企业的资产负债表存在系统性差异。具体来看，在银行和企业融资市场均存在金融摩擦时，货币政策冲击通过信贷渠道的金融加速器效应，导致产能过剩程度不同的行业面临系统性差异的融资约束，实现对实体经济结构进行调控的功能。

  本文同时从理论与实证两个角度，对中国货币政策所具有的行业产能调整功能进行了探究。在理论研究部分，构建了包含企业抵押贷款约束和银行杠杆约束双重金融摩擦机制的 DSGE 模型，以解释中国货币政策对于产能过剩行业的去产能功能。研究结果表明：第一，货币政策的去产能效果既取决于货币政策对银行贷款总量供给的影响，也与不同行业类型企业的总体抵押能力密切相关。紧缩性货币政策会导致产能过剩行业企业的信贷获取量相对于其他行业企业出现系统性的边际减少，对产能过剩行业企业的投资产生更强的抑制效应，从而实现行业结构调整功能。第二，不同产权结构的企业面临不同的抵押贷款约束。相较于民营企业，国有企业受到紧缩性货币政策更弱的去产能作用，而金融加速器效应将放大这一产权结构异质性。此外，准备金等数量型工具与价格型工具相比具有更大的作用效果。在实证研究部分，应用宏观总量数据及微观上市公司面板数据对理论假说进行了验证。研究发现：第一，货币政策银行信贷渠道确实对行业产能调控具有长期的真实效应，这不同于货币政策仅具熨平短期经济波动功能的传统标准理论观点。第二，货币政策通过银行信贷渠道，对过剩行业中的国有企业与民营企业的产能波动均会产生显著影响，但扩张与紧缩性货币政策的效果具有非对称性。第三，利率调控面临由加速器效应引起的"次生损害"，数量型货币政策工具的产能调控效果优于价格型工具。

根据上述分析结论,得到以下三方面政策启示:第一,不同类型的政策工具具有不同的结构调控效果,这为通过进一步完善和创新分类调控政策思路,实现灵活精准、合理适度的货币政策操作路径提供了政策启示。第二,常规货币政策具有结构调控功能,通过创新货币政策调控方式推进供给侧结构性改革,并以此促进经济高质量发展战略,是必要与可行的。第三,在企业微观层面存在产权、资产负债特征等异质性时,仅靠利率市场化改革难以一举而竟全功,仍有必要深化发展金融市场的微观基础。

# 混频数据信息下的时变货币政策传导机制研究*

## ——基于混频 TVP-FAVAR 模型

尚玉皇　赵　芮　董青马

当前全球经济出现较大不确定性，金融市场脆弱性不断上升。中国宏观经济也面临着结构调整及金融风险集聚等问题，这使得货币政策、宏观经济及金融市场之间的关系呈现新的变化特征。与此同时，中国利率市场化的推进及金融科技的发展，使得货币政策操作面临复杂的金融大数据信息环境。在此现实背景下，有必要充分挖掘当前宏观经济及金融市场的大数据信息，深入研究货币政策传导机制的动态演化特征。这对于前瞻性地预调微调货币政策，健全货币政策和宏观审慎政策双支柱调控框架具有重要的现实意义。

货币政策传导是货币政策实施效果及最终目标的关键环节，因此，对货币政策传导的讨论受到广泛关注。众所周知，无论哪种货币政策传导机制均离不开现实的经济环境。受经济周期等因素影响，无论是价格型还是数量型货币政策常表现出时变特征。为充分挖掘并利用现实经济条件下丰富的数据信息，Bernanke 等主张利用 FAVAR 模型分析货币政

---

\* 原文刊载于《金融研究》2021年第1期。
作者简介：尚玉皇，经济学博士，教授，西南财经大学中国金融研究中心；赵芮，经济学硕士，西南财经大学中国金融研究中心；董青马，经济学博士，教授，西南财经大学中国金融研究中心。

策。该模型引入大量宏观数据以提取共同动态因子,该因子可以作为货币政策的中介指标,对产出和通胀具有较好的预测能力。随后,学者们进一步提出 TVP-FAVAR 模型,实现因子增广基础上的时变分析。TVP-FAVAR 模型既可以引入经济中高维信息含量,又能对货币政策机制进行时变分析,逐渐成为货币政策研究的主要方法。

值得关注的是,TVP-FAVAR 模型主要基于同频数据建模。但宏观经济数据的发布频率与金融市场数据截然不同,混频数据在实际经济活动中广泛存在。若为保持数据频率的一致性采用传统的同频数据,则会损失重要的高频数据信息。而这些包含丰富信息的高频数据对于揭示短期货币政策行为、及时微调货币政策具有重要意义。因此,如何有效利用混频数据信息构建 TVP-FAVAR 模型,进而分析货币政策传导机制,是我们面临的现实挑战,也是本文研究的方向。

针对这一问题,本文提出一种混频 TVP-FAVAR 模型即 MF-TVP-FAVAR 模型,利用可搜集的宏观及金融市场混频大数据信息展开讨论。我们将基于该模型刻画货币政策、核心宏观经济指标和高频金融市场变量间的动态作用机制。混频数据建模的方法近年来备受关注,已被应用到多个宏观经济分析领域,如金融形势指数构建、经济周期测度等。混频 TVP-FAVAR 模型的主要优势是最大限度地整合高频金融市场信息和低频宏观经济信息,并从大量信息中有效提取不可观测的潜在因子,从而更加准确及时地分析货币政策与宏观指标、金融市场指标的时变关系。

本文使用的混频数据信息具有前瞻性和多样性特征,主要包括中国季度宏观数据和月度宏观金融数据。其中,季度宏观数据包括季度 GDP 增长率;月度宏观数据包括 CPI 增长率、银行间同业拆借利率、货币供应量 $M_2$ 增长率;金融经济指标的选取主要来自信贷市场、股票市场、债券市场、房地产市场等,包括宏观景气先行指数、消费者信心指数、外汇储备资产、社会消费品贸易总额、上证综指收益率、发电量增长率、金融机构贷款余额和国房景气指数。考虑到数据公布时间的差异，我们最终选择的样本区间为：1997年1月到2017年12月。数据来源为国家统计局和Wind金融资讯数据库。

基于实证分析我们得到如下结论：第一，基于MF-TVP-FAVAR模型提取的金融形势指数较好地反映了中国金融状况的动态特征，其既可以作为我国经济运行状况的先行指标，也可作为货币政策中介目标的辅助指标。金融形势指数对利率及货币供应具有显著正向影响，而且该作用机制具有明显的时变特征。第二，混频TVP-FAVAR模型可以捕捉到月度观测频率上货币政策对宏观经济所呈现的显著时变特征，这一估计结果显著提高了货币政策传导机制分析的时效性。但价格型和数量型货币政策传导渠道在作用时滞性及影响幅度方面存在明显的差异性。第三，经济周期对货币政策效果产生显著影响。我们发现无论是产出效应还是价格效应，经济上行时期，货币政策传导机制都要比经济下行时期更加通畅。这意味着货币政策传导具有明显的周期特征。特别是，相比价格型货币政策，数量型货币政策更容易受到经济周期的影响。

基于上述研究结果，本文认为，在评估货币政策传导机制时，需要更多挖掘金融市场提供的混频数据信息流，结合不同频率的多维数据进行货币政策传导机制分析。混频大数据信息将会在未来货币政策实践中发挥重要作用。

# 新型货币政策担保品框架的绿色效应*

## 郭 晔 房 芳

2013年以来,央行大幅充实货币政策工具箱,创新推出短期流动性调节工具(SLO)、常备借贷便利(SLF)、中期借贷便利(MLF)、定向中期借贷便利(TMLF)等工具。随着新型货币政策的发展,对各种政策工具市场影响的探讨日益增多,但对新型货币政策的担保品框架仍缺乏足够研究。2018年6月,央行扩大了MLF的担保品范围,将绿色信贷和绿色债券纳入了担保品框架,这体现了当前加大对绿色经济领域支持力度,实现高质量发展和供给侧结构性改革的政策意图。那么,央行将绿色信贷资产纳入合格担保品框架是否能进一步提高绿色信贷企业的融资水平,降低绿色信贷企业的融资成本,值得研究与分析。

现有研究对新型货币政策是否具有结构调整效应尚未形成共识。尤其是在新型货币政策将绿色信贷资产纳入合格担保品框架的背景下,仍缺乏对新型货币政策是否能产生绿色效应的相关研究。本文认为新型货币政策可通过合格担保品渠道发挥定向调控绿色效应。一方面,央行的合格担保品政策意味着央行在通过MLF投放基础货币的同时要求商业银行提供绿色信贷资产等合格担保品,从而绕开商业银行负债端向资产端的传导关系,直接针对商业银行的资产端进行定向调控。另一方面,从特征企业的资产负债表来看,央行将某类信贷资产纳入合格担保品框架

---

\* 原文刊载于《金融研究》2021年第1期。
作者简介:郭晔,经济学博士,教授,厦门大学经济学院、王亚南经济研究院;房芳,博士研究生,厦门大学经济学院。

将提高此类资产的质权和稀缺性，相当于央行通过国家信用间接为特征企业进行"担保"，从而改善了特征企业的资产负债表状况，有助于提高绿色信贷企业的融资可得性并降低其借款成本。

本文选取CSMAR数据库中2013年第一季度至2019年第四季度A股上市公司的季度财务数据，基于双重差分法（DID）比较了央行担保品扩容对实验组和对照组企业影响的差异以识别因果关系。央行担保品扩容政策将绿色信贷资产纳入中期借贷便利的合格担保品范围提高了绿色信贷资产的质权和稀缺性，政策的主要作用对象为可以获得绿色信贷的企业。因此，能够作为央行合格担保品的绿色信贷资产是银行针对节能环保项目的专项信贷业务，并无行业的划分标准。单以行业作为实验组和对照组的划分标准可能会忽视绿色信贷对普通节能环保项目企业的影响，从而低估政策效果。为更准确地确定政策影响的目标主体，本文基于2013年原银监会发布的绿色信贷统计表中对绿色项目的描述，对上市企业公告进行文本分析，并对有绿色项目的实验组和没有绿色项目的对照组进行手工分类。

相关实证分析得出以下三个基本结论：第一，央行扩大合格担保品使用范围提高了绿色信贷企业的融资可得性，延长了绿色信贷企业的贷款期限结构，且融资可得性效应在民营企业中更为显著。第二，央行将绿色信贷资产纳入合格担保品框架降低了绿色信贷企业相对于非绿色信贷企业的融资成本，而且政策影响主要体现在国有绿色信贷企业中，而对民营绿色信贷企业依然要求了较高的风险溢价。商业银行对民营企业的信贷歧视并未打破，民营绿色信贷企业有效降低信贷融资成本仍存在一定困难。第三，央行的合格担保品扩张政策效应存在行业异质性。在环保行业中，政策效应主要体现在融资可得性上，而在重污染行业中，政策效应主要体现在融资成本上。

本文政策启示如下：一是进一步完善创新型货币政策框架，尤其是央行合格担保品制度，以充分发挥合格担保品制度定向支持绿色融资的资源配置功能。实证结果表明，此次央行合格担保品扩容确实具有绿色信贷效应，即增加了绿色信贷企业的融资可得性并降低了其融资成本。在当前"坚持绿色发展"及"创新结构性货币政策工具、引导金融机构优化信贷结构"的政策背景下，担保品扩容通过提高绿色信贷资产的质权和稀缺性在微观层面引入了激励相容机制。因此，应重视担保品框架对银行信贷偏好的调节作用，发挥担保品框架的最后贷款人功能。在支持我国经济绿色发展和结构调整的过程中，合理利用央行合格担保品框架的结构效应。二是在折损率设定中进一步体现绿色融资的正外部性效应。当前，我国绿色信贷资产作为担保品的折损率为50%~70%，相对于其他资产和国外标准来讲仍较高。因此，可考虑在风险可控条件下进一步降低民营绿色信贷企业的折损率，以更好发挥央行担保品制度在降低民营绿色信贷企业融资成本方面的作用。三是重视担保品扩容的风险防范，加快央行合格担保品的内部评级等配套制度的建设，更好发挥新型货币政策的绿色资源配置功能。

本文主要研究了我国扩大货币政策担保品框架所产生的绿色金融效应，而此类新型货币政策的绿色效应是否能进一步传导到绿色生产，新型货币政策与绿色发展是何种关系，仍有待进一步探索。

# 人口老龄化、养老保险基金缺口弥补与经济增长*

吕有吉　景　鹏　郑　伟

伴随人口老龄化程度的不断加深，中国城镇职工基本养老保险基金缺口问题日益严峻，经济增长也面临较大下行压力。党的十九届五中全会提出的"系统观念"要求加强全局性谋划，经济平稳较快增长是养老保险制度可持续运行的重要基础，有必要将弥补养老保险基金缺口置于经济增长框架下进行讨论。那么，不同的养老保险基金缺口弥补方式将对人口老龄化背景下的经济增长带来何种影响？结合中国现实，应如何科学选择弥补养老保险基金缺口政策工具？

本文构建一个包含财政支出和公共债务的世代交叠模型，以养老保险基金缺口弥补为核心内容，考察人口老龄化对经济增长的影响，并探讨何种养老保险基金缺口弥补方式更有利于促进经济增长。研究发现：第一，若采用财政补贴方式弥补养老保险基金缺口，生存概率上升和生育率下降均会提高长期经济增长速度。第二，若采用发行公债方式或财政补贴与发行公债两者兼用方式弥补养老保险基金缺口，当人力资本产出弹性较小时，生存概率上升和生育率下降均会提高长期经济增长速度；当人力资本产出弹性较大时，长期经济增长速度随生存概率上升呈倒"U"

---

*原文刊载于《金融研究》2021年第1期。

**作者简介**：吕有吉，经济学博士，讲师，南开大学金融学院；景鹏，经济学博士，副教授，西南财经大学保险学院；郑伟，经济学博士，劳合社讲席教授，北京大学经济学院。

形变化趋势，随生育率下降而提高。第三，养老保险基金缺口弥补方式是影响长期经济增长的重要制度因素，当人力资本产出弹性较小时，发行公债、财政补贴、发行公债和财政补贴两者兼用这三种方式对应的长期经济增长速度排序为"发行公债＞两者兼用＞财政补贴"；当人力资本产出弹性较大时，排序为"财政补贴＞两者兼用＞发行公债"。

本文主要有三点贡献：第一，在研究思路上，以养老保险基金缺口为切入点，实现了人口老龄化、养老保险基金缺口弥补方式与经济增长三者的有机结合，厘清了人口老龄化和养老保险基金缺口弥补方式对经济增长的影响机理。第二，在模型构建上，综合考虑了弥补养老保险基金缺口对生产性公共支出和私人物质资本的替代效应，探讨了经济均衡的稳定性、动态有效性及债务可持续等核心问题。第三，在研究结论上，刻画了不同养老保险基金缺口弥补方式下人口老龄化与经济增速的演变特征，给出了在不同条件下最有利于促进经济增长的养老保险基金缺口弥补方式。

基于上述结论得到二点政策启示。

第一，理念层面，应认识到人口老龄化挑战与机遇并存，以更积极的态度应对潜在挑战。近年来，我国人口老龄化程度持续加深，人口红利逐步消失，养老保险基金缺口问题日益凸显，如何在弥补养老保险基金缺口时兼顾经济增长和民生保障无疑是政府面临的一项挑战。但也要看到，如能顺应人口结构变迁趋势，实现从扩大劳动力规模到提升劳动力质量的转变，完成从"制造"到"智造"的转型，经济有望在长期实现较快增长，养老保险基金缺口问题将迎刃而解。

第二，制度层面，应在系统观念指导下结合我国国情做好弥补养老保险基金缺口的制度探索和政策储备工作。现行制度安排下，大规模减税降费将限制财政收入规模，而日渐扩大的养老保险基金缺口则要求政府不断提高财政补贴力度，这无疑会降低生产性财政支出份额，如基础建设支出和公共教育支出，从而抑制长期经济增长。考虑到当前我国经济增长的主导力量仍是物质资本，人力资本产出弹性相对较小，探索包含发行公债等在内的多种养老保险基金缺口弥补方式有助于更好地优化经济社会长期发展路径，实现养老保险制度与经济增长的良性互动。

第三，技术层面，应在量化基础上动态确定弥补养老保险基金缺口的政策工具组合，进一步提升国家治理效能。当前我国正进行新一轮的新基建投资，这有赖于财政的有力支持，与此同时，不断扩大的政府债务规模将影响我国经济的稳定性。因此，在采用财政补贴和发行公债两者兼用的养老保险基金缺口弥补方式时，既要考虑到财政补贴对于其他生产性财政支出的替代效应，又要考虑到发行公债对私人物质资本的替代效应，在量化分析上述两种替代效应的基础上，结合具体政策目标合理确定不同政策工具在弥补养老保险基金缺口上承担的比例。特别地，引入发行公债方式时，政府应采取有效措施规避由债务规模扩张导致的经济稳定性下降问题，从而实现经济平稳较快增长。

本文构建了人口老龄化、养老保险基金缺口弥补方式与经济增长三者关系的理论分析框架，但对个人人力资本投资动机的设定及债务规模调控方式的探索存在局限性，未来的研究至少可从两方面进行拓展。第一，考虑到子女赡养仍是中国个人养老的重要组成部分，可引入"养儿防老"机制更好地刻画个人进行人力资本投资的动机。第二，债务规模扩大会削弱经济稳定性，这对政府的债务管理能力提出了更高要求，如何调控债务规模以实现经济在不同均衡间的平稳过渡是亟待解决的关键问题。

# 老龄化、消费结构与服务业发展[*]

颜 色  郭凯明  段雪琴

多数走上工业化道路的经济体的发展历史表明,经济发展过程也是人口年龄结构和产业结构不断变迁的过程。人口年龄结构变迁会呈现老龄化程度加深态势,主要是以生育率下降、预期寿命提高为特征的人口转变过程导致的。产业结构变迁会呈现库兹涅茨事实,即农业经济比重下降、服务业经济比重上升、工业经济比重先上升后缓慢下降的发展趋势。中国经济演化路径也大致符合这些发展规律,但同时存在着一些矛盾和问题。

一方面,中国人口老龄化程度快速加深,老龄化率(65 岁及以上人口占总人口比例)和老年抚养比(老年人口与劳动年龄人口之比)分别由 1982 年的 4.9% 和 8.0% 提高到 2020 年的 13.5% 和 19.7%,但中国还处于上中等收入国家水平,未富先老与经济发展矛盾突出。另一方面,中国服务业比重不断提高,服务业产出比重和就业比重分别由 1978 年的 24.6% 和 12.2% 上升到 2019 年的 53.9% 和 47.4%,但服务业发展仍相对滞后,结构也有待优化升级。

事实上,老龄化加深和产业结构变迁并不是独立发生的现象。利用近几十年的跨国数据,本文发现,老龄化和服务业比重的相关关系取决于经济发展水平,伴随着经济发展,老年抚养比与服务业比重的关系由负转正。

---

[*] 原文刊载于《金融研究》2021 年第 2 期。
作者简介:颜色,经济学博士,副教授,北京大学光华管理学院;郭凯明,经济学博士,副教授,中山大学岭南学院;段雪琴,经济学硕士,中国工商银行广州分行。

本文在包含收入效应和价格效应的两部门模型中引入人口年龄结构，研究了老龄化对服务业发展的影响。本文提出，老龄化会通过收入效应和价格效应两个渠道影响服务业发展。在收入效应渠道上，老龄化的影响方向取决于不同年龄群体对工农业产品的最低消费水平，影响程度取决于人均消费水平；在价格效应渠道上，老龄化的影响方向取决于相对价格对不同年龄群体的影响程度。如果老龄化在收入效应渠道上对服务业比重的影响为负，在价格效应渠道上对服务业比重的影响为正，那么老龄化对服务业比重的影响就取决于这两种渠道影响程度的相对大小。在人均收入较低时，收入效应渠道的影响程度较大，老龄化对服务业比重的影响为负。但随着人均收入提高，收入效应渠道的影响程度逐渐减小，价格效应渠道转而成为主导机制，因此老龄化对服务业比重的影响也会由负转正。

本文结合1995—2010年跨国数据定量评估了不同环境下老龄化对服务业比重的影响，发现老龄化的影响还取决于老龄化程度和不同产业的相对生产率。并且，在年轻人关于两个产业部门产品的替代弹性较低、老年人关于两个产业部门产品的替代弹性较高，或老年人的工农业产品最低消费水平较低时，老龄化加深更可能提高服务业比重。改变产业部门消费率和劳动力转移成本等因素后，定量结果仍保持了较高稳健性。

本文结论既解释了随经济发展水平变化，老龄化程度对服务业发展的影响由负转正的跨国事实，也有助于评估老龄化加深在特定国家对产业结构的影响。在中国等发展中国家，人均消费水平较低，未富先老不利于服务业发展；在欧美等发达国家，老龄化加深对服务业发展的影响会存在差别，这又取决于这些国家的老龄化程度。因此，不同国家评估老龄化对产业结构的影响，应结合不同年龄人群的消费偏好、人均消费水平和老龄化程度等因素综合进行分析。

本文结论也为中国应对老龄化和发展服务业提出了针对性的政策建议。

一是坚持扩大内需,持续提升消费水平。继续保持人均收入稳定增长、提高居民消费比重,能够有效缩小老龄化对服务业发展的负面影响,且在老龄化程度较高时更为有效。缩小区域城乡发展差距和不同群体收入差距,使共同富裕取得更为明显的实质性进展,不断提升公共服务质量和水平,能够充分释放巨大的内需潜力,促进消费水平显著提升,通过需求侧消费结构升级拉动服务业发展。

二是优化投资结构,推动投资服务业化。投资结构伴随着经济发展呈现出服务业化趋势,不断提高投资品中服务业附加值所占比重,有助于吸纳更多劳动力到服务业生产投资品。加大自主研发投入规模,不断延伸产业链和供应链,加强金融业和商业服务业对实体经济的支持力度,稳步提升无形资产投资在总投资中的占比,通过需求侧投资结构优化推动服务业发展。

三是发展生产性服务业,提高服务业生产率。通过提高服务业生产率降低服务相对价格,能够缩小老龄化对服务业发展的负面影响,特别是在老龄化加深的经济中更为有效。发展生产率相对较高的生产性服务业,推动先进制造业与现代服务业深度融合,稳妥扩大服务业对外开放程度,能够快速提升服务业生产率,通过供给侧技术进步推动服务业发展。

四是深化劳动力市场改革,降低劳动力流动成本。缩小产业间劳动工资差距,降低劳动力向城镇地区服务业转移的制度壁垒,有助于提高服务业就业比重。建立整合高效的全国统一市场,深化户籍制度改革,放开放宽大中城市落户限制,消除就业歧视,通过供给侧劳动配置效率提升推动服务业发展。

# 智能化对中国劳动力市场的影响：
# 基于就业广度和强度的分析*

周广肃  李力行  孟岭生

  自动化和智能化是当今社会经济发展的重要趋势，将会对生产效率和经济增长起到重要作用。随着互联网及大数据、云计算等技术的发展，人工智能的理念和技术正在全球范围内掀起一场深刻的技术革命。自动化、智能化技术在拉动经济增长动力的同时，也对很多传统职业产生了冲击，越来越多的工作岗位可能在智能化的浪潮中被机器和自动化技术替代。已有研究表明，中低技能劳动者就业率和工资的下降在很大程度上可归结于智能机器的发展和应用。近几年人工智能产业的高速发展及人口老龄化社会的加速到来，更是引起了各界对智能化如何影响劳动力市场这一问题的关注。不同于以往三次技术革命中机器设备对于体力劳动的替代，智能化是逐渐将"智力"融入生产流程中，其不仅要求机器的灵巧度要逐步接近人类的能力，更重要的是使得机器逐步拥有人类"思考"的能力。机器经历的"自动化—智能化—人工智能"的系列转变，将会对劳动力市场产生进一步冲击。具体到我国，智能化和自动化对劳动力市场的影响可能更明显，这一方面是因为我国处于智能化技术发展前列，另一方面与我国人口众多的现状和劳动密集型产业为主的产业结构相关。

---

\* 原文刊载于《金融研究》2021年第6期。
  作者简介：周广肃，经济学博士，副教授，中国人民大学劳动人事学院；李力行，经济学博士，教授，北京大学国家发展研究院；孟岭生，经济学博士，研究员，香港中文大学经济系。

本文将美国劳工部标准职业代码与中国职业代码相匹配，基于 Frey 和 Osborne（2017）对美国各种职业被智能化替代概率的估计结果，估算了各职业被智能化替代的概率。匹配结果显示，不同职业被智能化替代的概率存在较大差异：一些程序化、高重复、低技能的工作被替代的概率较高，如机械制造加工人员、食品饮料生产加工及饲料生产加工人员等；而另一些特殊化、高技能、创造性的工作岗位被智能化替代的概率较低，如各类技术人员、企事业单位负责人等。接下来，利用多个年份的人口普查和家庭调查微观数据及欧盟的机器人使用数据，本文将个体劳动者被替代的概率加总得到城市层面的工作岗位被替代指标，并在城市层面和个人层面估计了智能化对就业广度（就业人数）和就业强度（工作时长）的影响。研究发现，智能化对我国劳动就业产生了明显的替代作用，一方面减少了就业人数的增长，另一方面增加了在职劳动力的工作时间，根据不同样本的回归分析发现，女性、低教育劳动者、大龄劳动者、移民等劳动力市场中相对脆弱的群体所受的冲击更大，且随着时间推移，影响效果呈增大趋势。

相比已有文献，本文可能的贡献如下。首先，大部分关注智能化影响的文献以发达国家数据为基础，而本文补充了发展中国家劳动力市场被智能化影响的证据。其次，估算了我国各职业被智能化替代的概率，全面地评估了智能化对劳动力市场可能产生的替代性影响。再次，估算了智能化对就业广度和就业强度的影响，并进行了根据不同劳动力特征的差异性分析，有助于客观全面地评估智能化对劳动就业和相关福利所产生的影响。最后，使用欧盟机器人的数据作为中国智能化的替代性指标，考察了智能化的不同方面对于劳动力市场的影响。

本文的研究尽管侧重于相关分析而非因果关系的推断，但也为讨论自动化和智能化对中国劳动力市场带来的冲击提供了重要的实证证据，具有明显的政策含义。我国在大力推动人工智能等新技术发展的同时，需注意其对劳动力市场产生的潜在冲击。首先，需要全面评估智能化对劳动力市场产生的影响，因为智能化并不是一种中性的技术进步，其对于不同行业、不同特征的劳动力将会产生差异性影响。其次，对劳动力市场中相对弱势的群体（如女性、低教育劳动者、大龄劳动者、移民）给予更多关注，通过进行职业教育或职业培训努力提高其劳动技能和人力资本，以应对智能化对其就业机会的负面影响。最后，关注智能化对劳动时间等劳动者福利所带来的影响，尤其警惕智能化可能带来的收入和社会阶层的极化现象，在利用技术进步促进经济发展的同时提高劳动者福利，维护社会公平。

# 资本回报、产权保护与区域资金集聚*

曹廷求　张翠燕

改革开放四十多年来，中国经济取得举世瞩目成就的同时也面临诸如发展不平衡、不充分等问题。区域间经济发展差距受金融资源配置的影响得到了学者的广泛认同。为解决区域不平衡问题，党的十九届五中全会明确提出坚持实施区域协调发展战略，但我们也应认识到"完善产权制度和要素市场化配置"，实现"要素自由流动"是实现区域协调发展的必要条件。

区域要实现协调发展需依托金融资源的支持，结合我国实际，从区域视角看一个地区可获得资金的渠道除金融渠道外，还应包括财政渠道、外商投资渠道及其他资金。区域资金的流动究竟受何种因素驱动？资金具有天然的逐利性，这种逐利性会驱动资金流向资本回报率较高的地区，但国际间的资本流动并未遵循这一模式，因此出现了著名的"卢卡斯悖论"。有学者认为法律环境、制度质量、经济结构等因素的差异可以部分解释国际资本流动中的"卢卡斯悖论"，其中产权保护是一个重要因素。对我国而言，产权制度是社会主义市场经济的基础性制度，为企业提供市场化的营商环境，而完善的契约制度为企业之间契约的高效执行提供一定的法治化保障，因而产权保护可以看作是衡量区域风险的一个重要指标。根据资源配置效率理论，相同的风险水平下，资金逐利避险

---

*原文刊载于《金融研究》2021年第2期。

作者简介：曹廷求，管理学博士，教授，山东大学经济学院；张翠燕，经济学博士，山东大学经济学院。

的特性会促使资金流向资金效率高的领域,而同等的资金效率水平下,资金逐利避险的特性又驱使资金流向风险低的领域。总的来看,本文将资本回报、产权保护置于同一框架下分析我国区域资金集聚的驱动因素,而如何准确测度一个地区的资金集聚是其中的关键性问题。

已有关于区域资金的研究可能存在以下几个问题:(1)研究某一类资金虽能反映地区资金吸引力的部分情况,但是不全面;(2)"货随钱走"的测度相对能反映资金的流动情减,但也是一种间接测度方法,并且无法得出某一个地区的资金流动的绝对数值;(3)基于投资与储蓄相关性研究资本流动在我国的适用性有待验证;(4)时间跨度周期短,不能完全反映我国经济的发展历程。区别于已有研究中对资本流向的考察通常采用资本存量指标,本文关注的资金是从地区融资视角而非投资视角,比较而言,以固定资本形成额计算的资本存量是从投资视角考察,二者有本质性区别。区域资金依据资金来源渠道可分为金融渠道、财政渠道、外商投资渠道及其他资金,随着各类年鉴的出版、数据的公开透明,直接计算各地区每年聚集的资金成为可能,且直接法下估算相对更加准确。

本文从地区融资视角而非投资视角,采用直接法依据资金来源渠道对1985—2017年我国省级层面吸引的资金进行测算,统计发现,我国地区资金吸引力并非一成不变,区域间的资金流动在30多年间发生了较大变化,东西部地区资金差异逐渐缩小,但就个别地区而言,存在两极化趋势。从资金来源结构看,中西部地区资金来源中中央项目和转移支付占比较高,而东部地区以贷款和证券市场融资为主。

我们利用固定效应模型(FE)及面板固定效应的工具变量(IV)估计方法,从逐利性和产权保护两个视角探讨区域资金流动的动机,总体上资金与资本回报率间呈"U"形关系,当资本回报率较低时,资金不具有逐利性,但超过临界值资金则会凸显逐利性。受资金来源结构影响,东部地区资金的逐利性更强,而非东部地区则不具有逐利性。从资金与产权保护的关系看，总体上完善的契约制度比产权制度更能吸引资金集聚，但东部地区产权制度是吸引资金集聚的关键因素，非东部地区则是契约制度。从资金的异质性看，契约制度更能吸引市场化资金。

在当前我国着力构建高质量发展的国土空间格局背景下，应意识到东部地区资本回报率较高，资金逐利性强，会促使市场化资金进一步由西部流向东部，长此以往不利于东西部经济协调发展。资金大量流向东部会加剧东部过度金融化，并导致"脱实向虚"；西部由于缺乏资金，融资约束问题会阻碍经济发展。地方政府应结合本地实际情况，将有效市场和有为政府更好地结合，推动要素合理流动和高效集聚，东部地区应进一步提升产权制度建设，做好"放管服"改革，优化市场化营商环境，发挥市场化营商环境吸引资金的优势；中西部地区则需完善法律制度保障力度，优化法治化营商环境，借助法治化营商环境吸纳更多市场化资金。在保安全的基础上，将资本回报率控制在一定范围内，为经济增长吸纳长期稳定的资金支持，从而促进区域协调发展。

# 产业政策、创新行为与企业加成率*
## ——基于战略性新兴产业政策的研究

诸竹君　宋学印　张胜利　陈丽芳

党的十九届五中全会提出，坚持创新在我国现代化建设全局中的核心地位，把科技自立自强作为国家发展的战略支撑。发展战略性新兴产业成为"围绕产业链部署创新链、围绕创新链布局产业链"的重要组成。我国战略性新兴产业深受产业政策和宏观经济环境影响，2010年正式出台的《国务院关于加快培育和发展战略性新兴产业的决定》及在"十二五""十三五"时期陆续颁布了一系列发展规划，产业政策对构建现代产业体系、推动战略性新兴产业高质量发展的支撑引领作用更加凸显。《中华人民共和国国民经济和社会发展第十四个五年规划和2035年远景目标纲要》对发展战略性新兴产业提出了"各具特色、优势互补、结构合理"的新要求和新目标。如何实现产业政策实施效果由数量导向型向提升企业质量效益和核心竞争力转型？这是具有较强理论价值和实践意义的重要学术问题。

目前关于产业政策实施效果的研究并未获得一致结论，实证研究表明产业政策实施效果可能存在异质性。竞争性产业政策能提高企业资源配置效率，培育产业发展新优势、新动能，带动上下游产业发展，提升

---

\* 原文刊载于《金融研究》2021年第6期。
作者简介：诸竹君，经济学博士，副教授，浙江工商大学经济学院；宋学印，经济学博士，副研究员，浙江大学经济学院；张胜利，经济学博士研究生，浙江大学经济学院；陈丽芳，经济学博士，讲师，厦门国家会计学院。

国家整体产业创新能力；能激励企业增加研发投入，提高竞争优势。同时，产业政策也可能恶化行业和企业的生产率及降低资源配置效率，政府补贴可能对企业研发创新激励并不显著。因此，本文通过探究2010年《国务院关于加快培育和发展战略性新兴产业的决定》这一战略性新兴产业政策实施对企业加成率的影响效应，试图从动态层面提供产业政策实施的有效空间。

本文可能的创新之处如下：理论上，研究了产业政策对企业加成率的作用机理，结合我国后发型大国特征对产业政策理论进行了适应性修正，构建了以技术差距作为衡量指标的产业政策实施空间。实证上，分析了战略性新兴产业政策引致的加成率效应，刻画了企业主体异质性对加成率效应的影响，揭示了战略性新兴产业政策由于"选择性"特征对不同企业的作用效果存在差异，总体上对企业竞争力的提升效果还有较大的上升空间。政策上，为产业政策最优实施空间提供了经验证据，从技术差距视角提供了优化政策实施空间和促进政府由"开辟者"转向"赋能者"动态演进的有效路径，对改善产业政策实施效果和促进创新高质量发展具有一定参考价值。

具体来看，本文基于1998—2013年我国工业企业数据库、海关数据库和专利数据库的匹配数据（接近200万个样本），根据战略性新兴产业政策实施的准自然实验，检验了其对企业加成率的影响程度和作用渠道。研究发现：（1）战略性新兴产业政策总体上选取了生产率和研发水平相对较高的行业，并显著增加了企业专利申请量，为经济高质量发展提供了重要的产业支撑。（2）从企业加成率看，战略性新兴产业政策通过成本渠道和价格渠道影响企业加成率。由于影响企业加成率的成本效应大于影响产品质量的价格效应，导致政策一定程度上降低了企业加成率。（3）行业技术差距对战略性新兴产业政策的加成率效应具有显著负向调节作用，随着行业技术水平接近前沿，政策实施效果呈优化趋势。

（4）由于企业主体异质性，战略性新兴产业政策具有的"选择性"特征会引致"重数量轻质量"的创新陷阱，这是造成企业加成率下降的重要原因。

　　本文的政策含义如下：第一，坚持将产业发展水平、质量效益作为产业政策实施的重要目标。可放宽对专利总量和人均数量的考核，不设约束性指标，减少对相关产业的事前选择性补贴，强化对专利实施效果的动态追踪，对产业化效果好、市场化程度高的专利成果给予后期奖励。同时，将产业政策实施与行业技术差距相结合作为参考依据。第二，将优化市场环境和政府职能作为提升战略性新兴产业发展质量的重要策略。在产业发展萌芽期，主要依靠提供优质的营商环境和竞争中性的市场环境促进战略性新兴产业发展，政府主要做好市场竞争"规制者"。在产业发展至与前沿技术差距相对较小时，做好市场竞争和创新驱动"赋能者"，探索建立科技成果转化的"绿色通道"，充分发挥市场在资源配置中的决定性作用，更好地发挥政府作用，推动有效市场和有为政府更好地结合。第三，坚持将战略性新兴产业与各产业深度融合发展作为产业政策的优化方向。依托战略性新兴产业高质量发展，补齐产业链供应链重要产品和关键核心技术的短板，引导战略性新兴产业瞄准上游核心环节，打造创新链和产业链有效联动的关键部门，更好地提升产业链供应链的现代化水平。

# 02　金融稳定与风险防范

# 中国企业杠杆：一个周期性问题？*

陆　婷　徐奇渊

在我国宏观杠杆率的构成当中，企业部门一直占据重要地位。理解经济周期与企业杠杆率之间的关系，不仅有助于加深对微观企业融资行为的认知，更有助于探索货币政策和宏观审慎政策的协调配合关系，从而预防和化解企业杠杆率动态变化过程中可能引发的风险。

一般认为，宏观经济周期能够通过多种渠道影响企业杠杆率。它不仅会改变企业的融资需求，也会改变企业所面临的融资环境及企业朝目标杠杆率调整的速度。然而，在既有的关于经济周期和企业杠杆率关系的经验研究中，判断企业杠杆率是顺周期还是逆周期变化时，主要依赖于经济周期哑变量或某个宏观经济变量（如 GDP 增长率）估计系数符号。这种做法被 Halling 等（2016）批评为一种假设"其他条件不变"的判断方式，忽略了经济周期对杠杆率决定因素的影响，相当于考察一个利润、规模等特征完全不变，只是突然发现自己处于衰退期的企业杠杆率变化。

为实现对企业杠杆率随经济周期变化的整体把握，本文沿袭了 Halling 等（2016）的理念，在构建企业资本结构动态局部调整模型的基础上，通过观察经济周期哑变量前的估计系数来确定经济周期对企业杠杆率的直接影响，同时通过允许解释变量和模型参数变动来捕捉经济周期对企业杠杆率的间接影响，这些被允许变动的变量和参数包括企业特

---

* 原文刊载于《金融研究》2021 年第 2 期。
作者简介：陆婷，经济学博士，副研究员，中国社科院世界经济与政治研究所；徐奇渊，经济学博士，研究员，中国社科院世界经济与政治研究所。

征、企业特征和杠杆率之间的函数关系及企业实际杠杆率朝目标杠杆率调整的速度。

利用我国规模以上工业企业数据库 1996—2013 年的年度数据（共计 1 450 941 个样本），我们测算了经济周期对企业杠杆率的影响，研究发现，在同时考虑经济周期的直接和间接影响后，企业杠杆率总体为顺周期变动，但对经济周期的敏感度远低于只考虑经济周期直接影响的情况。也就是说，经济周期的直接影响会促使企业杠杆率出现大幅度的顺周期调整，与既有研究结果相一致，但其间接影响同时会有一个反向作用，持续且稳健地推动企业杠杆率逆周期变动。因此，总体上企业杠杆率虽然还是呈现出顺周期特征，但顺周期程度却被显著削弱了。

通过区分企业产权性质，我们还考察了经济周期对企业杠杆率的影响是否在不同产权企业中存在差异。结果显示，国有企业杠杆率对经济周期的敏感度显著低于民营企业，经济周期给国有企业杠杆率变动带来的贡献极低。这解释了为何我国国有企业和民营企业杠杆率之间的分化具有时变性。民营企业杠杆率具有较强的顺周期性，杠杆率会随着经济周期而变化，而国有企业杠杆率几乎不随经济周期而变动。国有企业和民营企业杠杆率对经济周期敏感度的差异导致二者之间的杠杆率差距时而收窄时而扩大，使杠杆率分化程度在时间维度上出现变化。

一方面，本文对企业杠杆率随经济周期动态变化的既有研究形成补充和扩展。通过企业特征、企业特征与杠杆率之间的关系、杠杆率调整速度随经济周期而变化，我们发现经济周期对企业杠杆率的直接和间接影响会共同在企业杠杆率变动过程中发挥重要作用的证据，在此基础上，更细致地测算了经济周期对企业杠杆率变化的整体贡献，为现有文献中的"企业杠杆率是顺周期还是逆周期变化"之争提供了有益补充。同时，与国内相关文献大都使用上市企业数据不同，我们在实证研究中使用了工业企业数据库。我国能够上市融资的企业比例较低，且上市企业融资行为与证券市场定价效率密切相关，因而具有一定特殊性，使用工业企业数据库能更好地反映大多数融资渠道"受限"企业的行为决策，从而避免由上市所造成的偏差。

另一方面，本文研究为思考"双支柱"调控框架的分工与协调提供了一定的微观基础。在全面考虑了经济周期的直接和间接影响后，我国企业杠杆率呈顺周期变动的特征，因此货币政策在维护物价水平稳定、熨平经济周期波动时，能够对企业杠杆率稳定产生一定的正向溢出效应。从这个角度而言，"双支柱"调控框架具有内在的一致性，存在协调配合、形成政策合力的基础。然而，企业杠杆率的顺周期性较弱，经济周期波动的平复并不能完全使企业杠杆率稳定。因此，想要在保持物价和经济增长稳定的同时实现稳杠杆，货币政策和宏观审慎政策都不可或缺，二者须相互协调和配合。

本文一个可行的拓展方向是，探究宏观和微观层面企业杠杆率决定因素在经济周期不同阶段作用机制的差异，以及其对企业杠杆率的非对称影响效果，这有助于政策制定者在稳定企业部门杠杆率的同时，进一步将经济周期纳入考虑范畴，对"双支柱"调控框架下的政策实践具有参考意义。

# 监测系统性金融风险[*]

## ——中国金融市场压力指数构建和状态识别

### 李敏波 梁 爽

  监测金融市场运行状况对中央银行维护金融稳定和进行宏观审慎管理至关重要。一方面，金融机构的稳健性高度依赖金融市场的运行状况。另一方面，中央银行的货币政策、宏观审慎政策的实施不仅有赖于金融市场传导，有时政策本身就是对金融市场运行状况的响应。加之金融市场价格变量具有较强的前瞻性，金融体系乃至经济体系的一些重要变化，比如重大政策调整，甚至货币、债务、银行危机等压力事件，均会以不同形式体现在金融市场价格信号中。中央银行从事前选择政策实施窗口、事中相机调整政策实施力度、事后评估政策实施效果的角度，也需密切监测金融市场的运行情况。

  金融市场工具众多，不同工具之间差异性较大，如何从纷繁复杂的金融工具价格变量中选择有代表性的变量来表征金融市场的总体运行情况，是监测金融市场面临的主要挑战。通过选择金融市场代表性指标，用适当方法构造金融市场压力指数，以此表征金融市场承受的总体风险压力水平，已被证明是一个监测金融市场运行的可行方案。国外学者和机构在金融市场压力指数构建方面进行了诸多探索。近年来，国内学者

---

[*] 原文刊载于《金融研究》2021 年第 6 期。
  作者简介：李敏波，经济学博士，中国人民银行金融稳定局；梁爽，经济学硕士，中国人民银行金融稳定局。

在构建金融压力指数方面也有较多研究。总体来看，目前国内文献编制的金融市场压力指数，基本能有效识别区域内的金融市场压力事件，但在指数编制方法和压力状态识别方面还存在一定缺陷。由于数据可得性和编制方法等方面原因，以往文献研究构建的金融压力指数频率较低，从监测金融风险角度看，及时性有所欠缺；部分文献选取了银行部门不良贷款率等指标，数据有一定滞后性，且可能被操纵。我们认为，完全采用金融市场数据构建金融市场压力指数，有利于弥补既往文献编制金融压力指数在底层数据质量、及时性等方面的不足。而且，随着利率市场化改革推进，基于金融市场数据构建的金融市场压力指数对系统性金融风险的代表性和有效性将得到进一步提升。

本文参考以往文献的通行做法，将金融市场压力指数的构建分为两个层次，一是单个子市场压力指数的构建，二是在子市场压力指数基础上合成整个金融市场压力指数。根据中国金融市场特点，本文选取债券市场、股票市场、货币市场和外汇市场上共17个有代表性的指标，采用日频交易数据，运用经验累积分布函数法分别构造各子市场的压力指数，以监测各子市场的风险状况。在此基础上，考虑以各子市场之间时变的相关关系刻画系统性金融风险的跨市场传染特征，采用相关系数矩阵对子市场压力指数进行加权，合成金融市场压力指数，以监测整个金融市场的风险状况，特别是系统性金融风险状况。

编制金融市场压力指数的最终目的是监测、评估金融市场的压力状态，能够恰当识别金融市场的高压力状态至关重要。部分文献采用压力指数当期值超过其历史数据均值若干倍标准差的方式定义压力状态，但这种定义方式一般在金融市场压力指数服从单峰薄尾分布时才会有较为明确的含义。在多峰厚尾分布中，变量当期值与均值的偏离在若干倍标准差之外的概率未必较小，以此定义的高压力区间未必真的代表了高压力状态。部分文献通过对比金融压力指数与危机时压力指数取值高低来划分压力状态，这种方法有一定可行性，但其划分压力状态的阈值依赖于危机时的指数取值，仅使用了少量信息，稳健性不足。Hamilton（1989）提出的马尔科夫区制转换模型为识别金融市场压力状态提供了有益思路。本文假设金融市场承压状态可分为高压力状态和中低压力状态，通过分析金融市场压力指数分布初步支持了该假设，进而建立马尔科夫两区制转换模型，对金融市场的历史压力状态进行识别。

通过对金融市场压力指数状态识别效果的回溯分析可以发现，金融市场压力指数能有效反映样本域内的压力事件，例如2003年证券公司大范围出险、国际金融危机、欧洲主权债务危机、2013年6月银行间流动性紧张、股市异常波动、中美贸易摩擦、新冠肺炎疫情等事件。同时，构建金融市场压力指数的基础——四个金融子市场压力指数也能够有效反映局部压力事件。这将方便金融管理部门和市场参与者在关注整个金融市场压力状态的同时，对局部性压力事件亦保持关注，以便更全面地评估风险。

本文编制金融市场压力指数兼具稳健性、能逐日监测等优点，为监测评估系统性金融风险、选择政策实施窗口和评估政策实施效果等提供了有力工具。但应看到，本文构建的中国金融市场压力指数基于市场交易数据，并未就具体的风险成因和风险源头进行追溯。因此，在对金融市场压力状况进行判断识别后，需配合其他监测、评估和分析工具，有针对性地进一步分析压力的来源和成因，以期达到更好的监测评估效果。

# 资产透明度、监管套利与银行系统性风险*

陈国进　蒋晓宇　刘彦臻　赵向琴

党的十九届五中全会将健全防范化解重大风险的体制机制列为"十四五"规划的主要目标之一。其中,防范化解系统性金融风险是攸关我国经济高质量发展的核心问题之一。近年来,全球经济金融形势严峻,我国坚持全面整治金融乱象。在此背景下,监管部门更加重视金融机构不透明、违规监管套利等风险隐患,要求强化市场约束机制。很多研究认为,银行资产缺乏透明度及由此导致的监管套利是导致金融危机的重要原因。资产不透明的金融机构会过度依赖批发性融资进行监管套利,这不利于系统性风险的防控。充分的信息披露可以降低银行破产概率或系统性风险。高透明度的银行向外界传达偿付信息的能力更强,从而更容易吸引外部再融资,不透明则导致偿付能力不确定,可能引发银行危机。因此,深入探究资产透明度、监管套利对银行系统性风险的影响机制,有利于守住不发生系统性风险的底线,提高金融服务实体经济的能力,也为完善宏观审慎调控框架、实施穿透式监管提供理论参考与实证依据。

---

\* 原文刊载于《金融研究》2021年第3期。
　作者简介：陈国进,经济学博士,教授,厦门大学王亚南经济研究院,厦门大学经济学院;蒋晓宇,金融学博士,厦门大学经济学院,中国人民银行金融研究所;刘彦臻,金融学博士,厦门大学王亚南经济研究院;赵向琴,经济学博士,教授,厦门大学经济学院。

目前，关于资产透明度和监管套利对银行系统性风险影响的理论或实证研究还比较少。本文关注同业批发性融资与零售性存款在存款人市场监督上的差异及利用批发性融资（以同业存单为代表）进行监管套利的问题。一些监管措施主要基于资产负债表内业务（比如银行资本充足率的监管），银行产生了将资产负债业务从表内移到表外的动机，进而规避金融监管以获得监管套利。银行批发性投融资不同于存贷款等传统资产负债，绕开投资者和存款人监督，规避监管限制，使得银行资产透明度下降。银行有动机通过同业通道规避监管限制进而引发过度关联和更高的风险。

本文首先在经典银行道德风险模型的基础上引入关联性，从资产透明度和监管套利的视角对银行系统性风险累积的内在机理进行理论分析。然后基于中国上市银行的数据，利用滚窗估计对资产透明度进行测度，利用 SRISK、MES 等方法对系统性风险进行测度，在充分控制可能影响银行系统性风险的银行层面特征、宏观经济因素的情况下，实证分析银行资产透明、监管套利等对银行系统性风险水平的影响，探讨其影响机制。

根据相关分析，本文得出以下结论：一是资产不透明、监管套利的增加会提高银行的系统性风险水平。二是监管套利弱化了资产透明度和资本监管机制对银行系统性风险承担的约束作用。资产透明度与资本监管机制在约束系统性风险承担中的协调作用不明显。三是以大银行为主的债权银行受到监管套利的影响相较于资产透明度更明显。

本文主要的学术贡献如下：（1）大量文献从个体风险角度进行研究，本文是银行层面的系统性风险研究，放松独立性设定，在异质投资组合情形下（允许关联性）引入资产透明度，从而在一定程度上丰富了资产透明度如何影响银行系统性风险这一研究领域。（2）利用关联性和债权债务银行的设定，我们研究了系统重要性银行对存款市场监督的非对称性反应。（3）相比于零售性存款市场领域，本文增加了批发性融资市场、银行系统性风险视角的研究，也填补了影子银行、互联网金融等批发性融资在银行透明度方面的研究。

基于上述研究结论，本文得到如下政策启示：第一，在利率市场化改革稳步推进过程中，银行存在一定的借同业通道规避监管的行为，这种监管套利不利于系统性风险防范。银行的资产不透明可能是造成风险累积的重要因素。设定更高的金融机构信息披露标准、提高银行交易投资透明度是防范金融风险的有效手段之一。第二，监管部门可结合我国金融系统特点，注重规范银行间市场债务债权方的投融资行为及商业银行同业债权类资产认定范围与条件。对信息披露提供考核激励，增设资产透明度指标，进而对商业银行实施全面、持续和穿透性监管。第三，充分利用高质量信息披露强化市场约束机制，通过加强金融机构的公司治理水平提高金融风险防范的预判性和前瞻性，守住不发生系统性风险的底线。

# 我国金融机构尾部风险影响因素的非线性研究*

## ——来自面板平滑转换回归模型的新证据

杨子晖　陈雨恬　林师涵　关子桓

在"十四五"规划开局之际,我国的金融风险形势面临着新的挑战,防范风险仍是金融业的永恒主题。在影子银行、地产金融、金融控股公司等新型金融业态快速发展的背景下,全球中小金融机构的尾部风险事件频发,我国中小银行的风险隐患也开始凸显,部分中小金融机构相继出现风险暴露。此类风险事件引发了全球监管机构对"太大而不能倒"这一传统理念的重新审视,如何准确识别现阶段银行体系的风险薄弱环节、有效防控尾部风险成为各国政府与学术界关注的核心问题。就我国而言,在资本市场不确定性与经济下行压力加大、资本市场改革进程加快的背景下,准确剖析我国银行规模与尾部风险间的作用关系,同时深入探讨尾部风险的影响因素等问题具有重要的学术价值与现实意义。

首先,综观该领域的研究,现有的国内文献主要集中在探讨金融机构间的风险传染情况,而较少结合中国实际经济条件考察"太大而不能倒"理论在中国的适用性。其次,在探讨银行规模对尾部风险的作用方向时,

---

\* 原文刊载于《金融研究》2021年第3期。

作者简介：杨子晖,经济学博士,教授,中山大学岭南学院、中山大学高级金融研究院；陈雨恬,博士研究生,中山大学岭南学院；林师涵,博士研究生,中山大学高级金融研究院；关子桓,博士研究生,中山大学岭南学院。

现有文献仍未达成一致意见。相关研究表明,这种作用关系往往会受到金融机构基本面因素影响(Buch等,2019),因此结合金融机构基本面指标考察其尾部风险驱动因素十分必要。再者,国内外文献大多采用线性基准回归模型考察金融风险的驱动因素,而忽略了风险传导的强度与方向常呈现明显的非线性转变,且对金融系统的负面冲击达到一定阈值后更是将对其稳定性造成严重冲击(Acemoglu等,2015)。因此,在传统的线性框架下对变量间的作用关系进行分析,可能导致结论出现较大偏差。最后,需要进一步指出的是,现有研究在考察变量间的非线性关联时,忽略了我国经济改革存在明显的"渐进式"趋势。因此,如何有效考察规模对尾部风险的异质性影响,并准确刻画这一关系随着各影响因素而产生的渐进转变,是结合我国实际经济条件考察尾部风险驱动因素过程中必须考虑的重要问题。

本文选取44家上市金融机构展开实证研究,其中11家为上市银行,33家为上市非银行金融机构,样本区间为2008年1月至2020年6月。第一,采用相对重要性分析技术方法,考察机构规模及基本面因素对我国上市银行等金融机构尾部风险的贡献程度,发现在我国银行系统中,机构规模是尾部风险的重要影响因素,而不良贷款率、个人住房贷款比率、非利息收入比率等指标也明显影响着我国银行系统的风险水平。第二,采用边际效应分析技术剖析规模对风险的异质性效应,结果显示,对于不同规模的银行机构,各因素对尾部风险的作用力度存在显著差异,其中较高的杠杆率与非利息收入比率能够增加小银行的尾部风险,而特许权价值指标对银行的尾部风险存在正向影响。第三,进一步基于面板平滑转换估计模型(PSTR),考察机构规模对尾部风险的非线性作用,结果表明,上市银行规模的增加能够有效缓释我国银行业的尾部风险,但该影响将随着银行基本面指标的变化而出现显著的非线性转变。具体而言,资产质量较差、成本管理水平较低等问题将加剧金融机构的脆弱性,而改善银行收入结构能够有效提升银行业的稳定性，非利息收入比率、手续费收入比率等指标的上升则增强了大型金融机构的风险抵御能力。第四，拓展样本分析表明，我国金融机构规模与尾部风险存在明显的负向关联，但相比银行业，金融机构规模与尾部风险的非线性关系更易受到各类因素的扰动，偏离原有的平滑转化态势。

基于以上研究结论，提出三点启示：第一，金融管理部门应对不同规模的银行实施差异化监管，有效改善中小银行的风险控制能力和治理水平。而在利率市场化持续推进、银行业竞争日益加剧的背景下，应重点关注中小银行的成本管理水平，通过将成本收入比率纳入压力测试范围等手段，进一步加强针对中小银行相关经营风险暴露的监管力度。第二，稳步推进金融稳杠杆工作，避免过度、过快去杠杆而引发系统性金融风险。面对新冠肺炎疫情期间由逆周期金融调节政策所引起的不良贷款隐患，应密切监控银行企业贷款垫款比率、个人住房贷款比率等指标的运行区间，对我国银行可能出现的不良资产反弹做好前瞻性应对准备，充分防控银行的流动性风险。第三，监控银行混业经营风险，加强混业监管的协调与统筹工作。本文分析表明，包含银行业、证券业、其他金融业在内的金融机构规模与尾部风险的非线性关系易受到各类因素的扰动。因此，应完善穿透式监管工作，对各类金融机构及其经营活动实施风险全覆盖监管，进一步提升证券业、其他金融业等行业的风险抵御能力，填补跨行业、跨市场、跨部门的监管漏洞，防范交叉领域的潜在金融风险。

# 金融周期对房地产价格的影响*

## ——基于 SV-TVP-VAR 模型的实证研究

钱宗鑫 王 芳 孙 挺

进入 21 世纪以来，作为城镇化进程重要载体的房地产业在国民经济中位置突出，成为拉动经济发展的主要引擎之一。由于房地产是银行信贷的重要抵押品，广义信贷等金融周期指标与房地产价格的相互影响机制将金融与实体经济进一步紧密联系起来。然而，2008 年国际金融危机爆发后，随着我国经济从高速度增长逐渐转变为高质量发展，以及货币政策与宏观审慎政策"双支柱"调控框架的确立，特别是在住房金融宏观审慎政策付诸实施的情形下，金融周期对房地产价格的影响是否有所不同就成为一个有趣的问题。与此同时，尽管许多研究认为我国的房地产市场和金融部门是紧密联系在一起的，但关于我国房地产部门和金融部门之间动态关系的研究却较少。本文试图填补这些研究空白。

本文以股票市场价格变量、市场利率变量、资本流动变量、金融杠杆变量和货币供应变量作为基础变量构建我国的金融周期指数，用以描述金融市场景气程度。在此基础上，以金融周期综合指数、房地产价格指数、实体经济产出为变量，构建并使用马尔科夫链蒙特卡罗（MCMC）法估计一个带有随机波动性和时变参数的结构向量自回归模型（SV-

---

\* 原文刊载于《金融研究》2021 年第 3 期。
   **作者简介**：钱宗鑫，经济学博士，教授，中国人民大学财政金融学院；王芳，经济学博士，教授，中国人民大学财政金融学院；孙挺，经济学硕士，中信建投证券股份有限公司资本市场部。

TVP-SVAR），以研究我国金融周期对房地产价格的动态影响。

本文构建的 VAR 模型有以下特征：允许模型回归系数随时间改变；允许经济冲击的大小随时间改变；用递归识别法识别模型的结构化经济冲击。基于以下原因，上述三个特征十分重要：首先，我国的经济发展特点使得房地产部门和金融部门的动态关系可能存在结构性的变化，允许 VAR 模型的系数随时间改变能够较好地捕捉到这些变化；其次，国内外经济环境及经济不确定性的来源随时间改变，因此，模型中内生变量的冲击大小可能随时间变动，使用 VAR、SVAR 等传统定量分析方法对既有明显周期性又附带时变特征的我国房地产市场和金融市场进行分析可能会遗漏关键的时变信息；最后，简单地把简化式 VAR 模型的误差项理解为经济冲击忽略了内生变量之间的当期相关性，进而容易导致错误结论。在此 SVAR 模型中，变量排序如下：实际经济活动指标（产出）、房价指标、金融周期指标。如此排序的假设是：房地产价格和金融周期对实际经济活动的影响存在滞后性；金融市场的变化对房地产价格的影响存在滞后性；金融市场状态对房地产市场和实际经济活动的变化反应迅速。

本文使用 2004—2016 年的季度数据估计模型。在构建我国的金融周期指数时，我们用上证 A 股指数度量股票市场表现，用固定资产投资来源中的贷款额占总投资的比例作为杠杆率的度量指标，用资本和金融账户的差额占 GDP 的比重作为资本流动的度量指标，用 $M_2$ 季度同比增速作为货币供给的度量指标。在 SV-TVP-SVAR 模型中，我们使用 GDP 季度同比增速作为实际经济活动度量指标，用考虑了房屋质量差异的"中国典型城市住房同质价格指数"度量房地产价格。

在金融周期指标构建及模型估计中，本文得到以下三个主要的结论：第一，本文构建的金融综合指数可以较为准确地反映金融市场的运行情况，与我国经济金融市场的拟合度较高。第二，我国经济冲击的大小随时间改变。实际经济活动的波动性在2009年达到峰值,然后逐渐下降;房价的波动率表现出下降趋势,但在2014—2016年有所上升;金融周期指数的波动性缓慢上升,意味着这段样本期间中的金融风险值得注意。第三,金融周期对房地产价格的影响具有明显的时变性。2008年之前,金融市场繁荣对房地产价格有稳定的推升作用,但国际金融危机后该影响持续弱化;与之类似,实际经济对房价的影响也从2008年以后逐渐变弱;金融周期、房地产价格冲击对产出的影响均逐渐减小。这意味着,在经济增长方式转变和经济结构调整的过程中,我国房地产价格对经济金融冲击的敏感度已经大幅下降。

根据以上分析,本文提出了以下政策建议:首先,要充分认识到金融周期对房地产价格、实体产出影响表现出明显的时变性。与2008年国际金融危机前相比,当前我国金融市场冲击对房价及产出的影响均大幅降低,金融刺激政策可能难以再通过房地产市场有效带动实体经济的繁荣。相反,其可能导致银行贷款不良率的攀升,在金融系统内积累系统性风险。其次,国家针对房地产的宏观调控政策不仅对控制银行贷款不良率的提高体现出积极作用,而且有助于产出和房价随机波动率的下降及风险防控。近年来,我国加强了防范和化解系统性金融风险的政策举措,房地产金融化、泡沫化势头得到遏制,未来应继续坚持将房地产宏观调控政策作为宏观审慎政策框架的重要组成部分。

# 基于共同冲击和异质风险叠加传导的风险传染研究*

## ——来自中国上市银行网络的传染模拟

徐国祥　吴　婷　王　莹

金融是国家重要的核心竞争力，防范化解金融风险特别是防止发生系统性金融风险，是金融工作的根本性任务。近年来，我国防范化解金融风险攻坚战取得关键进展。党的十九届五中全会强调"坚持系统观念""注意防范化解重大风险挑战"。现代金融体系和经济环境日趋复杂，坚持系统观念显得愈加重要，站在整体和全局高度观察、思考和防范重大金融风险具有重要的学术价值和现实意义。

系统性风险是一个被广泛使用的术语，但很难定义和量化，它经常被视为一种"当我们看到它时"就存在的现象。外生或内生冲击及各类因素主导的传播渠道和传播次序，使得系统性风险的产生和演变形成"黑箱"。学术界为了简化这些因素组合，通常将注意力限制在三种风险形式：异质风险的系统内部传染，外部共同冲击引发的风险，随着时间推移积累引起的失衡风险。上述风险形式并不是相互排斥的，相反，在真实危机中，风险的交互叠加更加普遍。识别系统性风险事件的一个重要

---

\* 原文刊载于《金融研究》2021年第4期。
　作者简介：徐国祥，经济学博士，教授，上海财经大学统计与管理学院，上海财经大学应用统计研究中心；吴婷，经济学博士，讲师，上海立信会计金融学院保险学院；王莹，经济学博士，阿里巴巴集团。

因素是潜在的"系统状态"及事件进一步改变"系统状态"的能力。例如，当系统遭遇外部冲击而整体被削弱时，即使是暂时或较小的异质风险，也可能持续反馈产生严重的影响。可见，从风险源头来看，外部共同冲击引发的整个系统"脆弱"在极大程度上决定了异质风险的传染深度和广度。鉴于此，本文将银行系统遭遇外部共同冲击作为研究起点，建立了一个共同冲击和异质风险交互传导和放大的简化模型。根据特定阶段中所占主导地位的风险因素不同，抽象出一个包含"原始冲击""增量冲击"和"违约冲击"传导的系统性风险传染模型，刻画了外部共同冲击削弱整体系统状态背景下，异质风险沿着金融市场和银行间债权债务链交互溢出，并与共同冲击叠加反馈的动态过程。

一直以来，系统性风险的研究文献集中探讨交易对手方风险外部性（Counterparty Risk Externality）和相关外部性（Correlation Externality）[①]。自2008年国际金融危机之后，学界也日益关注相关外部性对风险传染机制的影响，例如 Acharya 和 Yorulmazer（2008）指出，潜在的信息溢出会增加风险决策之间的相关性，从而促进内生性共同冲击风险。事实上，已有一些文献对异质风险传染和共同冲击传染进行比较分析，采取不同的研究方法均得出共同冲击传染更加重要的结论。本文模拟了共同冲击和异质风险交互作用下的风险传染过程，其实也属于两者的对比研究。与已有文献相比，本文的贡献体现在以下方面：第一，对外部共同冲击传导进行微观解构，可能有助于系统性风险的早期预警和干预；第二，基于风险相关性构建直接和间接网络，不仅能更好捕捉到风险传染的各个阶段，还未过度依赖银行的历史违约数据；第三，度量不同"触发银行"引起的系统性风险。与一次性离开（Leave-One-Out，LOO）方法中直接

---

[①] 交易对手风险外部性是指由于直接因果相关导致的风险溢出，最典型的是债权债务关系链引发的多米诺传染。相关外部性是指由于间接因果相关（如共同风险因素）导致的风险溢出，包括宏观风险、市场风险等。

去除单个银行相比,本研究的"触发银行"一直被保留在模拟网络中,叠加验证其发生偿付能力破产为止,更贴近真实的风险情形。

本文基于风险相关性建立了两类银行网络,一是基于2018年我国15家上市银行的股票收益率和2016—2018年的银行评级数据构建贝叶斯分层图模型,用于模拟原始冲击和增量冲击;二是基于15家上市银行的2018年年报相关数据构建银行间市场拆借矩阵,用于模拟违约冲击。在此基础上,本文利用蒙特卡罗模拟上述"三阶段"系统性风险传染模型,通过冲击交互和损失叠加动态验证每个银行的偿付能力,破产银行的损失会继续传染,直至系统实现相对稳态(即偿付能力破产银行数量不变),并进一步测度了不同触发银行引发的系统性损失、单个银行的系统性风险杠杆能力(文中称为"传染乘数")及政府监管介入的效果。

模拟结果显示:共同冲击损失远大于异质风险损失(银行间市场拆借违约风险);规模和网络关联性是决定传染乘数的两个重要因素,且当规模因素不突出时,网络关联性对传染乘数的决定作用相对更强,极容易出现小规模、高关联性银行具有较高的传染乘数;当银行风险资产损失率在10%至25%之间时,造成系统性损失的杠杆能力普遍增强。此外,政府在金融资产抛售环节的监管介入能较好地降低系统性风险。

根据上述分析结论,本文得到以下三方面政策启示:第一,为了从源头上控制系统性风险,建议增加银行系统共同风险敞口的评估,并重视对中小规模银行的网络高关联的识别与评估。第二,鉴于触发银行的传染乘数存在拐点现象,建议可适当增加系统性风险的"阻断"干预机制,比如设置一个风险加权资产损失率预警值以严防风险的升级。从本文的模拟结果来看,可尽量将损失率控制在10%以内。第三,虽然在资产抛售环节监管介入能明显降低损失,但由于我国银行系统可供出售金融资产的占比较低导致介入时点的敏感度不够明显,未来随着可供出售金融资产的占比上升,可能会存在介入节点的减损差别效益。

# 03 银行经营与企业融资

# 定向降准、贷款可得性与小微企业商业信用*

## ——基于断点回归的经验证据

### 孔东民 李海洋 杨 薇

全面扶持小微企业发展,为我国经济高质量发展注入活力与新动能,是我国经济平稳运行和转型升级的必然要求。然而,"融资难、融资贵"一直严重制约着小微企业成长,使小微企业不得不诉诸非正式融资制度(如商业信用)来获得资金。党的十九届五中全会明确提出,支持小微企业成长为创新重要发源地,完善促进小微企业发展的政策体系。其中,实施"精准滴灌"式的货币政策,对小微企业成长尤为重要,有助于进一步加强金融服务实体经济的功能。我国央行自2014年6月推出定向降准这一结构性货币政策工具,旨在鼓励商业银行等金融机构向小微企业等国民经济重要部门和薄弱环节提供信贷支持,疏通小微企业通过正式制度(如银行贷款)进行融资的渠道,以缓解这些企业的融资约束。

不同于传统"一刀切"式的全面降准政策,定向降准通过对符合一定条件的商业银行等金融机构下调存款准备金率,引导信贷资源更多地流向小微企业等重点、薄弱经济部门,以优化信贷资源配置结构,实现

---

\* 原文刊载于《金融研究》2021年第3期。
作者简介:孔东民,管理学博士,教授,中南财经政法大学金融学院、华中科技大学经济学院;李海洋,金融学博士,中南财经政法大学金融学院;杨薇,金融学博士,讲师,华东理工大学商学院。

经济结构转型升级。因此，定向降准本质上是"精准滴灌"式的数量型货币政策工具，旨在定向支持小微企业通过商业银行等获得信贷资源。定向降准自实施以来，备受学术界关注，并研究评估定向降准的政策效果。

然而囿于数据可得性、研究视角及研究方法，鲜有研究评估定向降准对微观企业其他融资方式的影响。对于小微企业而言，由于其经营风险较大，信息披露不健全，企业规模较小，往往难以获得银行信贷。在这种情况下，为维持正常的投资生产活动，小微企业经常使用商业信用缓解资金困难。定向降准政策的实施有利于银行贷款更多地流向小微企业，可能影响小微企业的商业信用。

使用国泰安 CSMAR 数据库中全国中小企业股份转让系统披露的企业财务数据，基于小微企业不得不诉诸于非正式制度（如商业信用）来缓解融资困难的现实，根据《中小企业划型标准规定》对小微企业明确的规定，采用模糊断点回归设计，借助定向降准这一自然实验，本文评估银行贷款可得性对小微企业商业信用的影响，检验正式融资制度对非正式融资制度的替代效应。研究发现，受定向降准政策冲击，小微企业贷款可得性上升，进而对商业信用的需求显著下降；不同的模型设定与稳健性检验，均得到一致的结论；银行信贷资源配置往往与银行的价值发现功能相一致，银行倾向于发现优质企业，对其进行授信并进行有效监督。因此，定向降准的作用存在于融资约束较弱、市场实力较强的优质小微企业，这些企业更有可能获得定向降准释放的信贷资源，银行贷款可得性更有可能提高，进而对商业信用产生负向影响。

本文的主要贡献在于：基于正式融资制度与非正式融资制度的视角，研究了小微企业贷款可得性对商业信用的影响，评估了定向降准对小微企业融资决策产生的实际效果；银行贷款和商业信用是企业资金来源的重要组成部分，许多因素对这两种融资方式产生共同作用。本文使用断点回归设计，基于定向降准政策和明确的企业划型标准，克服内生性问题，识别了贷款可得性上升对小微企业商业信用的负向因果效应，为银行贷款与商业信用之间的替代关系提供了来自中国小微企业的证据，丰富了货币政策对企业商业信用影响的相关研究。

本文对定向降准的评估具有明晰的政策启示：一方面，由于小微企业是促进我国经济结构优化的新动能，同时小微企业融资难的困境短期内难以得到完全解决，因此应坚持实施定向降准政策，进一步提高小微企业银行贷款可得性，加大力度缓解小微企业融资约束；另一方面，定向降准的政策效应主要存在于融资约束较弱、市场势力较强的优质小微企业，有必要进一步推出金融扶持政策，将信贷资源直接分配于弱势小微企业，尤其在新冠肺炎疫情这一特殊背景下，创新直达实体经济的货币政策工具对于弱势小微企业的生存发展至关重要。

囿于数据可得性和局限性，本文研究的样本来自新三板的企业，然而小微企业遍布全国各地，随着我国信息披露制度的不断完善及数据收集和存储能力的不断提升，未来需要进一步考察小微企业融资决策问题，为小微企业发展提供更多精准参考。

# 银行竞争提高了企业投资水平和资源配置效率吗？*

## ——基于分支机构空间分布的研究

### 李志生 金凌

2006年以前，我国银行分支机构设立受到严格管制，无论是在审批程序还是准入条件上，监管部门都对股份制商业银行和城市商业银行异地设立分支机构进行严格把控。在此背景下，国有商业银行在银行市场中占据主导地位，以贷款业务为例，其市场份额占比超过65%。为更好地服务实体经济发展，银监会于2006年和2009年先后颁布了《城市商业银行异地分支机构管理办法》和《关于中小商业银行分支机构市场准入政策的调整意见（试行）》，放宽了股份制商业银行和城市商业银行异地设立分支机构的条件。上述政策调整后，股份制商业银行和城市商业银行的贷款业务份额和分支机构数量占比大幅上升，银行分支机构空间分布发生了较大变化，网点覆盖率不断扩大，银行业竞争水平和服务经济社会发展的能力明显提升。

银行体系不仅在我国金融系统中占据重要地位，也在企业生产经营和经济发展的资金融通中发挥着举足轻重的作用。已有研究表明，银行竞争有利于提升企业信贷可获得性和信贷资源配置效率。考虑到企业生

---

\* 原文刊载于《金融研究》2021年第1期。
**作者简介**：李志生，金融工程博士，教授，中南财经政法大学金融学院；金凌，金融工程博士研究生，中南财经政法大学金融学院。

产经营与融资状况密切相关，企业投资与投资效率势必受银行分支机构空间分布和银行竞争水平的影响。投资是实体企业最重要的生产经营活动之一，其效率不仅是企业内部资源配置效率的集中体现，更是供给侧结构性改革关注的重点。鉴于此，准确评估银行分支机构空间分布和银行竞争水平变化对企业投资和投资效率的影响，具有较好的政策意义和现实针对性。

本文基于企业和银行分支机构的地理位置，采用企业周边银行分支机构数量度量银行竞争水平，通过2001—2012年国家统计局工业企业数据（300 269家工业企业1 054 210个年度样本），研究银行竞争对企业投资水平和投资效率的影响。研究结果表明，企业周边银行分支机构数量的增加显著提高了企业的投资水平和投资效率。如果企业周边20公里半径内分支机构数量由0家增加至10家，企业投资增长0.96%，非效率投资下降0.73%，经济意义显著，企业内部资源配置效率明显改善。在替换指标度量方法、控制区域差异和潜在的双向因果关系、采用2009年政策变化作为外生冲击等检验中，结果表现出较好的稳健性。进一步研究表明，银行分支机构数量增加（竞争水平上升）对企业投资效率的提升作用主要表现在投资不足的企业和非国有企业中，企业融资约束程度的降低和代理冲突的减弱是银行竞争提高企业投资效率的主要原因，其中银行竞争对企业融资约束的缓解效应强于对代理冲突的遏制效应。

本文对已有文献的贡献和拓展主要体现在以下三个方面：一是在中国问题研究方面，已有文献较多关注银行竞争对宏观层面的资源配置效率及微观层面的企业信贷资源获取和融资约束的影响，对企业如何将获取的信贷资源用于投资和资源分配层面的关注有所不足，本文从企业投资水平和投资效率的角度系统评估了银行竞争的经济效应。二是在银行竞争水平的度量上，国内外研究大多采用银行市场结构指标（如行业集中度或赫芬达尔—赫希曼指数）或放宽银行分支机构设立限制这一准自然实验，但两者都难以区分同一地区不同微观企业面临的真实的银行竞争水平及其异质性，同时，市场结构指标则往往与地区宏观经济等因素密切相关。本文采用企业周边一定半径内银行分支机构数量度量银行竞争水平，在有效区分不同企业面临的真实银行竞争水平的同时，将统计范围限定在企业周边，较大程度上缓解了地区宏观因素导致的潜在内生性问题，有利于更加精准地评估银行竞争的经济效应。三是现有银行分支机构空间分布的相关研究集中于宏观经济增长和银行绩效等方面，鲜有文献以微观企业生产经营为研究对象。本文基于企业投资水平和投资效率的视角展开研究，从研究样本和研究维度上对相关文献进行了有益补充。

　　根据研究结论，本文有以下政策启示：在供给侧结构性改革的进程中，应进一步加强金融基础设施建设，不断扩大金融服务的覆盖面和可得性，培育银行市场良性竞争环境，充分发挥市场配置资源的作用，引导信贷资金进入实体企业，在提高银行系统服务实体经济能力的同时，助力高质量发展。

# 融资租赁、银行信贷与企业投资\*

## ——基于2004—2016年中国上市公司的实证研究

### 赵 娜 王 博 张珂瑜

近年来，融资租赁作为集融资与融物于一体的融资方式得到较快发展，成为与实体经济联系较为紧密的金融工具之一。融资租赁为民间资本流入正规融资渠道提供了可能性，同时也通过放宽对企业资信水平、经营状况等方面的限制，为民营企业、中小企业带来融资机会，成为解决我国中小企业融资难题的有益探索。作为同样重要的外部融资渠道，融资租赁与银行信贷之间是何种关系，以及融资租赁能否作为传统融资渠道的有效替代方式等问题都值得深入思考。

目前关于融资租赁与银行信贷之间关系的研究，国内外文献主要集中在以下两个方面。一是基于 Myers 等（1976）的债务替代理论，认为企业增加融资租赁会减少借贷融资。二是由 Lewis 和 Schallheim（1992）从承租人视角提出的互补理论。但我国目前租赁市场交易总额中约有90%以上为融资租赁，其中售后回租又占据了较大比例，2015年甚至高达83.9%，而经营性租赁交易占比仅为12.5%。因此，根据我国租赁业的发展现状和租赁交易税收制度安排特点，我国企业融资租赁和银行信贷之间的互补理论机制较难实现。

---

\* 原文刊载于《金融研究》2021年第1期。
作者简介：赵娜，经济学博士，副教授，南开大学经济学院；王博，金融学博士，教授，南开大学金融学院；张珂瑜，硕士研究生，中国人民大学汉青经济与金融高级研究院。

本文通过手工整理我国沪深两市 2004—2016 年全部 A 股上市公司的年度报告，获得融资租赁数据和财务指标等进行实证检验（最终得到 2 261 个上市公司 11 827 个样本点）。研究结果表明：融资租赁和银行信贷都能够显著提升公司投资率，并且融资租赁对于银行信贷具有显著的替代效应。由于融资约束在融资租赁与银行信贷之间的替代关系中扮演着十分重要的角色，所以本文选取企业资产有形性、资产负债率及企业所有制性质作为企业融资约束程度的衡量指标，通过实证分析探究其在企业融资租赁和借贷融资的替代关系中所发挥的作用。结果发现，企业的有形性资产净值率较低、资产负债率较高或为民营企业，即企业的融资约束程度越严重，融资租赁对银行信贷的替代作用就越大。

本文在以下三方面对已有文献形成补充和扩展：第一，国内有关融资租赁的研究多集中于宏观视角，微观层面的研究相对较少（史燕平和徐晓兰，2013）。本文从企业微观层面实证检验了融资租赁对银行信贷具有替代效应，以及融资约束在两者替代关系中的影响机理，为客观评估融资租赁对经济发展的影响提供了微观证据，丰富和拓展了融资租赁的研究范畴。第二，已有研究文献多是讨论融资租赁与银行信贷之间的数量变化关系（Deloof 和 Verschueren，1999；Lin 等，2013），但考虑到这种数量变化可能会受到企业资产结构等因素的共同影响，从而可能导致内生性问题和估计偏误，同时，仅从数量上分析融资租赁与银行信贷的关系，也无法体现出两者关系存在的基础。因此，本文基于融资租赁与银行信贷共有的特点——"融资"属性，从企业投资视角来检验两者的替代关系是否成立，即当一种融资渠道的成本提高时，另一种融资渠道对企业投资的促进效果是否会增强。第三，本文从资产有形性、财务杠杆水平和所有制性质三个方面分析融资约束对融资租赁替代效应的影响，结果表明，面临较强融资约束的企业，融资租赁对银行信贷的替代作用更加明显，这为我国进一步完善金融市场体系建设提供了参考。

根据上述分析结论,得到以下政策启示:积极引导融资租赁发挥其"产融结合"的优势优化金融供给,促进融资租赁"融资"和"融物"双重属性的有效发挥,不断提高其精准服务实体经济的能力,为缓解小微企业融资难题贡献力量。同时,针对融资租赁尤其是售后回租的"类信贷"功能,积极完善融资租赁的相关政策,规范和引导其回归本源、扬长避短,在充分发挥其独特优势的同时防范化解相关金融风险。

# 去产能政策与融资租赁*

史燕平　杨　汀　庞家任

党的十九大报告强调，我国经济已由高速增长阶段转向高质量发展阶段。党的十九届五中全会进一步指出，要"以推动高质量发展为主题"来"加快建设现代化经济体系"。在我国经济从"高速度"向"高质量"的转型背景中，产能过剩问题一直是困扰经济转型过程的沉疴。为治理产能过剩，近十余年来相关部门多次出台去产能政策，政策工具涵盖金融、财税、市场准入等多方面。其中，金融政策的目标是从资金源头上调整产业之间的资源配置，限制产能过剩企业的融资渠道，从而达到让企业减产的目的。去产能政策颁布之后，相关金融机构通过压缩贷款、限制资本市场融资等方式协助实现去产能。然而，在产能过剩企业的银行贷款等融资方式下降的同时，这些企业通过融资租赁获取的资金在持续增加。这一现象背后是否隐藏了某种套利行为？这种套利行为又会给去产能政策的实施效果带来怎样的影响？本文试图从理论上对去产能政策和融资租赁之间的相互影响机制提供一种可能的解释，并通过实证研究来验证理论解释。

具体来看，考虑到我国融资租赁业从2007年开始再次发展，本文手工收集了2007—2016年我国上市公司的融资租赁交易信息（共计14 679

---

*原文刊载于《金融研究》2021年第4期。
作者简介：史燕平，经济学博士，教授，对外经济贸易大学国际经济贸易学院；杨汀，经济学博士，讲师，北方工业大学经济管理学院；庞家任，经济学博士，副教授，清华大学经济管理学院。

个样本点），并利用双重差分法（Difference in Differences，DID）来识别去产能政策和融资租赁之间的相互关系。实证研究结果显示，去产能政策显著推动了融资租赁规模的扩张，而融资租赁规模的扩张又反过来在一定程度上削弱了去产能政策的效果。进一步分析表明，去产能政策从需求端和供给端同时推动了融资租赁规模的扩张。从需求端角度看，去产能政策出台后，产能过剩企业的长期资金来源显著减少，导致出现长期资金缺口。一方面，银行对产能过剩企业的信贷结构进行调整，大幅收紧对其发放的贷款特别是长期贷款规模，融资期限越来越趋于短期化。另一方面，去产能政策对产能过剩企业使用债券、股权融资等长期融资方式做了明文限制。为弥补长期资金缺口，产能过剩企业需要寻找可替代的长期资金，而融资租赁的一些特点使其成为可能的备选方案：首先，融资租赁的期限较长，一般为3~5年；其次，融资租赁机构所受监管相对较松。综上所述，去产能政策限制了产能过剩企业从主流融资渠道获得长期资金的能力，激发了其对融资租赁的需求，从而推动了融资租赁规模的扩张。从供给端角度看，虽然去产能政策限制银行向产能过剩企业发放贷款，但部分产能过剩企业仍具备还款能力，为其提供融资依然有利可图，因此银行也有较强动机进行监管套利，即可以通过受监管较弱的融资租赁子公司间接为这些企业提供资金。根据是否由银行控股，融资租赁机构可分为银行系租赁公司和非银行系租赁公司。相较于后者，银行系租赁公司在为产能过剩企业提供融资租赁时具有两方面优势。一是信息优势，由于母公司（银行）与产能过剩企业之间的借贷关系，银行系租赁公司对这些企业的熟悉和了解程度更高，信息不对称问题相对较轻。二是资金优势，由于有母公司（银行）支持，银行系租赁公司的资金更为充足，贷款成本更低。相关分析也表明融资租赁扩张的资金主要来自银行系租赁公司。

根据上述分析结论，得到以下两方面政策启示：第一，制定产业政策时应考虑影子银行渠道。随着融资租赁等形式的影子银行规模日益扩张，制定产业政策时不仅要考虑银行贷款等主流融资渠道，还应兼顾影子银行渠道，否则可能会存在漏洞而滋生监管套利行为，导致政策效果被削弱。在经济高质量发展目标下，应充分考虑产业政策与金融体系间的相互作用，实现产业政策与金融体系的良性互动。第二，引导融资租赁业回归本源。融资租赁包括直接租赁和售后回租两种交易形式。在直接租赁中，承租人选定设备后，出租人向供货商购买设备，出租给承租人使用并收取租金。在售后回租中，企业将自身部分资产卖给租赁公司以获得融资，再从该出租人处租回已售出资产并支付租金。这两种融资租赁交易模式的主要区别是，直接租赁的最终交易目的是"融物"，即为承租企业引进设备；而售后回租的交易目的是"融资"，即为承租企业提供资金融通，是一种类贷款的融资形式。融资租赁的本源是基于直接租赁的设备融资业务。发达国家的融资租赁业务以直接租赁为主，而我国企业则以售后回租为主。直接租赁在促进制造业产融结合、推动实现"一带一路"倡议方面大有可为，因此，相关部门应鼓励发展直租业务，引导融资租赁业回归本源，为实体经济发展提供更多支持。

# 04 企业改革与创新发展

# 国企"混改"与企业金融资产配置*

叶永卫　李增福

2013年11月,党的十八届三中全会提出"积极发展混合所有制经济"。自此,国有企业改革进入"混合所有制改革"的历史新阶段。在这一背景下,混合所有制改革对国有企业行为的影响迅速成为学术界和实务界关注的焦点。本文所关注的中心问题是:混合所有制改革是否影响了国有企业的金融资产投资行为?厘清这一问题,不仅有助于全面了解混合所有制改革产生的经济效应,而且对于如何制定相关措施以引导金融更好地服务实体经济具有积极意义。

从理论上来说,在国有企业混合所有制改革过程中,非国有股东的进入可能会对企业的治理结构和资源禀赋产生影响,进而作用于国有企业的委托代理冲突和融资约束。一方面,由于非国有资本的逐利性,非国有股东具有强烈的动机去监督企业经理人,强化经理人的薪酬(或解聘)与绩效的敏感性,完善公司治理结构,进而提升国有企业的公司治理水平。在此背景下,企业经理人将更加注重企业的长远发展而非短期利益,从而进行更多有利于企业价值提升的实体投资(诸如研发创新等)。然而,研发创新等投资高投入、长周期的特征使其面临更多的不确定性和更高的调整成本,一旦中断,必将给企业带来巨大损失,因此企业经理人有动机借助金融资产的"蓄水池"效应,来减少未来不确定性和高额调整

---

\* 原文刊载于《金融研究》2021年第3期。
　　**作者简介:** 叶永卫,经济学博士研究生,上海财经大学公共经济与管理学院;李增福,经济学博士,教授,华南师范大学经济与管理学院。

成本对企业实体投资的影响，本文将这一作用路径称之为治理效应路径。另一方面，伴随非国有资本的进入，国有股权占比下降，国有企业承担的政策性负担和任务也将相应减少，这在一定程度上会削弱与国有股权相伴而生的资源效应，进而强化企业所面临的融资约束。因此，基于预防性储蓄动机，企业经理人会配置更多的金融资产来平滑企业的实体投资，以避免融资约束导致实体投资项目陷入资金困境，本文将这一作用路径称之为融资约束路径。综上可知，无论是基于治理效应路径还是基于融资约束路径，国企"混改"均可能促进国有企业的金融资产投资。

为验证上述理论推断，本文利用2010—2017年中国沪深A股上市公司的面板数据（共计6 150个样本），考察了国企"混改"对企业金融资产配置的影响，并重点分析了国企"混改"过程中企业进行金融资产配置的动机。研究结果显示，非国有股东参股显著促进了国有企业的金融资产投资。作用机制检验发现，非国有股东参股通过治理效应路径和融资约束路径共同影响了国有企业的金融资产配置行为，具体表现为非国有股东参股带来的监督治理效应和融资约束强化效应均增强了国有企业配置金融资产的预防性储蓄动机，进而促使国有企业增加金融资产投资。上述研究结果表明，非国有股东参股推动的国有企业金融资产投资并非出于短期利益追逐，更多是为了平滑企业投资进行的预防性储蓄。

相较于已有文献，本文的边际贡献主要体现在如下三个方面：第一，对于混合所有制改革的经济后果，目前已有较多的文献进行了研究，其中既有正面之词，也不乏负面之说。遵循前期文献的研究脉络，本文探究了混合所有制改革过程中，非国有股东参股对国有企业金融资产配置的影响，并重点分析了非国有股东参股背景下国有企业金融资产配置的动机。这一工作有助于丰富和拓展国有企业混合所有制改革经济后果的相关研究。第二，现有文献大多集中于对企业金融资产投资经济后果的讨论，而较少关注企业金融资产投资的驱动因素。本文从非国有股东参股的视角研究国企金融资本配置的驱动因素，是对企业金融资产投资驱动因素研究文献的一个补充。第三，本文研究结论证实，非国有股东参股推动的国有企业金融资产投资并非出于短期利益追逐，更多是为了平滑企业投资进行的预防性储蓄。因此，在制定相关政策以解决企业金融资产投资乱象时，应当甄别两种动机的差异并加以区别对待，避免因一概而论给企业正常的投融资活动带来不利影响。

# 非国有股东治理与国有企业去僵尸化*

## ——来自国有上市公司董事会"混合"的经验证据

马新啸　汤泰劼　蔡贵龙

近年来,在经济结构转型升级和全面深化改革的背景下,如何更好地处置僵尸企业在顶层设计、学术研究及社会实践领域都是一个广受关注的话题。在我国的转轨进程中,部分企业长期亏损、盈利无望、生产停滞,却依靠财政补贴、低成本银行信贷等一直勉强存活,这类企业通常被称为"僵尸企业"。僵尸企业的存在不仅影响非僵尸企业的正常经营、形成"挤出效应",而且会降低市场配置资源的效率和阻碍技术进步,最终妨碍经济社会高质量发展。其中,国有企业作为中国特色社会主义的重要物质基础和政治基础,在我国经济高速发展和战略目标实现,特别是"十三五"规划完成的过程中发挥着不可或缺的关键作用,然而部分国企呈现出较为严重的僵尸化现象,限制了其国民经济中流砥柱作用的发挥。因此,如何更好地治理国有僵尸企业和促进国企高质量发展,已成为全面深化改革的重要环节。

2013年11月,党的十八届三中全会通过了《中共中央关于全面深化改革若干重大问题的决定》,明确指出要"积极发展混合所有制经济"。2017年10月,党的十九大报告指出要"深化国有企业改革,发展混合

---

\* 原文刊载于《金融研究》2021年第3期。
作者简介:马新啸,会计学博士研究生,中山大学管理学院;汤泰劼,会计学博士研究生,北京大学光华管理学院;蔡贵龙,会计学博士,助理教授,中山大学管理学院。

所有制经济，培育具有全球竞争力的世界一流企业"。2020年10月，《中共中央关于制定国民经济和社会发展第十四个五年规划和二〇三五年远景目标的建议》明确提出"深化国资国企改革，做强做优做大国有资本和国有企业。加快国有经济布局优化和结构调整，发挥国有经济战略支撑作用。加快完善中国特色现代企业制度，深化国有企业混合所有制改革"。作为国企改革的关键突破口，混合所有制改革的目的在于通过引入非国有股东，在国有企业中形成更加制衡的股权结构和多元化的董事会结构，健全更加有效的内部监督与治理机制，从而使得国有企业在全面建设社会主义现代化国家新征程中的支柱作用行稳致远。

在此基础上，本文以我国沪深两市2008—2015年国有上市公司为样本（合计6 357个观测值），通过手工整理年报披露的前十大股东性质、持股比例与股东委派高管数据，分别从股权结构和高层治理两个维度刻画非国有股东参与国企治理的程度，研究其对国企去僵尸化的影响作用。研究发现：非国有股东参与国企高层治理可以显著降低冗员规模和提升资本密集度，进而降低国企成为僵尸企业的可能性，这种效果在国企高管的影响力较弱，即非国有股东参与国企治理的能力相对较强时更为明显，而仅持股等股权结构维度的治理影响较弱；进一步地，通过细分僵尸企业识别指标，本文发现非国有股东治理可以在抑制低息贷款获取和改善盈利能力两方面降低相应国企的僵尸化程度，促使其正常经营运转；最后，经过良好治理的国有企业生产能力和市场价值得到显著提升。

本文主要有如下两方面贡献。第一，丰富了僵尸企业治理和国有企业混合所有制改革的相关研究。具体而言，本文针对我国僵尸企业现象中更加亟须解决的国有企业僵尸化现象，从股权制衡和高层治理的双重视角，探讨体现市场化运作的非国有股东治理能否及如何对国有僵尸企业产生影响作用，对僵尸企业治理和国有企业混合所有制改革的文献进行了有益补充。第二，本文具有一定的政策参考价值。国有企业在促进社会主义公有制经济发展壮大、维护国家经济安全、实现国家战略目标等诸多方面发挥着不可替代的重要作用。国有企业是中国特色社会主义的重要物质基础和政治基础，是党执政兴国的重要支柱和依靠力量，必须做大做强。因此，本文研究如何在不失去国有股东控制权、不造成国有资产流失的前提下实现国有企业去僵尸化，更加具有现实意义和参考价值：在国企混改背景下，更要在以董事会"混合"为代表的诸多治理模式上进行深层次配套改革，由此可以更好地完善国企治理和抑制国有僵尸企业现象，促使国有企业在全面建设社会主义现代化国家新征程中发挥日益重要的作用。

本文的研究具有以下三点启示。第一，本文的结论为做好处置僵尸企业工作提供了一种可行的解决途径，非国有股东参与国企高层治理可以明显改善国企僵尸化现象。第二，在国企的混合所有制改革过程中，不能为"混"而"混"，仅有简单的股权混合难以较好发挥非国有股东的治理作用，通过更好地保障非国有股东委派董事、监事和高管进入国企高层参与治理，让非国有股东拥有充分的话语权，有助于实现国有资本与非国有资本的混合由"量变"引发"质变"。因此，各层级的国有企业在进行混合所有制改革时应在实质上确保非国有股东实现应有的权利。第三，非国有股东要发挥积极的治理作用面临诸多的约束条件，国有企业管理层过高的影响力容易出现"一言堂"现象，会大大削弱非国有股东"发声"空间，因此，为了进一步提升非国有股东的话语权，可以相应限制国有企业管理层过大的控制权，从而更好地保障改革有效推进。

需要指出的是，囿于数据收集的局限性，本文样本期未能覆盖到僵尸企业现象更加受关注的2016年及以后，这可以作为进一步的研究内容。

# 债务结构优化与企业创新：
# 基于企业债券融资视角的研究*

江轩宇 贾婧 刘琪

党的十九届五中全会指出，"我国已转向高质量发展阶段"，要"坚持创新在我国现代化建设全局中的核心地位，把科技自立自强作为国家发展的战略支撑"。企业是科技创新的主体，提升企业的创新能力是实现高质量发展目标的重要驱动力。然而在新时期，错综复杂的国际形势和新冠肺炎疫情冲击等因素增加了经济发展的不确定性，导致宏观杠杆率重新呈现攀升态势。宏观杠杆率的过快上升容易累积风险，而宏观杠杆率的下降又不利于发挥金融对实体经济的支持作用。在此背景下，研究债务结构优化与企业创新的关系，对于维持企业杠杆率稳定，实现创新驱动发展战略，处理好稳增长和防风险的关系具有重要的理论和现实意义。

本文从债券融资视角出发，考察企业是否能够利用债券市场提高直接融资比重、优化企业债务结构，进而促进企业创新。从理论上看，债券融资对于企业创新的影响存在一定的不确定性。一方面，作为企业债务主要的直接融资及长期融资渠道，债券融资可以通过降低债务融资成本、延长债务期限等方式，在负债水平不变的情况下优化债务结构，进

---

\* 原文刊载于《金融研究》2021年第4期。
作者简介：江轩宇，管理学博士，副教授，中央财经大学会计学院，中国管理会计研究与发展中心；贾婧，博士研究生，中央财经大学会计学院；刘琪，硕士研究生，清华大学经济管理学院。

而促进企业创新。另一方面，债券作为交易型债务，与银行贷款这一关系型债务相比，既具有更强的债务契约刚性特征，又容易给予经营者较高的控制权，不利于发挥负债的治理效应，进而抑制企业创新。

因此，本文以2006—2017年沪深两市A股上市公司为样本（共计12 915个样本），分别从专利数量和专利引用率两个维度衡量企业的创新水平，对债券融资是否及如何影响企业创新展开研究。实证结果发现，债券融资与企业创新显著正相关，表明债券融资优化企业债务结构、促进企业创新能力提升的积极作用占据主导地位。进一步研究表明：（1）债券融资不仅通过降低整体债务融资成本、延长整体债务期限结构促进企业创新，还通过对银行贷款的溢出效应，即降低银行贷款成本、延长银行贷款期限，对企业的创新活动提供支持；（2）产品市场竞争和代理问题会在一定程度上削弱债券融资对企业创新的促进作用；（3）不同类型的债券对创新活动的影响存在异质性。相比于公司债、企业债与可转换债券，短期融资券和中期票据对企业创新的促进作用更加显著，这说明债券发行的便利性在促进企业创新的过程中发挥了重要作用。

本文的研究贡献主要体现在三个方面。第一，丰富了企业创新影响因素的相关研究。首先，从微观角度来看，现有研究主要探讨了负债水平与企业创新的关系，却忽略了负债结构对企业创新的影响。本文则是在假设企业负债水平一定的前提下，探讨企业能否利用债券融资成本低、期限长的特征及债券融资渠道减少银行的"敲竹杠"行为，对自身的债务结构进行优化，进而促进企业创新。其次，从宏观角度来看，现有文献主要从信贷市场发展及股票市场发展的角度探讨了金融发展与企业创新的关系，但对债券市场发展在其中发挥的作用关注不足。本文在一定程度上反映了债券市场发展对企业创新的积极作用。第二，丰富了企业债券融资经济后果的相关文献。继社会融资成本、银行贷款成本、现金股利政策和企业创新绩效之后，本文聚焦于专利产出数量及引用率，探讨了债务融资与企业创新的关系，能够从创新规模和质量的双重视角更好地展现债券融资对企业创新水平影响的全貌。同时，本文在考虑债券融资的特性之外，还分析了直接债务融资渠道（债券融资）对间接融资（银行贷款）的溢出效应，即企业的债券融资行为是否有助于改善银行贷款条件（包括贷款成本和期限结构），进而促进企业创新，并且为相关作用机理提供了充分的经验证据，有助于更为全面地揭示债券融资影响企业创新的作用机理。第三，揭示了债券融资影响企业创新所需要的条件。本文发现，不同类型的债券对企业创新能力的作用存在异质性。与限制相对较多而且融资便利性相对偏低的公司债、企业债和可转债相比，融资便利性更高的短期融资券和中期票据对企业创新的促进作用更强。

在政策启示方面，本文的研究结论说明，企业需要认识到债券融资的重要性，要在风险可控的前提下，充分利用债券市场，通过加大直接债务融资比例优化债务结构，进而促进创新水平的提升；同时，应进一步推动债券市场的发展，完善债券市场的制度建设，不断提高债券融资的便利性，为企业更好地优化债务结构、提升创新能力创造条件。如此，才能更好地发挥金融对实体经济的支持作用，推动实现创新驱动发展战略，促进经济持续健康发展。

# 股票流动性与中国企业创新策略：
# 流水不腐还是洪水猛兽？*

林志帆　杜金岷　龙晓旋

创新是引领发展的第一动力，是建设现代化经济体系的战略支撑。作为中国经济最具活力的一环和提高资源配置效率的重要平台，资本市场在助力企业研发创新、驱动经济增长中扮演着关键的角色。当前除主板、中小板、创业板三个主流交易市场之外，科创板、中小企业股份转让系统、区域性股权交易市场、券商柜台交易市场等平台蓬勃发展，多层次资本市场体系建设正加快推进。在此背景下，本文探讨了股票流动性对上市公司创新战略的影响。

自 2005 年的股权分置改革开始，资本市场的股票流动性开始呈现明显增强的趋势。而后，2010 年融资融券制度启动并逐步扩容、2014 年"沪港通"开通、2016 年新三板分层制度试行、2017 年"H 股'全流通'试点"、2020 年创业板实施注册制和新股涨跌幅限制放宽等改革举措，无不反映了我国提升上市公司股票流动性、提高资金流动效率的决心。探索股票流动性对企业创新的影响对当前多层次资本市场建设中如何通过合理的制度设计来实现"以金融助实体、以改革促发展"具有重要的启示意义。

---

\* 原文刊载于《金融研究》2021 年第 3 期。

作者简介：林志帆，经济学博士，特聘副研究员，北京师范大学人文和社会科学高等研究院；杜金岷，经济学博士，教授，暨南大学经济学院；龙晓旋，经济学硕士，珠海华发集团有限公司战略发展中心。

理论文献指出，股票流动性对企业创新可能有两种截然不同的影响。有文献认为较高的股票流动性能够激励企业创新，这是因为：股票流动性越高，投资者"用脚投票"的交易成本越低，也就更利于大股东和机构投资者进入和退出。而大股东和机构投资者一旦减持就很可能在市面上形成"风向标"，这种明显的负面信号将带动中小投资者抛售股票，"滚雪球"般下滑的股价表现可能导致管理层被问责甚至解聘。并且，如果企业管理层的薪酬与股价挂钩或包含股票期权，他们的个人财富也可能蒙受损失。可以推知，股票流动性较高所带来的"退出威胁"及一系列连锁反应将使管理层更加注重治理表现，着力提升企业价值，有效地治理管理层卸责的"委托—代理"问题，激励研发创新这种有利于企业长期价值活动的开展。这可以归纳为股票流动性对企业创新的"激励机制"假说。

另外，还有文献认为较高的股票流动性会抑制企业创新，可归纳为"压力机制"假说。这是因为：其一，较高的股票流动性会加剧企业被恶意收购的风险，当股票流动性较高时，大额交易引发的股价波动较小，恶意收购方更容易掩盖其在二级市场大量买入的行为。这便使管理层需要花费更多的时间和精力去监控股票市场交易、应对恶意收购方取得一定"筹码"后召开临时股东会议、提议罢免经理人或安插高管的滋扰，挤占了对研发创新的关注。其二，管理层还需要将股价维持在较高的水平以抬高恶意收购方的操作成本，这可能迫使企业削减高风险、高投入且回报周期长的研发创新活动以保证财务表现的稳定性。其三，较高的股票流动性也会使得"快进快出"的交易成本降低，吸引短期投资者买卖股票。短期投资者热衷于题材炒作，也没有动机去监督企业决策，这往往会催生管理层的短视行为，与研发创新的长期价值导向背道而驰。

鉴于此，本文综合使用上市公司分类专利的申请、授权、终止数据进行实证研究，结果发现：一方面，股票流动性使企业发明专利申请数量显著增加，但能通过实质审查的授权增长极少，说明申请质量下滑；另一方面，股票流动性使创新含量较低的实用新型与外观设计专利显著增加，但这些专利拖累了企业未来的盈利表现，并使企业"重申请轻维持"，揭示了资本市场压力下企业专利数量的增长实际上是一种策略性行为。分样本检验发现，创新策略的扭曲集中体现于民营、传统行业及长期机构投资者持股比例低的企业。

  本文的研究发现并不意味着我们需要"因噎废食"地遏制市场流动性的提升。针对"专利泡沫"现象，应加强投资者教育，使其意识到正确的投资决策应关注企业的实质性研发创新能力与长期价值，减少跟风炒作、追涨杀跌等非理性投资行为；也可以逐步引入社保养老金等具有较长投资视野的资金入市，稳定上市公司管理层的心理预期，使其更加关注企业长期价值的提升，通过市场力量强化企业创新质量，激励真正具备创新价值乃至引领国际的技术出现，实现企业盈利表现的持续提高。

# 中国金融扩张下的本土企业创新效应

## ——基于倒"U"形关系的一个解释

张 杰 吴书凤 金 岳

现阶段,我国经济发展过程中产生的金融资金"脱实向虚"及资金在金融体系内部自我循环现象,引起高度关注(苏治等,2017;李扬,2017)。这可能挤占以制造业为主的实体经济部门的贷款机会,提高实体经济部门的贷款成本,从而影响本土企业的创新行为和决策。

客观上讲,判定我国是否存在金融业增加值占GDP比重相对快速扩张现象,较为科学合理的依据是检验金融业部门自身规模的扩张及其金融产业链向影子银行体系的延伸,是否有效匹配或支撑了本土企业的自主创新能力提升,以及是否已经偏离甚至脱离了以制造业为主的实体经济部门可持续发展的内在需求。事实上,金融业增加值占GDP比重的持续扩张是包括我国在内的发展中国家经济发展阶段中不可避免的。当前我国金融业增加值占GDP比重的相对快速扩张,既具有经济发展的合理性因素,也可能包含着金融发展深度相对不足及金融结构转化相对滞后的深层次风险因素。

本文基于微观企业创新数据,在归纳和界定我国金融业增加值占GDP比重相对快速扩张特征事实的基础上,利用2005年后放松银行业务

---

\* 原文刊载于《金融研究》2021年第4期。
作者简介:张杰,经济学博士,教授,中国人民大学中国经济改革与发展研究院;吴书凤,博士研究生,中国人民大学经济学院;金岳,博士研究生,中国人民大学经济学院。

管制和经营范围管制等政策冲击的准自然实验，借鉴 Stevenson（2010）、Ahern 和 Dittmar（2012）构造工具变量，实证探究了中国各地区金融扩张对地区内本土企业创新活动的影响效应及其作用机理。研究结论表明，金融业增加值占 GDP 比重持续扩张与本土企业创新投入呈现稳定的倒"U"形关系，从而验证了我国各地区金融扩张会对地区内微观企业创新活动造成两面性影响效应。具体而言，金融合理扩张有利于本土企业的创新活动，但其相对过快扩张则可能对本土企业创新活动造成显著的抑制效应，且这种抑制效应主要作用于 31.55% 的本土企业，尤其是 45.98% 的私人所有企业的创新活动方面；进一步区分企业内源创新和外源创新活动，发现这一抑制效应分别体现在 31.38% 的本土企业和 55.66% 的私人所有企业的内源创新活动方面，以及独立法人企业和私人所有企业的外源创新活动层面。

本文政策含义如下：一方面，现阶段制造业增加值占 GDP 比重持续下滑，应坚定并强化制造业在国民经济体系中的基础性地位，构建与本土企业自主创新能力全面提升发展目标相匹配、相适宜的多层次、多样化的现代金融体系，这将是健全社会主义市场体制和推动重大要素市场化改革的基础性目标，是建设中国特色的现代金融体系的核心任务（张杰，2020）；另一方面，通过加快推进银行盈利模式和金融监管体制的根本性改革，限制和消除我国以银行主导的间接融资型金融体系中不合理的金融工具创新和产业链扩张现象，应作为我国今后一段时期内深化金融体制改革必须坚持的重要方向（张杰，2018）。在我们看来，构建与本土企业发展的各个环节各种形式的融资需求相匹配、能够有效覆盖我国制造业产业链和创新链融合发展体系中所产生的各种融资需求的现代银行体系，尤其是发展地方性、专业化、全能制的股份制中小商业银行体系，可能是破解如何有效促进金融体系为实体经济服务困局的重要改革突破口。

# 数字金融与区域技术创新水平研究*

聂秀华　江　萍　郑晓佳　吴　青

　　党的十九届五中全会指出，在当下重要的战略机遇期，面对错综复杂的国际形势、艰巨繁重的国内改革发展稳定任务特别是新冠肺炎疫情的严重冲击，"砥砺前行、开拓创新"仍然是战胜各种风险与挑战、继续乘风破浪的总基调，要"坚持创新在我国现代化建设全局中的核心地位"。然而，我国自主研发现状不容乐观，创新能力仍不充分适应高质量发展要求。同时，受传统发展模式及旧有经济体制的影响与制约，我国金融市场发展尚不完善，传导机制不健全、资源配置效率低、深层次结构性矛盾突出等不平衡和发展不充分等问题影响了微观主体为其创新项目融资的可能性，遏制了区域内技术创新水平的提高。数字金融作为一种高效、覆盖面广的全新金融服务模式为解决企业技术创新的融资约束问题带来了潜在契机。那么，在新的经济金融发展背景下，数字金融的跨越式发展能否助力区域技术创新进程？

　　尽管现有文献从多角度、多层次证实了传统金融对企业技术创新的显著作用，但关于数字金融这一新金融服务模式是否能克服传统金融体系发展中的问题，发挥其服务实体经济、激励地区企业技术创新等领域效能，还存在争议与进一步研究的空间。基于此，本文实证检验了数字

---

\* 原文刊载于《金融研究》2021年第3期。
　　作者简介：聂秀华，金融学博士研究生，对外经济贸易大学国际经济贸易学院；江萍，金融学博士，教授，对外经济贸易大学国际经济贸易学院；郑晓佳，管理学博士，讲师，对外经济贸易大学国际经济贸易学院；吴青，经济学博士，教授，对外经济贸易大学国际经济贸易学院。

金融与区域技术创新水平之间的关系，并主要从以下几个方面形成创新点：一是从数字金融这一新型金融模式入手，探究金融发展对区域创新的作用，验证数字金融影响区域创新的两个可能路径，检验了金融发展对技术创新的非线性作用，对金融功能领域文献作出重要补充；二是综合采用动态面板模型、工具变量法及动态门限面板模型等多种方法探讨数字金融发展与技术创新水平的线性与非线性关系，从研究方法上丰富了已有的创新领域文献，也充分保证了研究结论的稳健性；三是使用发明授权专利的市场价值指标以有效衡量区域技术创新水平和质量，从全新维度综合考察了数字金融发展对区域技术创新产出、效率的影响。

基于2011—2018年省级面板数据，本文考察了数字金融与区域技术创新的关系。一是构建基准线性回归模型，验证数字金融以及其分指标对区域技术创新的影响。考虑到数字金融对创新的作用可能受到诸多因素的影响，采用动态门限面板模型进一步探究基于指数自身变化特征、制度质量和内部技术吸收能力（人力资本水平）等异质性条件下两者可能存在的非线性关系。二是深入探究了金融发展影响区域技术创新的两种可能机制：缓解企业融资约束和促进产业结构升级。三是考虑到我国显著的地域差异特征及数字金融本身阶段性发展特点，本文进一步探究了数字金融创新激励效应在空间与时间维度上的可能变化。研究结论如下：第一，数字金融可通过缓解企业融资约束和促进地区产业结构优化、升级等方式促进区域技术创新水平提升。第二，数字金融对区域技术创新的作用受到其自身完善程度、制度质量、人力资本水平等因素影响，具体来说，在较完善的数字金融发展阶段、较好的制度质量和较高的人力资本水平情况下，数字金融对区域技术创新水平将产生更为显著的"激励效应"。第三，数字金融对技术创新的促进作用在空间和时间维度上存在显著差异，在东部地区及在推动数字金融发展的变革性事件后，数字金融的创新"激励效应"更加突出。

政策建议如下：首先，通过金融科技的运用加快传统金融机构数字化改革步伐、提高现有数字金融在新技术场景的应用能力，同时坚持市场化、法治化、国际化原则的统一，稳定发展步调，将金融活动全面纳入监管，保证金融系统的安全性与稳定性，优化金融服务实体经济的功能和效率。其次，完善地区制度质量、人力资本等关键辅助性因素，助力数字金融发展。一方面，完善已有的知识产权保护法律法规系统，提高执法效率，建立多层次的法律宣传体系；另一方面，构建多元化人才培养模式和强化技术创新研发团队的建设，依据不同地区发展状况制定适宜的人力资本激励措施、环境制度安排等，以最大限度发挥数字金融驱动地区技术创新水平提升的效果与优越性，推进创新驱动发展战略，实现社会主义现代化远景目标。最后，应加快创新模式转变，提升地区创新质量审核水平与完善创新评价体系构建，谨防"虚假性"或"策略性"创新行为出现，提升金融支持与产业政策等推动创新发展措施的有效性。

# 地方政府人才引进政策促进了区域创新吗？*

## ——来自准自然实验的证据

钟 腾 罗吉罡 汪昌云

在当前人口老龄化、经济发展由物质资本驱动转向人力资本驱动的新阶段下，高技能人力资本（以下简称"人才"）成为国家之间、地区之间争相抢夺的稀缺资源，人才对于中国经济转型的重要性不言而喻。在我国，人才与创新一直受到高度重视，党的十九届五中全会提出，坚持创新在我国现代化建设全局中的核心地位，深入实施科教兴国战略、人才强国战略、创新驱动发展战略，激发人才创新活力，完善科技创新体制。本文深入探讨各地人才引进政策与地区创新之间的关系，有助于发掘人才战略与创新之间的内在联系，为相关政策提供参考。

自 2008 年开始，我国中央政府和地方政府大量出台人才引进政策，各地的人才争夺日益激烈。然而，人才引进政策，尤其是地方层面的政策，是否能够起到促进创新的作用，仍是一个存有争议的问题。一方面，人才引进的初衷在于吸引优秀人才流入，引进先进理念和技术，加快当地创新升级和产业转型，而其所带来的政策补助也会直接提高企业利润和

---

\* 原文刊载于《金融研究》2021 年第 5 期。

作者简介：钟腾，经济学博士，副教授，对外经济贸易大学金融学院；罗吉罡，硕士研究生，复旦大学经济学院；汪昌云，金融学博士，教授，中国人民大学中国财政金融政策研究中心。

生产率，从而促进区域创新；另一方面，当前的人才引进政策尚存在"重引进""轻培养"等特征，与地方的产业特征和财政状况并不完全匹配，个别地区甚至出现为了维持人口红利和政绩工程而扭曲人才制度或财政补贴下的寻租等情况，可能对创新产生负面影响。本文通过地方政府人才政策相关数据进行系统的实证研究，考察地方政府人才引进政策对区域创新是否起到显著推动作用，是否存在政策扭曲，并探究背后的作用机制，以期为优化地方人才引进政策及更好实现创新发展提供借鉴。

本文贡献主要包括：第一，以往文献大多关注国家层面的人才政策的作用，且以定性分析为主，而本文将关注点和数据细化到城市，通过较为严格的实证分析，探究了地方层面的人才引进政策对创新的影响；第二，不仅关注政策的直接效果，也对其作用机制进行了探讨，更加全面而深入地刻画了政策的作用路径；第三，当前中国面临劳动力减少和经济增速放缓的问题，人才成为各地经济发展亟须的新动能，本文对地方政府优化人才激励政策、实施创新驱动发展战略具有政策参考价值。

本文以2009—2012年39个城市集中出台的地方人才引进政策为准自然实验，利用多期双重差分法来探究地方政府人才引进对区域创新的作用。首先，根据2013年国家科技部国际合作司编写的《中国各省市引进海外科技创新人才政策指南》，确定各个城市出台人才引进政策的时间，将各地的政策视为一次准自然实验；为与实验组形成对照，采用倾向得分匹配法，从城市的特征变量入手，通过一对一最邻近匹配，构造出与实验组城市的特征最为接近的另一组城市作为对照组，由此形成包含39个实验组城市和39个对照组城市的样本，样本时间跨度为2006—2015年。用两个指标作为城市创新水平的反映，一是各城市历年的有效专利申请数量，该指标从专利数量的角度衡量区域创新能力；二是复旦大学产业发展研究中心发布的"中国城市创新指数"，该指标从专利价值的角度衡量区域创新能力。

基于以上设定，通过双重差分回归来考察政策出台前后实验组城市与对照组城市在创新能力上是否表现出显著差异，结论如下：（1）总体上看，地方政府人才引进政策对区域创新起到了促进作用，既提升了地区内的专利数量，也提升了地区内的专利价值，且政策效应随时间推移而变强。（2）政策的作用机制为通过扩大研发投入来促进创新，但创新效率并未显著提高。（3）政策效果在不同地区呈现出异质性。在营商环境较差的地区，政策效应侧重于提高专利数量，营商环境较好的地区则侧重于提升专利价值；政策在科教投入力度较弱的地区效果更明显，在投入力度较大的地区则效果不明显；在知识产权保护程度弱的地区，政策效果更多体现为提高专利数量，保护程度强的地区，政策效果则侧重体现为提升专利价值。

本文的政策建议为：地方人才引进政策应贯彻党的十九届五中全会稳中求进的基调和坚持新发展理念的精神，完善创新体制机制。一方面，科教基础雄厚、创新补助充足的地区，不宜再把创新发展更多寄托在政策激励效应上，而应着力于引导外来人才和技术与当地产业经济的融合，攻克创新效率的瓶颈，实现创新模式的转变；另一方面，科教基础薄弱、创新补助缺乏的地区，应以人才政策出台为契机，大力扶持当地科教和创新产业，培养创新的土壤，带动大众创业积极性，扩大人才队伍和研发规模，补足资金投入的短板。从根本上看，要完善市场竞争机制，发挥市场在研发资源配置中的决定性作用，建立以市场竞争促进高质量区域创新的健康发展模式，政府对创新项目补助的指标设立也应尽量符合市场规律，同时着力进一步优化营商环境，完善知识产权保护，为企业高质量创新营造良好的外部制度环境。

# 开发区层级与域内企业创新：
# 激励效应还是挤出效应？*

## ——基于国家级和省级开发区的对比研究

蔡庆丰 陈熠辉 林海涵

开发区建设是中国改革开放 40 年的成功实践，对经济起飞和高速增长起到重要推动作用。进入新时代，中国经济已由高速增长阶段转向高质量发展阶段，经济发展不平衡、不充分问题仍然突出，创新能力还不适应高质量发展的要求。党的十九届五中全会提出"坚持创新在我国现代化建设全局中的核心地位""加快发展现代产业体系，推动经济体系优化升级"。在这样的时代背景下，各地各层级开发区建设能否满足新的发展要求，促进域内企业研发创新，形成新的聚集效应和增长动力，既关乎开发区自身的可持续发展，也关系各地区能否顺利完成"十四五"规划目标、实现新旧动能转换和高质量发展。

截至 2018 年底，中国共有各类型开发区 2 543 家，其中国家级开发区 552 家，省级开发区 1 991 家。两类开发区表面上只是审批机构的差异，但在实际运作中，规模设施、政策支持和管理体制上的差异使得不同层级开发区对域内企业的影响也存在较大差异：首先，国家级开发区的规模普遍大于省级开发区的规模，且发育更为成熟，域内基础设施也会相

---

\* 原文刊载于《金融研究》2021 年第 5 期。
作者简介：蔡庆丰，经济学博士，教授，厦门大学经济学院；陈熠辉，经济学博士，助理教授，湖南大学金融与统计学院；林海涵，硕士研究生，厦门大学经济学院。

对完善。相较于省级开发区，国家级开发区更易形成集聚效应，各种创新要素的聚集也更容易激发企业的创新意识；而省级开发区往往规模较小，与国家级开发区相比，较难形成集聚效应，对地区经济发展起到的带动作用也较为有限。其次，国家级开发区在税收优惠、政府补贴等政策支持力度上会明显优于省级开发区，通常直接给予区内企业税收和财政补助；而省级开发区更多是以地税返还和财政奖励的手段进行激励。最后，在设立目的和管理模式上，国家级开发区的设立大多遵从国家层面的区域发展战略，有利于形成灵活高效的管理体制和运行机制，也会更注重培养企业的创新能力；而设立省级开发区的目的则更多是基于地方提升 GDP 总量、引领产业发展、推动招商引资及土地资源的开发利用。因此，省级开发区的发展更容易受到地方 GDP 与产业竞争以及地方经济发展目标的影响。那么，各层级开发区建设究竟会对微观企业的创新行为产生怎样的影响呢？

与既有研究主要聚焦于国家级开发区不同，本文以 2007—2018 年上市公司为样本，结合手工收集整理的开发区域内企业信息，对比研究了国家级和省级开发区对域内企业创新活动的影响。研究表明，与国家级开发区显著促进域内企业创新投入不同，省级开发区表现出负向抑制作用。国家级和省级开发区对域内企业创新的影响机制也存在明显差异：国家级开发区通过税收优惠、政府补助和融资支持等政策效应，以及金融资源、研发人才和经济主体的集聚效应激励企业创新；而省级开发区的发展则更容易受地方经济竞争的影响而挤出企业的创新投入。进一步，国家级开发区对域内企业创新的促进作用在市场化程度较高的地区和中央国有企业中更明显，而省级开发区的抑制作用则在地方国有企业中更明显。

本文的贡献主要体现在以下三个方面：第一，基于企业创新的视角，丰富了开发区这一地方常用的参与经济模式与微观企业行为的相关研究。

现有关于开发区的研究大多聚焦于区域经济总量层面，而本文聚焦于对域内企业创新活动的影响，并揭示其影响机理。第二，基于国家级和省级开发区的对比研究，进一步对开发区建设这一中国改革开放的实践进行深入讨论。以往关于开发区研究的文献基本集中于国家级开发区，对于国家级和省级开发区的差异化影响还没有研究提供相应的理论支撑和经验证据，也没有探究其背后导致差异的原因。国家级和省级开发区之间的对比研究对于理解地方行为与区域GDP和产业竞争等现象也有所启发。第三，拓展了政府干预与企业创新的相关研究。虽然这一领域的研究近年来受到学术界的关注，但既有研究更多的是直接从财税支持、官员更替与国企行为等方面展开的，本文从开发区建设这一视角切入，丰富了这一领域的相关研究。

结合本文的研究结论，我们可以获得以下几点政策启示：第一，开发区的"创新提升"有赖于激活域内企业的创新活力，形成新的聚集效应和增长动力，进而提升区域创新能力。在这一方面，国家级开发区运作模式与体制机制优于省级开发区。因此，我国在开发区建设进程中应该进一步发挥国家级开发区的示范作用，推动省级开发区的管理模式和体制机制向国家级开发区看齐，促使其更加重视并支持域内企业的研发创新活动。第二，本文的机制检验和异质性分析也表明，在开发区建设中以往适应增量经济发展的地区经济竞争模式会带来粗放式发展等问题，不利于企业创新和区域活力，在我国经济转向高质量发展阶段的背景下，如何推动有效市场和有为政府更好地结合，也是当前经济改革亟须思考的问题。

# 05　金融市场

# 央行货币政策报告文本信息、宏观经济与股票市场[*]

姜富伟　胡逸驰　黄　楠

近年来，中国人民银行（简称央行）对货币政策沟通日益重视，央行沟通也成为金融学界、政界和业界的高度关注的热点问题。许多学者就央行沟通的度量、央行沟通与通货膨胀预期等问题开展了许多有意义的研究，但现有文献对央行沟通对我国金融市场资产价格的影响研究还稍显不足：

一是仅关注央行沟通中透露出的货币政策倾向，忽视了货币政策沟通文本中包含的其他定性信息；二是多通过人工阅读的方法来分析央行货币政策沟通文本，技术手段单一，结果主观性较强。

本文使用前沿的人工智能文本大数据分析技术，对2001年第一季度至2018年第三季度共71篇央行货币政策执行报告（以下简称"报告"）进行研究，计算出报告的文本情绪（Tone）、文本相似度（Similarity）和文本可读性（Readability）等文本指标，探究报告的文本信息与宏观经济和股票市场的关系。本文基于姜富伟等（2021）开发出的中文金融情感词典，结合央行沟通的遣词造句习惯，用情绪单元法计算出报告的文本情绪，用TF-IDF加权的余弦相似度来表征报告的文本相似度，用平

---

[*] 原文刊载于《金融研究》2021年第6期。

作者简介：姜富伟，金融学博士，教授、博导，中央财经大学金融学院；胡逸驰，硕士研究生，北京大学经济学院；黄楠，经济学博士，嘉实基金管理有限公司。

均句子长度来表征报告的可读性，计算并描述我国央行货币政策报告的文本特征。

然后，本文对报告文本特征与宏观经济和股票市场的关系进行了实证分析，检验了报告文本情绪和经济增长、通货膨胀、利率变动等宏观经济金融指标的关系，并将文本情绪、文本相似度和文本可读性指标加入 EGARCH 模型，探究报告文本指标是否会影响发布后第一个交易日的股票市场收益率和波动性。本文还将报告内容分解为经济金融基本面和央行政策指引两部分，分别计算两部分指标的文本情绪，探究报告的基本面描述部分和政策指引部分是否都能对股票市场产生显著影响。

实证分析结果表明，报告文本情绪与经济增长、通货膨胀、就业水平等诸多宏观经济指标有显著相关性，且文本情绪值较高预示着宏观经济向好，文本情绪值较低预示着宏观经济下行。在控制经济增长和货币政策等变量后，报告文本情绪对报告发布后股票市场的收益率有显著正向影响。报告文本相似度越高，股票市场波动性越小；反之股票市场波动性越大。报告文本可读性高低对股票市场波动性的影响并不显著。进一步研究发现，报告文本情绪中对股票市场有显著影响的是其反映央行政策指引的部分，而反映宏观经济金融基本面的部分对股票市场影响并不显著。这表明，报告的文本情绪影响股票市场，本质上是央行的政策指引在起作用，而不是宏观经济金融历史信息的作用。

本文贡献主要体现在以下几方面。首先，使用前沿的人工智能文本大数据分析技术对报告文本进行了全方面多维度分析，开发了货币政策文本情绪词典，并用计算机自动计算出政策文本情绪等指标。其次，弥补了中文经济金融文本情绪研究中关于央行沟通情绪分析的欠缺，探索了我国央行沟通文本情绪分析，为将来围绕央行沟通开展更加全面和深入的研究提供基础。最后，对央行沟通文本情绪影响金融市场的机制进行实证研究，结果表明能够显著影响市场的是文本情绪中反映央行货币政策指引的部分，而非反映宏观经济基本面的部分。报告的文本情绪能够影响股票市场，本质上是央行的政策指引改变了市场预期。

在我国政府日益强调防范化解系统性金融风险、建立健全货币政策和宏观审慎管理政策双支柱调控框架的背景下，本文的研究结论对强化金融监管和促进宏观审慎管理有一定启示。本文实证结果表明，央行的货币政策沟通能够显著地影响股票市场的收益率和波动性，有力地证明了我国央行沟通的有效性。通过与市场进行充分的沟通，央行可以影响资产价格，从而达到货币政策调控和维护金融稳定的目的。另外，本文也指出央行报告的文本情绪中真正影响市场的部分是反映央行对未来经济形势的判断和政策前瞻的部分。基于这一结论，央行可有效利用自身权威性和影响力，通过及时公布和清晰阐释对下一阶段经济金融形势的预判和货币政策思路，更加有效地管理市场预期。

# 多重信用评级与债券融资成本 *

## ——来自中国债券市场的经验证据

陈关亭　连立帅　朱　松

我国债券市场自1981年重新发行国债起,历经四十年的迅猛发展,市场持续扩容,债券种类不断增加。截至2020年11月末,我国债券市场托管余额为115.7万亿元,已经跃居为全球第二大债券市场。党的十九大报告提出"提高直接融资比重,促进多层次资本市场健康发展"。一方面,作为提供直接融资的主要资本市场之一,债券市场在我国金融市场中的作用和地位不断加强,在金融市场改革及金融领域对外开放中扮演着排头兵的角色。另一方面,投资者对债券市场的积极性是债券市场发展的关键因素,发行人与投资者之间信息不对称带来的发行人道德风险和投资者的逆向选择问题,则是影响投资者积极性的重要原因。

债券信用评级是缓解发债企业与投资者信息不对称和保护投资者的重要机制,对投资者的决策有着重要影响。一方面,准确且及时的信用评级有利于投资者获取发债企业信息,降低其面临的信息不对称,促进债券市场健康发展;另一方面,由于信用评级在债券发行及债券融资成本中的重要作用,发债企业会主动寻求高估的信用评级,这会降低信用评级质量,导致投资者对信用评级的准确性与合理性产生质疑,影响其

---

\* 原文刊载于《金融研究》2021年第2期。
　作者简介:陈关亭,经济学博士,副教授,清华大学经济管理学院;连立帅,管理学博士,副教授,华东师范大学经济与管理学部;朱松,管理学博士,教授,华东师范大学经济与管理学部。

对整个债券市场的积极性，不利于债券市场的健康发展。因此，如何构建合理的信用评级制度，提高投资者对债券市场的信任度和积极性，是一个十分重要的话题。

目前中国债券市场绝大多数公司采用单一评级制，但也有部分公司选择两家或两家以上信用评级机构对同一评级对象分别进行信用评级，并在债券募集说明书中公开披露相应的评级信息，本文将后者称为多重信用评级（以下简称"多重评级"）。在政策层面，2012年银行间债券市场重启信贷资产证券化时要求实施双评级制度，鼓励探索采取多元化信用评级方式。对于多重评级的理论解释，主要有信息生产假说、评级意见购买假说与认证假说。Kronlund（2020）认为，与单一评级相比，多重评级更难以实施评级购买，因而当发行人披露单一评级时更可能存在评级购买问题。借鉴上述观点及相关文献，本文使用信息生产和信用认证假说来发展研究假设，排除了信用评级购买假说。根据信息生产假说，多重信用评级向市场传递了更多指标与维度的增量信息，投资者会综合不同的信息，判断发债企业风险水平，从而获取企业的真实价值信息，降低其面临的信息不对称程度，并进一步影响债券融资成本；根据信用认证假说，发债企业聘请多家信用评级机构获取多个信用评级，可以弥补单一评级机构在市场中的信誉不足而向市场传递更多信号，有助于增强信用评级的认证强度与效度，并影响债券融资成本。

基于2004—2018年中国信用债市场的评级样本（共计14 929个样本），本文主要采用OLS方法，研究发现：多重评级有利于降低债券融资成本，表明面对不同评级机构的评级结果差异，发债企业可以通过多重评级向市场传递更多和更具效度的评级信息，以弥补单一信用评级的信息不足和评级结果失准，从而减少投资者决策的不确定性，降低债券融资成本。相对于不一致的多重评级，一致的多重评级更有利于降低债券融资成本。在多重评级中，相对于评级机构均为"发行人付费"模式，兼有"投资者付费"模式的信用评级更有利于降低债券融资成本。此外，当多重评级存在评级不一致的情况时，平均评级的信息含量最高，即综合不同信用评级包含的多种信息比任何单一信用评级的信息更加具有信息含量。进一步分析发现，多重评级对于降低融资成本的效果在非上市公司和声誉较高的评级机构中更为明显。最后，基于2012年我国银行间债券市场重启信贷资产证券试点时监管部门推动实施双评级制度这一外生事件，本文还发现当强制要求实施多重信用评级之后，在发债企业评级购买动机与评级膨胀程度下降的情况下，多重评级仍能降低债券融资成本，即强制性的双评级制度对债券融资成本的降低效果非常明显。

本文主要政策启示如下：第一，双评级尤其是不同付费模式评级机构实施的多重评级向市场传递了更多信息，有利于提高信用评级的准确性与合理性，因此，有必要逐步扩大强制性"双评级制度"的施行范围，并推广嵌入"投资者付费"评级机构的多重评级模式；第二，鉴于多重评级有利于降低债券融资成本，且不论评级结果是否一致都能体现上述效果，因此，发债企业可以考虑聘请多家信用评级机构实施多重评级，以弥补单一信用评级的信息不足与结果失准；第三，良好的声誉在降低发债企业融资成本的同时，也可赢得企业信任与市场份额，因此，信用评级机构应该像鸟儿爱惜羽毛一样维护评级声誉。

# 私有信息、评级偏差和中国评级机构的市场声誉*

寇宗来　千茜倩

信用评级机构在债券市场中扮演着重要角色，理应凭借专业化的信息收集和处理能力，对企业乃至债券进行分类评级，从而尽可能降低资本市场中的信息不对称程度，为广大投资者提供相对可靠的决策依据。但随着一系列国内外债务违约事件的陆续发生，市场对评级机构产生了越来越多的质疑，认为信用评级机构并没有起到资本市场守门人的作用，甚至有可能与发债企业沆瀣一气，将风险过度转嫁到投资者身上。

本文旨在考察我国的评级机构是否具有市场声誉。如何测度评级机构的市场声誉是一个颇具挑战性的问题。从概念上讲，这涉及一个"悖论"：一方面，评级机构要建立市场声誉，就必须借助其专业化的信息收集和处理能力向市场提供可靠的决策信息；另一方面，只有当评级机构可以通过提供虚假信息而误导市场时，它才算是真正具有市场声誉。的确，如果评级机构策略性地提高信用评级并不能对投资者行为或企业的发债成本造成显著影响，其所给出的评级将最多是一个并不能愚弄市场的"橡皮图章"，或者说该评级机构本质上是没有市场声誉的。基于以上逻辑，本文分两步研究我国发行人付费评级机构的市场声誉：第一步，

---

\* 原文刊载于《金融研究》2021年第6期。
**作者简介：** 寇宗来，经济学博士，教授，复旦大学中国社会主义市场经济研究中心；千茜倩，经济学博士，助理教授，西安交通大学经济与金融学院。

构造评级机构的"评级偏差";第二步,考察评级偏差和机构特征如何影响企业的发债成本。

为了检验评级机构的市场声誉,我们需从可观测评级中提取出"评级偏差"部分,相较于已有文献,本文有两方面改进。首先,既有文献常见的做法是将评级与债券的各种基本面信息进行回归,然后将"回归残差"作为评级偏差的量度。但考虑到可观测的评级都是由最终赢得评级竞争的评级机构所给出,上述"回归残差"既有可能反映了评级偏差,也有可能反映了赢得评级竞争的评级机构获得了关于发债企业及其债券的私有信息。因此,我们需要在上述回归残差中进一步剔除私有信息部分,才能得到真正所需要的评级偏差,这也正是本文的核心工作和关键贡献之一。

参考 Tian(2011),本文引入各评级机构到发债企业的空间距离来控制私有信息及由此带来的选择偏误,因为空间距离会影响评级机构的信息收集成本及确认信息是否有误的监督成本。与 Tian(2011)所不同的是,我们不但引入了发债企业到所有评级机构(最近分支机构)距离的均值,还引入这些最短距离的方差。直观上,平均距离越大,评级机构越难监督发债企业,对发债企业的信息劣势越大,从而更倾向于给出较低评级。进一步,给定均值,方差越大意味着各评级机构在私有信息方面的差异越大,而距离越近的评级机构越有可能准确了解发债企业的真实情况。如果发债企业为高质量企业,则近距离的评级机构给出相对更高的评级,进而更有可能在评级选购机制下赢得竞争;但如果发债企业为低质量企业,则近距离评级机构会给出较低评级或退出竞争,而发债企业将会选择远处的评级机构。总体而言,距离方差越大,发债企业实际所获评级的预期值越高。基于上述分析,与既有文献相比,通过引入发债企业到各评级机构最短距离的"均值"和"方差",将能较好地控制评级中的私有信息部分,而由此所得到的"回归残差"也就能更加准确地度量"评级偏差"。

对每只债券我们只能观察到最终赢得评级业务的评级机构所给出的实际评级。因此，要准确度量"评级偏差"的关键之处就是为每只债券构造一个比较公允的"基准评级"。但考虑到不同债券之间可能存在很大差异，因而以全体债券样本为基础的回归预测值作为基准可能会带来较大的误差。对此给出的解决方案是，对每一只债券都按照债券和发债企业的所有公开信息及发债企业到各评级机构的距离信息，利用倾向得分匹配方法（PSM）找到与之特征相似但由其他评级机构评级的多只债券作为控制组进行回归，相应的处理效应就更加准确地度量了"评级偏差"。

按照上述理论逻辑，本文以2009年1月至2017年10月公开发行的企业债和公司债为研究样本进行分析（共计6 073个样本），有以下发现：

首先，发债企业与评级机构间平均距离越大，其所获评级越低；发债企业到评级机构间距离方差越大，其所获评级越高；平均距离和距离方差都会对实际评级造成影响，但影响机制不同。这表明，加入距离因素的确有助于控制和剔除私有信息，进而由此得到的"回归残差"也就主要包含了"评级偏差"部分。

其次，我们又考察了"评级偏差"和评级机构虚拟变量对发债成本的影响，并得到三个重要结论：第一，"评级偏差"能够显著降低企业的发债成本。这意味着，尽管我国评级机构受到广泛质疑，但平均而言，它们依然具有"引导"市场的能力，即具有显著的市场声誉。第二，各评级机构的声誉存在显著异质性。这意味着，对于不同评级机构给出的同等评级，市场投资者是区别对待的；进一步地，不同评级机构将信用评级向上扭曲相同的幅度，其对市场投资者造成的影响也是不同的。第三，考虑到评级机构与发债企业在选址上可能会有集聚效应，我们基于高铁开通事件做了双差分检验，表明本文结论是稳健成立的。

# 资本市场开放能否提高企业信息披露质量？*

## ——基于"沪港通"和年报文本挖掘的分析

阮 睿 孙宇辰 唐 悦 聂辉华

在党的十九届五中全会通过并公布的"十四五"规划建议中，推进金融双向开放是"建立现代财税金融体制"工作部署的重要内容。经验表明，较高的上市公司信息披露质量是成熟金融市场的重要特征之一，且信息披露质量能够显著影响资本市场效率。本文以"沪港通"这一重大资本市场开放事件为契机，研究扩大资本市场开放对提高上市公司信息披露质量的作用。

2014年11月17日，沪港股票市场交易互联互通机制（以下简称"沪港通"）开通，这是中国资本市场开放的重要举措之一。在这一机制下，香港投资者能够买卖规定范围内的上交所股票，同时内地投资者能够买卖规定范围内的联交所股票。既有研究表明，资本市场开放会对金融市场发展产生积极影响，如降低融资成本，改善公司治理，提高公司绩效等。特别地，Yoon（2021）发现，"沪港通"机制带来的资本市场开放增加了公司私下信息沟通次数，但公开披露的次数没有增加。然而，私下沟

---

\* 原文刊载于《金融研究》2021年第2期。
作者简介：阮睿，经济学博士，中央财经大学中国财政发展协同创新中心；孙宇辰，经济学博士，对外经济贸易大学金融学院；唐悦，金融学博士，西南财经大学经济与管理研究院；聂辉华，经济学博士，教授，中国人民大学经济学院。

通仅仅增加了部分投资者的信息,而对公司公开信息披露行为的作用有限,广大中小投资者难以从中受益。本文把研究视角转向公开信息披露的质量,希望探讨的问题是,资本市场开放是否能够提高公司公开信息披露质量,从而改善公司整体的信息环境？

本文将2014年开通的"沪港通"机制作为一个准自然实验,并利用2010—2019年A股上市公司的数据,研究资本市场开放对上市公司信息披露质量的影响。参照已有文献,本文计算常用词占比和文本确定程度等可读性指标,用于衡量公司信息披露质量。本文将A股市场中受到"沪港通"机制影响的公司作为实验组,其余公司作为控制组,综合运用匹配、双重差分及合成控制等技术,探讨资本市场开放带来的境外投资者参与对公司信息披露质量的影响。

本文的实证结果得出了以下两个结论：一是资本市场开放改善了相关公司的年报文本可读性,使企业的信息披露质量显著提高。该结果对加入公司治理及信息环境控制变量、考虑"深港通"机制以及采取渐进DID估计等方法均稳健。二是通过进一步的异质性分析表明,文本可读性的改善在盈余操纵水平较高、股价信息含量较低的企业中更加显著,这表明资本市场开放可以促使原本治理水平和信息披露质量较差的企业努力改善其信息披露质量。

相对于已有文献,本文的主要贡献有如下三点。

第一,给定资本市场开放这一外生冲击,本文将研究视角由上市公司的信息披露数量转向信息披露质量。研究发现,"沪港通"的实施提升了相关企业年报文本的可读性,企业公开信息披露质量得到了改善,表明资本市场开放是提升市场整体信息质量的有效途径。

第二,本文利用文本挖掘技术构建文本可读性指标,从而丰富了信息披露质量的相关研究。既有文献已使用的信息披露质量衡量方法包括操纵性应计绝对值、分析师预测误差、跟踪分析师数量等。这些指标从不同的方面反映了企业的信息披露质量，但因为指标自身定义的原因，不可避免地受到较多外界因素或模型设定的影响。本文通过对年报文本的挖掘分析，为信息披露质量提供了一种更为直观而较少依赖于外界因素的度量方法，从而有利于深入理解资本市场开放对信息披露质量的影响。

第三，本文为资本市场开放对企业行为和绩效的影响提供了新的实证证据。利用"沪港通"开通这一外生事件，本文发现资本市场的开通有助于提升企业的公开信息披露质量。在市场整合后，内地受影响企业面临着提升信息质量和治理水平的压力，从而促使它们更主动地向公司治理水平相对较高的成熟企业看齐。本文的实证研究有助于我们更清晰地认识资本市场开放对促进金融市场发展的重要作用，并为我国资本市场进一步扩大开放的政策提供了理论支持。

本研究对资本市场开放和资本市场制度建设的政策启示有以下几点。第一，中国资本市场应进一步对外开放，扩大资本市场容量，充分利用国际国内两个市场的资源，促进企业提升自身治理水平。第二，扩大金融开放也对监管水平提出了更高的要求，监管部门要相应加强对信息披露质量的重视程度，积极引导企业主动提高信息披露质量，特别是公开信息披露质量。第三，引导企业主动提高年报的信息披露质量。企业要关注披露文本的理解难度，尽量减少以故弄玄虚、模棱两可的语句误导投资者的情况。监管部门可以通过去函问询的方式，要求个别公司对年报中表述不清的文字加以澄清，从而督促上市公司提高信息披露质量。

# 卖空机制能够约束内部人减持吗？*

## ——基于融资融券制度的经验证据

**马云飙　武艳萍　石贝贝**

自2005年股权分置改革以来，我国上市公司大股东获得了在二级市场减持股票的权利。与此同时，越来越多的民营企业登陆中小板和创业板，且广受市场追捧，因此，持有公司股票的内部人减持、套现动机比较强烈。通过整理数据发现，2006—2016年我国A股市场共发生内部人减持68 490次，减持金额总计高达20 603亿元，减持数量合计1 814亿股，减持规模和数量在2015年达到高峰。在此背景下，内部人减持会对企业自身及资本市场带来怎样的影响？这一问题引起学术界和实务界的高度关注。

学者们普遍发现，上市公司内部人往往利用自身估值优势或采用其他一系列手段，比如盈余管理、规避坏消息、操纵股价等，在企业价值被市场高估时，减持变现，从而获得超额收益。这种出于私利目的的减持行为具有很强的负外部性，不仅损害了外部投资者的利益，也危害了实体经济的发展。具体来说，上市公司内部人减持会向市场传递企业估值偏高或发展前景不佳的信号，造成股价下跌，给外部投资者带来损失，挫伤投资信心。而作为补偿，外部投资者之后会要求更高的回报，从而

---

\* 原文刊载于《金融研究》2021年第2期。
　作者简介：马云飙，管理学博士，讲师，中央财经大学会计学院；武艳萍，会计学博士研究生，中央财经大学会计学院；石贝贝，管理学博士，讲师，对外经济贸易大学国际经济贸易学院。

增加公司的融资成本，降低企业资金可获得性，减弱企业"投资—投资机会"敏感性，降低企业投资规模，最终损害实体经济发展。

尽管监管部门高度重视内部人的减持行为，并且颁布了多项规章制度以抑制大股东及董监高等内部人的减持行为。然而，一些大股东及董监高等内部人为了减持套现甚至刻意寻找漏洞，进行恶意减持。那么，能否通过制度层面的设计，提升市场定价效率，降低股价被高估的程度，从而减少上市公司内部人减持行为？

卖空交易机制的启动，是近年来我国证券市场的一次重大创新与突破。在不存在卖空的条件下，即使一部分具备强大信息收集、处理与分析能力的投资者意识到企业的价值被高估了，也无法将负面信息充分、迅速地反映在股价中。此时，内部人可以通过减持获得较高收益。而当融资融券业务展开后，允许投资者卖空时，一部分专业的投资者可以通过挖掘企业的负面信息，通过卖空股票来获利。这一机制加速了负面信息融入股价的程度和速度，能够促使股价更加准确地反映公司基本面信息，降低股价被高估的程度，从而减少内部人通过减持获取的变现收益。随着收益的降低，内部人减持的动机也会降低。

基于上述论断，本文以我国放松卖空管制为视角，探究其对内部人减持的影响。研究发现，卖空机制能够抑制企业内部人减持行为。机制分析发现，卖空对内部人减持的抑制作用是通过缓解股权高溢价实现的。进一步研究表明，卖空能够抑制大股东、董事及管理层减持，但对监事减持无影响；卖空能够降低内部人减持的获利程度，并且在内部人减持动机更大时，对内部人减持的抑制作用更强；卖空通过约束内部人减持提升了股票定价效率，还有助于降低内部人增持行为。

根据上述分析和发现，本文有以下三方面贡献和政策启示：第一，本文的研究结论丰富了上市公司内部人减持的相关研究。已有关于内部人减持的研究主要集中在减持的动机及减持的经济后果两方面，鲜有文献探讨如何通过合理的市场机制抑制上市公司内部人减持行为。本文从我国融资融券启动这一视角，研究放松卖空管制对内部人减持行为的影响，丰富了内部人减持领域的文献。第二，本文为进一步厘清融资融券的经济后果提供新的经验证据。融资融券业务启动后，学者们对这项交易机制的实施效果展开了深入探讨。一部分研究肯定了我国融资融券业务开展的成效，认为卖空机制能够提升市场定价效率，降低股价波动性，有利于市场的稳定健康发展；同时，也有学者指出，融资融券制度会增加股市下跌风险，降低企业创新质量。可见，现有研究对这项交易机制的经济后果尚存在一定争议。本文从上市公司内部人减持的角度研究卖空机制的治理效应，为进一步厘清融资融券的经济后果提供了新的经验证据。第三，为证券监管部门进一步完善制度层面设计，保护中小投资者利益提供了有益的政策启发。由于减持规定难以做到事无巨细，加之受到强烈的套现动机引导，企业内部人会想方设法寻找规则漏洞。因此，抑制内部人不合理的减持行为，还需要市场机制调节。本文从我国融资融券业务启动这一视角出发，研究放松卖空管制后，股票定价效率提升对减持行为的影响，为证券监管部门进一步完善制度层面设计，保护中小投资者利益提供了有益的政策启发。

# 中国股市羊群效应的区制转移时变性研究*

郑挺国　葛厚逸

中国股市自1990年开市以来，经历了多轮牛熊转换和市场环境的变迁，价格波动幅度较大一直是挥之不去的阴影。任泽平等（2019）认为羊群效应是造成中国A股"暴涨暴跌"的重要因素。而已有的国内研究也表明，中国股市的不稳定性与国内投资者的羊群行为紧密相关，投资者的羊群行为往往会加速股市泡沫的形成与破灭（刘祥东等，2014；陶瑜，2017）。识别并剖析中国股市羊群行为特征对于强化风险识别和提升风险防控具有重要的理论和现实意义。

目前国内关于羊群效应的检验普遍采用静态模型的方法，假设羊群行为不随时间推移或独立于经济状态。然而这种假设是牵强的，投资者羊群行为可能呈现时变特性。为此，一种更自然的方法便是将静态模型扩展为动态模型，使其更好地适用于现实情况，从而捕捉到羊群效应的结构性变化。作为传统静态模型向动态模型推广的一种典型方法，马尔科夫区制转移模型在羊群效应研究中已经得到了应用。例如，Bohl等（2016）利用嵌套马尔科夫区制转移的羊群效应检验模型讨论了美国股市的动态羊群行为。然而这些文献关于羊群时变行为的研究均以西方发

---

\* 原文刊载于《金融研究》2021年第3期。
　作者简介：郑挺国，经济学博士，教授，厦门大学经济学院；葛厚逸，金融学博士研究生，厦门大学经济学院。

达国家股市的制度安排为基础,但不同国家的市场发展程度和制度安排之间存在巨大差别,因此西方有关羊群时变行为的研究结论对于广大发展中国家并不一定适用。特别地,中国股市结构较为特殊,包括沪深A股市场、沪深B股市场、中国香港股市和中国台湾股市,不同股市之间的制度设计和发展程度存在很大差别,其羊群行为也可能形态各异。因此,在分析中国股市羊群行为时,必须将现有理论和研究方法与中国特有的国情相结合,使其更好地适用于中国现实情况。本文基于中国不同股市的异质性背景,力图设计更加符合中国现实的实证模型和检验,对中国股市时变羊群行为和时变交叉羊群行为进行全面的分析。这种探索对于加强羊群效应理论在中国的研究具有一定的理论意义,同时对监管机构强化风险监测和预警,尤其是应对开放经济下的风险传染也具有重要的指导意义。

为此,本文基于1997年1月至2019年12月的中国股市日频交易数据,利用马尔科夫区制转移模型,探讨中国股市羊群效应的时变特征。首先,本文基于传统检验羊群效应的静态CCK模型实证结果,发现羊群效应在沪深A股市场、沪深B股市场和中国台湾股市中普遍存在,但并未发现中国香港股市存在羊群效应的证据。其次,基于马尔科夫区制转移模型的实证结果表明,中国股票市场运行周期可以被明确地划分为两种区制,分别呈现出低波动和高波动的行情特征。羊群效应表现出明显的区制依存性,沪深A股市场和沪深B股市场在高波动区制中,羊群效应表现得更为强烈,但其区制持续期较短,而在低波动区制中,羊群效应表现得较为和缓,但其区制持续期更长;中国台湾股市的羊群行为依存于高波动区制,相应的区制持续期较短,而在持续期较长的低波动区制中不存在羊群效应;中国香港股市在不同区制中均不存在明显的羊群行为。最后,本文检验了中国股市对美国股市及中国内地股市对中国香港股市可能存在的交叉羊群效应,实证结果表明,中国沪深A股市场在低波动区制中对美国股票市场和中国香港股票市场存在明显的交叉羊群效应。

相比已有文献，本文的研究贡献在于：首先，本文考虑到中国股票市场的特殊结构，综合探讨了不同制度和市场环境下的股市羊群效应，这为我们全面而深入地认识与比较沪深 A 股市场、沪深 B 股市场、中国香港股市和中国台湾股市羊群效应的静态和时变特征提供了经验证据。其次，本文研究也丰富了开放经济条件下金融风险传染的相关文献。我们从金融市场联动视角出发，将用于检验一个国家（地区）封闭市场羊群效应的传统 CCK 模型扩展到可以检验跨境交叉羊群效应的 CCK 模型。通过对中国股市交叉羊群效应的实证分析，本文从行为金融学视角揭示了美国股市和中国香港股市对中国沪深股市风险传染的交叉羊群效应路径。这一发现不仅为理解美国股市和中国香港股市对中国内地股市的风险传导机制提供思路，而且能够为开放经济下金融市场风险监测和有效监管提供重要参考。最后，为了确保马尔科夫区制转移模型应用的合理性和研究结论的可靠性，本文在实证分析中提供了必要的参数检验，这也为后续学者的研究提供了参考与借鉴。

# 信息不对称、过度自信与股价变动*

宫汝凯

信息传导非同步和投资者情绪变化是股票市场的两个典型特征，前者会引发投资者之间出现信息不对称问题，后者主要体现为投资者过度自信，两者共同作用影响股票价格变动。因此，将投资者的心理偏差和行为特征纳入经典金融市场定价理论分析框架深入探讨股价变动的内在逻辑具有很高的理论价值。同时，结合中国股票市场发展的现实，投资者获取和理解信息的能力可能存在明显的差异。在这一背景下，探讨信息传导过程中内生的信息不对称和投资者潜在的心理偏差双重因素驱动的股票定价模型具有重要的现实意义。

现有文献已经关注到这一问题，主要集中于信息在金融市场中的传导过程和投资者情绪对股票价格的影响两个方面。而较少涉及信息传导过程中内生出的信息不对称问题，更是鲜有关注投资者在新信息处理和更新中可能出现的过度自信情绪，两者共同作用促使股价变动，势必会影响传统股票定价模型的解释力。在现实市场上，信息传导往往是非同步的，自然地将投资者分成两个群体：一类是尚未获取新信息的投资者，其仍保持上一期的状态，按照历史信息进行投资决策；另一类是获取新信息的投资者，综合考虑新信息和历史信息进行投资决策。在多期的投资环境下，随着到期收益的实现，投资者将实现收益与上一期对该期收

---

\* 原文刊载于《金融研究》2021年第6期。
　作者简介：宫汝凯，经济学博士，副教授，东华大学旭日工商管理学院。

益的预期进行对照：若实现收益与预期收益存在显著的不一致且前者小于后者（即投资失败），投资者将其归结为运气差等外部因素所致，不影响本期的投资决策；若两者没有出现显著差异或前者大于后者（即投资成功），投资者则将其归功于"出色"的个人能力。在"自我归因偏差"的心理作用下，实现的超额收益将会提高投资者的信心，可能触发投资者产生过度自信情绪。此时，市场上会出现未获取信息、获取信息但未出现过度自信和获取信息且出现过度自信三类投资者。随着新信息的逐步流动，三类投资者的比例及过度自信程度将会发生改变，引起整体市场情绪变化，引发股票成交量和价格变动。可见，更为现实的情形是，信息的非同步传递会内生出信息不对称，进而使得投资者产生异质信念；同时，超额收益的实现可能引发投资者出现过度自信倾向，两者共同作用影响投资者的投资决策，引发股价变动。

有鉴于此，本文将信息不对称和投资者过度自信置于同一个分析框架研究现实市场上信息传导过程中股价变动的内在机制。参考 Easley 和 Hara（2004）的模型思路，采用信息渐进流动来刻画信息传导过程，进而内生出投资者之间的信息不对称问题；在此基础上，引入投资者过度自信这一典型的心理特征，建立两阶段动态序贯定价模型，探讨由信息不对称和投资者过度自信双重因素驱动的股价变动逻辑。结果表明，第一，面临新信息的进入，投资者对股票收益预期的调整与股票均衡价格呈正相关关系：提高投资者对股票的收益预期将使得股票均衡价格上涨，反之则相反。第二，面对有利消息时，具有过度自信倾向投资者的比例变大，股票的均衡价格上涨，股票收益下降；面对不利消息时则相反。第三，随着过度自信投资者比例和过度自信程度升高，市场风险溢价将下降。第四，投资者群体在信息传导过程中出现分化，形成异质信念，未获取信息和获取信息但未出现过度自信的投资者认为股价被高估，获取信息且出现过度自信的投资者认为股价被低估，引发市场成交量和股价变动。

第五，过度自信投资者比例与过度自信程度提高均会对市场效率产生正向影响，而对市场深度具有负向效应。第六，采用理论结果对现实市场上的非对称效应和波动持续性等典型的波动性特征进行了解释。

  本文的贡献主要体现在以下三个方面：第一，考察信息在股票市场上的渐进流动过程，内生出投资者之间潜在的信息不对称问题，探讨股票均衡价格的形成过程和变动机制，作为现有关于股票市场上信息传导方面研究的有益补充；第二，基于自我归因偏差理论，在信息传导过程中引入投资者过度自信这一典型的心理偏差，考虑更为现实的市场环境，探讨信息不对称和投资者过度自信双重因素驱动下股价形成和变动的内在机制，扩展了现有关于股票定价和价格变动等相关方面的研究；第三，采用理论结果对市场价格波动的非对称性和持续性等典型特征进行了行为金融学视角的解释，增强了对现实市场中股价变动机制的认识和理解。

# 基金网络能够提高投资绩效吗？*

陈胜蓝　李璟

以公募基金为代表的机构投资者，经历了快速的发展。党的十九届五中全会提出：构建金融有效支持实体经济的体制机制，提升金融科技水平，增强金融普惠性。基金作为金融业的重要组成部分，基金经理如何进行投资决策是构建、强化基金有效支持实体经济体制机制的关键，值得重点关注。最近研究表明由于信息结构的互补性，社会网络在基金经理资产配置和多元化决策过程中起着重要作用。本文重点关注基金共同持股形成的动态社会属性网络及其如何影响基金投资绩效。

在理论上，基金持股网络会如何影响投资绩效存在两种不同的观点：一种观点认为，网络会产生信息扩散效应，处于基金网络中心的基金经理会较早收到信号，更快获得更有价值的信息。与处于网络外围的基金经理相比，处于网络中心的基金经理持有的信息会更及时准确，从而会对基金的投资绩效产生正向影响。另一种观点认为，基金网络会诱发基金经理的"搭便车"行为。相比处于网络外围的基金经理，处于网络中心的基金经理更具有"搭便车"的条件，这意味着基金网络会对基金绩效带来负向影响。

本文以中国资本市场股票型基金 2005 年 1 月至 2018 年 9 月的数据为研究样本考察基金网络对基金投资绩效的影响。研究结果表明，基金

---

\* 原文刊载于《金融研究》2021 年第 6 期。
**作者简介**：陈胜蓝，管理学博士，教授，浙江工业大学经济学院；李璟，应用经济学博士研究生，内蒙古大学经济管理学院。

在基金网络中的中心地位越高,基金的投资绩效越高。以程度中心度、邻近中心度和特征向量中心度分别测量基金在基金网络中的地位,平均而言,程度中心度、邻近中心度和特征向量中心度分别每增加一个标准差,其投资绩效分别提高 54.43%、51.15% 和 50.93%。

接着,本文考察了基金网络影响基金投资绩效的渠道,结果表明,基金网络主要通过提高基金的选股技能、资产配置技能和资产管理技能来影响投资绩效。

最后,本文考察基金网络对基金份额的影响。基金网络为信息的传播与交流提供了渠道,位于网络中心地位的基金经理可以更快收到更有价值的信息,促使基金进行高质量的投资组合管理和产品差异化策略,这正是促使基金获得市场份额的关键。本文的检验结果表明,基金网络对其市场份额有显著的正向影响。

本文的研究贡献主要在以下两个方面。

第一,丰富了机构投资者持股互动的相关文献。已有大多数研究假定机构投资者是同质的,而缺乏对机构投资者异质性及其之间互动的研究。本文通过构建动态的基于持股的基金网络对此进行了扩展。基金持股网络反映了机构投资者持股之间的互动,并从网络位置这一角度将机构投资者持股进行了区分,利用一系列中心度的测量方法考察了持股网络中不同位置的基金在获取信息、采取行动上的差异。

第二,丰富了社会关系影响投资绩效的相关研究。之前的研究大多数考察社会静态属性特征形成的社会互动,但这样构建的网络中心度指标不能随时间变化,且没有进一步打开社会互动影响投资绩效的渠道。本文从动态的机构投资者持股互动的角度构建基金网络,考察其对基金投资绩效的影响。研究发现,在基于持股的基金网络中,积极的信息扩散效应较消极的抑制效应占主导地位,从而导致持股关系联系更多的基金有更好的投资绩效。进一步地,网络中基金之间的社会互动是通过提高基金的选股技能、资产配置技能及资产管理技能最终影响基金的投资绩效。

  本文研究结论还具有一定的现实意义。从基金经理角度，应当关注社会网络带来的正面影响，构建更加有效的社会网络，提高投资绩效。从个体投资者角度，关注基金网络特征有助于判断基金的投资价值，进一步深化金融普惠性。

# 名义价格幻觉*

——基于证券分析师目标价格预测的经验证据

何贵华　崔宸瑜　高　皓　屈源育

投资者潜意识里认为名义价格低的证券上涨空间大而名义价格高的证券上涨潜力小的行为偏误被称为"名义价格幻觉"（Birru 和 Wang, 2016）。大量文献从企业财务政策和资产价格等间接视角对中国 A 股市场的名义价格幻觉现象进行了研究（何涛和陈小悦，2003；李心丹等，2014；俞红海等，2014；罗进辉等，2017），发现散户投资者倾向于购买名义价格低的证券。

然而，在上述研究中，投资者是否因为股票名义价格而对股票回报产生了有偏的预期是无法直接观测的，因此并不能可靠地区分投资者对低价股的偏好究竟是面临预算约束时的理性最优选择，还是由名义价格幻觉引起的行为偏差。由于在我国股票市场，股票以"手"即100股为单位交易，散户投资者在资金量有限的情况下，购买高价的证券必然会挤占其他资产的配置空间，限制资产配置可行域的大小，进而影响投资组合的整体效果。由此可见，散户投资者青睐低价股，很可能是因为低价股可以使投资者有更灵活的选股空间，而不是因为名义价格幻觉引起的行为偏差。

---

\* 原文刊载于《金融研究》2021 年第 6 期。
**作者简介**：何贵华，管理学博士，讲师，中南财经政法大学会计学院；崔宸瑜，管理学博士，讲师，对外经济贸易大学国际商学院；高皓，管理学博士，清华大学五道口金融学院；屈源育，经济学博士，副教授，对外经济贸易大学金融学院。

本文利用目标价格这一可以直接反映证券分析师股票回报预测的研究场景，通过检验证券分析师做出的股票未来回报预测与股票名义价格之间的关系，对名义价格幻觉是否影响了证券分析师判断提供了直接体现心理预期的经验证据。本文研究设计的一个重要优势是可以排除投资者预算约束的干扰，因为预算约束虽然会影响投资者投资组合的构建，但却不影响投资者对股票回报的预期。

　　与名义价格幻觉的理论预测一致，本文研究发现，即使在控制了公司的基本面信息、股票的贝塔系数及其他与股票回报相关的公司特征之后，证券分析师对低价股未来回报的心理预期显著高于高价股。且这一现象在规模小、上市时间短、股票收益的波动性大、财务透明度低和无形资产占比大等难以估值的股票中表现得更加明显。本文还借助股票送转引起的股价"机械性"下降，为名义价格幻觉提供了进一步的证据。结果发现，股票除权后，证券分析师对送转股未来回报的心理预期显著高于没有进行送转的配对股票。

　　后续研究表明，证券分析师对低价股做出显著高于高价股的股票回报预测，确实是证券分析师心理预期的如实反映，而不是因为：（1）证券分析师跟踪的低价股比高价股有更好的投资机会，在未来能够实现更大幅度的价格上涨；（2）证券分析师有意揣度其他投资者的心理，发布迎合投资者心理的目标价格，以最大化所在证券公司的利益。

　　本文的学术贡献主要体现在以下几个方面：第一，本文使用证券分析师预测的股票目标价格数据，为名义价格幻觉是否显著干扰了证券分析师判断提供了直接的大样本证据支持。此外，本文的研究发现，为围绕名义价格幻觉探讨A股市场异象、A股投资者交易行为和A股上市公司财务政策等问题的学术文献（何涛和陈小悦，2003；李心丹等，2014；俞红海等，2014；罗进辉等，2017）提供了更加坚实的微观基础。第二，证券分析师领域的学术文献主要关注盈余预测与荐股评级，本文则对证券分析师目标价格预测的影响因素进行了研究，发现证券分析师目标价格预测的准确性显著受到了名义价格幻觉的影响。已有文献（Hilary 和 Menzly，2006；Hribar 和 McInnis，2012；Cen 等，2013；Pouget 等，2017；Hirshleifer 等，2019）研究表明，证券分析师的工作容易受到过度自信、投资者情绪、锚定效应、验证偏差和第一印象等常见心理偏误的影响，因此本文也丰富并拓展了证券分析师行为偏差的学术研究。

此外，我们的研究发现也有较大的实践价值，在专业的证券分析师尚且受到名义价格幻觉影响的情况下，缺乏财务知识和专业技能的散户投资者更需要进行自我提醒，尽量避免名义价格幻觉对投资决策的干扰。此外，监管机构应关注名义价格幻觉对股票市场的潜在影响，对上市公司利用股票送转投其所好的行为加强监管，保护散户投资者的利益。

# 06 国际经济与贸易

# 双边出口全球价值链实际有效汇率弹性理论测度及解析*

彭红枫  刘海莹

2020年6月以来,得益于我国有力的疫情防控举措和稳定的经济复苏态势,人民币汇率呈现出持续升值趋势,但出口也呈现出快速增长趋势。传统宏观经济学假设的汇率升值抑制出口理论受到挑战。近年来,汇率与出口弱相关现象引起广泛关注。许多学者研究发现汇率对出口的影响弱化了(杨雪峰,2013;Ahmed等,2015),甚至出现了"汇率贬值抑制出口"等传统经济理论无法解释的悖论(田侃等,2019)。造成这一现象的主要原因是,在全球价值链背景下,各国通过中间品贸易产生了供给侧联系。当前,全球价值链深入发展改变了传统贸易形式,中间品贸易日益频繁,通过嵌入全球价值链进行中间品贸易获取增加值收益已成为主流贸易方式(王直等,2015)。而基于Armington需求理论只考虑各国需求侧联系的传统实际有效汇率在衡量一国国际价格竞争力方面存在缺陷,反映一国相对价格竞争力与出口的关系时存在方向和数量上的误导(Bems和Johnson,2012)。

Bems和Johnson(2012,2015,2017)充分考虑了全球价值链背景下的供给侧联系,基于全球价值链下的投入产出关系构建了新的模型框

---

* 原文刊载于《金融研究》2021年第2期。
作者简介:彭红枫,经济学博士,教授,山东财经大学金融学院;刘海莹,金融学博士研究生,山东财经大学金融学院。

架对实际有效汇率进行测算。倪红福（2018）将这一模型进一步扩展到双边出口，文章考虑了第三国的影响，提出全球价值链背景下计算双边实际有效汇率的新方法，该方法可以准确衡量双边出口价格竞争力的变化。我们进一步应用该指标，对双边出口全球价值链的实际有效汇率弹性进行了理论测度和结构分解，通过引入第三国汇率效应和供给侧联系，纠正传统汇率作为相对价格竞争力衡量指标在解释与出口关系时存在的数量和方向偏误。

本文的主要贡献有以下两点：一是以 Bems 和 Johnson（2012，2015，2017）、Patel 等（2014）和倪红福（2018）的模型为基础，充分考虑全球价值链背景下的供给侧联系和第三国汇率效应，从对传统汇率指标进行修正的研究转向对双边出口汇率弹性的研究。从模型构建角度出发对双边出口全球价值链实际有效汇率弹性做出测度及分析。对当前研究中存在的"出口汇率不相关之谜"和"汇率对出口影响弱化"甚至"贬值抑制出口"现象做出解释。二是对弹性模型做出拓展，从相对价格变动引起的最终产品结构变动、中间产品结构变动及中间投入和增加值替代结构变动三个方面对双边出口全球价值链实际有效汇率弹性变动做出分解，这有助于理解弹性变动背后的结构性因素。

基于 Bems 和 Johnson（2012，2015，2017）、Patel 等（2014）和倪红福（2018）的研究成果，结合研究目的，本文建立了局部均衡模型，推导得出了双边出口全球价值链实际有效汇率弹性并做出了结构性分解。本文利用 WIOD 数据库提供的 2000—2014 年世界投入产出表数据进行测算。研究结果表明：（1）中国对主要贸易伙伴出口的全球价值链实际有效汇率弹性绝对值在 0.729~0.883 之间，全球价值链的深入发展在一定程度上降低了双边出口对全球价值链实际有效汇率变动的敏感性，但"汇率对出口影响弱化"并没有传统汇率表现得那么严重，以至于出现"贬值抑制出口"的情况。传统汇率在描述双边相对价格竞争力变动和出口关系时的确在方向和数值上都存在较大偏误。从区域来看，我国与日本和美国等主要发达国家的进出口量对全球价值链实际有效汇率的变动更敏感。（2）双边出口全球价值链实际有效汇率弹性结构分解结果显示，相对价格变动引起的中间产品结构变动和最终产品结构变动在双边出口全球价值链实际有效汇率弹性中的贡献度最高。对中国出口而言，伴随我国在全球价值链中参与度和地位的提升，中国对主要贸易伙伴出口中由相对价格变动引起中间产品结构变动对总弹性的贡献不断提升。此外，在分解中我们发现，在与中国贸易过程中，一些国家和地区的结构分解贡献度具有数值和变动上的相似性，例如韩国和中国台湾，日本和美国。

通过研究分析，可以得到以下几点政策启示：第一，为准确评估出口贸易状况，增强出口贸易政策制定效率，纠正传统汇率弹性测度偏误，有必要对双边出口全球价值链实际有效汇率弹性做出测算并关注该指标的异常变动。第二，为更有效地应对全球价值链实际有效汇率变动对双边出口造成的冲击，要找到弹性变动背后的结构性因素。在双边贸易过程中要重点关注最终产品和中间产品的结构变动情况，及时调整最终产品和中间产品进出口结构以减轻相对价格变动对出口的冲击。第三，对中国出口而言，伴随我国在全球价值链中地位和参与度的提升，中间品在贸易中的地位日益凸显。要重点关注我国与出口贸易国及第三国的中间产品贸易结构变动情况。当冲击发生时短期内可以通过寻找替代贸易伙伴方式来平抑出口波动，但长期仍要靠结构调整和政策沟通等方式来解决冲击。

# 遭遇反倾销与多产品企业的出口行为：
# 来自中国制造业的证据 *

许家云 张俊美 刘竹青

改革开放以来，我国的对外贸易经历了前所未有的快速发展，在规模和体量方面，已连续多年位列全球第一。但在新一轮贸易保护主义浪潮席卷的背景下，长期得益于经济全球化的我国在海外市场遭遇的反倾销贸易壁垒也愈发严重。据世界贸易组织统计，1995 年至 2020 年 6 月全球发起的反倾销调查案件有 6 139 起，我国遭遇的反倾销调查案件高达 1 440 起，占总案件的 23%，年均遭遇反倾销调查超过 55 起，并且涉案产品行业分布广，涉及各种所有制企业。2019 年 11 月 19 日，我国发布了《关于推进贸易高质量发展的指导意见》，强调优化贸易结构，实现贸易高质量发展的重要性。提高出口企业的市场竞争力、增强出口企业应对国外反倾销调查的能力，无疑是实现出口贸易高质量发展和"双循环"新发展格局的重要方式。基于此，本文尝试回答以下几个问题：反倾销究竟会对我国出口企业产生怎样的影响？其作用机制如何？

从理论上看，遭遇反倾销对出口企业的影响是多方面的：一方面，遭遇反倾销提高了出口企业的生产成本，削弱了价格优势，降低了利润，因此对出口产生不利影响；另一方面，遭遇反倾销威胁了出口企业的生存，

---

\* 原文刊载于《金融研究》2021 年第 5 期。
作者简介：许家云，经济学博士，副研究员，南开大学 APEC 研究中心；张俊美，经济学博士生，南开大学经济学院；刘竹青，经济学博士，副教授，福建师范大学经济学院。

加剧了其面临的竞争压力,会"倒逼"企业改变策略实现转型升级,从而提高企业自身效率和产品质量,从根本上增强企业的产品竞争力。因此,遭遇反倾销对我国出口企业的影响是一个实证问题。鉴于此,本文首先就反倾销影响多产品企业出口行为的相关作用机制进行梳理;然后构建计量模型,采用倍差法全面考察反倾销对我国多产品企业出口及生产率的影响;在基准分析的基础上,进一步考察全球价值链嵌入其中的作用,并基于马氏距离配方法、GMM方法等进行相应的稳健性检验,证实了本文结论的稳健性。此外,本文还考察了反倾销对多产品企业出口的异质性影响及对企业生产率的影响。

本文的研究特色主要体现在如下几个方面:第一,在研究视角上,本文尝试结合厂商和产品的异质性贸易理论,使用我国多产品出口企业的微观数据,从企业内部出口产品结构的视角探究遭遇反倾销对多产品企业出口行为的影响。与已有大多数文献所不同的是,本文不仅考察遭遇反倾销对企业出口规模、出口数量、出口产品种类的影响,还考察了遭遇反倾销对企业出口价格、出口产品集中度及出口市场多元化的影响,这不仅丰富了有关评估遭遇反倾销的出口效应的研究文献,而且也深化了我们对遭遇反倾销影响企业出口行为作用机制的理解。第二,在研究维度上,本文不仅采用PSM-DID方法考察了遭遇反倾销对企业出口行为的平均影响效应,而且还进一步将全球价值链纳入本文的分析框架,通过测算企业的全球价值链上游嵌入度、下游嵌入度及地位指数,深入考察企业在全球价值链中的位置在企业遭遇反倾销时对其出口行为的作用,检验发现,遭遇反倾销对企业出口行为的影响受到企业全球价值链上游嵌入度、下游嵌入度及地位指数的制约,而既有关于遭遇反倾销贸易效应的研究较少关注全球价值链的作用。第三,本文还进一步从企业内出口产品再配置的视角考察遭遇反倾销对多产品企业生产率的影响,发现遭遇反倾销通过促进企业出口产品组合向其更具竞争优势的核心产品转变，显著提高了多产品出口企业的生产率，并且上述效应随着遭遇反倾销程序的推进逐步凸显，这一发现也在一定程度上丰富了遭遇反倾销的出口效应研究。本文研究既是对已有贸易理论、贸易政策文献的有益补充，又是对我国出口企业面临重大问题的深度解析，对我国在全球价值链背景下如何有效实现对外贸易高质量发展，具有重要的现实意义。

本文在多产品企业贸易理论的框架下，从多产品企业内部产品配置的角度全面探究了遭遇反倾销对企业生产率的影响，为反倾销与企业贸易行为的研究提供了来自企业—产品层面的经验证据。本文研究结论表明，遭遇反倾销在降低企业出口数量的同时，可以加速企业出口产品之间的优胜劣汰，促使企业集中核心优势生产并出口其最具竞争力的产品，长远来讲有益于提升我国企业的生产效率和竞争力升级。同时，我国出口企业中存在着大量的加工贸易企业，这些从事简单加工或组装活动的企业，最容易受到反倾销的制约，而处于价值链上游的企业由于能够创造较高的附加值而处于主动地位，因此，我国出口企业应充分利用反倾销的竞争压力，积极推动技术创新，加大自主品牌的研发和设计，掌握核心竞争力，实现出口企业尤其是加工贸易型出口企业从价值链下游向上游的逐步攀升，不断提升企业生产率。

# 金融结构如何影响外资进入方式选择？*

景光正　盛　斌

近年来，受"逆全球化"浪潮兴起的影响，全球价值链分工体系正处于深度重构过程，随着国际投资体制碎片化趋势的加剧，作为主要载体的外商直接投资（Foreign Direct Investment，FDI）行为受到明显冲击。与此同时，我国的引资竞争也面临发达国家"制造业回流"和传统生产要素优势不明显等诸多挑战，导致对外资吸引力下降。2019年3月15日《中华人民共和国外商投资法》颁布实施，进一步表明"加大外资吸引力度，在更高水平上扩大开放"，仍是我国长期不变的政策基调，同时也要求我国在改革开放的基本理论与战略思路上有更多创新和突破。已有研究较多关注外资引入之后的经济绩效问题，鲜有研究从外资进入方式的选择出发，基于优化外资进入内部结构的动机，考察东道国何种因素影响了外资进入方式的选择。

外资进入东道国市场的多元化方式选择主要包括绿地投资和跨国并购两种。外资进入方式选择问题作为跨国公司在进入东道国市场时的核心决策之一，不仅直接关系到企业自身跨国经营的成败，也对东道国的经济绩效产生显著影响。其中，金融是现代经济的核心，东道国能否通过完善的金融体系吸引外资进入，以实现前沿技术扩散、推动其全球价值链地位升级，日益成为学术界重点关注的问题。与此同时，营商环境

---

\* 原文刊载于《金融研究》2021年第5期。
作者简介：景光正，经济学博士，南开大学经济学院、跨国公司研究中心、国际经济研究所；
盛斌，经济学博士，教授，南开大学经济学院、跨国公司研究中心、国际经济研究所。

作为当前和预期的政策、制度及行为环境，不仅直接影响到跨国投资的回报与风险，还通过影响不完全契约条件下金融资源的配置效率，间接影响外商直接投资收益（Antras 和 Helpman，2004）。目前已有一些文献探讨了金融发展与外资进入之间的关系，但鲜有文献在各国营商环境差异的背景下研究金融结构与外资进入方式选择之间的关联。

本文基于 Levine（2002）的方法，构建金融结构指标体系，试图在以下方面有所贡献：第一，研究视角上，从金融体制视角切入，深入考察了不同金融结构对外资进入方式选择的影响，并基于国际投资相关理论，系统梳理了金融结构对外资进入方式的影响机制，进而为我国金融供给侧结构性改革和提高外资引入质量提供有益参考。第二，研究方法上，采用"法源"作为分组依据的工具变量对金融结构和外资进入方式选择关系进行了内生性处理；此外，进行了机制检验，从而深化了对金融结构与外资进入方式选择之间关系的理解。第三，基于不完全契约理论，将营商环境纳入研究框架，不仅考察了营商环境对外资进入方式选择的直接影响，还运用门限效应模型，间接检验了营商环境的调节效应，从而为评价金融供给侧结构性改革和引资结构优化提供一个相对严谨的实证分析框架。

本文分析得出三个基本结论：第一，相较于银行主导型金融结构，市场主导型金融结构更有利于外资选择跨国并购方式进入，发达国家金融市场的促进作用明显优于发展中国家。第二，传导机制检验发现，技术创新引致和国家风险管控是金融结构影响外资进入方式选择的重要渠道，其中，细分国家风险渠道检验发现，金融结构主要通过降低经济金融风险影响外资进入方式选择。第三，营商环境的改善不仅对外资进入具有直接促进作用，也能间接调节金融市场对外资进入结构优化的提升作用，且发达国家营商环境发挥的作用显著大于发展中国家。

本文的研究结论具有明晰的政策含义。首先，继续深化金融供给侧结构性改革，切实推动金融市场化、自由化与国际化，有效降低外资企业进入和经营成本；适时调整引资政策，不断完善外商投资准入前国民待遇加负面清单管理制度，兼顾绿地投资和跨国并购两种外资进入方式的政策，以此实现外资结构和质量双升级。其次，进一步强化技术创新和防范国家风险。一方面，创新激励政策要实现从重"数量"到重"质量"转变，增强金融服务实体经济的能力，创新绩效评价也要实现科学性和灵活性的统一；另一方面，在全球经济不确定性不断加剧的背景下，要健全金融风险防范机制，有效管控和化解国内外企业共同面临的系统性和非系统性风险。最后，引资政策制定应致力于营商环境改善，遵循国民待遇意义上的竞争中性原则，建立和完善外商投资促进机制，营造稳定、透明、可预期和公平竞争的市场环境。

# 汇率不确定性与企业跨境并购*

孟 为  姜国华  张永冀

在国际经济形势复杂多变和汇率市场化改革的背景下，世界各国之间汇率相对波动已呈常态，未预期汇率波动引致微观企业面临的财务风险与经营风险增加，并对一国经济可持续发展产生深远影响。目前，世界经济走势、全球供应链、各国经济政策、国际机构发展等均存在一定程度的"不确定性"，而微观企业的生存与发展也依存于各类不确定性。

在经济全球化背景中，引导国际经济合作、深入全球价值链与产业链、促进企业参与国际竞争成为发展外向型经济的重要途径。跨境并购是世界范围内对外直接投资的主要形式，也是我国企业走出国门的重要途径。相对境内并购，企业在跨境并购中面临着三种额外不确定性：一是国际经济发展中的逆全球化、贸易争端和保护主义、地缘政治冲突等带来的不确定性，二是我国与目标企业所在国家之间相互关系的不确定性，三是目标企业所在国家内部的经济、政治、安全、法律等方面的不确定性。特别地，汇率作为国际价格，反映了一国竞争力，未预期的汇率波动蕴含于上述不确定性中，进而影响企业决策，尤其是涉外财务决策。

本文聚焦汇率不确定性在企业跨境并购层面的微观经济后果，旨在更加深入地认识错综复杂的国际环境带来的新矛盾和新挑战，以进一步

---

\* 原文刊载于《金融研究》2021 年第 5 期。

作者简介：孟为，管理学博士，博士后（讲师），北京大学光华管理学院；姜国华，管理学博士，教授，北京大学光华管理学院；张永冀，管理学博士，副教授，北京理工大学管理与经济学院。

增强机遇意识和风险意识。本文定义"汇率不确定性"为历史趋势和公开信息不能预期的汇率波动,即来源于无法对未来汇率波动方向、波动范围和分布概率进行准确预测的情境。在汇率不确定性下,作为经济开放载体的企业在国际贸易、跨境投融资中的交易质量和风险控制显得越发重要。那么,汇率不确定性是否以及通过什么途径影响我国企业跨境并购决策?

汇率因素直接作用于涉外交易成本与外币结算成本,进而影响持有外币资产或承担外币负债企业的价值、企业进出口行为或跨境投融资业务。基于此,本文提出汇率不确定性影响企业跨境并购的两种机制:(1)实物期权效应,即汇率不确定性通过提升交易成本和预期收益不确定性、增加外部融资约束等途径抑制企业跨境并购决策;(2)风险对冲效应,即汇率不确定性加剧了市场竞争程度与企业面临的经营风险,促使企业通过跨境并购利用国际资源、增强竞争力,进而实现对冲汇率风险的目标。为检验两种机制的作用效果,本文以2000—2019年A股上市公司宣告的跨境并购交易为研究对象(共计34 592个样本),实证分析发现:(1)人民币兑美元名义汇率不确定性显著降低了我国企业跨境并购的可能性,实物期权效应占主导作用;人民币名义有效汇率不确定性与企业跨境并购决策显著正相关,风险对冲效应起主导作用。(2)横截面检验发现,人民币兑美元名义汇率不确定性对企业跨境并购的抑制作用在汇率交易风险和折算风险更高以及存在融资约束的企业中更为明显;同时,有效汇率反映一国贸易条件,处于竞争激烈行业以及自身汇率经济风险更高的企业,在人民币名义有效汇率不确定性加剧时更有可能进行跨境并购。(3)结合金融摩擦和风险承担的中介效应检验进一步证明,人民币兑美元名义汇率不确定性和人民币名义有效汇率不确定性分别通过实物期权和风险对冲机制影响企业跨境并购决策。(4)对企业跨境并购经济后果的检验表明,在人民币兑美元名义汇率与人民币名义有效汇率不确定性较高时期，企业进行的跨境并购拥有相对较好的财务绩效，汇率风险约束使并购行为更为审慎高效；跨境并购有利于缓解公司股价对人民币名义有效汇率变化的敏感程度，明显降低汇率经济风险，但对人民币兑美元名义汇率的风险敞口没有显著缓解作用。

本文有以下三个方面贡献或启示：第一，本文区分了双边汇率（人民币兑美元名义汇率）与有效汇率的作用机制差异，拓展了汇率波动的微观经济后果及外部不确定性影响企业行为的研究范畴。本文为企业积极参与国际分工和经济合作提供参考，尤其提醒企业跨境决策时应注意汇率风险，在不确定性中寻找确定性。第二，本文对对外直接投资、企业并购尤其是跨境并购影响因素的文献进行了补充，在现有法律制度、金融发展、社会关系、会计准则、公司战略、企业文化等因素研究之外，提供了汇率不确定性对企业并购行为影响的解释，有利于全面认识并评价企业跨境并购决策的效果。第三，汇率未预期波动会诱发国际资本套利，加剧金融市场动荡，甚至导致金融危机。本文从资本市场视角探究汇率不确定性的外溢效应，在微观层面进一步厘清资本市场与外汇市场的互动关系，为新发展格局下我国推进高质量对外开放与汇率市场化改革提供参考。

# 07 财税政策与地方政府行为

# 房价调控、地方政府债务与宏观经济波动*

梅冬州　温兴春　王思卿

　　1998 年住房制度改革以来，我国经历了房价的急剧上涨。不断上涨的房价在吸引大量的社会资金和银行贷款进入房地产行业的同时，也推动了地方政府利用土地储备向银行大规模举债，造成地方政府债务高企。在房价与地价、地价与地方政府偿债能力高度相关的背景下，对房价的调控不当极有可能触发地方债务（毛捷和曹婧，2019）。那么，调控房价能否使资金流向制造业部门？房价调控与地方政府债务风险又有何联系？

　　通过梳理中国宏观经济的特征事实，我们发现在当前地方政府融资模式下，地方政府的收入高度依赖于"土地财政"，地价的高低影响了地方政府的收入，决定了地方政府的偿债能力。管控房价会影响地价，地价下降又会影响地方政府的偿债能力。当地方政府无法偿还债务，且地方政府债务规模太大或中央政府缺乏救助意愿时，地方政府可能出现违约，这将通过金融系统对经济造成严重的负面影响。基于这些事实，本文建立了一个多部门的 DSGE 模型。首先，为刻画房价与土地财政、地方政府债务之间的关系，我们将地方政府及其土地财政行为嵌入模型。

---

*  原文刊载于《金融研究》2021 年第 1 期。
　作者简介：梅冬州，经济学博士，教授，中央财经大学国际经济与贸易学院；温兴春，经济学博士，讲师，对外经济贸易大学金融学院；王思卿，应用经济学博士研究生，清华大学经济管理学院。

模型中地方政府依赖土地出让和土地抵押借贷为自己的开支融资，地价和房价的变动直接影响了地方政府偿还债务的能力。其次，为刻画地方政府借贷行为对金融部门的影响，参考 Iacoviello（2015）和 Bernanke 等（1999）的研究，我们在模型中引入两类金融摩擦：一方面，由于将存款转化为贷款需要耗费贷款成本，且金融部门受外部监管约束，导致基准贷款利率高于存款利率，即存在"存贷溢价摩擦"；另一方面，由于信息不对称，企业融资能力受净资产限制，即存在"外部融资溢价摩擦"。

数值模拟结果表明，房价管控导致地价下降，从而降低了地方政府收入，直接影响了地方政府偿还债务的能力。如果地价下降没有触发地方政府债务违约，那么地价下降将带来两方面的影响：一是导致地方政府收入下降，从而影响地方政府支出，使基建部门产出下降，降低了总产出；二是导致地方政府抵押借贷额下降，金融中介流向地方政府的资金减少，金融部门的存贷溢价下降，其他部门从金融部门获得贷款的成本下降，并通过金融加速器效应进一步放大，从而带来非基建部门投资上升、产出扩张。但如果地价下降触发地方政府债务违约，即地价下降造成的地方政府收入下降使其无法偿还金融部门贷款，且地方政府债务规模太大或者中央政府缺乏救助意愿，那么由此带来的债务违约将导致金融部门资产受到损失，使金融中介减少贷款、存贷溢价大幅上升，整个经济中所有部门获得资金的成本急剧上升，并通过金融加速器放大，造成经济中所有部门的投资和产出大幅下降。

在房价调控对经济波动的影响中，与金融部门的资产负债表直接相关的存贷溢价摩擦起到关键作用。如何在管控房价时不引发地方政府的违约和产出大幅下降？进一步的政策反事实分析表明，在采取债务置换避免地方政府违约的情况下，应使用财政资金补充银行资本金或降低银行准备金率，以降低金融中介的存贷溢价摩擦，从而在避免地方政府违约的同时，降低整个社会的融资成本，将房价调控对经济的负面影响降到最低。

与之前研究相比，本文存在以下几点创新：首先，地方政府债务问题一直是房价调控不可回避的焦点问题，已有研究也多为定性分析且缺乏系统性。对此，本文通过在一个多部门的DSGE模型中引入地方政府的土地财政行为，将房价如何影响地价，地价变动如何影响地方政府的偿债能力，进而对地方政府和金融中介的行为产生影响结合起来，梳理了房价与地方政府债务的影响路径，并对决定两者关系的关键因素进行了研究。其次，房价调控如何影响经济波动，现有研究多为定性分析，本文构建了一个多部门的DSGE模型，从一般均衡的角度对房价调控影响经济波动的各个渠道进行刻画，并讨论了各因素的作用。有助于理解当前房价调控的作用路径和影响效果，可为相关政策的制定提供有益参考。最后，如何在稳定房价使资金流向制造业部门的同时不触发地方政府债务违约，本文在通过模型分析理清相关思路的基础上，尝试探讨这一问题，并提出了相关对策建议。

# "税费替代"：增值税减税、非税收入征管与企业投资*

赵仁杰　范子英

近年来，全球范围内税率普遍下降，通过减税促进企业投资成为各国刺激经济的重要手段。从 2018 年 5 月开始，我国增值税 17% 和 11% 两个档次的税率分别下调一个点，2019 年 4 月 1 日后增值税两个档次的税率分别从 16% 降至 13%、从 10% 降至 9%，一年之内增值税税率下降了 1/4，这是该税种在我国设立以来最大分度的减税措施，税率的下调直接降低了企业税负。同时，在增值税、企业所得税等方面，我国还出台了专门针对小微企业的减税政策。提振企业投资和促进经济增长也是我国此轮大减税改革的关键目标，尤其是增值税税率的大幅下调和小微企业的减税政策在促进企业投资上被寄予厚望。从政策实施效果来看，2019 年上半年民间投资未出现明显增加，受增值税减税影响最大的制造业，其 2019 年上半年的投资增速同比也偏低。因此，在大减税改革的背景下，一个亟待回答的关键问题是减税政策的效果如何？从企业投资的角度来看，哪些因素可能会影响减税政策的效果？

在我国主体税种为共享税的情况下，大减税政策会同步带来地方财政减收，减税力度越大对地方财政压力的影响会越明显。在减税政策影

---

\* 原文刊载于《金融研究》2021 年第 1 期。
作者简介：赵仁杰，经济学博士，副教授，西北大学经济管理学院；范子英，经济学博士，教授，上海财经大学公共经济与管理学院。

响下，地方为了缓解财政压力会通过其他方式筹集收入，其中最具代表性的就是非税收入。分税制改革后我国绝大部分非税收入的征管权和收入被划归给地方，面临减税政策带来的财政收入冲击，地方可以通过加强非税收入征管来缓解减税政策带来的财政压力，进而可能导致在地方财政收入和企业负担上体现出税减少、费增加的"税费替代"效应，这使得减税政策实施后企业综合税费负担变化的不确定性增强，有可能会弱化减税政策促进企业投资的效果。

本文在"税费替代"的逻辑框架下，利用我国增值税减税的政策冲击，研究减税对企业非税负担的溢出效应及其对企业固定资产投资的影响。增值税是我国的第一大税种，也是中央地方共享税，在我国引入增值税制度之初，固定资产价值中的税款以及折旧不允许在税前扣除，这导致企业固定资产投资的税负较重。2004年我国开始在东北三省的八大行业试点增值税转型政策，允许新购机器设备中的税款在税前扣除，2008年这一政策被推广到汶川地震受灾严重的地区，2009年1月1日开始，增值税转型在全国所有地区、所有行业一次性推开。增值税转型使得企业固定资产投资中的进项税款可以在税前扣除，极大降低了企业固定资产投资的税收负担，但也会导致政府增值税收入减少，这为研究减税政策对政府非税收入征管的影响提供了机会。

我们利用2008—2011年城市层面的数据（1 000多个样本量），研究发现，2009年的增值税转型改革会显著降低地方政府的增值税收入，尤其是在改革前对增值税收入依赖度比较高的地区这一效应更加明显。增值税转型在导致城市增值税收入缩减的同时，会显著提高政府的非税收入，对增值税依赖度越高的城市其非税收入提升越明显，在地方收入层面验证了"税费替代"假说。

企业是税费的承担主体，增值税转型政策直接降低了企业的增值税税负，而地区层面的研究结果显示这项改革也同时增加了地方的非税收入。基于 2008—2011 年企业层面的数据（每年约 70 万家），本文利用双重差分方法研究了 2009 年增值税转型改革对企业税费负担的影响，从"税费替代"角度揭示税费不确定性对企业固定资产投资的作用。实证分析的结果表明：第一，增值税转型在总体上降低了企业综合税费负担，尤其是显著降低了企业增值税税负，达到了向企业减税的效果。第二，增值税转型在减税的同时，也提高了企业的非税负担，企业所在地对增值税收入的依赖度越高，增值税转型导致企业非税负担上升的效应越明显。第三，增值税转型对企业非税负担的正向作用主要体现在小型、微型和民营企业上，对大中型企业和非民营企业的影响并不显著，这说明增值税减税的"税费替代"效应在不同企业间具有非对称性特征。第四，小型、微型和民营企业非税负担上升会显著抑制这些企业的固定资产投资，促使这些企业通过持有更多现金和减少流动性负债等方式来应对减税政策实施后企业税费负担的不确定性。

根据上述分析结论，本文得到以下三方面政策启示：第一，在推行大减税政策的同时，应充分考虑地方面临的财政压力，通过完善央地收入补偿机制、减少地方事权等配套改革，降低减税政策给地方财政造成的冲击；第二，在针对小微企业减税的同时，需要进一步规范地方对小微企业的非税项目征管，通过更大力度的降费措施防止减税的同时小微企业非税负担上升，确保减税政策的实际效果；第三，在财税体制改革中减轻企业税费负担，需要不断推进非税收入的规范化和法治化改革，通过非税收入划转改革、非税收入立法等途径降低地方对非税收入的弹性征管，逐步实现中央税费统管。

# 减税降费的价格和福利效应*
## ——引入成本传导率的投入产出价格模型分析

倪红福　闫冰倩

"减税降费"作为积极财政政策的重要组成部分，在激发经济活力方面发挥着重要作用。2020年的新冠肺炎疫情对全球经济造成巨大短期冲击，还将产生长远影响。该影响持续时间越长，全球价值链断裂风险越大，越可能会导致全球化倒退、产业链崩溃等危机。为应对经济下行压力和支持疫情防控，企业更需要税费优惠政策。然而，用减税降费来减轻企业负担的目的能否成功与企业税费成本向生产者价格传导的效率密切相关，因此考察减税降费问题时须同时将成本传导率考虑在内。从宏观角度整体看，若税费成本部分传导，引起生产者价格下降，使企业中间品投入价格下降，进一步降低企业生产成本，从而也可提高企业利润，即通过中间投入的网络联系渠道进一步放大减税降费的降负作用。但企业出厂生产者价格还受多种因素影响，例如市场需求旺盛，需求大于供给，产品价格就可随之上涨。那么中国实施的减税降费政策（尤其是2019年）的价格效应究竟如何，进而又如何影响福利值得深入研究。鉴于影响生产者价格的因素较多，本文只能抽象其他影响因素，考虑在不同成本传导率情形下，减税降费的价格效应和福利效应。

---

\* 原文刊载于《金融研究》2021年第2期。
　　作者简介：倪红福，经济学博士，副研究员，中国社会科学院经济研究所；闫冰倩，经济学博士，副研究员，中国社会科学院财经战略研究院。

本文通过构建引入成本传导率的投入产出价格模型，在投入产出模型中嵌入抵扣机制的增值税、社保费、其他生产税等间接税费，重点分析减税降费的价格和福利效应，并通过设计不同的结构性减税降费情景模拟分析不同减税降费政策方案的优劣。相对于已有文献，本文的主要边际贡献有以下三点：（1）引入成本传导机制，构建带有增值税、社保费和其他间接税的成本非完全传导的投入产出价格模型。传统的投入产出价格模型假设价格是完全前向传递的，即认为生产成本（税费、中间品成本）的变动会完全传递到产品价格。然而现实经济市场中，大多是非完全竞争市场，企业拥有一定垄断势力并在生产成本上实施价格加成，从而使生产成本的冲击并不一定完全反映在产品价格中。（2）分析了不同成本传导率情景下，实际减税降费政策对 PPI 和福利的影响。结合税务局各行业的实际减税率数据，考虑到税收征管能力，反事实模拟分析了实际减税降费的价格效应和福利效应。（3）结合税率简化和促进资源有效配置的税率改革原则，模拟分析了三种结构性减税降费情景的影响，为进一步推进税收制度改革和宏观政策制定提供参考。

本文研究结果表明：（1）减税降费使得各行业产品价格降低，对第三产业的价格影响最为明显。减税降费对卫生行业、其他制造业产品业和批发业的价格影响最大，而对房地产价格的影响最小。（2）成本传导率越高，产品价格的下降幅度越大。当成本传导率分别为 1/3、2/3 和 1 时，各行业产品价格的平均下降幅度分别为 0.32 个、0.93 个和 2.66 个百分点。（3）较为合理的中国整体成本传导率约为 1/3，减税降费是 2019 年中国 PPI 下降的主要因素之一。当成本传导率为 1/3 时，模拟计算的 PPI 下降幅度与国家统计局公布的 2019 年 PPI 下降幅度（−0.3%）非常接近。（4）在福利效应方面，减税降费使消费者价格下降，居民福利得以提升，且城镇居民福利改善高于农村居民的福利改善。随着价格传导率增大，城镇居民与农村居民的人均福利改善差距扩大。

基于研究结论，可以得到以下主要政策启示。第一，减税降费能够有效降低生产者价格指数，减轻企业成本负担，同时提升消费者福利。当前我国经济面临国内外巨大风险挑战，须为企业卸掉重负，将减税降费落到实处，确保国家支持新冠肺炎疫情防控、复工复产。稳定外贸、扩大内需的税费优惠政策落实到位。第二，在设计减税降费政策时需要考虑到行业部门的成本传导率情况，防止其削弱政策实施效果。应预估行业部门的成本传导率，设计减税降费的幅度和大小，真正减轻企业负担。第三，结构性减税降费政策更利于获得好的政策效果。从本文对三种结构性减税降费的方案分析可知，"仅降费"方案的福利效应最高，且对财政收入的影响最小；"简并税率的全覆盖＋无降费"方案可最大程度地降低生产成本，而"对服务业简易征收＋无降费"方案对国家财政收入的冲击最大，不宜作为未来税改的方向。第四，虽然减税降费会一定程度上提高居民的福利水平，但减税降费总体上对城镇居民福利改善程度大于农村居民。因此，在进行减税降费政策设计时，需适当出台一些配套政策，避免减税降费政策拉大城乡差距。最后，本文仍然存在一些不足之处，值得未来进一步研究。如限于数据可获得性，本文对所有行业部门的成本传导率都设定为同一数值，显然实际中不同行业部门的成本传导率不同，可探索如何估计不同行业的成本传导率，并改进本文引入成本传导率的投入产出价格模型。此外，本文也可扩展到带有投入产出结构的一般均衡模型。

# 政府间收入分成与财政收入预算偏离*

吕冰洋　陈志刚

　　财政是国家治理的基础和重要支柱，而预算是财政制度的基础。预算偏离又在较大程度上反映了政府的预算管理水平。所谓预算偏离，指的是政府预算和决算的差异，具体可定义为（决算－预算）/预算，这包括收入预算偏离和支出预算偏离，本文主要关注收入预算偏离。

　　自分税制改革以来，我国政府的预算偏离程度长期处于较大状态。尽管低收入国家的预算偏离程度普遍高于高收入国家，但我国各省的收入预算偏离程度在 2000—2014 年的平均值为 9.38%，不仅大于一些发达国家，甚至高于许多发展中国家。预算本身是一种收支计划，应该允许决算数与预算数存在一定差距，而且在预算编制过程中会特意留有一定余地。但如果差距过大，就会带来一系列问题。如果预算偏离过大的状况一直持续下去，政府预算编制就失去了其科学性和权威性，现代预算制度进而现代财政制度的建立也会在一定程度上受到挑战，从而影响财政对经济社会的调节效果。因此，理解导致收入预算偏离的原因并提出有针对性的措施，对于建立现代预算制度，提高政府财政管理活动的绩效乃至推进国家治理现代化都具有重要的意义。

　　从既有关于预算偏离的研究来看，国外文献侧重从收入预测的角度进行讨论，国内文献则超出了预测范畴，更加关注预算执行层面的问题。

---

\* 原文刊载于《金融研究》2021 年第 5 期。
　作者简介：吕冰洋，经济学博士，教授，中国人民大学财政金融学院；陈志刚，经济学博士，助理教授，深圳大学经济学院。

关于预算偏离的成因，当前文献主要从技术、经济及制度等方面进行了分析，但鲜有研究关注到政府间财政关系对预算偏离的影响。鉴于此，本文系统分析了财政收入分成对收入预算偏离的影响。基于我国财政收入分成和预算管理的制度背景，本文认为政府收入分成对财政收入预算偏离的影响机制如下：我国政府间财政收入划分广泛采用分成办法，在财政压力和财政扩张机制下，财政收入分成对决算的影响程度大于对预算的影响程度；地方政府面临财政收入分成比例改变后，会选择调整政府行为以改变财政决算，从而影响财政预算偏离。进一步地，本文构建了一个简单的静态模型，模型分析表明，财政压力和财政扩张两种机制的存在使得政府间收入分成的变化对预算偏离产生两种截然相反的影响。其中财政压力机制是指地方政府面临的财政压力会随着财政收入分成比例的下降而上升，为缓解财政压力，地方政府会加强税收征管或者大力发展经济，从而财政决算收入会上升，最终导致收入预算偏离上升；财政扩张机制是指地方政府通过提高税收努力来增加财政收入的意愿会随着财政收入分成比例下降而下降，从而财政决算超出预算的程度也将变小，最终导致收入预算偏离下降。

通过手工收集各省在人代会上的预算报告，本文整理了2000—2013年我国30个省（市、区）的（收入）预决算数据和收入分成数据[①]。具体处理上，本文将省以下政府当作一个整体，并运用双向固定效应模型实证检验了政府间收入分成对财政收入预算偏离的影响，结果支持财政压力机制：财政收入分成降低1个百分点，收入预算偏离会增加0.3个百分点。其可能的原因在于，财政扩张是边际影响，而财政压力是总量影响。财政压力就像一个最低的要求，即使上级政府给下级政府的收入分成比

---

[①]2000年之前各省份预决算报告存在较多缺失，同时，我们预测的省以下收入分成数据截至2013年，且其在2000年之前的数据量也较少。

例再小（即对财政扩张的影响再弱），它也会通过加强税收努力或者促进经济发展等方式，增加自身的收入，以满足财政压力这一总量的需要。只有在不存在财政压力的前提下，下级政府才可能会考虑税收分成比例的调整带来的财政扩张的变化。进一步的实证结果较好地支持了上述解释：相比省级政府，市县政府面临更大的财政压力，因而，财政收入分成对收入预算偏离的影响在市县层面显著为负，而在省本级层面为正但不显著；相比经济发达地区，经济落后地区面临的财政压力更大，因而随着经济发展水平的提高，收入分成对收入预算偏离的影响变小。在改变收入预算偏离衡量方式、控制转移支付变量、考虑内生性问题、加入预算偏离滞后项及考虑变量间空间影响的情况下，本文结论依然稳健。

我国"营改增"之后，以共享税为主的政府间收入分成改革已是箭在弦上。根据本文研究所得出的政策建议是，为有效降低地方政府收入预算偏离，政府间收入划分的改革方案要兼顾长期稳定性与财力支持性，改革既要能够缓解地方政府的财政压力，又要保持财政收入分成办法的稳定性。

本文的主要贡献包括：第一，研究预算偏离问题面临的重要挑战是数据问题，以往研究或是数据缺乏而不深入或是数据的获取还有待完善，本文利用各省人代会上的预决算报告收集了全省和市县加总层面的预算偏离数据；第二，以往文献讨论预算偏离影响因素时，多是从在理论层面多角度探讨，具体因素的分析不够深入，也缺乏相应的实证检验，本文则从理论和实证两方面系统阐述和检验了财政收入分成对收入预算偏离的影响；第三，财政收入分成的变化对地方政府行为的影响会产生两种相反的作用机制——财政压力和财政扩张，以往文献多是分析其中的一种机制，本文则同时考虑了两种机制变化对预算偏离的作用。

# 地方公共债务与资本回报率*

——来自新口径债务数据和三重机制检验的经验证据

冀云阳 毛 捷 文雪婷

近年来,地方公共债务在稳投资、补短板、促增长过程中发挥日益重要的作用。截至2019年末,地方公共债务余额已经上升至21.3万亿元,相比2013年增长了一倍多。党的十九大报告指出,我国经济已由高速增长阶段转向高质量发展阶段,必须坚持质量第一、效益优先;同时提出防范化解重大风险等三大攻坚战部署。在此情况下,未来的财政政策须"提质增效",保证公共投资的合理性、有效性,并进一步提高财政资金的配置效率。那么,大规模的债务性投资是否能够形成有效投资?债务性投资的增加对我国经济增长潜力的影响如何?是否会导致债务风险的积累?这些问题事关我国经济高质量发展和系统性风险防范,而回答上述问题必须考虑各地区资本回报率的变化。这是因为,资本回报率是判断投资是否过度和效率高低的关键指标(Bai等,2006;柏培文和许捷,2017)。与此同时,资本回报率也决定了政府债务能否促进经济增长。当资本回报率高于实际利率时,增加公共债务可以挤入私人投资,加速资本积累,从而促进经济增长;但随着资本不断积累,投资回报率逐渐降低,此时增加公共债务反而会抑制经济增长。债务风险的积累也与资

---

\* 原文刊载于《金融研究》2021年第6期。

作者简介:冀云阳,经济学博士,助理教授,湖南大学经济与贸易学院;毛捷,经济学博士,教授,对外经济与贸易大学国际经济贸易学院;文雪婷,经济学博士,泰康资产管理有限责任公司。

本回报率密切相关，这是由于我国地方政府往往通过举债融资的方式进行城市建设投资，如果资本回报率低，则意味着政府投资可能起不到改善投资环境、带动私人投资的作用，从而无法产生足够的投资收益或租税收入用以偿还债务本息，这容易引发偿债风险。由此可见，系统分析地方公共债务扩张与资本回报率变化之间的关系具有重要的研究意义。

然而，通过文献梳理发现，已有研究尚未对上述问题开展深入的理论分析和实证检验。本文力图弥补这一不足，在理论分析基础上，通过使用新口径的地方公共债务数据以及测算城市层面的资本回报率（全国179个地级市，2006—2015年），实证检验地方公共债务扩张对资本回报率的影响及其地区异质性表现，并从宏观、中观和微观三重视角对其作用机制进行综合分析，最后，提出深化地方政府投融资体制改革的政策建议。

本文研究的边际贡献主要体现在以下三方面：第一，数据方面，本文尝试使用地级市层面的新口径公共债务和资本回报率的匹配数据进行分析，为实证检验提供更具代表性的基础数据；第二，内容方面，尽管现有文献已经对我国资本回报率的影响因素进行了多方面探讨，但均未考虑当前我国地方公共债务扩张对资本回报率的影响效应，本文弥补了此项不足，验证了两者之间的关系及其地区异质性表现和作用机理，丰富了有关资本回报率影响因素的文献；第三，机制方面，本文以资本错配为逻辑起点，从宏观层面的基础设施投资效率、中观层面的房地产行业投资占比、微观层面的企业投资挤出效应三个角度，全面分析了地方公共债务影响资本回报率的中介机制，为深刻理解地方公共债务与资本回报率的内在关联提供了新证据。

本文的研究结论表明：第一，地方公共债务扩张显著降低了资本回报率。第二，地方公共债务对资本回报率的负面影响主要通过降低基础设施投资效率、提高房地产业投资占比、挤出企业投资这三个作用机制实现。简言之，地方公共债务扩张导致了资本配置效率的下降。进一步分析表明，地方公共债务扩张主要降低了基础设施投资的规模效率，并且由于地方政府债务融资强化了企业融资约束，从而降低了企业投资效率，这是地方公共债务导致资本错配的微观表现。第三，地方公共债务对资本回报率的负面影响在非城市群、非大中城市和土地融资依赖度更高的城市表现更为突出。

以上研究结论对理解我国经济增长模式和可能存在的风险隐患具有参考意义，并为深化地方政府投融资制度改革提供政策参考。第一，加强地方公共债务的限额管理，持续推进地方政府债券市场化发行制度改革，发挥市场主体对地方债券发行和使用的监督作用，强化地方政府债券融资过程中的合理性、资金使用的有效性。第二，加强地方政府债务资金支出的配置管理和债务项目的绩效治理，提高基础设施投资效率、债券资金配置效率和使用效益，逐步建立全生命周期的地方债务项目绩效管理制度。第三，加快地方政府投融资体制改革，改变"重发行、轻绩效"的投融资理念。立足于对债务风险的防控，将规范地方政府债券市场化发行和改善企业投融资环境统筹考虑，促进投资主体多样化，实现公共投资和私人投资的合理匹配。第四，注重地区差异，创新地方政府债券的分类绩效管理体制，更加强调债券资金的使用效率。加快地方税体系建设，改变地方政府过度依赖土地融资的收入结构，调整地方经济发展依赖房地产投资的单一结构，促进经济高质量发展。

# 财政引导金融机构支农的激励政策产生效果了吗？*

行伟波　张思敏

"农业、农村、农民"问题一直是中央一号文件的工作重点之一，设计相关支持政策以解决"三农"问题是我国当前经济持续发展的关键。目前我国农业处于关键的转型期，农业生产方式正在由劳动密集型转向资金和技术密集型，这意味着要靠有效率的资金投入来推动农业发展。然而，长期以来我国农村地区存在普遍的资金供求缺口，农村信贷市场信息不对称、农村金融市场失灵问题严重。因此，包括农业信贷在内的各类涉农贷款，成为对农村地区进行开发式扶贫的主要政策工具。

历年来，我国中央政府颁布了大量支持农村贷款和农业经济发展的财政政策和金融政策，近期一系列政府决策表明我国开始尝试利用财政手段引导金融资源向农村配置。例如，为了激励金融机构加大涉农贷款力度，财政部发布的县域金融机构涉农贷款增量奖励政策自2009年起在全国进行了多轮试点，是将财政政策与信贷政策有机结合的重要举措。

本文论述了农村金融理论与农业贷款对农业经济增长的作用机制，为实证研究提供了一定的理论基础，并针对涉农贷款奖励政策对各地区农业经济发展的影响程度进行了较为准确的评估，另外探索了涉农贷款

---

\* 原文刊载于《金融研究》2021年第5期。

作者简介：行伟波，教授，博士生导师，对外经济贸易大学国际经济贸易学院；张思敏，经济学硕士，对外经济贸易大学国际经济贸易学院。

影响农业经济发展的内在机制。对进一步完善财政支农和金融支农政策、促进解决"三农"问题具有一定的参考意义。

具体来讲,由于2009—2014年有25个省(区、市)先后进入奖励政策试点,本文建立了一个渐进双重差分模型来评估外生的奖励政策对各地区农业经济发展的作用,实证模型以2006—2018年我国各省(区、市)的相关农业经济数据作为研究样本。首先,分别以粮食产量、农民收入为被解释变量,以试点政策变量为核心解释变量,在控制气候条件、要素投入、地方支农财政支出、地方金融发展和农业产业化等变量后进行回归分析。其次,为了保证实证结果的可靠性和严谨性,进行稳健性检验。再次,为了评估奖励政策对不同地理位置省(区、市)的影响是否具有明显的异质性,本文在渐进双重差分模型中加入地理位置特征与政策变量交互项,进行异质性检验。最后,识别了涉农贷款奖励政策影响农业经济的机制路径,分别检验了奖励政策对涉农贷款余额及农业机械总动力、农村农户固定资产投资额、交通基础设施、水利基础设施建设等被解释变量的影响。实证部分数据来源为历年《中国统计年鉴》、万得数据库和国泰安数据库。

实证结果表明:第一,涉农贷款增量奖励政策显著地促进了各省(区、市)粮食产量、农民收入等指标增长,促进了农业经济的发展,且这一结论在进行稳健性检验后仍然成立;第二,涉农贷款增量奖励政策对不同地理位置省(区、市)的农业经济的影响具有明显的异质性,其中中西部省(区、市)受到的影响更大,这可能是由于东部地区第一产业比重较低、金融市场相对完善,且东部省(区、市)的奖励资金由地方财政分担的比例较大,因此奖励政策对东部省份农业经济的促进作用最小;第三,进一步的机制识别检验发现,涉农贷款增量奖励政策主要是通过促进涉农贷款的发放,进而提高农业机械化水平、优化道路交通和水利建设等农村基础设施的方式促进了当地农业经济的发展。

本研究的创新与贡献体现在以下三个方面。第一，采用的研究样本较为准确。以往研究大多利用 2008 年之前的样本，而部分使用跨越 2008 年前后样本的研究由于农业贷款数据统计口径发生变化，回归结果会存在偏差。本文的政策评估避免了直接使用农业贷款数据，而是利用 2009 年后政策试点变化来研究农业贷款与农业经济增长的关系，可信度较高。第二，采用的研究方法较为精准。以往文献大多利用协整检验、误差修正模型等方法，本文则选择使用渐进双重差分法，以外生政策事件发生前后的变化为研究对象，消除了内生性问题。第三，深入探讨了影响机制。以往的研究文献仅仅分析农业贷款是否对农业产出、农民收入产生影响，本文则评估了涉农贷款增量奖励政策具体影响农业经济的数项渠道。

本文仅将我国分为东、中、西部三个区域以分析奖励政策的异质性，未来可进一步深入探讨试点省（区、市）地形特征等内部差异；另外，农业贷款对于农业经济发展的整体影响可能比本文解释的三个机制复杂，今后还需要进一步创新。

根据实证结论提出以下政策建议：当前应继续推进财政激励金融支农政策，充分发挥财政和金融政策的协调配合，确保贷款贴息、担保、税收减免、费用补贴等多项财税杠杆政策及支农再贷款、贷款利率等多项货币政策工具的统筹协调和密切配合，实现金融机构和农户农企的双赢。通过差别化的财政支持政策，鼓励金融机构重返农村、增设网点，对新型农村金融机构的贷款给予定向费用补贴和税收优惠。此外，建立政策性涉农贷款风险补偿机制，对高风险低收益的涉农贷款提供财政贴息，降低涉农企业及各类组织的贷款风险，健全农村金融体系，形成财政资金与金融资金的良性互动。

# 08 家庭金融、普惠金融与社会发展

# 住房财富对中国城镇家庭消费的影响*

尹志超 仇 化 潘学峰

现阶段，中国正迎来经济转型升级的新时期，机遇与挑战并存。党的十九届五中全会提出要加快形成以国内大循环为主体、国内国际双循环相互促进的新发展格局。"内循环"市场以消费为主，关键目标在于拉动消费，发挥消费作为经济增长主要动力的作用。在过去几十年里，人民收入实现了快速而稳定的增长，这也增加了家庭对住房的需求。如今，住房已经成为中国家庭财富的重要组成部分。一方面，住房可通过财富效应促进家庭消费，另一方面，住房价格较高也会增加家庭抵押贷款负担，产生"房奴效应"，降低家庭消费。因此，住房财富对家庭消费的影响方向并不确定。探究住房财富变化对中国家庭消费的影响具有理论意义和现实意义。

本文基于2013—2019年中国家庭金融调查数据，研究了住房财富对家庭消费的影响，并检验了住房财富影响家庭消费的可能渠道。中国家庭金融调查（CHFS）自2011年在全国范围内开展，每两年采集一次数据。调查样本覆盖中国除新疆、西藏、港澳台地区以外的29个省（区、市）。问卷问题涵盖了受访者房产、各类收入、消费、信贷约束等具体情况，数据代表性好、质量高，为本文研究住房财富对家庭消费的影响提供了数据支持。本文使用2013年、2015年、2017年和2019年的CHFS数据，

---

\* 原文刊载于《金融研究》2021年第2期。
作者简介：尹志超，经济学博士，教授，首都经济贸易大学金融学院；仇化，博士研究生，首都经济贸易大学金融学院；潘学峰，经济学博士，助理教授，对外经济贸易大学金融学院。

构建有效样本为13 328户的平衡面板数据。考虑到本文研究住房财富变动对家庭消费的影响时，可能会因为遗漏变量和逆向因果导致内生性问题。不随时间变化的不可观测变量（如观念、习惯）在截面数据估计中无法识别，使用工具变量也难以有效解决。因此，本文使用固定效应模型进行估计。除此之外，为解决逆向因果带来的内生性问题，本文使用2012年、2014年、2016年和2018年的省级房价作为工具变量，使用固定效应—工具变量法进行估计。

研究结果表明，中国家庭的住房财富显著促进了家庭消费，住房财富对家庭消费的边际影响为0.02。拥有较高住房财富显著提高了家庭享受型消费占比，降低了家庭的恩格尔系数，改善了家庭消费结构。进一步研究发现，住房财富能有效缓解家庭流动性约束，改善财务状况，降低家庭流动性约束的概率，使家庭投入更多资金用于消费。异质性分析表明，对于不同类型的家庭消费，住房财富的作用存在差异。相比于日常消费，住房财富对非日常消费的促进作用更大。中西部地区家庭在拥有较高住房财富后，提高家庭消费水平的程度更高。除此之外，对于只拥有一套房的家庭，住房多是为了满足居住刚需，住房财富促进消费的作用较小。

相较于以往文献，本文可能的创新点和贡献在于：一方面，更充分地解决内生性问题，估计了住房财富对家庭消费的影响系数为0.02。另一方面，研究了住房财富对家庭流动性约束的影响。虽然中国尚未正式实施住房净值抵押贷款，但住房财富仍能缓解家庭信贷约束和流动性约束，这证明了抵押贷款渠道的普遍性。

研究结论表明，在合理控制房价和防范风险的前提下，可发挥既有住房财富对平滑家庭消费的积极作用，进一步推进家庭消费升级。

未来研究可基于银行数据，进一步探索信用卡等在住房财富促进消费中发挥的作用。此外，其他资金来源（如民间借贷）对住房财富效应的影响也值得探讨。

# 住房公积金与家庭风险金融资产投资*

## ——基于 2013 年 CHFS 的实证研究

### 陈选娟　林宏妹

股市有限参与问题全球普遍存在，我国的情况尤其突出。"十四五"规划和 2035 年远景目标纲要提出，要多渠道增加城乡居民财产性收入。金融产品投资作为重要渠道之一，哪些因素影响了我国居民家庭风险金融资产投资？

高房价是其中一个主要原因。国家统计局数据显示，2000—2019 年我国房价增长迅速，2000 年全国住宅商品房平均售价为 1 948 元/平方米，2019 年则高达 9 287 元/平方米。与此同时，我国居民家庭投资房产的热情却不减。房产投资占用了大量资金，对家庭风险金融资产投资形成了挤出效应（吴卫星和齐天翔，2007）。

为了提高居民住房购买能力，我国借鉴新加坡的中央公积金制度，于 1994 年开始在全国推行住房公积金制度。住房公积金可从两方面影响家庭可支配收入。一方面，住房公积金缴纳和提取都不需要缴纳个人所得税，相当于增加了居民的远期收入，有助于提高居民的终身财富水平；另一方面，拥有住房公积金的家庭要承受公积金缴存施加的流动性约束，还要承担公积金存款的利息损失。

---

\* 原文刊载于《金融研究》2021 年第 4 期。
　作者简介：陈选娟，金融学博士，教授，上海财经大学金融学院；林宏妹，金融学博士，上海财经大学金融学院。

但区别于养老保险，有房和无房家庭在公积金政策中的处境并不相同，无房家庭不能使用公积金支付购房首付或者偿还房贷，即使可以提取公积金支付房租，额度也十分有限。因此，公积金对不同家庭的影响存在异质性：有房家庭可提取公积金，可支配收入增加，从而促进其风险金融资产投资；无房家庭缴纳公积金，可支配收入减少且利息受损，尤其是有购房意愿但尚未攒够首付的家庭，有公积金并不能降低其住房储蓄，缴存公积金反而可能抑制其风险金融资产投资。

目前，关于住房投资挤出效应的研究比较全面，却鲜有文献研究住房公积金如何影响家庭风险金融资产投资。本文尝试探究住房公积金对家庭风险金融资产投资的影响，并据此提出相应的政策建议。具体研究三个问题：首先，在考虑房产投资的同时，住房公积金如何影响家庭风险金融资产投资决策，以及住房公积金如何影响家庭风险金融资产投资比重；其次，分析其中的影响机制，探究住房公积金通过哪些渠道影响家庭风险金融资产投资；最后，讨论住房公积金对不同类型家庭的影响差异。

本文数据来自西南财经大学中国家庭金融调查与研究中心2013年的"中国家庭金融调查"（China Household Finance Survey，CHFS），该调查涵盖全国29个省（区、市）的262个县（区、市），共有28 000多个样本家庭。研究方法上，首先使用Probit模型检验住房公积金对家庭是否投资风险金融资产的影响，然后使用Tobit模型检验住房公积金对家庭风险金融资产投资比重的影响，最后使用中介效应模型检验其中的影响机制。为了解决潜在的内生性问题，采用工具变量法进行检验，同时采用Heckman两步法、面板固定效应模型进行稳健性检验。实证结果表明：住房公积金能显著提高有房家庭风险金融资产投资的可能性和投资比重，但是对无房家庭的风险金融投资则无显著影响。研究其影响机制发现，住房公积金会提高家庭可支配收入、增加户主风险偏好，从而促进家庭风险金融资产投资。

本文从住房公积金的角度研究家庭金融资产配置问题,发现了制约家庭风险金融资产投资的新证据,为多渠道增加居民财产性收入拓展了切入点,也有助于政府部门完善住房公积金政策,健全多层次社会保障体系。据此,本文得到以下三方面的政策启示:(1)可引导居民家庭合理地投资住房,降低住房的投资属性,增强其居住属性,从而减少住房投资对风险金融资产投资的挤出。(2)可在平衡房价的同时扩大住房公积金覆盖范围,让更多居民家庭享受住房公积金保障,引导居民家庭合理投资股票等风险金融资产。尤其是增强住房公积金对无房家庭的支持,适度放宽无房家庭提取公积金的条件和额度。(3)可强化住房公积金增值保值功能,将大体量的住房公积金余额合理投资,尽量减少缴存住房公积金给居民家庭造成的流动性约束和利息损失。

本文的研究贡献在于:第一,首次将住房公积金与家庭风险金融投资联系在一起,探究住房公积金影响家庭风险金融资产投资的机制。本文证实了住房公积金能够提高家庭可支配收入、增加户主风险偏好,从而促进有房家庭风险金融资产投资并为家庭股市有限参与之谜提供了新的解释,拓展了住房公积金相关问题的研究,为后续研究提供了新方向。第二,本文实证结果表明住房公积金不仅有住房保障的功能,还有调节家庭风险金融资产投资的作用,此研究结论为实现多渠道增加居民财产性收入、促进多层次金融市场发展提供了社会保障层面的切入点。第三,住房异质性分析表明,公积金对无房家庭的风险金融投资并无显著影响,这有利于政府部门正确认识住房公积金制度运行中存在的不公平性问题,对完善住房公积金制度具有实践意义。

# 传统家庭观念抑制了城镇居民商业养老保险参与吗？*

## ——基于金融信任与金融素养视角的实证分析

### 郑 路 徐旻霞

近年来，随着我国人口老龄化的快速发展，社会养老负担日益加重。面对这一形势，党的十九届五中全会提出要实施积极应对人口老龄化的国家战略，发展多层次、多支柱的养老保险体系。2020年中央经济工作会议提出要"规范发展第三支柱养老保险"。现阶段，以商业养老保险为代表的第三支柱个人养老金成为解决我国养老问题的重要突破口，商业养老保险产品将成为居民拓展新的养老模式、满足多元化养老方式的重要渠道。

目前，我国居民的商业养老保险参与度严重不足。既有研究从政策制度、市场供给及个人与家庭特征三个角度对这一现象进行了深入讨论，认为养老金资产管理不足、政策体系不完善、养老金融产品和服务的需求导向不足、供给不足等原因制约了居民参与商业养老保险。同时，个体年龄、教育水平、社会资本、家庭规模和家庭人口结构等因素也会影响其购买商业保险。但这些研究大都从理性经济视角出发，没有考虑金融行为背后的文化要素，忽视了居民的主观金融态度及需求。

---

\* 原文刊载于《金融研究》2021年第6期。

**作者简介**：郑路，社会学博士，长聘副教授，清华大学社会科学学院、社会与金融研究中心；徐旻霞，社会学博士研究生，清华大学社会科学学院。

文化是影响金融活动的重要因素，会通过塑造非制度约束，影响正式制度安排，影响个体的风险偏好、时间偏好、消费偏好和投资偏好等途径对个体金融决策产生影响。我国传统文化推崇家庭本位，强调"养儿防老"，传统的亲子反馈养老观念在现代城市居民中仍有相当的分量，这会深刻影响我国居民的商业养老保险参与情况。此外，对金融产品、金融机构和金融制度体系的信任、对金融市场的认知水平、获取金融信息并进行相应金融决策的能力也是影响个体金融行为的重要文化因素。

因此，本研究采用中国家庭金融调查（CHFS）2015年数据，考察传统家庭文化观念如何塑造我国城镇居民的金融信任和金融素养水平，并进一步影响其商业养老保险的参与情况。中国家庭金融调查是一项开始于2011年的全国大型综合社会调查，每两年进行一次，2015年第三轮调查样本分布在全国29个省（区、市）的363个县的1 439个村（居）委会，对家庭经济、金融行为进行了全面细致的刻画，包括其收入、消费、金融资产、住房资产和债务情况等。本研究从CHFS 2015调查数据的所有样本个体中，保留了15 659个信息较为完整的城镇居民个体，构成本研究的分析样本。

首先，我们通过因子分析法构建传统家庭观念的测量指标。其次，通过Logistic和OLS方法分别考察金融素养、金融信任和传统家庭观念这三个变量与商业养老保险参与的关系，采用因果步骤法、Sobel中介效应检验、KHB检测和Bootstrap检测来检验金融信任与金融素养的中介作用，使用工具变量处理研究中可能存在的内生性问题，通过改变变量测量方式、分样本回归等方法进行稳健性检验，进行分地区、教育水平和职业的异质性讨论。

实证结果表明，"养儿防老"等传统家庭文化观念会抑制我国城镇居民参与商业养老保险，这一影响在控制了内生性后依然显著；进一步研究发现，传统家庭观念（养儿防老等）会削弱居民的金融信任，减少居民对金融信息的关注，不利于居民金融素养的提升，进而降低其商业养老保险参与度；异质性分析表明，传统家庭观念（养儿防老等）对居民商业养老保险参与的负向影响在中西部地区和受教育水平偏低的群体中更加突出。

理论方面，区别于以往研究采用的经济理性视角，本研究提供了一个解释金融发展的文化观念视角，揭示了影响城镇居民商业养老保险参与及我国养老金融市场发展的文化因素。实践方面，本研究所得结论对我国养老金融市场的发展及养老体系的健全和完善具有一定的政策启示。

首先，受中国传统家庭文化观念的深远影响，子女养老和居家养老仍是我国居民首选的养老方式。我国未来可以探索更多居家养老、社区联合养老等创新型养老模式，以最大程度满足居民的养老需求。其次，金融信任和金融素养是传统家庭观念对居民商业养老保险参与产生影响的重要途径。因此，有关社会主体应当进一步拓宽居民的金融信息渠道，加强金融知识宣传，不断提升居民的金融素养；增强金融市场监管，完善金融制度体系，进一步提高居民对金融市场和金融体系的信任，助力推动商业养老保险及其他养老金融产品的发展；同时，也要注重对中西部地区的金融扶持，缩小金融发展的地区和城乡差异，增强金融发展的普惠性。最后，积极发展商业养老保险，发展多层次多支柱养老保险体系，健全多层次社会保障系统。未来我国养老金融市场面临着巨大的发展空间，各市场主体应当充分抓住机遇，迎接挑战，不断推进养老体系三大支柱的充分、均衡、高质量发展。

# 回不去的家乡？*

## ——教育公共品供给与人口回流的实证研究

### 李 明 郑礼明

近年来，我国人口出生率持续下降，老龄化程度不断加深，存量人口再配置意义越发突出。当前我国流动人口规模仍然庞大，同时出现了回流到家乡地的新趋势。如何回应流动人口关切，加速移除劳动力流动的体制机制障碍，畅通流动人口自由发展渠道，已成为亟须思考的重要问题。随着收入水平的提高，人们对公共服务的需求逐渐提升，城市公共品供给对人口回流的作用值得高度关注。Tiebout最早提出居民会综合考虑各地的公共品和税收后定居于最符合其偏好的地区，基于发达国家的研究表明，这一机制是存在的。但由于中国统一的税制和一定程度上限制人口流动的户籍制度，Tiebout机制在中国是否适用一直存在争论。对流动人口而言，家乡公共品的供给，特别是教育公共品的供给状况是否会对回流决策产生影响，尚未有确切回答。传统上，使用微观数据研究上述问题有一定困难。首先，一旦个体回到家乡，便不再属于流动人口监测范围；其次，回流作为一个追溯性的迁移活动，需要掌握个体历史迁移行为信息。受数据和方法所限，已有文献对人口回流的研究大多集中于理论分析，或利用有关监测数据考察影响流动人口回流意愿的因

---

\* 原文刊载于《金融研究》2021年第4期。

作者简介：李明，经济学博士，教授，对外经济贸易大学国际经济贸易学院；郑礼明，经济学博士研究生，对外经济贸易大学国际经济贸易学院。

素，对公共品供给状况是否影响实际回流行为则缺乏直接证据。

本文基于 2001 年起实施"撤点并校"政策外生冲击，结合 2005 年全国 1% 人口抽样调查微观数据和城市特征数据，实证研究了家乡教育公共品供给状况对流动人口回流决策的影响。我们利用 2005 年全国 1% 人口抽样调查数据中居住地址和"五年前常住地"信息，构建流动人口是否回流的动态变量。"撤点并校"是一项 2001 年至 2011 年在中国推广的公共政策，地方政府基于各种原因，撤并了远远大于学生减少比例的小学数量，可以视为一次主动减少基础教育公共品的行为。我们根据各地执行"撤点并校"政策强度的不同，构造教育公共品供给变动的代理变量。按照准自然实验的方法，本文选择五年前在外、家中至少有一个未成年子女的劳动者作为研究样本，考察家乡教育公共品供给情况对其回流决策的影响。若子女年龄为 6 至 10 岁（国家法定小学入学年龄为 6 岁，2001 年政策实行时的 6 岁儿童在 2005 年时为 10 岁，故在此年龄区间内的儿童受撤点并校政策影响）为实验组，否则为控制组，并由此构建截面数据双重差分模型。该模型衡量的并不是处理组与控制组在政策实施前后的差别，而是两组个体在不同政策实施强度地区回流概率的平均差异。

本文研究发现，首先，教育公共品减少显著阻碍了流动人口回流，减少幅度越大阻碍越严重。这一结论在放松样本选择限制、以家庭为单位定义回流、检验入学年龄设置是否合理、将回流定义在户籍地所在省等稳健性检验后依然成立。通过增加控制变量和工具变量法克服潜在内生性问题后，结果与基准回归基本一致。其次，异质性分析结果表明，这种阻碍倾向不分户口类型，但对家中有男孩及家庭规模较小的流动人口更加明显。最后，我们基于代际视角，考察了教育公共品供给对流动人口群体家庭中未成年子女随迁行为的影响，发现供给减少增加了适龄入学儿童迁出的概率。这意味着教育公共品供给状况影响两代人迁移。

除进一步证实Tiebout机制外，本文可能的创新和贡献还有以下两方面。首先，实证研究了城市公共服务在人口回流中的作用，弥补了相关文献的空白。已有文献探讨公共服务对人口迁移的影响大多基于人口流出视角，对回流缺乏关注；受限于数据，人口回流领域文献对公共品的讨论大多集中于理论。本文提供的证据有助于加深对人口流动规律的认识。其次，在研究方法上有所创新。本文尝试基于截面数据研究动态人口回流，并从家庭角度对人口普查数据进行了适当挖掘和应用，为后续研究提供一种新的思路。

本文结论具有丰富的政策意义。当前，我国正处于深入推进高质量发展的关键时期，加强市场在劳动力资源配置中的决定性作用，破除阻碍劳动力流动的体制机制障碍已成为各界共识。改进公共资源配置方式，优化教育等公共品供给水平，不仅有助于破除劳动力流动障碍，促进人口合理、有序流动，还能提高生产要素配置效率，并进一步促进经济增长和提高人民生活水平。对希望吸引更多人口流入的城市来说，在落户、补贴等政策之外，努力提高公共服务水平也是重要的财政投入方向。本文结论为通过加大公共服务投入，破除人口流动障碍，加快推进中国特色城镇化道路提供了经验证据。本文重点考察的是教育公共品供给数量变化的影响，未来可基于公共品供给质量及其他公共品供给状况（如医疗）开展研究，从更多角度探讨公共品供给影响人口流动的规律。

# 转入土地、农户农业信贷需求与信贷约束*

## ——基于中国家庭金融调查（CHFS）数据的分析

路晓蒙　吴　雨

《中华人民共和国国民经济和社会发展第十四个五年规划和2035年远景目标纲要》中提出，要巩固完善农村基本经营制度，完善农村承包地所有权、承包权、经营权分置制度，进一步放活经营权。土地流转是放活经营权、促进农村土地资源优化配置的重要一环。农地"三权分置"的改革，不仅能推动土地经营权的流转，更能通过改变承包权益的实现形式，释放和激发土地活力，实现土地价值，为农户积累土地资本、取得货币收益，进而从根本上改变农业的弱势地位（洪银兴和王荣，2019）。

在土地流转和规模经营中，融资问题至关重要。土地流转规模的大小、流转方式的选择、流转速度的快慢等问题很大程度上取决于融资问题的解决（北京天则经济研究所《中国土地问题》课题组，2010）。当前，关于农户土地流转问题的研究多集中在土地流转影响因素及土地流转绩效上，对农户信贷的研究主要集中在信贷行为和信贷对农户的重要性上，但鲜有文献对农户在土地流转过程中产生的信贷需求和约束问题进行探讨。

---

\* 原文刊载于《金融研究》2021年第5期。
作者简介：路晓蒙，经济学博士，副研究员，西南财经大学中国家庭金融调查与研究中心；
吴雨，经济学博士，副研究员，西南财经大学中国家庭金融调查与研究中心。

本文基于西南财经大学中国家庭金融调查与研究中心 2015 年和 2017 年在全国范围内开展的大型微观调查数据，在当前实行土地集体所有权、农户承包权和土地经营权三权分置的大背景下，从转入土地的视角对农户的信贷需求、信贷约束和信贷满足度等问题进行了深入研究。结果显示，转入土地对农户信贷的影响主要表现为：（1）相比未转入土地农户，转入土地农户的农业信贷需求更强烈，但非农信贷需求并没有显著增加；（2）转入土地农户的农业信贷发生比例显著增加，但面临信贷约束的比例也显著增加。对获得农业信贷的农户进一步研究发现，转入土地农户的信贷满足度也较低，信贷约束的缺口较大。在分析农户的转入土地规模时，本文发现上述现象在转入土地规模较大的农户中表现更为明显。

本文的学术贡献在于以下几点：（1）丰富了农户土地流转和信贷行为方面的文献。已有关于农户信贷的研究主要集中在信贷对农户的重要性和农户信贷行为上，关于土地流转的研究也主要集中在土地流转影响因素和绩效上。本文研究了农户在土地流转过程中的信贷行为，是对已有文献的有益补充。（2）已有关于农户信贷行为的研究多集中在农户的信贷约束和信贷需求上，本文研究了农户的信贷满足度问题，对已有研究进行了深化。（3）农户信贷领域的经验研究对数据要求非常苛刻（Diagne 等，2000），本文使用了全国范围内的抽样调研数据研究农户的信贷行为，研究结论更具代表性。

本文的政策意义主要有以下两点：第一，土地流转制度的建设不仅有利于放活经营权，更能促进农村土地资源的优化配置。虽然近些年来国家出台了诸多农村金融政策，如农户小额信贷政策等，但本文研究发现，信贷问题依旧是转入土地农户面临的重大难题。本文的结论有助于理清土地流转过程中农户面临的信贷约束问题，从而更好地促进土地流转市场的健康发展。第二，我国决战脱贫攻坚已取得全面胜利，巩固提升脱贫攻坚成果是"十四五"规划的首要任务。在此过程中，金融的作用不容忽视。本文研究发现,农户在转入土地过程中面临较严重的信贷约束问题,政府应持续加大对转入土地农户的信贷扶持力度,缓解其信贷约束,助推农户盘活农村发展,建立健全巩固拓展脱贫攻坚成果的长效机制,进一步实现乡村振兴。

# 义务教育能提高代际流动性吗*

陈斌开 张淑娟 申广军

阶层固化影响国家长治久安,提高代际流动、促进机会均等对经济社会健康发展至关重要。改革开放以来,中国经济取得了快速发展,人民生活水平显著提高,"让一部分人先富起来"的愿景已经基本实现。但正如党的十九大报告所指出的,我国当前发展仍存在"不平衡不充分"问题,成为满足人民日益增长的美好生活需要的主要制约因素。不平衡不充分的发展在静态上表现为收入差距不断扩大,动态上表现为代际流动性减弱。在过去的30年里,中国的代际教育和收入的相关系数持续上升,说明代际流动性不断下降。

现有的研究大多集中在测量和描述代际流动方面,而对公共政策如何提高社会流动性的研究较少。1986年颁布的《义务教育法》,逐步免除了小学和初中的学费,降低了出身贫寒的孩子进入小学和初中的门槛,已有研究证实义务教育政策提高了人们的受教育年限。本文进一步分析了政策实施对社会流动和长期公平的影响。使用2013年中国家庭收入调查和2005年全国1%人口抽样调查数据,利用1986年颁布的义务教育法在不同省(区、市)的实施时间差异作为外生冲击,采用双重差分方法探究义务教育政策对于代际流动的影响及其作用机制,发现义务教育政策确实显著提高了代际之间的教育流动性。

---

\* 原文刊载于《金融研究》2020年第6期。
作者简介:陈斌开,经济学博士,教授,中央财经大学经济学院;张淑娟,经济学硕士,工程师,深圳市大数据研究院;申广军,经济学博士,副教授,中山大学岭南学院。

进一步探究义务教育对代际流动性的提升机制，发现其大幅度提高了父母教育水平较低群体的受教育年限。这些父母因其职业层次、收入水平较低，不能或不愿投资于子女的人力资本积累，而义务教育政策解除或者缓解了这些家庭面临的约束和限制。而教育水平较高，从而职业层次、收入水平也高的父母，本来就会投资于子女的教育，因此义务教育政策并没有显著影响。

本文选用代际之间的教育流动性作为研究对象，还有两方面的好处。首先，现有关于代际流动性的文献中，社会学研究倾向于职业流动性，而经济学研究更多考虑收入流动性（阳义南和连玉君，2015）。教育作为最重要的人力资本，在很大程度上决定着个人的职业选择和收入水平，因而教育流动性也发挥着更基础的作用。其次，收入流动性的测度存在两个缺陷：第一，调查数据报告的当期收入可能会受到某些随机因素的冲击，而用暂时收入代替永久收入度量代际流动可能存在测量误差，即生命周期偏误（Black and Devereux，2011）；第二，目前可得的微观数据库中，一般只能找到共同居住的父子收入状况，存在样本选择偏误问题。本文使用中国家庭收入调查数据的教育变量来测度流动性，一方面，教育变量测量误差更小，且能较好地反映一个人的持久收入；另一方面，调查者直接询问户主及户主配偶父母的教育情况，有效避免了父子两代分开居住造成的选择性偏误。

与现有文献相比，本文主要有四方面贡献。第一，以教育代际流动性为研究对象，弥补了现有文献多局限于收入或职业流动性的不足；第二，现有代际流动性研究多以测度和描述为主，对代际流动性背后的影响因素缺乏深入研究，本文细致考察了义务教育对代际流动性的影响及其作用机制；第三，研究流动性影响因素的难点在于因果关系识别，本文以义务教育法为外生冲击，识别了公共政策对社会流动性的影响；第四，义务教育政策对教育回报率和健康等方面的影响讨论较多，本文将中国义务教育政策影响的研究拓展到代际流动性,与现有文献形成互补,并为义务教育政策调整提供借鉴。

  本文的研究结果的政策含义如下。首先,本文发现九年制义务教育对促进教育流动性有积极影响,主要是由于该政策通过缓解家庭的约束,显著促进了家庭社会经济地位较低的儿童接受教育。因此,这一政策在改革开放初期有效地促进了人力资本积累,并为后续的经济社会发展奠定了良好基础。近年来,我国经济社会高速发展,对更高素质的劳动力需求增加,但我国的社会流动性整体仍呈现下降趋势。延长义务教育年限,可同时缓解这两方面的压力,对实现教育公平,提升整体国民素质至关重要。其次,真正发挥教育作用,改变贫困学生命运。一是提高义务教育质量,使教育与经济社会发展的需求更加匹配,进而通过教育回报吸引人们接受更多教育;二是增强社会性培训或职业培训的可及性,为错过正式学校教育的或者职业技能需求更高的劳动者,提供科学、系统的职业技能训练机会。应进一步发挥公共政策在改善代际流动方面的作用,通过教育机会的均等化促进社会公平和正义。

# 企业精准扶贫行为影响企业风险吗?*

甄红线 王三法

精准扶贫作为国家战略,是针对我国特殊国情提出的一种创新扶贫形式。企业参与精准扶贫既可发挥产业扶贫的先天优势,实施"造血式"扶贫,也能获得创造价值的更大平台。因此,企业精准扶贫是打赢脱贫攻坚战的重要环节,也成为企业履行社会责任的新形式。2016 年 11 月,国务院印发《"十三五"脱贫攻坚规划》,明确要求国有企业强化帮扶责任,同时积极鼓励和引导民营企业等其他类型企业参与扶贫工作。上市公司作为资本市场的主体及国民经济发展的重要推动力量,是履行精准扶贫社会责任的重要群体,那么,资本市场是否关注上市公司的精准扶贫行为?企业参与精准扶贫如何影响企业风险?

关于企业社会责任对企业风险影响的研究,有两种截然不同的观点:风险降低假说和风险增加假说。风险降低假说认为,企业积极承担社会责任,能够为企业获取政府补助、项目支持和外部融资等提供便利,向外界传递企业经营情况良好的信号,提高品牌知名度和树立良好的公众形象,为企业后续发展营造稳定的外部环境。企业履行社会责任能够与利益相关者建立密切联系,实现企业与投资者之间的价值融合,获取对企业发展必不可少的人力资本、组织能力、声誉资本、客户忠诚度等竞争性资源。企业社会责任履行较好的企业,更容易获取投资者和合作伙

---

\* 原文刊载于《金融研究》2021 年第 1 期。
**作者简介:** 甄红线,会计学博士,教授,东北财经大学会计学院,中国内部控制研究中心;
王三法,会计学博士研究生,东北财经大学会计学院,中国内部控制研究中心。

伴的青睐，提高企业对财务环境变动的应对能力，降低财务风险。积极承担社会责任形成的道德资本和声誉资本对企业具有"声誉保险"作用，可减缓危机事件对企业发展的负面冲击。此外，社会责任信息披露向市场传递了公司大量非财务信息，具有"信息沟通"效应，能够提高企业的信息透明度，降低企业风险。

就风险增加假说而言，新古典经济学认为，企业承担社会责任偏离了股东价值最大化目标。在企业现金流有限的条件下，过多承担社会责任会占用企业资源，可能导致企业被迫降低研发投入和长期性投资等战略性投资，削弱企业竞争力，降低企业价值，从而增加企业风险。委托代理理论认为，管理者存在机会主义倾向，积极履行社会责任可能是其为了提高个人声誉和社会影响力，进行与企业自身发展无关的社会活动。将企业有限的资源浪费在与股东价值创造无关的社会活动上，会削弱企业竞争力，导致企业风险增加。经理人出于自利动机，可能利用社会责任工具转移负面消息，掩盖企业经营业绩中的问题，使企业社会责任只具有"工具特征"而非"创值特征"。另外，企业履行社会责任，虽可积累企业未来发展的声誉资本，但耗时较长、成本较高，可能得不偿失，导致企业风险增加。那么，企业精准扶贫作为企业履行社会责任的新形式，在中国资本市场是符合风险降低假说还是风险增加假说，有待探究。厘清这一问题，有助于地方政府制定相关政策引导企业持续参与扶贫事业，建立减贫的长效机制。

本文基于中国A股市场非金融类上市公司2016—2018年精准扶贫投入数据，实证研究企业精准扶贫参与水平对企业股票市场风险的影响及作用机制，进一步检验企业信息透明度与地区制度环境对二者关系的调节作用，得出以下结论：一是企业精准扶贫参与水平与企业股票市场风险显著负相关，这说明企业精准扶贫参与水平越高，资本市场投资者越看好该企业未来的发展前景，给予企业积极、正面的评价，降低了企业股票的市场风险，企业参与精准扶贫在中国资本市场适用于风险降低假说。二是企业信息透明度越低，精准扶贫行为对股票市场风险的降低作用越强，说明企业信息透明度越低，企业精准扶贫行为的"信息沟通"作用越强。三是在制度环境越薄弱的地区，企业精准扶贫行为对股票市场风险的降低作用越强。

本文的主要贡献为：首先，从精准扶贫视角研究企业社会责任对企业风险的影响，丰富了企业社会责任与企业风险的研究范畴。其次，基于股票市场风险角度，发现投资者关注企业精准扶贫行为，识别了企业精准扶贫的战略意义，上市公司积极参与精准扶贫既响应了国家脱贫攻坚号召，也有利于降低企业风险，获得承担社会责任与规避风险的"双赢"结果。这丰富了企业精准扶贫经济后果的相关研究，对理解我国企业精准扶贫动机也有一定启示意义。最后，分别从声誉效应、资源效应和信息效应的角度，探索了企业精准扶贫影响企业风险的作用机制，为有关部门建立减贫的长效机制和企业风险防范提供了经验证据和理论参考。

# 绿色投资者发挥作用吗?*

## ——来自企业参与绿色治理的经验研究

### 姜广省 卢建词 李维安

随着我国进入工业化、城市化高速发展的阶段,生态环境问题更加凸显,党的十八届五中全会首次把"绿色"作为"十三五"规划五大发展理念之一,党的十九大又进一步指出"人与自然是生命共同体""人与自然和谐共生"。不可否认,"天人合一"的绿色治理观,不仅强调经济活动应顺应生态法则,而且坚持与自然环境和谐共生的科学发展状态的"和谐共生"理念,已成为我国经济高质量发展的必然选择。

2016年《关于构建绿色金融体系的指导意见》强调"建立健全绿色金融体系""推动证券市场支持绿色投资",党的十九届五中全会提出2035年远景目标是"广泛形成绿色生产生活方式""发展绿色金融""推进重点行业和重要领域绿色化改造"等。这一系列绿色金融相关政策引出了一批特殊的机构投资者——绿色投资者,他们主要以投资可持续为目的,顺应可持续发展战略,综合考虑经济、社会、环境等因素,促使企业在追求经济利益的同时,积极承担相应的社会责任。在绿色投资者看来,企业参与绿色治理具有双重效应:从经济效应上来讲,能够降低企业的股权成本和债务成本,在一定程度上可以提高企业的财务绩效,

---

\* 原文刊载于《金融研究》2021年第5期。
作者简介:姜广省,管理学博士,讲师,天津财经大学商学院;卢建词,管理学博士,讲师,天津财经大学商学院;李维安,管理学博士,教授,天津财经大学中国公司治理研究院。

增加企业的经济价值；从社会和环境效应来讲，有助于改善利益相关者之间的关系，创造共享价值，促进社会和环境的共同发展，实现投资可持续的目标。但从企业来看，企业作为自然资源消耗和污染物排放主体，虽然是绿色治理的重要主体和关键行动者，但实际上，参与绿色治理属于一种公共事务性活动，企业实施这些活动还需要得到其他利益相关者的支持，并且除保证自身发展之外，还需要抽取部分资源用于绿色治理行为。同时，参与绿色治理具有长期性和不确定性，所以，一些具有短期收益偏好的管理者可能并不情愿主动实施绿色治理。

从现实来看，近年来我国绿色投资者持股规模越来越多，2006—2016年年均增长率为9.6%，其如何影响我国企业参与绿色治理，是一个有趣的话题。因此，在已有研究基础上，本文基于现有研究对绿色投资者的界定，着重探究绿色投资者和企业参与绿色治理之间的关系，并在以下两方面对已有文献形成补充和扩展：一是从企业层面探究绿色治理的影响因素，这为企业践行绿色治理理念的研究提供了一个新的视角。以往研究从理论上指出绿色治理是企业履行社会责任的一种思路及企业在参与绿色治理过程中是重要主体和关键行动者，而从实证上探讨企业参与绿色治理影响因素的研究还比较少，并且较多集中于考察消费者等不同利益相关者对企业从事社会责任活动的影响，未上升到关注其绿色行为实施情况的绿色治理层面。因此，本文探索性地将企业参与绿色治理作为考察对象，探究绿色投资者的影响作用，丰富了企业参与绿色治理的相关研究。二是有关绿色投资者的研究主要集中在增加市场收益和降低资本成本等经济效应层面，忽略了从绿色投资者的绿色投资理念出发考察其影响企业社会行为的有效性，尤其是对企业参与绿色治理方面的探究。本文从绿色投资者的投资目的和绿色理念出发，结合"用手投票"和"用脚投票"的影响途径，探究绿色投资者对企业参与绿色治理的影响机理，是对现有研究的有益补充。

具体来看，本文从企业层面探究绿色投资者对企业参与绿色治理的影响，基于2006—2016年我国沪深A股上市公司数据（共计71 882个样本），研究发现：一是存在绿色投资者的上市公司实施绿色行动的发生比较高，是不存在绿色投资者企业的1.65倍，且绿色投资者能够促使企业增加绿色支出约63.64%（0.56/0.88），以及提高绿色治理绩效约52.17%（0.024/0.046）。绿色行动和支出均显著正相关于绿色治理绩效，且绿色行动的影响程度较强。二是在是否属于重污染企业、不同所有制形式和处于不同环保意识地区的企业，绿色投资者对企业参与绿色治理和绿色治理绩效的影响程度均存在较大的差异。绿色投资者对绿色行动的促进作用在弱环保意识地区的企业中更加明显，对企业绿色支出的促进作用在重污染企业和国有企业中更加明显，而对企业绿色治理绩效的提升作用在非重污染企业、弱环保意识地区和国有企业中更加明显。三是企业参与绿色治理和较高的绿色治理绩效能够获得绿色投资者的认同并增加其持股量，虽然绿色支出不利于改善企业经营绩效，但绿色行动和绿色治理绩效均能提高企业经营绩效。

本文为我国绿色金融发展和企业参与绿色治理提供了一定参考：一是完善相关规定和制度，进一步发挥绿色投资者的绿色公司治理作用；二是引导企业以新发展理念为指导，树立绿色可持续发展理念，建立健全与绿色投资者等利益相关者的沟通渠道，努力识别社会参与者对企业可持续发展的认识要求与期待。

# 09　公司治理与公司金融

# 员工薪酬竞争力与上市公司员工持股*

张会丽　赵健宇　陆正飞

员工队伍决定企业战略决策的执行力，对企业发展的重要性不言而喻。构建和谐劳动关系被提升至我国经济社会发展的重要战略地位。中共中央、国务院在《关于构建和谐劳动关系的意见》文件中指出，在新的历史条件下，努力构建中国特色和谐劳动关系，是加强和创新社会管理、保障和改善民生的重要内容，是经济持续健康发展的重要保证。证监会颁布的《关于上市公司实施员工持股计划试点的指导意见》（以下简称《指导意见》）强调，上市公司实施员工持股计划试点，有利于建立和完善劳动者与所有者的利益共享机制。《指导意见》颁布后，上市公司踊跃出台员工持股计划。

从员工持股相关理论来看，缓解劳资矛盾及通过资本共享构建劳资方的利益共同体是员工持股的基本理念。依据社会公平理论，员工对收入分配的满意度，往往取决于其通过社会比较获得的公平性认知，比较后的薪酬竞争力往往成为劳动方与资本方矛盾冲突的根源。所以，随着劳动力市场流动性的不断提高，员工薪酬的竞争力强弱成为影响企业员工队伍稳定及员工积极性的重要因素。那么，缓解员工薪酬竞争力不足是否是我国企业推出员工持股的重要考虑因素之一？明确这一问题将对

---

\* 原文刊载于《金融研究》2021年第1期。
　作者简介：张会丽，管理学博士，副教授，北京师范大学经济与工商管理学院；赵健宇，管理学博士，讲师，中央财经大学会计学院；陆正飞，管理学博士，教授，北京大学光华管理学院。

监管机构厘清我国员工持股的现实趋势进而优化员工持股政策环境具有重要意义。

国外基于员工持股理论框架研究企业实施员工持股动机的直接经验证据还相对欠缺，且发达国家的结论未必适用于新兴市场国家。国内企业实施员工持股的动机可能纷繁复杂，目前尚未有研究结合员工持股的理论基础来检验其实施动机。本文结合我国现阶段的劳动关系特点，运用大样本研究考察员工薪酬竞争力是否是企业实施员工持股的重要动机，丰富和扩展了国内外相关研究文献。

本文以2006—2017年我国A股上市公司为样本，从企业所处行业地位的薪酬相对值比较和行业薪酬绝对值水平比较等两个维度对员工薪酬竞争力进行量化，构建实证回归模型，并在回归模型中控制公司财务和治理等其他可能的影响因素。实证结果显示，员工薪酬竞争力强弱与企业是否实施员工持股二者存在显著的负相关关系，即员工薪酬竞争力越弱，企业越可能实施员工持股。且员工薪酬竞争力对员工持股的实施形式也会产生一定影响，表现为员工薪酬竞争力越弱，企业实施员工持股的锁定期限越长、覆盖人数越多及员工股占比越高；进一步研究发现，员工薪酬竞争力强弱与企业是否实施员工持股可能性的负相关关系只在外部劳动力市场流动性压力较大和内部人力资本重要性较高及融资约束程度较高的样本企业中显著。上述结论表明，缓解因薪酬竞争力不足对企业运营可能产生的负面影响，是企业实施员工持股的重要动机之一。

本文的可能贡献在于：第一，为我国实施非高管员工持股的企业内在动机提供了来自薪酬竞争力视角的经验证据，且结论表明我国企业在利用员工持股改善劳动关系的做法与监管部门的政策思路相契合。第二，通过明确和厘清我国企业实施员工持股的主导动机之一，为我国相关政策对员工持股制度作出进一步规范和完善提供了经验证据支持。2020年10月，国务院在《关于进一步提高上市公司质量的意见》中提出，进一步完善上市公司股权激励和员工持股制度,在对象、方式、定价等方面作出更加灵活的安排。本文的研究结论对优化我国员工持股政策环境和企业创造内部员工的和谐氛围具有重要意义。第三,拓展和丰富了学术界关于员工持股、职工薪酬、收入分配等相关话题的讨论。鉴于本文的结论表明员工持股可能是薪酬竞争力不足的替代机制,后续涉及职工薪酬、收入分配相关领域的研究,有必要对可能存在的员工持股因素加以考虑。

# 股权质押下的控股股东增持：
# "价值信号"还是"行为信号"？*

徐龙炳　汪　斌

近年来，不少上市公司控股股东纷纷增持了本公司股票。若从公司发布的增持公告解读来看，控股股东对于增持目的的表述，大多为基于对公司股价未来上升空间的信心，以及对公司未来发展前景的看好。但仔细调查后发现，不少控股股东增持背后都有股权质押的影子。股权质押下的控股股东为何热衷于增持？不同背景下的增持行为，其传递的信号性质是否有所区别？市场如何解读这一信号？

传统信号理论认为控股股东增持传递了公司基本面及未来发展状况的信号，理性投资者在收到这一信号后会对公司价值作出判断，认为现时股价与内在价值存在背离，从而达到信号传递的效果。而根据行为金融学，投资者是有限理性的，他们在决策时存在参考点依赖与代表性偏差，当传统的信号传递在他们脑中成为一种判断习惯后，就会变成一种行为信号。行为信号也归属于信号传递框架，与传统信号不同，该信号并不传递公司的价值信息，而是借助于投资者的判断习惯来影响其投资决策，从而达到不同的信号传递效果。与传统信号理论相似，行为信号也会对市场参与者产生影响。本文认为股权质押下控股股东的增持更多是一种

---

\* 原文刊载于《金融研究》2021 年第 1 期。

作者简介：徐龙炳，经济学博士，教授，上海财经大学金融学院；汪斌，博士研究生，上海财经大学金融学院。

行为信号，控股股东有动机利用增持对投资者的行为信号作用来稳定股价，从而缓解股权质押风险。

与其他市值管理方式相比，增持具有如下优势：首先，在股价下跌特别是暴跌时，股权质押下的控股股东会面临股票被强制平仓的巨大压力，所以有很强的紧迫感去维稳股价，而增持公告往往能在短期内引起市场正向反应，故会被控股股东所采用。其次，尽管中国资本市场在不断发展，但投资者结构仍然以散户为主，其过高的换手率和投机性交易也显著区别于发达国家的资本市场。在此背景下，现有研究发现投资者对公司更名、资本运作、股票高送转、策略性媒体披露等行为反应较大，从而使股价在短期内明显上涨。增持作为内部人交易行为，往往会被投资者认为是价值信号，因而控股股东有动机利用投资者的这种认知偏差，通过增持达到短期内提振股价的目标。最后，已有股权质押的文献发现，控股股东进行股权质押的公司会通过盈余管理、税收规避、股票高送转、信息披露操纵等公司层面的手段来应对控制权转移风险，但盈余管理往往要缴纳更多税款，且实施过程较长，在时间上存在滞后，不一定能及时化解危机；股票高送转会导致股价长期反转，加剧股价的波动程度，且股票高送转公告一般发生在季末，在一年内使用次数也有限制，当平时遇到突发事件时，难以及时实施。与前述几种市值管理手段相比，控股股东增持虽需一定成本，但其操作方式相对灵活，增持计划可以通过临时公告的形式向投资者披露，除了法定禁止的时间段内，控股股东可以在任意时间通过增持来维稳股价，缓解股价下跌风险。因此有理由相信，控股股东作为内部人，有动力通过增持股份的形式向市场发送行为信号来缓解质押平仓压力。

本文选取2008—2017年A股上市公司样本，实证检验了股权质押下控股股东增持的动机、短期市场反应和增持后公司长期经济表现。研究发现：股权质押下控股股东更有可能增持，并且质押比率越高，增持可能性越大，说明控股股东有动机利用增持来缓解控制权转移风险；短期内，增持公告产生了正向的市场反应，其程度在非质押组和质押组间无显著差别；而长期来看，保持其他变量不变，增持后质押组的长期股价及经营绩效均弱于其对照组，而非质押组则好于其对照组，说明股权质押下的增持并不是价值信号，而是行为信号。进一步分析发现，股权质押对增持的正向效应在高平仓压力组、低质量公司组及监管环境较宽松的欠发达地区更显著。拓展性检验表明，在考虑减持影响后，股权质押下控股股东更倾向于净增持，并且管理层与其他大股东也会迎合控股股东的增持行为。最后本文排除了价值低估假说、政治动机假说、增强控制权假说及过度自信假说对上述结论的替代性解释。

本文的贡献主要体现在以下三个方面：首先，本文深化了股权质押领域的研究。以往关于股权质押的文献，大多集中在公司层面股权质押所带来的经济后果，如控股股东进行股权质押的公司会通过盈余管理、税收规避、股票高送转、信息披露操纵、股份回购、开发支出会计政策隐性选择等公司层面的手段来应对控制权转移风险，鲜有考虑股权质押背景与内部人交易的关联。本文将股权质押与内部人交易联系起来，拓展了股权质押的研究视角。其次，本文为行为公司金融学研究提供了来自中国的新证据。已有研究指出，市场上理性的参与者会利用另一些参与者的有限理性，通过公司更名、公司资本运作公告、股票高送转、策略性媒体信息披露等行为来谋取私利，实现财富转移。本文从行为信号视角出发，发现股权质押下控股股东的增持行为正是利用了投资者心理的代表性偏差，通过发送行为信号，使得短期内股价上升，以缓解控制权转移风险。最后，本文结论对各市场参与主体也具有现实意义。对于监管部门而言，需进一步完善股东增持制度和股权质押信息披露制度，加强对股权质押下控股股东增持的监管；对于股权质押的控股股东，则应努力提高自身业绩来应对控制权转移风险，规范自身增持行为；对于投资者而言，应该理性对待股权质押下控股股东的增持行为。

# 高管团队内部治理与企业资本结构调整*

## ——基于非 CEO 高管独立性的视角

张 博 韩亚东 李广众

自 Modigliani 和 Miller（1958）资本结构无关理论与融资决策权衡理论提出以来，企业资本结构选择的理论与实证研究一直是公司金融学研究的热点。资本结构合理与否直接影响到企业的经营决策和长远发展，对企业价值具有重要影响。优化企业融资结构也是深化金融供给侧结构性改革的重要内容。但是对于资本结构的动态调整行为，现有研究仍然是不充分的。具体包括企业负债率普遍低于最优水平、资本结构调整速度的不对称性及局部均衡调整模型在不同资本结构调整成本下的适用性等问题。Morellec 等（2012）从股东与经理人代理问题的角度对这些现象作了理论分析，他们认为传统权衡理论往往假设经理人和股东利益完全一致，很少考虑股东与经理人之间的利益冲突。在信息不对称与利益冲突条件下，所有权与经营权的分离不可避免地产生委托代理问题。自利的经理人可能通过偷懒、浪费或过度投资等损害股东利益的行为实现个人利益最大化。由于负债能够减少企业现金流，约束经理人现金浪费行为，对经理人具有较强的约束效应。因此，自利的经理人往往倾向于选择一个低于股东利益（公司价值）最大化对应的最优资本结构的负债

---

* 原文刊载于《金融研究》2021 年第 2 期。
  作者简介：张博，会计学博士，副教授，中国人民大学商学院；韩亚东，管理学博士研究生，中国人民大学商学院；李广众，经济学博士，金融学博士，教授，中山大学商学院/管理学院。

水平，向上调整资本结构的速度相对较慢。

针对股东与管理层之间的代理冲突及内外部公司治理机制如何影响资本结构决策，学者们分别从公司外部治理机制、董事会监督和高管薪酬契约等角度对此问题进行研究。研究发现，完善的治理机制可以缓解股东与管理层代理冲突所导致的企业资本结构普遍低于最优资本结构水平问题。在公司高管如何影响企业资本结构方面，现有研究大多将CEO个人作为管理层的代表，侧重CEO个人特征以及董事会、股东监督的治理效应。然而，作为企业经营决策的重要参与者——非CEO高管在企业资本结构决策过程中的作用尚未得到充分关注。

高阶理论（Upper Echelons Theory）认为非CEO高管对公司决策的制定具有重要影响。作为企业各个项目的具体实施者，非CEO高管拥有动机与能力约束CEO的自利行为。具体而言，CEO是企业的决策者，而决策的具体实施需要非CEO高管的协调与配合。由于企业的绩效与长远发展直接关系到非CEO高管的个人利益，当非CEO高管察觉到CEO决策出于其自利动机或者CEO决策不利于企业的长远发展时，非CEO高管将采取消极工作、拒绝提供信息或"建言"等方式对CEO的自利决策进行间接干预，甚至通过拒绝执行决策或者否决决策的方式进行直接干预，从而对CEO的自利行为产生治理作用。这种高管团队内部非CEO高管对CEO"自下而上"的监督治理机制被称为高管团队内部治理（Internal Governance）。

本文采用2001—2017年中国沪深A股上市公司为研究样本，通过非CEO高管相对于CEO的独立性来衡量高管团队内部治理效应。具体而言，我们采用非CEO高管是否在CEO任期内上任来衡量非CEO高管的独立性，在CEO任期之前上任的非CEO高管比例越高（低），非CEO高管相对于CEO的独立性就越强（弱），高管团队内部治理效应就越强（弱）。研究发现，当企业负债不足时，高管团队内部治理效应能够显著提高企业的负债水平,进而降低企业实际资本结构与目标资本结构偏离程度,高管团队内部治理对资本结构偏离度的影响在非国有企业中表现更加明显。进一步研究发现,高管团队内部治理效应在第一类委托代理问题比较严重及非CEO高管监督动机较强的企业中更加显著。作用机制分析表明,高管团队内部治理效应通过减少第一类代理成本来降低企业资本结构的偏离程度。

本文的贡献主要有以下几个方面:第一,以往关于股东与管理层代理冲突治理机制对企业资本结构影响的文献主要侧重考察董事会监督、薪酬契约等传统公司治理因素的影响。本文尝试从高管团队内部治理的视角考察企业资本结构的影响因素,有助于拓展公司治理与资本结构研究的相关文献。第二,国有企业和非国有企业在融资及高管的劳动力市场、激励和约束机制等方面存在差异。本文研究发现,高管团队内部治理效应对企业资本结构偏离程度的影响集中体现在非国有企业中。这一研究结论对加深高管团队内部治理效应有效性的认识具有较好的参考价值。第三,本文的研究结论具有较强的应用价值。考虑到非CEO高管相对CEO的独立性在公司治理中的重要作用,投资者、监管机构、独立审计机构对此应该给予密切关注。在改善公司内部治理方面,本文提出在企业进行非CEO高管选聘时,适当限制CEO对选聘过程的影响能够在一定程度上提升公司治理水平,优化企业资本结构。

# 商业信用与合作型客户关系的构建*

## ——基于提供给大客户应收账款的经验证据

江 伟 底璐璐 刘诚达

  随着供应链呈现出日益复杂化的趋势,如何管理供应链相关风险成为企业高管面临的一个重要课题。现有研究表明,当企业能够与客户之间建立合作型而不是保持距离型客户关系时,双方之间信息交流与合作的增强不仅能够在一定程度上缓解由于客户过于集中可能导致的要挟问题和经营风险问题,而且可以通过增加关系专有化投资、降低销售和管理费用及降低审计收费等提高企业会计业绩与市场价值。然而,现有文献对企业如何与客户特别是大客户建立与维护合作型关系的关注还相对较少,只有少数学者从资本结构、会计政策、盈余管理等方面提供了有限的经验证据。

  作为一种被广泛采用的交易方式,商业信用的高低反映了企业与客户交易时对收益与风险的权衡。在目前关于商业信用的研究中,大部分学者集中考察了商业信用的融资功能,而忽略了提供给客户的商业信用即应收账款所具有的产品质量担保功能在构建合作型客户关系中的作用。由于一般很难获取大样本的商业信用具体产品和条款信息,现有针对应收账款产品质量担保功能的经验研究非常有限,而且这些研究都是间接

---

\* 原文刊载于《金融研究》2021 年第 3 期。
  **作者简介:** 江伟,管理学博士,教授,中国人民大学商学院;底璐璐,管理学博士,讲师,西南财经大学会计学院;刘诚达,管理学博士,讲师,浙江工业大学管理学院。

地通过考察供应商或者客户特征对企业总体应收账款的影响来进行验证。考虑到在与大客户交易时面临的要挟问题与经营风险问题，企业是否及如何利用应收账款的产品质量担保功能来与大客户建立与维护合作型的客户关系同样缺乏直接的经验证据。针对这一问题的研究对于推动我国企业供应链整合，促进供应链金融业务发展，进而提升我国经济全球竞争力也具有重要的现实启示意义。

本文的研究样本为 2005—2015 年在沪深证券交易所上市的公司。样本期间从 2005 年开始，因为从 2005 年开始才陆续有较多的公司自愿披露前 5 名客户的名称和销售额；在 2005 年之前，为了满足投资者对提高上市公司透明度的要求，我国上市公司已经对前 5 名应收账款欠款人的名称、欠款金额及账龄等信息进行了较为详细的披露。为此，本文手工收集了截至 2015 年上市公司前 5 名客户销售额及所占比重信息，以及前 5 名客户和前 5 名应收账款欠款人所在地区（省或者市）信息。

本文的研究结果表明，客户集中度越高，企业提供给大客户的信用政策越宽松，即应收账款金额越多，信用期限越长。与此同时，本文进一步考察了客户地理位置相似度、企业所处行业竞争状况、企业所处地区的营商环境三个因素对于上述关系的调节作用。研究结果表明，在与主要客户地理位置相似度较低的企业、处于竞争性行业的企业及营商环境较好的地区，上述两者之间的正相关关系有所增强。最后，本文发现，在与大客户构建合作型客户关系时，企业向这些大客户提供的应收账款越多，企业的业绩越好。

本文的研究贡献主要在以下两个方面。

第一，理论上，合作型客户关系有助于缓解客户过于集中所可能导致的要挟问题与经营风险问题，然而在现有的财务学和会计学文献中，学者们对于如何与客户尤其是大客户之间建立与维护合作型客户关系的关注还非常欠缺。目前只有少数学者从资本结构、会计政策、盈余管理等方面提供了有限的经验证据。在国内，虽然已有研究从上下游企业合作关系的角度考察了企业对外提供的商业信用，但是这些研究对于企业对外提供商业信用的动机，例如是迫于产品市场竞争的压力，还是利用应收账款的产品质量担保功能，基本不做明确区分。本文较为直接地考察了企业通过应收账款的产品质量担保功能与大客户之间构建合作型的客户关系，在一定程度上弥补了上述国内外文献的不足。

第二，在目前关于商业信用的研究中，大部分学者集中考察了商业信用的融资功能，而限于数据可得性，对产品质量担保功能的研究较少。本文利用我国上市公司对前 5 名应收账款欠款人信息及前 5 名大客户信息的披露这一独特数据，从直接提供给大客户应收账款的金额与信用期限两个方面，为企业利用应收账款的产品质量担保功能构建合作型客户关系提供了较为直接的经验证据。

本文的研究不足主要体现在以下两个方面：第一，在变量度量方面。未来可以考虑挖掘相关数据的可行性，从单笔赊销的对象、产品类型与质量、金额、信用期限等方面对合作型客户关系设计更为直接和精确的度量方法。第二，在研究维度方面。本文只是总体上考察了企业通过提供宽松的应收账款信用政策与大客户建立和维护合作型的客户关系，而没有深入探讨在合作型客户关系建立与维护这两个不同的方面，企业提供的应收账款信用政策是否有所不同。未来可以考虑对合作型客户关系建立过程与维护过程中的应收账款信用政策进行比较研究。

# 独立董事返聘与公司违规：
# "学习效应"抑或"关系效应"？*

杜兴强  张  颖

2001年8月，证监会颁布《关于在上市公司建立独立董事制度的指导意见》，要求上市公司修改公司章程聘任独立董事，并规定独立董事任期届满可连任，但连任时间不得超过6年。尽管存在这一限制，但仍有为数不少的独立董事，虽任期届满后离任，但经过一段时期后再次被原上市公司返聘。学术界对独立董事制度的经济后果做了多方面探讨，但现有文献并未对独立董事返聘现象进行系统分析。

资本市场中独立董事资源并不稀缺，但为何部分公司仍选择以往曾聘任过的独立董事？究竟是因为返聘的独立董事相比于其他独立董事对公司情况更为了解和熟悉，可以更好地履行监督和咨询的公司治理角色？还是返聘的独立董事经历"冷却期"，看似与公司内部无关系，但实则是"熟人好办事"？返聘的独立董事与首次聘任的独立董事相比，可能在知识经验积累方面更具优势（学习效应），但也可能与大股东或管理当局缔结更为亲密的关系（关系效应）。一方面，基于"学习效应"，返聘的独立董事在知识经验积累与缔结潜在关系获取内部信息方面可能区别于上市公司首次聘任的独立董事，所以能够更好地发挥监督与咨询作

---

* 原文刊载于《金融研究》2021年第4期。
作者简介：杜兴强，管理学博士，教授，厦门大学会计发展研究中心 / 厦门大学管理学院；
张颖，博士研究生，厦门大学管理学院。

用；另一方面，基于"关系效应"，返聘的独立董事则可能碍于"情面"，从而在履行监督和咨询职能时"流于形式"。

本文以 2003—2016 年沪深两市 A 股上市公司为研究对象，以上市公司财务违规情况作为独立董事监督咨询有效性的代理变量，检验独立董事返聘的前因后果，并比较有无返聘独立董事的上市公司之间的横向差异，研究独立董事返聘对公司违规的影响究竟是基于"学习效应"的抑制效果还是基于"关系效应"的助长效果。研究发现：（1）对独立董事返聘的公司而言，相对于冷却期，返聘期的公司违规显著更少（纵向对比）；（2）返聘的独立董事首任期间，公司违规要显著低于冷却期（纵向对比）；（3）相较无独立董事返聘、返聘人数更少的公司，返聘人数更多的公司违规显著更少（横向对比）。研究发现支持了"学习效应"假说，即独立董事返聘抑制了公司违规，并非是规避任期规定的手段。在进行敏感性测试，以及控制了可能存在的内生性问题后，本文结论依然成立。

本文可能的贡献包括：（1）基于独立董事返聘这一独特视角，尝试对独立董事与公司治理的相关文献作出补充。针对前期文献的不一致结果，本文采用独立董事返聘样本，分析返聘独立董事对公司治理的影响，力图为独立董事任期问题提供"他山之石"。此外，因为独立董事选择是一个内生决定变量，许多独立董事制度有效性的研究结论受到内生性问题影响。因此，本文对独立董事有效性文献的一个重要贡献，还在于通过返聘独立董事首任、离任、续聘三个期间的对比（纵向对比），在一定程度上缓解了独立董事选择受公司治理结构、公司业绩等变量影响的内生性问题。（2）对独立董事返聘经济后果及动因进行了探索。中国资本市场制度背景下，独立董事返聘并非个案特例，但目前文献并未系统剖析独立董事返聘现象的经济后果，也未对独立董事返聘现象的成因进行深入分析。本文对上述问题进行了有益的尝试，可以对相关文献形成一定补充。（3）本文自始至终主要使用独立董事返聘的样本，旨在揭示"返聘的独立董事,相比于离职期间接替其职位的独立董事是否在返聘期间具有更好的治理效果——更少的公司违规"。因此,本文力图回答"曾在公司任职的独立董事,任期届满或其他原因离职后,是否还应再次成为公司独立董事选聘的对象或是否应该被公司优先再次聘请为独立董事"。此外,本文发现在独立董事任期届满或其他原因离职后,经过"冷却期",若再次被返聘,公司违规概率显著更低。

本文研究结果具有一定的政策启示。首先,本文研究结论支持了独立董事的"学习效应"——返聘高质量独立董事可以有效抑制公司违规行为。基于此,公司可将曾在本公司任职的独立董事纳入候选人范围,比较独立董事在任期间履职表现,择优聘任。同时,本文结论也为上市公司提供了一条减少公司违规的参考路径。其次,本文研究研讨了独立董事返聘现象的经济后果和动因,可为监管部门从外部制度完善以及制度执行两方面强化对返聘独立董事的有效约束提供一定思路,避免公司为了避开6年任期监管规范、"技术性地轮换独立董事"、然后再进行返聘,由此导致独立董事独立性被削弱的情况。最后,本文对独立董事制度的有效性提供了一定支撑,对投资者理解独立董事作用的发挥及独董返聘现象提供了重要的经验证据。

# 大股东股权质押与上市公司资本运作*

陆 蓉 兰 袁

近年来，上市公司大股东利用股权质押进行融资成为我国资本市场的普遍现象。据 Wind 数据统计，截至 2018 年 6 月，A 股共有 3 349 家上市公司涉及股权质押，占全市场上市公司的 97.76%，累计质押市值达 5.7 万亿元。但是，2017 年下半年以来，A 股市场出现连续较大幅度的下跌，市场面临越来越大的质押爆仓压力。上市公司大股东股权质押危机成为资本市场关注的热点问题，甚至引发关于系统性风险的担忧。

股权质押表面上是股东自身的融资行为，但由于质押方处于上市公司大股东的特殊地位，一旦质押的股权被强制平仓，便会对公司的控制权、股价、经营业绩、信息披露等产生较大影响。因此，对公司大股东而言，当面临平仓风险时，存在着强烈的动机采取措施以稳定公司股价（廖珂等，2018）。相关措施包括信息披露操纵（谢德仁等，2016）、税收规避（王雄元等，2018）等。然而，鲜有文献对另一重要措施——资本运作进行研究。实际上，在中国的资本市场中，上市公司通过资本运作来稳定股价的案例屡见不鲜。资本运作主要包括资产收购、股权转让、资产剥离、吸收合并、债务重组、资产置换、要约收购等方式。

资本运作可能成为大股东为了缓解股权质押风险而采取的措施：一方面，上市公司经常利用资本运作的不确定性进行长期停牌，从而防止

---

\* 原文刊载于《金融研究》2021 年第 4 期。
作者简介：陆蓉，经济学博士，教授，上海财经大学金融学院；兰袁，博士研究生，上海财经大学金融学院。

股价的进一步下跌;另一方面,已有研究表明资本运作对上市公司是利好消息(张晓宇和徐龙炳,2017),可以提高股票的超额收益率。由此,本文提出并尝试回答:当大股东股权质押比例高或者股价达到平仓线时,上市公司是否会运用资本运作来缓解潜在的风险?如是,又会如何影响上市公司的资本运作?进一步,大股东运用资本运作缓解质押风险背后的机制是什么?

基于此,本文选取2007—2018年我国A股上市公司作为研究样本,考察了大股东股权质押对上市公司资本运作的影响及其作用机制。研究发现:(1)大股东股权质押比例越高,上市公司进行资本运作的可能性越大;这一关系在大股东质押股权面临的平仓风险越高和非国有控股的上市公司中更为显著。(2)随着质押比例的提高,大股东推动上市公司进行资本运作后的停牌时间越长,说明大股东利用停牌来避免股价的进一步下跌,从而为补充质押物争取时间。从股价提升的效果来看,资本运作在短期内能提高股价,缓解质押风险,但长期来看效果并不显著。(3)当面临平仓风险时,大股东主要通过资本运作来助推股价,反而会缩短停牌时间。(4)上市公司主要采取股权转让、资产收购和资产剥离的方式进行资本运作;其中,大股东主要利用资产收购和资产剥离增加停牌时间,利用股权转让助推股价。

本文的主要贡献体现在以下三个方面:第一,本文发现大股东股权质押与上市公司资本运作有密切关联。资本运作有缓解股权质押风险的作用,大股东有动机利用资本运作的市场反应及增加停牌时间以缓解质押危机。第二,本文拓展了上市公司停牌的相关研究。已有文献侧重于分析停牌产生的经济后果(石阳等,2019),本文则从上市公司停牌的动机出发,发现大股东主动利用停牌来实现自身的利益(例如,当质押物面临平仓风险需要时间筹措资金或阻止股价进一步下跌。第三,本文丰富了股权质押的相关研究。已有研究主要关注大股东面临股权质押风险时采取的措施，但对这些措施是否能真正化解质押风险的讨论较少。本文不仅补充了一种新的措施：资本运作，还对该措施的作用进行了剖析。研究发现，以资本运作来提升股价在短期内能缓解股权质押风险，但长期来看效果并不显著。

根据上述分析结论，本文的实践意义在于：一是规范大股东的股权质押行为，重点关注大股东质押比例高和面临平仓风险的上市公司，这些大股东很有可能进行资本运作，从而损害中小投资者的利益。二是重视上市公司随意停牌的现象。我国上市公司利用资本运作等重大事项进行随意停牌的现象较为普遍，这可能是大股东为了实现自身利益而主动发起的，降低了资本市场的运行效率。因此，监管机构应对停牌事由和时间等作出进一步规范。

# 避免亏损与公开增发盈余管理的识别与估计：来自聚束设计的实证证据*

## 张 红　汪小圈

党的十九届五中全会指出我国正处在重要战略机遇期，重点工作之一是全面深化改革，构建高水平社会主义市场经济体制。其中，加快金融体制改革，完善资本市场基础制度，提高上市公司质量是金融工作的重要内容。上市公司是资本市场健康发展的基石，近年来随着建立多层次资本市场体系的有序推进，我国上市公司数量稳步增长，已成为推动国民经济发展的重要力量。然而，我国上市公司依然存在许多问题，比如针对证监会退市政策的盈余管理行为，扭曲了资本市场发挥有效资源配置的功能，阻碍了资本市场资金流向高质量企业。因此，健全上市公司退出机制、提高上市公司治理水平是提高上市公司质量的重要方面。而这些工作开展的重要基础是对上市公司问题的客观认知，例如从宏观上识别我国上市公司盈余管理的动机和估计盈余管理程度。因此，本文从上市公司盈余管理问题出发，对以下几个问题进行研究：我国A股上市公司是否因为退市政策和公开增发股票政策而采取了盈余管理行为？如果是，有多少公司针对这两种政策进行了盈余管理？这些盈余管理行为会因企业特征呈现出怎样的异质性？

---

\* 原文刊载于《金融研究》2021年第4期。

**作者简介：** 张红，经济学博士，讲师，暨南大学产业经济研究院；汪小圈，金融学博士，助理教授，华东师范大学经济学院。

2001年，证监会正式取消PT制度，规定连续三年亏损的公司将在第三年年报公布之后十日内直接暂停上市。同年，证监会规定上市公司申请增发应满足最近三个会计年度加权平均净资产收益率平均不低于6%。在这一制度背景下，上市公司很可能为避免退市或实现公开增发而对盈余进行人为操纵。本文使用聚束设计方法对2002—2017年上市公司加权平均净资产收益率（ROE）分布在0（退市政策）和6%（增发条件）政策阈值处的盈余管理频率（多少公司进行了盈余管理）和盈余管理幅度（将盈余提高了多少）进行估计，以此来揭示盈余管理规模是否具有经济意义。

虽然已有诸多文献关注了盈余管理的估计，但是这些文献存在无法解决多个阈值情况下不同阈值之间相互关联的影响问题，也存在模型假设过多且无法给出假设直接证据的问题（吴联生和王亚平，2007），于是导致近十来年国内有关上市公司盈余管理程度估计的研究止步不前。另外，近十年来我国股市的政策也发生了许多变化，比如允许上市公司进行非公开增发和加强金融监管等措施。因此，本文试图运用一个新的方法——聚束设计来回答政策变化是否改变了原有结论，并同时估计两个阈值影响下的盈余管理频率。

与假设ROE分布密度函数的其他盈余管理文献不同的是，本文只使用聚束设计文献中常用的多项式函数和其他控制变量对无阈值影响区间中ROE分布密度进行数据拟合，然后利用拟合参数对阈值影响区间内的ROE分布密度进行反事实估计，最后利用阈值影响区间内反事实估计与现实ROE分布密度之间的差异计算出多少公司将ROE从阈值左侧操纵至了阈值右侧，即完成对盈余管理的估计。

本文使用聚束设计方法对盈余管理频率和幅度的估计结果显示，大约有3.184%的上市公司为了避免汇报亏损而进行盈余管理，占无阈值影响下存在亏损公司的59.25%；反事实估计ROE在[-1.5%, 0)的这些企业最可能参与盈余管理,在此区间内,近93%的公司有盈余管理行为;而其虚报的ROE大约分布于[0,3%),且在此区间观测到的公司中有近22.6%的ROE是盈余管理的结果;针对退市政策阈值0,进行盈余管理的公司平均意义上将ROE提高了2.115个百分点。与此同时,为了成功公开增发而进行盈余管理的上市公司,虽整体而言占所有公司的比例较小,仅有0.28%,但占股票公开增发公司的比例则高达58.13%,反事实估计ROE在[5%,6%)的这些企业最可能参与盈余管理,而其虚报的ROE大约分布于[6%,9.5%]。本文使用聚束设计同时估计两个阈值处的盈余管理频率和幅度,是对现有文献的一大贡献。

本文还对这些盈余管理行为进行异质性分析。首先,我们逐年估计了盈余管理的比例和程度。2002—2015年,上市公司避免退市的盈余管理动机一直比较稳定;而在2016年和2017年盈余管理的比例并不显著,这也许与证监会加强金融监管力度有关。为了公开增发而进行盈余管理的公司比例则仅在2002—2005年比较显著,此后盈余管理行为不仅不再显著、幅度也不断下降,我们猜测这与允许定向增发后公司公开增发需求降低有关。其次,我们发现ST企业的盈余管理频率是非ST企业的3.62倍。再次,杠杆率高的企业针对亏损和公开增发条件的盈余管理程度更为严重。

本文结论具有一定的现实启示:宏观层面,把会计指标作为硬约束来监管本意是希望淘汰盈利能力差的企业,并使得盈利能力强的企业可以有机会再融资,但这项政策无意中加强了企业为避免退市或为增发而进行盈余管理的动机。监管机构还需要辅以严格的信息披露监管才能达到应有的效果。微观层面,本文从分布上、从企业特征方面估计出哪部分盈余最可能是虚报的,监管机构则可以将这些上市公司作为重点审查和监管的对象。

# 高管宏观认知具有管理者"烙印"吗？*

## ——基于管理者风格效应的实证检验

### 罗勇根　饶品贵　陈　灿

党的十九大报告指出"我国经济已由高速增长阶段转向高质量发展阶段"。当前经济转型阶段面临着全球经济环境深刻变化、外部需求扩张变慢及国内经济增速放缓等多重挑战。由于企业所处宏观经济环境的复杂性，管理者需要面对大量复杂且模糊的信息，存在严重的信息过载现象。不同管理者受到不同认知结构的约束，无法完全处理并解释环境信息，导致在筛选和处理感知到的环境变化时，会出现个体之间的显著差异，进而表现出企业行为决策的异质性。本文研究的高管宏观认知（Managerial Macro-Cognition，MMC）是指在复杂多变的宏观环境下，管理者对宏观环境信息关注和解释，并将其运用于企业决策的认知结构与认知过程。高管宏观认知是管理者个人宏观认知能力的体现。管理者风格效应是指，管理者会将个人独特的问题处理方式与处理能力施加于企业，导致企业在重大决策行为时具有异质性，即企业行为存在明显的个体固定效应。由于不同企业高管对宏观环境的认知受个体所具有的经验、性格、思维和价值观等特征的影响，具有明显的高管个人特质，即具有管理者风格效应。

---

\* 原文刊载于《金融研究》2021 年第 5 期。

**作者简介：** 罗勇根，管理学博士，讲师，广东财经大学粤港澳大湾区资本市场与审计治理研究院/会计学院；饶品贵，管理学博士，教授，暨南大学管理学院；陈灿，管理学博士，助理教授，澳门大学工商管理学院。

本文从高管宏观认知的视角，研究高管宏观认知是否存在管理者风格效应，既有助于深化管理者风格在企业当中具体作用的理解，也为深入探究高管认知的形成机理提供经验证据。具体而言，本文以2001—2018年我国上市公司为样本，利用自然语言处理技术提取年报"管理层讨论与分析"（MD&A）中包含宏观经济词汇的描述，根据词频法构建高管宏观认知指标，即计算提取的宏观词汇占MD&A总词汇的比例。为检验高管宏观认知是否具有管理者风格效应，我们对比控制与不控制管理者个体固定效应，回归模型的拟合优度是否存在明显变化。如果控制管理者个体固定效应后，回归模型的拟合优度明显增加，则表明CEO的个体固定效应会显著增加模型的解释力度，说明高管宏观认知会受到管理者风格效应的显著影响。

实证结果发现：（1）企业层面的高管宏观认知具有明显的管理者"烙印"，会受到管理者个人风格的显著影响，表现为管理者风格效应。（2）管理者具体个人特征对高管宏观认知的管理者风格效应的影响表现为高管的学历及海外经历与管理者风格呈正相关关系，高管政府背景与管理者风格效应呈负相关关系。（3）管理者能力越强的企业，高管宏观认知的管理者风格效应越强，管理者越有可能将其决策理念与行为方式深植于企业。

本文的研究从以下几方面对已有文献形成补充和扩展。

第一，本文从高管宏观认知的角度，研究发现高管宏观认知同样存在管理者风格效应，说明不同企业之间存在管理者风格效应的差异。这一发现丰富了管理者风格效应对我国企业决策影响的相关研究，拓展了管理者个人特征及其相关属性的研究视角，为企业选择合适的管理者提供了参考，也为深入理解我国企业的决策行为提供经验证据。

第二，本文从高管对宏观环境变化的解释与判断能力出发，利用"管理层讨论与分析"的文本信息，构建高管宏观认知指标，研究了高管宏观认知能力形成的原因，丰富了高管能力的相关研究，也为高管宏观认知能力的异质性提供经验证据。

第三，本文拓展了管理者认知的相关研究。管理者认知的相关文献大多从个体人口统计学特征角度研究高管认知能力的高低。然而，尽管人口统计数据可以反映管理者从以往经验中积累的知识，但是它们不能反映对具体环境内容的解释。因此，本文从宏观环境的角度，衡量高管对宏观环境信息的认知，丰富了管理者认知的相关研究。

根据上述研究结论，本文得到以下启示：第一，在经理人市场存在信息不对称的情况下，企业可以根据高管的个人特征对其进行甄别，聘任宏观认知能力较高的管理者。第二，本文的研究结论也表明，除了财务数据信息之外，我们还应更加注重管理者个人特征等"软"信息，这些信息可用于分析和评价公司的经营风格和企业文化，判断和预测公司的行为，为更好地理解公司决策提供启示。

# 企业家前台化影响企业价值吗?*

## ——基于新浪微博的实证证据

### 孙 彤 薛 爽 崔庆慧

企业家在企业的发展过程中扮演着重要角色,其行为会对企业绩效及价值产生深刻影响。在传统意义上,企业家主要通过制定战略、影响内部管理等后台行为来影响企业价值。但互联网时代,信息传递方式与效率的改变带来了企业经营模式和管理方法的变革,企业家的角色也正在发生改变。越来越多的企业家从企业的幕后走向前台,积极主动地与公众沟通,希望通过人格化的个人行为向外界传递企业的战略、理念以及产品相关信息,即企业家前台化行为。2010 年以来,快速发展的微博为企业家前台化提供了一个更及时、更多元且低成本的平台。在微博中,用户之间无须互粉即可进行交流互动,同时通过关注、粉丝和互粉关系形成社交链。企业家开通个人微博后,信息可以从企业家处向外快速扩散,短时间内可以定向地传播给粉丝。粉丝的转发又会带来信息的加速传递和扩散。那么,企业家的前台化,如开通微博,对企业来说,是利还是弊?目前尚未有一致的结论。企业家开通微博是有成本的:第一,微博维护成本。企业家需要花费时间精力进行微博的发布、更新、互动等,而时间成本对于企业家这一类人群来说无疑是高昂的。第二,声誉

---

\* 原文刊载于《金融研究》2021 年第 5 期。
作者简介:孙彤,管理学博士,讲师,浙江万里学院商学院;薛爽,管理学博士,教授,上海财经大学会计与财务研究院,上海财经大学会计学院;崔庆慧,管理学博士研究生,上海财经大学商学院。

绑定效应。一旦企业家选择前台化，其个人声誉与所在的企业就会更加紧密地绑定在一起。第三，信息曝光风险。企业家曝光于人前，披露更多的私人信息意味着更大的风险。综上，企业家在考虑是否走向"前台"时，一定会权衡其收益与成本。那么，企业家前台化的收益表现在哪里？前台化是否会提升其所在企业的价值？如会提升，具体的路径又是什么？这是本文研究的出发点和关心的主要问题。

现有微博研究主要关注企业官方微博的信息传递作用，指出自媒体可以有效促进企业与投资者之间的双向沟通。有限的几篇企业家微博的研究试图从企业家形象或企业家精神的角度解释企业家前台化行为，但鲜有企业家个人微博对企业价值是否及如何产生影响的研究。有鉴于此，本文基于信息传递视角，实证检验了企业家前台化对企业价值的影响。具体地，本文选取 2010—2017 年中国 A 股上市公司为研究样本，借助 Python 网页搜索和文本分析技术获取企业家微博数据，通过构建多元线性回归方程，在控制行业固定效应和时间固定效应的情况下，进行了实证检验。并通过稳健性检验，缓解了反向因果、样本选择性偏差、内生性等影响。

研究结果表明：（1）企业家发布微博这一前台化行为有助于提升企业价值。从对价值影响的路径看，企业家微博发布后，企业经营性现金流增加，系统性风险降低；（2）对微博传递信息的内容进行文本分析，发现企业家微博中个性化微博比例越高、"艾特"人数越多及正向语调比例越高，其对企业价值的正向影响越显著；（3）相对于信息不对称程度较低的企业，在信息不对称程度较高的企业中企业家更倾向于发布微博。

本文的发现拓展了现有文献的研究成果，同时对处在互联网环境下的企业家行为决策也有着一定的借鉴意义。具体表现在以下几个方面：第一，本文将企业家前台化纳入信息不对称理论的框架中，阐明企业家前台化发挥着信息传递作用,不仅丰富了企业家前台化经济后果的文献,也拓展了自媒体在信息披露和信息传递方面的研究。第二,在互联网时代,企业内外部信息环境发生了重要变化,信息采集和传递的方式也发生了转变,企业家需要重新审视信息披露的方式方法。本文的发现对企业家是否及如何利用自媒体具有重要启示。第三,关于自媒体对企业影响的研究,现有文献的关注焦点为企业的官方微博。本文将对企业微博的研究下沉到企业家个人微博,是不同于企业官方微博的一个全新的视角。企业家微博信息更加多元化,了解企业家的性格特点、人生观、价值观等信息有助于投资者理解和预测他们的战略决策。第四,本文发现企业家会通过个人微博,直接或间接地传递与企业价值相关的信息,这一过程更有效率、更可持续,契合国家倡导的创新、绿色和共享的发展理念。

根植于网络的自媒体作为当下重要的信息媒介,其巨大的影响力往往超过我们的预期。创新、绿色、共享的理念不仅可以体现在生产环节,更可以应用于资本市场的信息沟通与传递过程。

Journal of Financial Research

## Brief Edition

(Volume Ⅰ · 2021)

# 01   Macroeconomics & Monetary Policy

## Industrial Revolution, Financial Revolution, and Systemic Risk Governance

CHEN Yulu

(The People's Bank of China)

This article studies the relationship among industrial revolution, financial revolution, and systemic risk governance by examining the three industrial revolutions in human history. The three industrial revolutions had significantly improved productivity, transformed industrial production and social relations. The advanced technology innovations and applications, transformation of economic structure and evolution of social environments promoted development and upgrading of the financial sector. Subsequently, rapid capital accumulation and effective intermediation were essential in turning technological progress into industrial revolution, and financial revolution became an important catalyst of industrial revolution.However, if the rules, institutional arrangements and regulations could not catch up with the revolution in financial sector, the imbalances will build up and systemic risks accmulate, which would in turn trigger financial crisis that would subsequently prompt major changes in the financial and regulatory systems.

The first industrial revolution established production process mechanization and industry specialization as the pattern of modem production and economic growth.Under the specific socio-economic environment in the UK, the swift industrial and business development drove the expansion of banking system and the emergence of a unified credit market that narrowed the credit spread among areas, and mitigated capital shortage in industrial areas. The first financial revolution, i.e. the rise of modem commercial banking system, provided massive fund support for the full-scale rise of the first industrial revolution. However, due to the weakness in risk management, rapid surge of bank credit accumulated massive risks in the financial system, which triggered frequent financial crises. After the financial crisis in 1825, the UK overhauled its financial system. The Bank of England gradually assumed central bank functions such as currency issuance, financial stability. The British financial industry entered into a century-long stable period thereafter.

During the second industrial revolution, the technological progress, economic expansion, and large-scale infrastructure building generated financing demands that stimulated the development of capital markets and investment bank business in the US. The second financial revolution, with the rise of modern investment banking system, restructured the capital foundation of the second industrial revolution. The development of capital market provided the financial infrastructure and capital for large-scale industrial development. The M&A deals helped optimize industrial and market structures, and facilitated the transformation of scientific and technological achievements into economic growth. But in the early stage of development, due to lack of regulation, speculation was rampant in the US capital market, stock price manipulation, insider-trading, and frauds went unchecked. Stock market panic occurred, frequently. After the Great Depression, the U.S. introduced multiple legislations, created regulatory agency and self-discipline organizations for the security markets, and established the separation of banking and investment bank businesses. Along with the gradual development of the financial market regulatory framework, the U.S. capital market entered into a regulated and recovery era.

In the process of the third industrial revolution, the United States, with a large weapons industry that expanded on orders from military forces of multiple countries, found it imperative to transform its economic institutions into civilian industries through rapid development of small or medium size enterprises. The existing financing pattern could not meet such needs in economic growth. The third financial revolution, with the emergence of venture capital investment system, created new driving forces for the third industrial revolution. Venture capital not only provided direct financing for high-tech firms in their early stages, but also offered non- financial supports, including business consulting, strategic advice, resource network, and etc. In the relatively light-touch regulatory environment, capital flocked into the venture capital system and greatly eased the difficulty in financing for the startup technology firms. However, due to the focus on growth and lack of attention to risk management in the US regulatory system, the expansion in the financial industry also led to "irrational exuberance" from 1995 to 2001 and the burst of 'dot-com bubble' . As the Nasdaq was in its early stage and accounted for a limited share in US capital market, the dot-com bubble caused limited damage on the economy. However, excessive risk-taking and lack of transparency of the venture capital system became more pronounced, the US regulatory authorities began to adjust rules on venture capital. In 2011, the SEC issued rules requiring venture capital funds to meet certain requirements, further tightening regulation of the venture capital system. In recent years, the speculation and pro-cyclical behaviors in venture capital investment became a topic of academic research.

The ongoing fourth industrial revolution is presenting historic opportunities for the financial industry. The integrated innovation of financial industry made possible by financial tecnology will become a feature of the fourth financial revolution. China is among the leading countries in financial technology development. We should learn from the past experience, and seek to balance development and security. With the progress of financial technology, the banking system, capital markets, venture capital system, and financial technology firms work together to support the real economy. At the same time, there should be measures to manage financial risks, to establish a dynamic and balanced financial regulatory system that is compatible with innovations in financial technology.

Such a system will guide financial institutions to stick to the proper way and make innovation under the precondition of serving the real economy and complying with regulatory requirements, prevent disorderly capital expansion, and prevent systemic risks.

# The Debt Repayment of the Boxer Indemnity and Its Impacts

WANG Xin    ZHANG Yi    WEI Lei

(Research Bureau, The People's Bank of China; Yangzhou Central Sub-branch,

The People's Bank of China)

In 1901, the Qing government was forced to sign the "Boxer Protocol" with western countries to pay 450 million "haikwan tael" of silver (the "Boxer Indemnity"). The research on the Boxer Indemnity is quite rich, but there are still some shortcomings. Previous studies are mainly based on traditional data and historical research methods, the application of new historical materials and new methods needs to be extended. Most studies treat the Boxer Indemnity as a separate event and are limited to commenting on the event and its impact, comparisons with other international indemnities of the same era and analysis of its connection with the global economic and financial markets are lacking.

This paper studies the Boxer Indemnity and its impact from the perspective of debt. Based on previous research results and related materials, this paper compiles a flow chart of the Boxer Indemnity payment, and concisely explains the payment process of the Boxer Indemnity. Furthermore, from the perspectives of currency purchasing power and international comparison, it analyzes the equivalence of the Boxer Indemnity to the proportion of economic aggregate and government fiscal revenue, the value of the Boxer Indemnity and its historical influence in public finance, banking, currency and other aspects.

The research findings of this paper include the following. First, the principal of the Boxer Indemnity is equivalent to 4.33 times of the Qing government's fiscal revenue in 1903. However, through the arrangement of debt repayment, the actual amount of the indemnity paid each year gradually decreased in its percentage to the fiscal revenue, avoiding the direct bankruptcy of the Qing government. Second, converted to the 1900 International dollar (Geary-Khamis Dollar) by the purchasing power parity, the Boxer Indemnity accounted for about 2.1% of China's GDP in 1900. In addition, due to the global depreciation of silver in the second half of the 19th century, the proportion of the Boxer Indemnity to the total indemnities in modern China is significantly lower when converted to the purchasing power of rice than in its silver amount. Third, compared with the domestic and foreign debt interest rates of the Chinese government at that time and the long-term sovereign debt interest rates of major countries around 1900, the 4% interest rate of the Boxer Indemnity is at a moderate level. Fourth, compared with Germany's war indemnity after World War I, the principal of the Boxer Indemnity is far lower in its proportion to the total national economic volume. However, China's actual payment each year is higher in its proportion to the fiscal revenue than that of the German indemnity. Unlike the German indemnity, the repayment of which produced unprecedented hyperinflation and exerted a great impact on the German history thereafter, the Boxer Indemnity did not bring hyperinflation to China. The main reason is that China did not have a real central bank and government credit paper money at the time, and the government could not relieve the fiscal pressure by issuing paper money indiscriminately, but the impact of the indemnity on China's financial system was more long-term. At last, the Boxer Indemnity had profound impact on China's finance, banking and currency. In terms of fiscal taxation, the Chinese Maritime Customs Service, which was managed by foreigners, took advantage of the Boxer Indemnity to expand its power, monopolized China's most important source of tax revenue and became "the second fiscal authority" independent from the Chinese government. In the financial market, foreign banks further strengthened their financial privileges and market advantages by handling the Boxer Indemnity business, and established their status as "recessive central banks" in China.

In particular, the power expansion of the HSBC and the Citibank is the most obvious. In terms of currency, the Boxer Indemnity did not change the "old system" of China's chaotic currency system, but gave birth to a "new cycle" and "new crisis" in currency circulation, which became an important fuse for the Shanghai "rubber wave" (financial crisis) in 1910.

Based on the above findings, this paper shows that the debt settlement of war reparations in modern history was not only dominated by political and diplomatic situations, but was also closely related to the transnational operations of financial institutions, especially banks. The economic impacts of war reparations depend not only on the total repayment amount, but also on the ability to govern the economy and the fiscal and financial systems.

# Liberalization Reform, Interest Rates, and Monetary Policy

LU Jun    HUANG Jia

(Lingnan College, Sun Yat-Sen University)

On October 29, 2020, the Fifth Plenary Session of the 19th CPC Central Committee adopted the Outline of the 14th Five-Year Plan (2021-2025) for National Economic and Social Development and the Long-Range Objectives Through the Year 2035, which clearly indicated the need to improve the market-based mechanism for selling and transmitting interest rates. After more than 20 years of interest rate liberalization reform, which has included increasing links between deposit interest rates, loan interest rates, market interest rates, and policy interest rates, China's monetary policy framework now has a unique and extremely important transmission channel for bank interest rates. There are two important issues to clarify in the discussion of the traditional interest rate transmission channel. First, it is necessary to recognize that monetary policy is directly related to bank interest rates. Second, various factors may create friction that blocks or interrupts the transmission from short-term nominal to real interest rates. Interest rate liberalization plays an important role in the allocation of financial resources if it allows central bank's policy interest rates to be smoothly transmitted to loan interest and deposit interest rates through market interest rate.

In the context of China's continuing interest rate liberalization reforms, this study treats the adoption of the monetary policy on bank interest rate transmission as a turning point, and comprehensively investigates the effects of two aspects of interest rate liberalization reform: the degree of interest rate liberalization and the monetary policy price rule.

This study constructs a partial equilibrium model that includes residents, manufacturers, and commercial banks to describe the time-varying characteristics of the degree of interest rate liberalization, and then discusses the endogenous relationship between the degree of interest rate liberalization and the transmission of monetary policy to bank interest rates. Both of these factors determine the efficiency of interest rate liberalization reform. Using the TVP-FAVAR model, this study then verifies the conclusion of the theoretical analysis. The data are from the China Financial Statistics Yearbooks, China Economic Network Statistical database, Wind, and Bankscope (renamed Moody's Analytics BankFocus). Public bank annual reports are used to supplement the databases.

This study offers two main conclusions. (i) China's interest rate liberalization reform is characterized by periodic fluctuations, and the progress of interest rate liberalization is not linear. (ii) The interest rate liberalization reform has a dynamic policy effect. Various reform policies increase the degree of interest rate liberalization, which in turn makes the transmission of monetary policy to bank interest rates smoother. However, the policy effects are not always marginally incremental.

The effect of the monetary policy price rule on interest rate liberalization reform could be strengthened, and the launch of the LPR formation mechanism reform in 2019 is a good opportunity. Therefore, this study suggests that there is a need to further improve the LPR formation, transmission, and regulation mechanism, improve the Funds Transfer Pricing mechanism so that bank interest rates meet market demand, encourage representative financial institutions to participate in the LPR, regulate the development of shadow banking businesses, exercise prudential supervision based on categories, ensure the effective transmission of monetary policy to bank interest rates, and strengthen the effects of interest rate liberalization reform.

The main contributions of this study are as follows. (i) Drawing on Ma and Wang (2014), this study considers the factors that create frictions between deposit interest rates, loan interest rates, market interest rates, and policy interest rates. The study also creates an index of the degree of interest rate liberalization based on time-varying characteristics and explores the endogenous relationship between the time-varying degrees of interest rate liberalization and the transmission of monetary policy to bank interest rates. The findings show that an objective and comprehensive evaluation of the effect of interest rate liberalization must consider both the degree of interest rate liberalization and the effectiveness of the monetary policy price rule. (ii) Drawing on Liu et al. (2018), this study estimates the degree of interest rate liberalization and its time-varying characteristics. Through the time point impulse response function, the lead time impulse response function, and the time-varying forecast variance decomposition, this study explores how to promote the reform by enhancing the effectiveness of the price rule at the macro level.

The deregulation of interest rates in China should not be the full extent of interest rate liberalization.It is necessary to continue interest rate liberalization reforms.Future research should explore the role of shadow banking and digital currency in the process of unifying the dual-track interest rates into one track.

# Can Monetary Policy Reconcile Sustaining Steady Growth with Preventing Risks in China? An Analysis Based on Dynamic Stochastic General Equilibrium Modeling

DONG Bingbing    XU Huilun    TAN Xiaofen

(School of Finance, Central University of Finance and Economics)

Macro leverage growth in China has been brought under control in recent years and has therefore stabilized. At the first meeting of the Central Committee for Financial and Economic Affairs in April 2018, it was proposed that China should stabilize its macro leverage and quickly reduce the leverage ratio of local government and state-owned enterprises (SOEs). However, stronger financial regulation and U.S.-China trade tensions imposed adverse shocks on the economy's driving force and on public confidence in the economy. The economy experienced increasingly downward pressure. In the face of the COVID-19 shock, the People's Bank of China strengthened counter-cyclical adjustments to monetary policy in 2020. These stronger counter-cyclical adjustments led to a temporary rise in the macro leverage ratio. Some researchers argue that stabilizing economic growth conflicts with stabilizing the macro leverage ratio in terms of counter-cyclical monetary policy adjustments. They therefore argue that monetary policy should now aim to enhance rather than stabilize economic growth.

However, monetary policy adjustment may not lead to such a conflict in terms of the economic meaning of the macro leverage ratio and structural deleveraging. In terms of improving credit allocation, when corporations with lower returns deleverage and those with higher returns leverage, resources can be redistributed to better performing corporates.Output productivity will therefore be promoted. This resource redistribution also helps to stabilize the macro leverage ratio and maintain economic growth.

We have three key questions. First, can monetary policy reconcile the stabilization of the macro leverage ratio with the maintenance of economic growth? Second, how can the structural monetary policy instrument cooperate with existing monetary policy instruments to channel funds precisely? Finally, how can monetary policy facilitate these two goals under the two-pillar framework of monetary policy and macro-prudential policy? We develop a two-sector New Keynesian dynamic stochastic general equilibrium (DSGE) model. The model includes an SOE sector and a privately owned enterprise (POE) sector, further incorporating collateral constraints for these two sectors' borrowing. We use Bayesian methods with economic data from China to estimate the model. We address the above questions by providing impulse responses, variance decompositions, and historical decompositions.

Our findings are as follows. First, maintaining economic growth and stabilizing the macro leverage ratio are not contradictory; rather, they can promote each other. If the central bank lowers interest rates and strengthens SOEs' collateral constraints, credit resources will be directed from SOEs to POEs. This redirection can promote credit allocation efficiency. This will help to maintain stable growth and stabilize the macro leverage ratio.These monetary policy adjustments can therefore enhance the effects of financing, serving the real economy and effectively preventing systemic financial risks. Second, the above effects are related to the borrowing costs of SOEs and POEs. The effects can be reinforced by bringing the SOE loan rate closer to the market rate and implementing structural monetary policy that aims to reduce POE loan costs. Third, collateral constraints on SOEs were the main factor in macro leverage from the second quarter of 2006 to the second quarter of 2018. The adjustment of interest rates has had a greater impact on macro leverage since 2017. Fourth, under the macro prudential policy framework, if the central bank targets the macro leverage ratio according to the Taylor rule, which varies over time according to policy background, then the rule will contribute to the balance between maintaining stable growth, making structural adjustments, and guarding against risks. If the central bank loosens interest rates and strengthens SOEs' borrowing constraints, the interest rate coefficient on the macro leverage ratio should be positive. Based on this Taylor rule setting, a decrease in the macro leverage ratio will make the central bank further reduce interest rates. This decrease will then reinforce the effect of lowering interest rates and strengthen the collateral constraints on SOEs.

We make three contributions in this paper. First, we add corporate heterogeneity to the DSGE model according to China's economic features. The model can therefore illustrate credit allocation and the monetary policy mechanism in the corporate sector. Second, we simulate the effect of monetary policy in different settings of corporate borrowing costs to show how the central bank can use structural monetary policy to promote credit allocation and strengthen the effects of financing serving the real economy. This paper provides theoretical insights into the impact of structural monetary policy. Third, we combine the theoretical model with macro leverage ratio data and identify the key factor that drives macro leverage ratio in China. Using counterfactual experiments, we also show how to facilitate the maintenance of economic growth and the stabilization of the macro leverage ratio under the macro-prudential framework.

# Investment Surges, Dual Financial Frictions, and Monetary Policy Transmission: Demystifying the Structural Adjustment Function of Monetary Policy During the Economic Transition

ZHAN Minghua   LI Shuai   YAO Yaojun   WU Zhouheng

(School of Finance, Guangdong University of Foreign Studies;
School of Finance, Zhejiang Gongshang University)

Investment surges are a typical phenomenon during China's current transitional period, as Justin Lin (2007) observes. Investment may systemically lean toward certain industries, due to either market distortions or government interventions. Investment leanings can lead to capital misallocation and excess capacity in some industries. To correct this imbalance, monetary policies have sometimes been successfully applied to de-capacitize these industries. Theoretically, however, monetary policy does not have structural adjustment functions, even when it is non-neutral in the long run. Therefore, explaining the industrial structural adjustment effects of Chinese monetary policy remains a great puzzle.

In this paper, we explain this puzzle from the perspectives of heterogeneous capacity features and property rights differences between enterprises in China. We construct a theoretical model with a dual financial frictions mechanism in the credit market to illustrate the de-capacitizing effects of monetary policy on excess industrial capacity. The dual financial frictions are the collateral constraint on enterprise and the leverage constraint on banks. The monetary policy transmission is marginally distorted by systematic differences in the balance sheet features of excess capacity industries and the property rights differences of enterprises.

We find first that the investments of excess capacity enterprises are more strongly repressed under contractionary monetary policies. Second, state-owned enterprises are less affected by contractionary monetary policies, as they possess better collaterals than private enterprises do. Third, quantitative monetary policy tools are more effective than price-based monetary policy tools.

We use macroeconomic aggregate data and A-share listed firm-level panel data from 2006 Q1 to 2017 Q3 to empirically verify the theoretical hypotheses. We find first that monetary policy has a significant de-capacitizing function. Second, the de-capacitizing function of monetary policy is mainly effective for excess capacity private enterprises.Third, quantitative monetary policy tools are more effective than price-based tools. Finally, expansionary and contractionary operations have asymmetric effects. State-owned enterprises are affected only by expansion.Private enterprises are affected by both expansion and contraction, and are more sensitive to contraction.

Our paper theoretically and empirically verifies that monetary policy has long-term industrial structural adjustment functions in China.It can have such functions when financial frictions and distortions prevail in the financial market, and when enterprises are heterogeneous in balance sheet features and in their ability to obtain external financing in the credit market.

Our work contributes to the literature in the following ways. First, we document and explain the long-term structural effects of monetary policy in transitional economies with financial frictions and institutional barriers. This is different from the traditional conclusion of monetary theories and studies regarding developed economies (Clarida and Gertler, 1999; Walsh, 2003). Second, our dynamic stochastic general equilibrium model clarifies the mechanisms of the de-capacitizing functions of monetary policy, identifying an interest rate channel and a credit channel. These channels fill the mechanism analysis gap in related literature on the de-capacitizing functions of monetary policy (Wei, 1993; Song, 1997; Zhou, 2004). Third, we discuss the effectiveness of interest rate tools and quantitative tools such as reserve requirements.Our paper therefore sheds light on the greater effectiveness of quantitatively based monetary policy tools in addressing structural problems.

Our research has important policy implications. First, different monetary policy tools have different structural adjustment effects.This implies that monetary authorities should choose and apply different tools according to their best marginal effects.Second, the structural adjustment functions of regular monetary policy tools should be considered in practice alongside other structural monetary policy tools. This is consistent with the creative application of monetary management identified by the communique of the fifth plenary session of the 19th Central Committee of the Communist Party of China.Third, the full functioning of interest rate marketization depends on the deep reform of microstructure financial markets due to microeconomic agents' heterogeneous features (Xu, 2018). Finally, the coordinated promotion of real economy supply-side structural reforms, interest rate marketization reform, and the construction of a high-level socialist market economy system are essential to a sound price-based monetary policy system.

# The Time-varying Transmission Mechanism of Monetary Policy with Mixed Frequency Data: Evidence from MF-TVP-FAVAR Model

SHANG Yuhuang   ZHAO Rui   DONG Qingma

(Institute of Chinese Financial Studies, Southwestern University of Finance and Economics)

The global economy is facing increasing uncertainty, and the financial market is becoming more fragile. China's macro-economy is also facing problems such as economic structural adjustment and financial risk agglomeration, which make the relationship between monetary policy and macro-economy more challenging. The gradual reform of Chinese interest rate marketization and the rapid development of Fintech are also leading to a complex financial big data environment in terms of monetary policy. To understand the dynamic behavior of the monetary policy-transmission mechanism, the available macroeconomic and financial market big data information must be utilized. Effectively analyzing the monetary policy mechanism through big data is thus a critical problem.

The transmission mechanism for monetary policies attracts extensive research attention. Some believe that the credit (quantitative) transmission mechanism is the main factor, while others suggest that the interest rate mechanism is more effective. Monetary policies typically exhibit time-varying features due to the business cycle, and thus a time-varying parameter vector autoregression (TVP-VAR) model is proposed to capture the behavior of monetary policies. The factor-augmented VAR (FAVAR) model is also used to analyze monetary policy, as it effectively utilizes real economic data.

The traditional TVP-FAVAR model uses only the same frequency data. However, the frequency of macroeconomic data is completely different from that of financial market data. Mixed frequency data are therefore widespread in actual economic activities. Effectively using such data to construct a TVP-FAVAR model and then analyze the monetary policy behavioral mechanism is therefore the challenge we face, and the aim of this study.

We propose a mixed frequency TVP-FAVAR (MF-TVP-FAVAR) model. We collect Chinese mixed frequency big data for our empirical study. The main advantage of the MF-TVP-FAVAR model is that it maximizes the integration of high-frequency financial market information and low-frequency macroeconomic information, and effectively extracts unobservable potential factors from a large amount of information. These advantages help us to more accurately analyze the time-varying relationships of monetary policy, macro indicators, and financial market indicators.

The mixed frequency data are mainly derived from China's quarterly and monthly macro data, and monthly financial data are also included. The sample period is from January 1997 to December 2017. The data sources are the National Bureau of Statistics and the WIND database.

The main conclusions of this paper are as follows.

First, based on the MF-TVP-FAVAR model, the Financial Condition Index (FCI) extracted from financial market big data can better establish the dynamics of China's financial situation. This index is a leading indicator that can be used to measure economic performance, and an auxiliary indicator of the intermediary target of monetary policy. The FCI has a significant positive impact on interest rates and money supply, and this impact shows time-varying features.

Second, based on the time-varying response function of monetary policy shocks, the MF-TVP-FAVAR model captures the time-varying features of the impact of monetary policy at a macroeconomic level. This impact can be identified through the monthly observation frequency, which significantly improves the timeliness of the monetary policy transmission mechanism. Unlike the money supply, the impact of interest rate transmission on output shows a lag effect. Interest rate transmission has become smoother with interest rate marketization, while the credit transmission mechanism is increasingly blocked by fiscal policy coordination.

Finally, the business cycle has a significant impact on the transmission mechanism of monetary policy. We find that both the output effect and the price effect of this mechanism are more fluent during an economic boom than in a recession. Thus, monetary policy transmission is obviously cyclical. However, compared with price-based monetary policies, quantitative monetary policies are more susceptible to the impact of the business cycle.

# The Green Financing Effect of The Expanded Central Bank Collateral Framework

GUO Ye  FANG Fang

(School of Economics /The Wang Yanan Institute for Studies in Economics, Xiamen University; School of Economics, Xiamen University)

Since 2013, China's central bank has greatly enriched its monetary policy toolbox and innovatively launched several policy tools such as short-term liquidity operations (SLO), standing lending facility (SLF), medium-term lending facility (MLF) and targeted medium-term lending facility (TMLF). Through such monetary policy tools, the central bank provides different maturities to commercial banks by means of pledge. With the development of the new monetary policy, there are more and more discussions on various policy tools. However, as a part of the new monetary policy, the collateral framework of the central bank still lacks sufficient research. In June 2018, the People's Bank of China gave priority to accepting green bonds and green loans as collateral, reflecting the intention of China's monetary policy to channel more funds into the green sector. Whether the central bank's inclusion of green credit assets into the qualified collateral framework can further improve the financing level of green credit enterprises and reduce their financing cost requires further research.

Based on existing studies, we believe that the collateral framework of the central bank may act on both the balance sheet of commercial banks and the balance sheet of characteristic enterprises. On the one hand, the collateral policy of the central bank means that when the central bank issues base money through MLF, it requires commercial banks to provide qualified collateral such as green credit assets, so as to bypass the transmission from the liability end of commercial banks to the asset end. On the other hand, the central bank's inclusion of a certain type of credit and financial assets into the qualified collateral framework will improve the pledge right and scarcity of such assets (Nyborg, 2017), which is equivalent to the central bank's indirect "guarantee" for characteristic enterprises through national credit.

Specifically, this paper selects the quarterly financial data of A-share listed companies in the China Stock Market & Accounting Research (CSMAR) database from the first quarter of 2013 to the fourth quarter of 2019, and excludes financial companies and companies that have issued green bonds during this period. Using difference-in-differences (DID) method, we compare the different effects of the central bank's collateral expansion policy on the enterprises in the experimental group and the control group to identify a causal relationship. The main target of the collateral expansion policy is the enterprises that can obtain green credit, but there is no clear industry standard. Therefore, identifying the experimental group and the control group only by industries may underestimate the effect of the policy and ignore the impact of green credit on ordinary enterprises with energy conservation and environmental protection projects. Therefore, to more accurately determine the target subjects affected by the policy, we analyze the annual reports of listed companies through text analysis method, and manually classify companies with green projects into the experimental group and companies without green projects into the control group based on the description of green projects in the "Green Credit Statistical Statement" issued by China Banking Regulatory Commission in 2013.

This study finds that the expansion of qualified collateral by the central bank of China improves the financing availability of green credit enterprises, and extends their loan maturity structure, and the financing availability effect is more significant for private enterprises. In addition, the expansion of qualified collateral reduces the financing cost of green credit enterprises, and this effect mainly exists in state-owned enterprises.Moreover, the effects of the expansion policy are heterogenous across industries. In the green industry, the policy effect is mainly on the financing availability, while in the pollution industry, the policy effect is mainly on the financing cost. The above conclusions indicate that the central bank should further improve the system of eligible collateral framework, attach great importance to the collateral framework for bank financing constraints and credit preference regulation, and give full play to the eligible collateral in its directional support for the green resource allocation function of the financial system.

This paper mainly focuses on the green financial effect of the monetary policy—the expansion of the collateral framework—in China. Whether this new monetary policy can be transmitted to the green production level needs further analysis. The relationship between the new monetary policy and green development still needs to be explored.

# Population Ageing, Pension Fund Gap Compensation and Economic Growth

LYU Youji    JING Peng    ZHENG Wei

(School of Finance, Nankai University; School of Insurance, Southwestern University of Finance and Economics; School of Economics, Peking University)

With the continuous deepening of the population ageing in China in recent years, the shortage of the Employees' Basic Pension Fund has become increasingly severe and the downward pressure on economic growth has become more significant. The "system concept" put forward by the fifth plenary session of the 19th Central Committee of the Communist Party of China calls for the strengthen of overall planning. As stable and rapid economic growth is essential for pension system's sustainable operation, it is important to discuss about the pension fund gap issue under the framework of economic growth.

This paper constructs an overlapping generations model that includes fiscal expenditure and public debt to examine the impact of population ageing on economic growth, and compares the methods of pension fund gap compensation in promoting economic growth. Our analyses reveal that: (i) if fiscal subsidies are used to compensate for the pension fund gap, both the raised survival probability and the declined fertility will increase economic growth; (ii) if public debts or a combination of fiscal subsidies and public debts are used to compensate for the pension fund gap, the above conclusion holds when the output elasticity of human capital is small, but the effect of the raised survival probability on economic growth follows an inverted U-shape pattern and the effect of the declined fertility on economic growth is positive when the elasticity is large; (iii) the way to compensate for the pension fund gap is an essential institutional factor for economic growth.

This paper has three main contributions. First, in terms of research ideas, this paper uses the pension fund gap as the breakthrough point to achieve an organic combination of population ageing, pension fund gap compensation methods, and economic growth, and clarifies the influencing mechanism of population ageing and pension fund gap compensation methods on economic growth. Second, in terms of model construction, this paper comprehensively considers the substitution effect of the compensation for pension fund gap on productive public expenditures and private material capital, and discusses several core issues of the overlapping generations model, such as the stability, dynamic effectiveness, and debt sustainability of the economic equilibrium.Third, in terms of research conclusions, this paper depicts the evolution characteristics of population ageing and economic growth under different pension fund gap compensation methods, and puts forward methods that are most conducive to promoting economic growth under different conditions.

Based on the above conclusions, this paper draws three policy implications. First, at the conceptual level, it should be recognized that population ageing is an issue with both challenges and opportunities, which needs to be addressed with a positive attitude.Second, at the institutional level, the institutional exploration and policy reserve of pension fund gap compensation methods should be done well under the guidance of the "system concept" and in combination with the specific national conditions.Considering that the leading force of China's economic growth is still the material capital, and the output elasticity of the human capital is relatively small, exploring ways to compensate for the pension fund gap, including issuing public debts, will better optimize the long-term development path of the economy and society, and realize a good interaction between the pension system and economic growth.Third, at the technical level, the combination of policy tools to compensate for the pension fund gap should be determined dynamically based on quantification to improve the efficiency of national governance. In particular, the government should adopt more active debt management policies when issuing public debts to avoid the decline in economic stability caused by the expansion of debt scale, so as to achieve steady and rapid economic growth.

This paper constructs a theoretical analysis framework of the relationship between population ageing, pension fund gap compensation methods, and economic growth.Future research can be expanded from at least two aspects. First, considering that children's support is still an essential part of old-age support in China, the mechanism of "raising children for old-age support" can be introduced in future studies to better depict the motivation of individuals to invest in human capital. Second, the expansion of the debt scale weakens economic stability, which puts forward higher requirements for the debt management ability of the government. How to regulate the debt scale to achieve a smooth transition of the economy between different equilibriums is a key issue to be solved urgently.

# Aging, Consumption Composition and the Development of Services

YAN Se   GUO Kaiming   DUAN Xueqin

(Guanghua School of Management, Peking University; Lingnan College, Sun Yat-sen University; Guangzhou Branch, Industrial and Commercial Bank of China)

Most economies that have undergone industrialization have found that the age structure of the population and the industrial structure have also changed. This change in age structure is known as the aging problem, and it is the demographic result of a lower fertility rate and longer life expectancy. The change in the industrial structure is known as "Kuznets facts", a set of trends that includes a rising share of services, a falling share of agriculture, and an inverted-u shaped share of manufacturing. The development of China's economy during the reform era has exhibited these trends, but with some critical problems. First, China's population is rapidly aging, but China is still a middle-income country. Thus, the onset of the aging problem before China becomes a high-income country may hinder further development. Second, although the share of services has grown steadily in China, it is still relatively low, and its structure should be improved. In fact, the processes of population aging and structural change are not taking place independently. Based on cross-country data from recent decades, this paper finds that the relationship between population aging and the share of services depends on economic development. As per-capita income rises, the relationship changes from negative to positive.

This paper incorporates the age structure into a two-sector model with an income effect and a price effect, and studies the effect of aging on the rise of services. In the model, people of different ages have various preferences for goods and services. In particular, elasticities of income for goods or services and the elasticity of substitution between them can change with age. The paper shows that aging can change the share of services through the mechanisms of the income effect and the price effect. For the income effect mechanism, the direction of the effect of aging depends on the survival level of consumption for goods, and the magnitude depends on per-capita consumption. For the price effect mechanism, the direction of the effect of aging depends on the magnitude of the effect of relative price on the consumption composition for people of different ages. When per-capita income is low, the income effect dominates, so the effect of aging on the share of services is negative. However, as per-capita income grows, the income effect diminishes, while the price effect becomes the dominant mechanism, causing the effect of aging on services to change from negative to positive.

We calibrate the model with cross-country data from 1995-2010, and quantitatively evaluate the effect of aging on the share of services in different circumstances. We find that the effect of aging also depends on the degree of aging and the relative productivity between sectors. Moreover, when the elasticity of substitution between goods and services is low for young people and high for old people, or older people's survival level of consumption for goods is low, a rising degree of aging is likely to increase the share of services. The results are robust if we change the consumption rate of sectoral output or the labor mobility cost.

We derive two policy implications from the findings.

First, our findings are helpful for evaluating the effect of aging on the share of services in different countries. The results not only explain the stylized fact that the effect of aging on services changes from negative to positive along with development, but also highlight the factors that influence the effect of aging in different countries. In developing countries like China, per-capita consumption is low, so aging before becoming a high-income country could hinder the rise of services. In developed countries, the effect of aging may differ, depending on its degree. Thus, to evaluate the effect of aging on industrial structure in different countries, it is necessary to pay attention to factors like the differences in the preferences of people of different ages, the level of per-capita consumption, and the degree of aging.

Second, we suggest that China's government should deal with the aging problem and develop services in the following ways. (i) ensuring that per-capita income grows steadily and increasing the share of private consumption could diminish the negative effect of aging on services. (ii) lowering the relative price of services by increasing the relative productivity of the service sector could also diminish the negative effect of aging on services. (iii) decreasing the wage gap between sectors and removing institutional barriers in labor mobility could promote the development of services. (iv) developing producer services to increase the value- added share of services in investment goods could attract more labor to produce investment goods in the service sector.

# The Impact of Automation and Artificial Intelligence on China's Labor Market: Quantity and Intensity of Employment

ZHOU Guangsu  LI Lixing  MENG Lingsheng

(School of Labor and Human Resources, Renmin University of China; National School of Development, Peking University; Department of Economics, the Chinese University of Hong Kong)

Automation and artificial intelligence (AI) are major trends in the workplace that have significantly improved production efficiency. Through the Internet +, big data, and cloud computing, AI has sparked a global technological revolution that has changed the traditional social order. While automation and AI have a positive impact on economic growth, they also negatively affect many traditional occupations. Many jobs may be replaced by automation. Studies show that the decline in the employment and wages of low-and medium-skilled workers can be attributed to the application of automation and AI. The rapid development of the AI industry and the aging of the population have drawn attention to how automation and AI affect China's labor market. Unlike the previous three technological revolutions in which machines and equipment replaced manual labor, automation and AI are being integrated into the production process. This not only requires machines to approximate human dexterity, but, more importantly, it means that machines are gradually developing cognitive abilities similar to those of a human. This transformation will have a significant impact on the labor market. In China, the impact of automation and AI will be more pronounced, partly because China is at the forefront of AI development, and partly because of its large population and labor-intensive industrial structure. However, little research (especially quantitative research) examines how China's labor market will be affected by automation and AI. This study estimates the effect of automation and AI on China's labor market and suggests relevant countermeasures.

Based on Frey and Osborne's (2017) estimation of the probability of computerization for 702 detailed occupations, this paper estimates the probability that each occupation in China will be replaced by automation.Based on these estimates, we use data from latest Census and China Family Panel Studies to estimate the automation-substitution probability by city, and gauge the macro impact of automation on China's labor market. Finally, we empirically examine the effect of automation on labor market outcomes, such as employment at the city level and individual working hours. The results show that automation has a significant and negative impact on employment but a positive impact on working hours. The effect is larger among vulnerable groups in the labor market, such as women, those with a low level of education, the elderly, and migrants.

The contributions of this paper are as follows. First, it shows how the labor market in developing countries is affected by automation. Second, it estimates the replacement probability for each occupation in China, and comprehensively assesses the possible substitution effect of automation. Third, it estimates the impact of automation on the quantity and intensity of employment and conducts a heterogeneity analysis using labor force characteristics, to provide a comprehensive assessment of the impact of automation. Finally, the paper uses data on EU robots as a proxy for AI in China to examine the impact of AI on the labor market from different perspectives.

Although this study focuses on showing correlations rather than inferring causality, it is nonetheless informative about the impact of automation and AI on China's labor market, and has important policy implications. While China promotes the development of new technologies such as AI, it needs to address their potential negative impact on the labor market. First, this impact needs to be comprehensively assessed, because its effect will differ across industries and workers.Second, more attention needs to be paid to vulnerable groups in the labor market (e.g., women, low-educated workers, older workers, and migrants). Efforts to improve their labor skills and human capital through vocational training are needed to alleviate the negative impact of automation and AI on them. Finally, attention needs to be paid to the impact of automation and AI on the welfare of workers, particularly the polarization of income and social class. Technological progress needs to be harnessed to promote economic development while improving the welfare of workers and maintaining social equity.

# Capital Return, Property Rights Protection and Regional Fund Agglomeration

CAO Tingqiu    ZHANG Cuiyan

(School of Economics, Shandong University)

Since the reform and opening up, China's economy has made remarkable achievements, but it also faces problems such as gradually widening unbalanced development gap and insufficient coordination of regions. It has been widely recognized that the gap is affected by the allocation of financial resources and the regional coordinated development cannot do without the support of financial resources, which come from domestic commercial and fiscal financing, foreign investment and other funds in China. According to the neoclassical theory, the profit-seeking nature of capital will drive funds to flow to regions with high return on capital.However, the international capital flow does not always follow this model, so the famous "Lucas paradox" appears. Then what factors drive the inter-regional capital flow in China? The theory of efficient allocation of resources indicates that under the same risk level, the profit-seeking and risk-avoiding characteristics of capital will prompt capital to flow to enterprises, industries and sections with high capital efficiency, while under the same capital efficiency level, it will drive capital to flow to those with low risks. This paper studies the driving factors of regional capital agglomeration considering both capital return and property rights protection, and accurately measures the degree of regional capital agglomeration according to the sources of capitals in China, which is practically important to realize the efficient market-oriented allocation of production factors, build a high-quality land spatial layout and promote regional coordinated development.

This paper constructs the capital agglomeration index based on the sources of capital, including bank loan, securities market financing, central project investment, transfer payment and foreign investment. By analyzing and counting the capital situation among provinces in China from 1985 to 2017, it is found that the inter-regional capital flows have changed greatly with the capital difference between the eastern and western regions gradually narrowed. As far as the source structure of funds is concerned, central projects and transfer payments are the main sources in the central and western regions, while loans and securities market financing in the eastern regions. Using the Fixed Effect model (FE) and the Instrumental Variable method (IV) of panel fixed effect to estimate the parameters, we find that there is a non-linear relationship between capital and return on capital, with U-shape in the eastern region and inverted U-shape in the non-eastern region, and a critical value condition for the occurrence of profit-seeking behavior of capital. The statistics of the critical value show that the returns on capital of most provinces in the eastern regions are on the right side of the lowest point, while those in the non-eastern region are on the right side of the highest point, indicating strong profit-seeking for the eastern capitals and weak for non-eastern capitals because of a high proportion of transfer payment in the central and western capitals. More capital is gathered in areas with good contracting institution while the property institution does not significantly promote capital agglomeration. The regional heterogeneity of the relationship between capital and property rights implies that the eastern region should pay attention to improving property rights institution, while the western region should focus on the improvement of contracting institution, so as to create a "wind vane" to attract capitals.

However, it must be realized that the higher rate of return on capital and the strong profit-seeking nature of capitals in the eastern region will drive the further flow of funds from the west to the east, which will widen the economic development gap in the long run. A large flow of funds to the east will aggravate the excessive financialization and cause funds to be diverted out of the real economy in the east, while serious financing constraints due to lack of funds will directly hinder western economic development. The local government should promote the reform of property right institution and the market allocation of factors according to the local actual situation, control the rate of return on capital within a certain range to absorb long-term stable financial support and make a better combination of efficient market and promising government for coordinated development of regions in China.

# Industrial Policy, Innovation Behavior and Firms' Markups: Research on the Policy of Strategic Emerging Industries

ZHU Zhujun　SONG Xueyin　ZHANG Shengli　CHEN Lifang

(School of Economics, Zhejiang Gongshang University; School of Economics, Zhejiang University; Xiamen National Accounting Institute)

During the 14th Five-Year Plan period, China has set forth new requirements for the development of strategic emerging industries and new goals of "characteristic development, complementary advantages and reasonable structure". Industrial development should focus on seizing opportunities for future industrial development and cultivating leading and pillar industries. However, it remains unclear how to develop strategic emerging industries and transform industrial policy support from quantity-oriented to quality-and efficiency-oriented.

This paper studies the mechanism and effective support space of industrial policy on firms' markups. The results show that first, the strategic emerging industry policy has significant positive effect, because firm's productivity and R&D are relatively high in this industry. Second, in terms of the mechanism, strategic emerging industry policies affect firms' markups through the cost and price channels. Currently (1998-2013), the negative cost effect is greater than the positive price effect, resulting in an overall negative effect. Third, in terms of heterogeneity, the industrial technology gap has a significant negative moderating effect on firms' markups, and a positive trend is observed between this effect and the technological convergence level. Fourth, further analysis shows that the innovation trap of focusing on quantity but neglecting quality, a consequence of support, is the main cause of decreasing overall markups.

This paper presents innovations in several areas.Theoretically, it explores the mechanism by which industrial policy affects firms' markups in the context of China's efforts to catch up with more developed economies. It amends industrial policy support theory and considers the technology gap in its conceptualization of the support space.Empirically, this paper reveals the effect of the strategic emerging industries policy on firm markups. Previous studies have obvious sample selection bias and fail to observe dynamic changes in markups (Lu et al., 2014; Liu, 2016). This paper uses industrial firm database records from 1998 to 2013 to study the effect of the strategic emerging industries policy, and it uses patent data with complete citation information to estimate patent quality. The innovation incentive of emphasizing quantity but neglecting quality, a consequence of the strategic emerging industry policy, is identified as the main cause of the negative markup effect. In terms of policy, this paper provides empirical evidence for the optimal implementation space of industrial policy. From the perspective of the technology gap, this paper provides an effective approach to oplimizing the policy implementation space and to promoting the dynamic evolution of government support from pioneering to enabling. This transition can enhance the effectiveness of industrial policy and promote the development of high-quality innovations.

This paper also has several policy implications. First, the levels of industrial development, quality and efficiency should be considered crucial targets of industrial policy support. Policymakers should consider relaxing the assessment of the total number of patents and number of patents per capita, not setting binding indicators, reducing selective subsidies, strengthening the dynamic tracking of patent implementation and rewarding patent achievements with a good industrialization effect and high degree of marketization at a later time. Also, the combination of industrial policy implementation and the industrial technology gap should be maintained.Second, optimization of the market environment and government functions is a crucial strategy to improve the quality of strategic emerging industries. In the early stage, industrial development mainly depends on a high-quality business environment and competitive neutral market environment, and the government effectively handles market competition as a regulator. When the technology gap is relatively small, the government should effectively manage market competition and drive innovation as an enabler. Third, the deep integration of strategic emerging industries and various industries should be targeted for the optimization of industrial policy. A reliance on high-quality innovations by strategic emerging industries should expand the number of important products and key core technologies in the industrial supply chain, focus on upstream core links and enhance the ability of the chain owner to lead and drive the industrial supply chain. Key departments should be created to effectively link the innovation and industrial chains and enhance modernization of the industrial and supply chains.

## 02　Financial Stability & Risk Management

### Corporate Leverage in China: Is it a Cyclical Problem?

LU Ting　XU Qiyuan

(Institute of World Economics and Politics, Chinese Academy of Social Science)

The business cycle can influence corporate leverage through various channels. It not only affects firms' financial needs, but also alters their financing environments and the speed of their adjustment to target capital structures. However, most of the empirical literature addressing the relationship between the business cycle and corporate leverage overlooks the potential indirect effects, and tends to draw conclusions about leverage dynamics merely from the coefficients of recession dummies or macroeconomic variables in empirical models. This practice is criticized by Halling et al. (2016), who regard it as a ceteris paribus approach that captures only the marginal effect of the business cycle on corporate leverage.

Based on a dynamic partial adjustment model of capital structure, this paper moves away from the ceteris paribus approach and presents a comprehensive empirical analysis of actual corporate leverage dynamics over the business cycle. Following Halling et al. (2016), we identify the direct effect of the business cycle by observing the estimated coefficient of the recession dummy and capture its indirect effects through variation in explanatory variables and model parameters such as the following: (i) changing firm characteristics; (ii) changing relationships between firm characteristics and leverage; and (iii) changes in the speed of adjustment to the firm's target capital structure.

We then quantify the impact of the business cycle on corporate leverage using the 1996-2013 annual data from the Chinese Industrial Enterprises

Database. Our results indicate that the direct effect of the business cycle on corporate leverage is pro-cyclical, as previous studies suggest, while the indirect effects consistently and robustly contribute to the counter-cyclical behavior of corporate leverage across all empirical specifications. Due to these counter-movements, the overall effect of the business cycle on leverage dynamics is statistically significant but economically trivial. In other words, the actual firm leverage exhibits a weak pro-cyclical characteristic.

We also categorize the firms according to their ownership and examine whether the impact of the business cycle differs between kinds of ownership. The leverage ratio of state-owned enterprises (SOEs) experiences even less cyclicality than that of private enterprises. This partially explains the time-varying divergence in leverage ratios observed in China between SOFs and private enterprises. The leverage ratio of private enterprises fluctuates as the economic environment changes, while the less financially constrained SOEs can maintain a more stable leverage ratio. The differences in their sensitivity to the business cycle cause variation along the time dimension.

Our paper contributes to and broadens the literature on business cycles and leverage dynamics. By decomposing leverage dynamics into different sources, we document that both the direct and indirect effects of the business cycle play important roles in causing leverage variations. We therefore quantify the overall influence of the business cycle on corporate leverage and provide new evidence for the cyclicality debate in leverage dynamics. Unlike many previous studies, which rely on data from listed companies, the dataset we use eliminates the bias caused by public offering. Our paper offers a more thorough investigation of the relationship between the business cycle and corporate leverage, and it improves our understanding of the mechanisms of leverage dynamics.

Most importantly, our study's empirical findings provide preliminary micro-foundations for reflecting on the division and coordination of the two-pillar framework. Countercyclical monetary policy works against the ongoing boom or recession trend and aims at eliminating the fluctuations associated with the business cycle.Therefore, the weak pro-cyclical characteristic of firm leverage suggests that countercyclical monetary policy will not automatically stabilize corporate leverage.Other policy tools, such as macro-prudential policies, are indispensable to keep leverage levels stable and prevent systemic risk. China needs to improve the two-pillar regulatory framework further to strike a balance between stabilizing growth and preventing risks.

# Monitoring Systemic Financial Risks: Construction and State Identification of China's Financial Market Stress Index

LI Minbo  LIANG Shuang

(Financial Stability Bureau, the People's Bank of China)

For the central bank to maintain financial stability and carry out macro-prudential management, it is essential to have timely and efficient monitoring of financial market conditions. The stability of financial institutions depends on the conditions of the financial market, and the effects of monetary policy and macro-prudential policy are transmitted through the financial market; the policies themselves are also responses to financial market conditions. In addition, financial market data contain highly forward-looking information.Major changes in the financial and economic system, such as policy adjustments and stress events, will be reflected in the financial market data. The central bank also needs to closely monitor financial market conditions to select the policy implementation window in advance, make adjustments during policy implementation, and evaluate the policy effect. A good method of monitoring the overall risk level of the financial market is to construct a financial market stress index with selected indicators of the financial market. Overseas researchers and institutions, and more recently domestic researchers, have extensively explored the construction of financial market stress indexes. Most financial market stress indexes constructed by domestic researchers can identify financial market stress events, but the index construction and stress state identification still show deficiencies.The frequencies of financial market stress indexes in the literature are relatively low, as they are limited by data availability and construction methods. Some studies use indicators such as the non-performing loan ratio of the banking sector, but the data have some lag and can be manipulated. We believe that constructing a financial market stress index with pure financial market data can address the deficiencies of the literature. Furthermore, as interest rate liberalization continues, the representativeness and effectiveness of a financial market stress index that measures systemic financial risk using financial market data will be further improved. In this paper, the construction of the financial market stress index involves two steps. The first is the construction of each sub- market stress index, and the second involves compiling the full financial market stress index based on these sub-market stress indexes. This paper selects 17 indicators, calculated with transaction data from China's bond market, stock market, money market, and foreign exchange market, to construct sub-market stress indexes using the empirical cumulative distribution function method. It then constructs the financial market stress index with the sub-market stress indexes, using the time-varying correlation between them to depict the cross-market contagion characteristics of systemic financial risk. The purpose of constructing the financial market stress index is to monitor and evaluate the stress level of the financial market, especially high stress states. Some studies define a high stress state as occurring when the current value of the financial market stress index exceeds the mean of its historical values by a specified number of standard deviations.Other studies determine stress states by comparing the current value of the financial stress index with its values during the financial crisis.None of these methods make sufficient use of the information contained in the financial market stress index. The Markov regime switching model proposed by Hamilton is a more proper method for identifying financial market stress states. This paper assumes that there are two stress states in the financial market—high and medium-to-low, which is preliminarily supported by the analysis of the historical distribution of the financial market stress index. It then establishes the Markov regime switching model to identify stress states.Through back testing, our financial market stress index is found to accurately reflect historical stress events; for example, the large number of securities firms on the verge of bankruptcy in 2003, the global financial crisis of 2007-2008, the European sovereign debt crisis, interbank liquidity strains in June 2013, abnormal stock market fluctuations in 2015, and the COVID-19 outbreak, Our financial market stress index, which has the advantages of robustness and high frequency, is a powerful tool to monitor and evaluate systemic financial risk, select a policy implementation window, and evaluate the policy effect.

# Asset Transparency, Regulatory Arbitrage, and Bank Systemic Risk

CHEN Guojin    JIANG Xiaoyu    LIU Yanzhen    ZHAO Xiangqin

(Wang Yanan Economic Research Institute/School of Economics, Xiamen University; Research Institute, The People's Bank of China)

Regulatory arbitrage and opacity of bank assets were important causes of the 2007-2008 global financial crisis. The full disclosure of information reduces the probability of bank bankruptcy and systemic risk.Banks with greater asset transparency are better able to convey solvency information to the outside world, which makes it easier to attract external refinancing. Conversely, the solvency uncertainty caused by asset opacity may lead to banking crises.Macroprudential regulation, such as bank capital adequacy ratio regulation, has focused on regulating business on balance sheets. In this context, banks are motivated to move business outside their balance sheets to avoid financial regulation and profit from regulatory arbitrage. There are currently few theoretical or empirical studies on the effects of asset transparency and regulatory arbitrage on banks' systemic risk.

This paper addresses the differences between interbank wholesale financing and retail deposits in depositor market supervision. It further addresses the use of wholesale financing (represented by interbank certificates of deposit) for regulatory arbitrage. Unlike traditional assets and liabilities such as deposits and loans, wholesale financing avoids both investor and depositor supervision and regulatory restrictions. This reduces bank asset transparency and makes banks take greater risks, and excessive connectedness.

This paper first introduces the classical bank moral hazard model in relation to the concepts of bank asset transparency and regulatory arbitrage (represented by correlated risk). We further analyze the effects of asset transparency and regulatory arbitrage on banks' systemic risk from the perspective of theoretical modeling. We also undertake empirical analysis of these effects based on our theoretical model.Drawing on the Wind and Bankfocus databases, we use the rolling window, SRISK and MES methods to measure the asset transparency and systemic risk of China's commercial banks. We fully control for bank level characteristics and macroeconomic factors that may affect systemic risk.

We find that regulatory arbitrage and low asset transparency lead to higher systemic risk. In the case of regulatory arbitrage, the correlation of bank risks and the risk externality of "rarely standing or falling alone" reduce the incentive for bank supervision. This results in collective failure and higher systemic risk. Banks no longer rely entirely on the deposit market for refinancing when interbank regulatory arbitrage occurs. The constraint of transparency on bank risk is weakened and the problem of moral hazard is further aggravated. As a lack of asset transparency weakens banks' financing ability in the deposit market, banks become more active in interbank regulatory arbitrage. Banks may opt for more opaque and risky investments.The homogeneity of assets and risk contagion from interbank certificates of deposit make the banking system more vulnerable. Regulatory arbitrage also weakens the effect of capital regulation on banks' systemic risk.

This paper's contributions are as follows. First, we study systemic risk at the bank level. This paper relaxes the independence setting and introduces asset transparency in the case of heterogeneous portfolios (allowing correlation). We also study the influence of asset transparency on banks' systemic risk. This paper therefore enriches research on the relationship between DELR and bank accounting choice and individual/systemic risk. It also details the mechanism of regulatory arbitrage and its coordination with capital regulation.Second, we study the asymmetric responses of systemically important banks to deposit market supervision using correlation and the setting of creditor and debtor banks. This is another way to support research on the distortion of retail deposit markets by "too big to fail" banks. Third, we add to the retail deposit market literature from the perspective of the wholesale funding market and banks' systemic risk. We also fill the gap in research related to bank asset transparency and wholesale funding such as shadow banking and Internet finance.

# Nonlinear Analysis of the Determinants of Tail Risk: New Evidence from the Panel Smooth Transition Regression Model

YANG Zihui    CHEN Yutian    LIN Shihan    GUAN Zihuan

(Lingnan College, Sun Yat-Sen University; Institute of Advanced Finance, Sun Yat-Sen University)

Small financial institutions frequently encounter tail risk events such as insolvency and significant decline in asset quality in the post-crisis period. These events challenge the traditional supervisory concept of "too big to fail". There is currently growing uncertainly in the capital market and increasing economic downward pressure. The Chinese capital market is also undergoing accelerating reform. It is therefore academically and practically important to investigate the intrinsic tie between bank size and tail risk and to explore the determinants of tail risk.

This paper complements and expands the literature with a high level of originality. First, most domestic literature addresses risk contagion between financial institutions. There is little discussion of whether the "too big to fail" theory can be applied under China's actual economic conditions. Second, there is currently little consensus regarding the direction of effect of bank size on tail risk. The literature suggests that the fundamental variables of financial institutions actually play an important role in this relationship (Buch et al., 2019). Research highlights the need to include fundamental variables in the model to evaluate the heterogenous impacts of institution size on risk-taking more efficiently. Third, linear baseline regression models are often used when researching driving factors of tail risk. However, examining the relationships among variables under the traditional linear empirical framework may result in great bias, as indicated by Acemoglu et al. (2015) and De Vita et al. (2018). This bias makes it difficult to identify the risk sources in the financial system. Finally, research is likely to overlook the fact that the economic reform process exhibits an incremental trajectory in China when analyzing the nonlinear interconnectedness among variables. It is therefore more appropriate to discuss the smooth evolution of tail risk in China under the panel smooth transition regression (PSTR) model.

Our sample consists of 44 Chinese listed financial institutions, comprising 11 banks and 33 non-bank institutions. The sample period runs from January 2008 to June 2020. MES is constructed to represent the tail risk level in this paper. All the data come from the Wind database.

Our paper uses the dominance analysis method developed by Israeli (2007) and Givoly et al. (2019) to investigate the contributions of bank size and other fundamental variables to banks' tail risks. We find that bank size is not the only main determinant of bank risk; variables such as the non-performing loan ratio, personal housing loan ratio, and non-interest income ratio are also significant in the model. We next introduce the marginal effect analysis technique and provide strong evidence of the heterogeneous effects of fundamental variables on tail risk conditional on bank size. Using the PSTR model proposed by Cheikh and Zaied (2020) and González et al. (2017), this paper further discusses the nonlinear impact of bank size on tail risk and the roles of other fundamental variables in this relationship. The result indicates that an increase in the size of banks reduces the tail risk of the financial system in a highly nonlinear way. The reduction of tail risk depends on fundamental variables such as franchise value, asset quality, leverage, cost, income structure, and loan portfolio. The conclusions remain consistent and robust even when we extend our sample to 44 financial institutions. We also find that the evolution of tail risk is more volatile in financial institutions than in the banking sector.

Our findings yield three important policy implications. First, the tail risks of small financial institutions deserve stronger supervisory attention and differentiated regulatory responses, especially at the level of cost management. Second, it is more appropriate to deleverage the financial sector gradually than in a rush.Finally, stronger integrated financial supervision is urgently needed to meet the emerging trend of cross mixed operation in the Chinese financial market. This paper thereby enhances insights into how to deepen financial reform and achieve high-quality economic development in China both theoretically and empirically.

# The Impact of Financial Cycle on Real Estate Prices: An Empirical Study Based on a SV-TVP-VAR Model

QIAN Zongxin    WANG Fang    SUN Ting

(School of Finance, Renmin University of China; China Securities)

Many papers, when constructing indices of China's financial cycle, include indicators of real estate market conditions as components. However, although many researchers believe that China's real estate sector and financial sector are closely related, there has been little research on this dynamic relationship. In this paper, we attempt to fill this gap by studying the dynamic impact of China's financial cycle on the real estate price. We do this in two steps.

In the first step, we construct an index of China's financial cycle that comprises five financial indicators: stock market performance, interest rate, capital flow, leverage, and money supply. We aggregate the five indicators as a simple average.

In the second step, we construct a three-variate vector autoregressive (VAR) model that includes an indicator of real activities, an indicator of real estate price, and our index of China's financial cycles. The VAR model has a few characteristics. First, we allow the regression coefficients to change over time. Second, we allow the size of the economic shocks to vary over time. Third, we use a recursive scheme to identify structural economic shocks. These characteristics are important for the following reasons. First, China's economy is continuously under reform. These reforms could cause structural changes in the dynamic relationship between the real estate and financial sectors, and omitting those structural changes could lead to misleading results. Allowing the coefficients of the VAR to vary over time should capture those structural changes. Second, due to the changing domestic and foreign economic environment, sources of economic uncertainty change over time. As a result, the size of the shocks to our endogenous variables might also change over time. Third, it is well known that simply interpreting the error terms of the reduced-form VAR as economic shocks omits contemporary correlations between endogenous variables, which can lead to misleading conclusions. Therefore, our VAR model is a structural vector autoregressive model with stochastic volatility and time-varying parameters. The variables in the model are entered in the following order: first, the indicator of real activities, second, the indicator of real estate price, and third, our index of China's financial cycle.

We estimate our model using quarterly data from 2004 to 2016. When constructing our index of China's financial cycles, we use the Shanghai stock market index as the indicator of stock market performance. We use the 7-day inter-bank market interest rate to represent interest rates; the ratio of fixed assets financed by credit to total fixed assets investment as the indicator of leverage; the ratio of the capital and financial account balance to GDP as the indicator of capital flow; and the year-on-year $M_2$ growth rate as the indicator of money supply. Our indicator of real activities is the year-on-year GDP growth rate. Our indicator of real estate price is the China Quality-Controlled Housing Price Index.

The results show that the structural economic shocks to China's economy vary in size over time. The volatility of real activities reached its peak in 2009 and then gradually declined. This suggests that China's macroeconomic policies have helped to stabilize economic growth since the global financial crisis. The volatility of the real estate price also demonstrates a declining trend. However, the trend reversed in 2014 and the real estate price volatility increased until 2016. These results suggest that China's real estate market was developing stably. However, uncertainty has increased in recent years (2015-2016). The volatility of our index of financial cycles gradually increases, suggesting that financial risk during the sample period deserves more attention.

The impact of financial cycle on real estate prices has obvious time-varying characteristics. Before 2008, financial market expansion had a stable influence on the promotion of housing prices, but since 2008, the impact has gradually weakened. Similar to financial shocks, the impact of the real economy on housing prices has also gradually decreased since 2008. This shows that regulatory policies have helped to greatly reduce the sensitivity of real estate prices to economic and financial shocks.The finding that the impact of financial cycles on the real estate price has weakened has important policy implications. A finance-led real estate boom is less likely, which means that the transmission from financial expansion to economic growth through the real estate sector has become less effective since 2008; instead, excessive financial risk-taking accumulates systemic risk. Macro-prudential policies regarding the real estate market are necessary.

# A Study of Risk Contagion Based on the Interaction Between Common Shocks and Idiosyncratic Risks: Evidence From the Simulation of Listed Banks in China

XU Guoxiang   WU Ting   WANG Ying

(School of Statistics and Management/Research Center for Applied Statistics, Shanghai University of Finance and Economics; School of Insurance, Shanghai Lixin University of Accounting and Finance; Alibaba Group)

"Systemic risk" is a widely used term that is difficult to define and quantify. The emergence and evolution of systemic risk resembles a "black box" with the process controlled by exogenous or endogenous shocks and where the contagion channels and orders dominated by various factors. To simplify the combination of factors involved, academics usually focus on three kinds of risk: internal contagion of idiosyncratic risk, extensive damage caused by external common shocks, and imbalance caused by the accumulation of risk over time. These three forms of risk are not exclusive, and usually occur simultaneously and interact with each other in real crises.

The key to identifying systemic risk events is to estimate the potential "system state" and evaluate the ability of these events to further change the "system state". The vulnerability of the entire system caused by external shocks determines the depth and breadth of idiosyncratic risk contagion. Thus, the results of this paper shed light on the effects of common external shocks on the banking system and establish a simplified interactive contagion model for common shocks and idiosyncratic risks. We introduce a systemic risk contagion model with three stages: original shocks, incremental shocks, and default shocks, based on their dominant risk factors.The model depicts the dynamic and interactive contagion process of common shocks and idiosyncratic risks, the effects of which spill over into the financial market and inter-bank debt chain.

The current paper has three main findings. First, losses caused by common shocks are much greater than those caused by idiosyncratic risks. Second, the key factors that determine the infection multiplier are size and network relevance, and network relevance has a stronger role in determining the infection multiplier when the size factor is not prominent.For example, it is often the case that small-scale and highly related banks have a higher infection multiplier. Third, the leverage that causes systemic loss is generally enhanced when the loss rate of the risk assets of the bank is between 10% and 25% . Furthermore, regulatory intervention by the government can effectively reduce the systemic risk.

This study makes the following contributions. First, we deconstruct common external shocks. We assume that there is a bank present to bear the external shock (called the "trigger bank").This bank's assets loss risk spills over in ordered layers throughout the banking network.The microcosmic simulation of common external shocks is helpful to depict the sensitivity of the systemic loss caused by the assets loss of a single bank (called the "infection multiplier"). As such, this finding will help to inform early warning systems and interventions in cases of systemic risk. Second, we build direct and indirect networks based on risk correlations. To distinguish the transmission paths of common risks and idiosyncratic risks, we construct a relationship network for common risk exposure and idiosyncratic risk exposure. The default order of banks is decided dynamically by mutual verification between the direct debt network of the interbank market and the indirect relational networks of common shock contagion models. Compared with the risk superposition model, this model not only better captures each stage of risk contagion, it also does not rely on the historical default data of banks. Third, we measure the systemic risk caused by different trigger banks. Compared with the leave-one-out method, which evaluates losses by directly removing a single bank one at a time, the trigger bank in this study remains in the simulation network until the solvency bankruptcy occurs. This more closely reflects a real risk scenario.

The conclusions of this study provide empirical evidence that will help to make regulatory decisions in the context of systemic risk. First, the results suggest that the assessment of common risk exposure in the banking system should be increased to control systemic risk from the source, and attention should be paid to the identification and evaluation of the network correlation of small and medium-sized banks. Second, in view of the inflection point, a phenomenon in which an infection multiplier triggers banks, we suggest that regulators intensify the blocking intervention mechanism against systemic risk, for example by setting an early warning rate of risk-weighted asset loss to prevent risk escalation.

## 03 Banking Operation & Financing

## Targeted RRR Cuts, Loan Availability, and the Trade Credit of SMEs: Evidence Based on Regression Discontinuity Design

KONG Dongmin    LI Haiyang    YANG Wei

(School of Finance, Zhongnan University of Economics and Law; School of Business, East China University of Science and Technology)

The smooth operation, transformation, and upgrade of the Chinese economy inevitably requires the comprehensive development of small and micro enterprises (SMEs). However, financing difficulties have severely restricted the growth of SMEs, causing them to resort to informal channels (such as trade credit) to obtain funds. The Fifth Plenary Session of the Nineteenth Central Committee of the Communist Party of China proposed to support the growth and transformation of SMEs into an important cradle of innovation and to improve policy to promote the development of SMEs. Among these efforts, the implementation of "precise drip irrigation" monetary policy is particularly important for the growth of SMEs and will help to further strengthen the function of financial services in the real economy. To encourage commercial banks and other financial institutions to provide more credit to SMEs and unblock the more formal channels (such as bank loans) through which SMEs can obtain financing, the People's Bank of China, China's central bank, began to implement targeted reserve requirement ratio cuts (TRRRCs) in June 2014.

In contrast to traditional "one size fits all" policies, TRRRCs lower the deposit reserve ratio for commercial banks and other financial institutions. This led to new loans to SMEs accounting for more than 50% of all new loans in 2020 in an attempt to incentivize the allocation of credit resources to weak yet important economic sectors such as SMEs. Therefore, TRRRCs are essentially a quantitative easing tool to improve access to finance for SMEs specifically.

While many studies have evaluated the effectiveness of TRRRCs, due to data availability and causal identification strategies, there is scant research evaluating the impact of TRRRCs on SMEs' other financing channels, such as trade credit, which is as important as bank loans for SMEs when obtaining funds. TRRRCs exert a significant influence on loan availability for SMEs whose sales fall below specific cutoffs. We can thus employ a fuzzy regression discontinuity design (RDD) and use the generated variation in loan availability to identify the impact of access to finance on the trade credit of SMEs. We conduct this RDD using the National Equities Exchange and Quotation's (NEEQ) financial disclosures data from the China Stock Market and Accounting Research Database. The results indicate that the demand for trade credit decreased significantly after the availability of loans for SMEs increased in response to TRRRCs. Furthermore, the allocation of bank loans is often consistent with the value discovery function of the bank. Banks can grant credit to high-quality companies and exert a supervisory function. Therefore, TRRRCs mainly improve loan availability for firms with fewer financial constraints and better market performance. The negative impact of loan availability on trade credit mainly exists among high-quality SMEs. The results are robust after choosing a different bandwidth, controlling for firm characteristics, sharpening the RDD, and excluding other sources of policy interference.

The contributions of this study are as follows. To the best of our knowledge, this is the first study to evaluate the effect of TRRRCs on SMEs' financing decisions. Moreover, the decision to obtain bank loans and trade credit for corporate financing is generally determined by various factors, and this may generate an endogeneity problem. By policy design, TRRRCs only target SMEs whose sales fall below a threshold. If the policy indeed changes loan availability, two kinds of firms whose sales are on the opposite side of the threshold but are otherwise similar will have different levels of financial access.Under this condition, we can use RDD to identify the impact of access to finance on trade credit. The results provide evidence that the substitution relationship between bank loans and trade credit dominates China's SMEs, which enriches the literature on the impact of monetary policy on corporate financing.

This study has clear policy implications. First, since TRRRCs improve SMEs' loan availability, this policy could be employed to ease the financing constraints on SMEs.Second, our results indicate that SMEs with fewer financial constraints decrease their trade credit due to the substitution of bank loans. Credit rationing leads to formal credit resources flowing into high-quality firms. Thus, policy makers are expected to introduce innovative financial policy tools that directly reach the real economy, in particular to help SMEs with severe financing difficulties.

One limitation of this study is that the sample is composed of firms listed on the NEEQ. However, SMEs are found throughout China. Improvements to China's financial information disclosure regulations and the development of data collection and storage capabilities will allow a more representative sample of the financing decision-making issues facing SMEs to be assessed in future research.

# Does Bank Competition Increase Firm Investment and Investment Efficiency? Evidence Based on the Geographical Distribution of Bank Branches

LI Zhisheng  JIN Ling

(School of Finance, Zhongnan University of Economics and Law)

  The five largest state-owned commercial banks dominated China's banking market before 2006, with more than 65% of the total lending business. This market was strictly regulated, and joint equity banks and local commercial banks were hard to establish branches outside the headquarter locations. Since the deregulations of 2006 and 2009, the China Banking Regulatory Commission has gradually relaxed the entry barriers for banks. The market share of joint equity banks and local commercial banks in lending thus increased from 13.10% in 2005 to 32.80% in 2017, and the proportion of their branches increased from 22.56% in 2005 to 41.87% in 2017. Bank deregulation also has major effects on the geographical distribution of branches, encouraging competition and enhancing banks' ability to support economic development.

  Previous research demonstrates that competition significantly enhances the ability of firms to obtain loans from banks and the efficiency of credit resource allocation. Due to the dominant role of the bank sector in China's financial system, bank loans are the most important source of the capital that fuels firm investment and local economic growth. Statistics from the People's Bank of China indicate that bank loans accounted for 71.19% of the social financing increment in 2017. Thus, changes in the geographical distribution of bank branches and the level of competition will have a major impact on firm investment and subsequent economic performance.

In this paper, we use the number of bank branches within a certain radius (i. e., 5, 10, or 20 km) around firms to measure the level of bank competition based on the address information of banks and firm headquarters. Using Chinese Industry Census data from 2001 to 2012, we investigate how changes in the geographical distribution and competition of banks affect firm investment and investment efficiency, and find that the number of bank branches around firm has a significantly positive effect. These findings are robust to a series of alternative empirical designs, such as changing the measures of bank competition, firm investment and investment efficiency, controlling for regional economic heterogeneity and potential reverse causality, and using the deregulation in 2009 as an exogenous shock. We also find that the positive impact of bank competition on investment efficiency is greater for a sample of underinvested and non-state-owned firms. Bank competition is also found to improve firms' investment efficiency, mainly by alleviating financial constraints and reducing agency conflicts.

This study makes various contributions to the literature. First, although research considers the relationship between bank competition and firms' ability to obtain loans from banks, few studies focus on the effect of bank competition on how firms utilize bank loans and their investment efficiency. Second, instead of the traditional bank competition indicators (i.e., concentration ratios or the number of banks in specific regions), we use the number of branches around a firm to evaluate its bank competition environment, which can effectively address the heterogeneity in competition faced by different firms in the same region. Third, although the influence of geographical distribution on macro-economic growth and bank performance is empirically investigated, few studies address the effect on micro-firms. Thus, we contribute to the literature by investigating the impact of bank branch geographical distribution on firm investment and investment efficiency using a large-scale micro sample.

Our work also has important policy implications. China is attempting to develop a market-oriented banking system with more accessible, more affordable, and higher-quality financial services. We find that the increase in bank branch coverage and bank competition has a positive impact on firm investment and investment efficiency. These findings provide empirical support for the marketization reform of China's banking industry and the development of inclusive finance. When conducting supply-side structural reform in the financial sector, China should continue to strengthen market mechanisms and institutions in the banking industry and facilitate high-quality development through market competition.

# Financial Leasing, Bank Credit and Enterprise Investment

ZHAO Na    WANG Bo    ZHANG Keyu

(School of Economics, Nankai University; School of Finance, Nankai University; Hanqing Advanced Institute of Economics and Finance, Renmin University of China)

Financial leasing has been developing rapidly and become one of the closest financial forces connected with the real economy in the context of new economic normal. It provides a possibility for private capital to flow into formal financing channels. It also provides financing opportunities for private enterprises and small and medium-sized enterprises, and makes up for the lack of state-owned banks' financing functions. As financial leasing and bank credit are equally important financing channels, their relationship and whether financial leasing can serve as an effective alternative to traditional financing channels to promote corporate investment are worthy of in-depth consideration. These issues are also very important for improving financing channels' ability to accurately serve the real economy, establishing a multi-level market system, ensuring stability on the six fronts and security in the six areas.

Domestic and foreign literature on the relationship between financial leasing and bank credit is mainly based on two theories: the debt replacement theory (Myers et al., 1976) and the complementary theory (Lewis and Schallheim, 1992). However, more than 90% transactions in China's current leasing market are financial leasing, of which sale-and-leaseback transactions account for a large proportion, reaching as high as 83.9% in 2015. Operating leasing transactions account for only 12.5%. Therefore, it is difficult to apply the complementary theoretical mechanism in China based on the current development of leasing industry and the characteristics of taxation arrangements. In this paper, we manually collect the financial leasing data from the annual reports of all A-share listed companies in China's Shanghai and Shenzhen stock exchanges during 2004 to 2016 for empirical testing.The results show that both financial leasing and bank credit can significantly increase company's investment rate, and financial leasing has a significant substitution effect on bank credit.Since financing constraints play a very important role, we select corporate asset tangibility, asset-liability ratio and corporate ownership as indicators to explore the role they play in the substitution relationship. We find that tighter financing constraints are associated with greater substitution effect of financial leasing on bank credit.

Our study contributes to the literature in the following three aspects. First, most domestic research on financial leasing focuses on macro-level analyses, while there are relatively few micro-level studies (Shi and Xu, 2013). We empirically examine the substitution effect of financial leasing on bank credit from the enterprise level and provide micro evidence for the impact of financial leasing on economic growth, which enriches and expands the research scope of financial leasing. Second, existing research mostly discusses the quantitative change relationship between financial leasing and bank credit (Deloof and Verschueren, 1999; Lin et al, 2013), but this quantitative change may be affected by common factors such as corporate asset structure, etc., which may lead to endogenous problems and estimation biases. Moreover, the quantitative analyses cannot reflect the existence of the substitution effect. Therefore, according to the nature of substitutes in microeconomics, and based on the common characteristics of financial leasing and bank credit-their "financing" attribute as financing channels, we start from the perspective of corporate investment to test whether the substitution relationship between the two exists. Third, we analyze the impact of financing constraints on the substitution effect. The results show that for companies facing stronger financing constraints, financial leasing has a more obvious substitution effect on bank credit, which suggests that financial leasing has a comparative advantage in alleviating corporate financing constraints.

Our findings have the following policy implications. With the advantage of "integration of industry and finance", the government should actively promote the effective use of the dual attributes of financial leasing, improve its ability to accurately serve the real economy, and provide strong financial support for the construction of a new development pattern. At the same time, in regard to the "credit-like" function of financial leasing, especially the function of sale-and-leaseback transactions, the government should actively improve the relevant policies, standardize and guide them to return to their original source, and promote the transformation of the risk prevention of leasing business from the credit of the lessee to the credit of the leased property to better prevent and resolve systemic financial risks.

# De-capacity Policy and Financial Leasing

SHI Yanping    YANG Ting    PANG Jiaren

(School of International Trade and Economics, University of International Business and Economics; School of Economics and Management, North China University of Technology; School of Economics and Management, Tsinghua University)

Since the 19th National Congress of the Communist Party of China (NCCPC), China's economic development goal has changed from "high speed" to "high quality".The Fifth Plenary Session of the 19th NCCPC further pointed out that it is necessary to "accelerate the construction of a modern economic system with the theme of promoting high-quality development".In the context of the economic transition from "high speed" to "high quality", overcapacity has always been a problem that plagued the process of economic transformation. In order to control overcapacity, China have repeatedly issued de-capacity policies in the past ten years with policy tools covering financial, fiscal taxation and market access areas. The goal of the financial policy is to adjust the allocation of resources among industries from the funding source, limiting the funding channels of overcapacity enterprise and achieving the purpose of reducing overcapacity. After the de-capacity policy was promulgated, relevant financial institutions restricted loans and capital market financing to assist in reducing overcapacity.However, while bank loans and other financing methods for overcapacity enterprises have declined, the funds obtained through financial leasing have continued to increase. Is there some kind of regulatory arbitrage behind this phenomenon? What consequences will such a regulatory arbitrage have on the implementation of the de-capacity policy? This paper attempts to provide a possible theoretical explanation for the interaction mechanism between the de-capacity policy and financial leasing, and to confirm the theoretical explanation through empirical research.Specifically, this paper manually collects information on financial leasing transactions of Chinese listed companies, and uses the Difference in Differences (DID) method to identify the relationship between the de-capacity policy and financial leasing.

Our empirical results show that the de-capacity policy has significantly promoted the expansion of the scale of financial leasing, which in turn weakens the effect of the de-capacity policy to a certain extent. Further analysis shows that the de-capacity policy has promoted the expansion of the scale of financial leasing from both the demand side and the supply side.On the demand side, the de-capacity policy restricts overcapacity enterprises from obtaining long-term funds, thus expanding the long-term funding gap and prompting them to actively seek alternative funding channels such as financial leasing.On the supply side, the main channel for overcapacity enterprises to obtain financial leasing is bank-affiliated leasing companies, implying that there are bank funds evading supervision through financial leasing and flowing to overcapacity enterprises.

The innovations of this paper include two aspects.First, this paper provides new evidence for the causal relationship between financing constraints and financial leasing.Existing literature has pointed out that alleviating financing constraints is an important motivation of financial leasing.Enterprises with stronger financing constraints will use more financial leasing.However, these studies often suffer from endogenous problems in the identification of the relationship between financing constraints and financial leasing. The de-capacity policy makes overcapacity enterprises face stronger financing constraints than non-overcapacity enterprises.At the same time, the policy is not under the control of enterprises, which can be seen as an exogenous impact that affects financing constraints and avoid endogenous problems. Therefore, this paper can provide robust causal evidence about financing constraints and financial leasing.Second, this paper can provide ideas for China to formulate more scientific and effective industrial policies, thereby promoting "high-quality" development.With the expansion of shadow banks such as financial leasing, the formulation of industrial policies should not only consider mainstream financing channels such as bank loans, but also consider shadow banking channels.Under the goal of high-quality development, China should fully consider the interaction between industrial policies and the financial system to achieve a benign interaction between industrial policies and the financial system.

## 04 Enterprises Reform & Innovation

## Mixed Ownership Reform and Financial Asset Allocation of State-Owned Enterprises

YE Yongwei　LI Zengfu

(School of Public Economics and Management, Shanghai University of Finance and Economics; School of Economics and Management, South China Normal University)

The Third Plenary Session of the 18th Central Committee of the Communist Party of China highlighted the necessity of actively developing a mixed ownership economy with the mutual integration of state- owned capital, collective capital, and non-public capital. It also recommended that private capital be allowed to participate in state-owned capital investment projects. The influence of mixed ownership reform on corporate behavior is gaining increasing academic attention. The central question addressed in this paper is whether mixed ownership reform affects state-owned enterprises' financial asset investments.

As state-owned enterprises undergo mixed ownership reform, the entry of non-state-owned shareholders may theoretically affect corporate governance structure and resource endowments. This in turn will affect agency conflict and the financing constraints of state-owned enterprises.

First, non-state-owned shareholders have a strong motivation to supervise managers as their capital enters state-owned enterprises due to the profit-seeking nature of non-state-owned capital. This motivation helps to alleviate the lack of supervision in state-owned enterprises. When making decisions in this context, a manager will pay more attention to the long-term development of the enterprise rather than short-term benefits. The manager will make more fixed asset investments, such as investments in innovation. However, fixed asset investments have long cycle characteristics. They are therefore subject to more uncertainty and higher adjustment costs. Fixed asset investments will inevitably cause huge losses if they are interrupted. Corporate managers are thus motivated to use financial assets' reservoir effects to reduce the impact of future uncertainty and adjustment costs on their fixed asset investments.

Second, the proportion of state-owned equity has continued to decline with the entry of non-state-owned capital. The policy burden on state-owned enterprises will also be reduced significantly. This change may weaken the resource effect associated with state-owned equity, which will increase the financing constraints faced by enterprises. Based on the precautionary savings motivation, corporate managers will therefore allocate more financial assets to smooth their enterprises' fixed asset investments. Their goal is to avoid financing constrains that would cause fixed asset investment projects to fall into financial difficulties.

Based on the above analysis, this paper uses panel data on China's listed companies from 2010 to 2017 to examine the impact of mixed ownership reform on state-owned enterprises' financial asset allocation behavior. The paper focuses on the motivations behind state-owned enterprises' financial asset investments during the process of mixed ownership reform. The results show that the entry of non-state-owned shareholders promotes state-owned enterprises' financial asset investments. By testing potential mechanisms, we show that both the governance effect and the strengthening effect of financing constraints caused by the entry of non-state-owned shareholders strengthen state-owned enterprises' precautionary savings motivation. State-owned enterprises will therefore increase their investments in financial assets. The above results suggest that it is not the interest-seeking motivation but the precautionary savings motivation that drives state-owned enterprises' financial asset investments in response to the entry of non-state-owned shareholders.

The paper's main contributions are as follows. First, many studies address the economic consequences of mixed ownership reform, but none examine these consequences from the perspective of financial asset allocation. This paper therefore enriches the literature in this area. Second, the literature mostly addresses the economic consequences of corporate financial asset investment, paying less attention to its driving factors. This paper studies the driving factors of enterprises' financial asset investments after the entry of non-state-owned shareholders, thus providing an effective supplement to the literature. Third, this paper's conclusions suggest that state-owned enterprises' financial asset investments in response to the entry of non-state-owned shareholders are driven not by the interest-seeking motivation but by the precautionary savings motivation. When attempting to unravel the complexities of corporate financial asset investments, we should therefore identify the different motives for corporate financial asset investment and treat these motives differently.

# Governance of Non-state Shareholders and De-zombification of SOEs: Evidence from the "Mixed" Board of Directors of listed SOEs in China

MA Xinxiao    TANG Taijie    CAI Guilong

(School of Business, Sun Yat-sen University; Guanghua School of Management, Peking University)

In recent years, how to deal with zombie firms has become a widespread concern in top-level design, academic research and social practice in the context of the new era of economic structural transformation and the comprehensive deepening of reforms. In the process of China's economic transition, some companies have suffered long-term losses, near-zero profits and stagnant production. However, they have been able to survive by relying on large financial subsidies and low-cost bank credit and are commonly referred to as "zombie firms". The existence of zombie firms not only affects the normal functioning of non-zombie firms and creates a crowding-out effect but also reduces the efficiency of resource allocation in the market, hinders technological progress and ultimately impedes high-quality economic and social development.

Furthermore, as an important foundation of socialism with Chinese characteristics, state-owned enterprises (SOEs) play a key role in the rapid development of the Chinese economy and the realization of strategic goals. However, issues such as "owner's absence" and "inner control" have created a relatively serious zombification problem in some SOEs, restricting their core role in the national economy.Therefore, how to better manage state-owned zombie firms and promote the development of high-quality SOEs has become a key element in the success of the comprehensive deepening of reforms in the new era.

On this basis, this paper studies the influence of non-state shareholders' governance on the de-zombification of SOEs in the context of the comprehensive deepening of mixed ownership reform in the new era.The results show that the participation of non-state shareholders in the high-level governance of SOEs can significantly reduce the number of redundant staff and increase capital intensity, thereby reducing the tendency of SOEs to become zombie firms. This effect is more pronounced when state-owned executives have relatively little influence over business decisions and when the equity structure dimension of governance is weak. By subdividing the indicators identifying zombie firms, this paper finds that the governance of non-state shareholders can reduce the degree of zombification of SOEs and promote their normal operation in terms of limiting the acquisition of low-interest loans and improving their profitability. Ultimately, the production capacity and market value of well-managed SOEs are significantly improved.

The findings of this article show that the governance of non-state shareholders plays a positive role in promoting the de-zombification and development of SOEs, which not only provides a useful supplement to the literature on zombie firms' governance and SOEs' reform but also helps China better coordinate the core role of SOEs in the new journey of building a modern socialist country. In fact, SOEs play an irreplaceable role in promoting the development and growth of the socialist public economy, safeguarding national economic security and achieving national strategic goals, which are paramount in the new journey toward a modern socialist country. This article explores how to achieve the de-zombification of SOEs without losing control of state-owned shareholders and without losing state-owned assets, which is important for practice and policy.

First, the findings of this article provide a workable solution for zombie firms. The governance of non-state shareholders can promote the development of

SOEs to a position of honor in the context of mixed ownership reform.

Second, in the mixed ownership reform process of SOEs, it is difficult to empower non-state shareholders to play a governance role by simply mixing equity. Only by better ensuring that non-state shareholders appoint directors, supervisors and senior executives to participate in the governance of SOEs can these shareholders have sufficient discursive power to mix public and private capital from "quantitative change" to "qualitative change." Therefore, SOEs at all levels of mixed ownership reform should ensure that these shareholders exercise their due rights.

Third, non-state shareholders face many constraints when playing an active role in governance. Top managers in SOEs often have undue personal influence over the enterprise, greatly weakening the voice of non-state shareholders. Therefore, to strengthen the voice of non-state shareholders, it is important to limit the influence of SOEs' managers, which will better ensure the effective progress of reform.

# Debt Structure Optimization and Corporate Innovation: A Study from the Perspective of Corporate Bond Financing

JIANG Xuanyu    JIA Jing    LIU Qi

(School of Accountancy, Central University of Finance and Economics; School of Economics and Management, Tsinghua University)

Enterprises are the main participants in scientific and technological innovation, and corporate innovation is a crucial driver of economic growth. However, the complex international situation and the impact of the COVID-19 pandemic have increased the uncertainty surrounding economic development, leading to a rise in the macro leverage ratio. A rapid rise in macro leverage might lead to the accumulation of risk, and a reduction in macro leverage does not support the real economy. In this context, the relationship between debt structure optimization and corporate innovation is an important topic. This relationship also has important relevance in the context of maintaining the stability of the enterprise leverage ratio, realizing innovation-driven development strategies, and handling the relationship between economic growth and risk prevention.

From the perspective of bond financing, we examine whether enterprises can use the bond market to increase the proportion of direct financing, optimize their debt structure, and promote corporate innovation. Theoretically, the impact of bond financing on corporate innovation is unknown. On the one hand, as a main direct and long-term financing channel of corporate debt, bond financing can optimize the debt structure and promote corporate innovation by reducing the cost of debt financing and extending debt maturity. On the other hand, compared with relationship debts like bank loans, bond financing, as a transaction debt, has a more rigid debt contract and is more likely to give operators greater rights to control, possibly weakening the effect of corporate governance of debt and impeding corporate innovation.

Based on sample firms listed on the Shanghai or Shenzhen Stock Exchanges during the 2006-2017 period, we use the number of patent applications and patent citations to measure corporate innovation to empirically test the relationship between bond financing and corporate innovation. We find that bond financing is significantly and positively correlated with corporate innovation, which indicates the positive role of bonds in enhancing corporate innovation ability through the optimization of the corporate debt structure. Our further findings are as follows. (i) Bond financing can promote corporate innovation by reducing the overall debt financing cost and extending overall debt maturity. Moreover, bond financing has a spillover effect on bank loans: bond issuance can promote corporate innovation by reducing the interest rate and extending the term of bank loans. (ii) Product market competition and agency problems can weaken the role of bond financing in promoting corporate innovation. (iii) The effects of different types of bonds on corporate innovation are heterogeneous. Compared with corporate bonds and convertible bonds, short-term commercial paper and medium-term notes play more significant roles in promoting corporate innovation, which indicates that the convenience of bond issuance is an important factor affecting corporate innovation.

The results of this paper contribute to the literature in the following ways. First, we extend the literature on the determinants of corporate innovation. From the micro perspective, existing studies mainly discuss the relationship between debt level and corporate innovation, ignoring the impact of debt structure. Given an assumed level of debt, we discuss whether and how the proportion of bond financing affects corporate innovation. From a macro perspective, existing studies mainly discuss the relationship between financial development and corporate innovation in terms of the credit market and stock market, ignoring the role played by the bond market.Our results reflect the positive effect of bond market development on corporate innovation. Second, we provide new evidence of the economic consequences of corporate bond financing. By assessing social financing cost, bank loan cost, cash dividend policy, and corporate innovation performance, we focus on corporate innovation and discuss the impact of bond financing on corporate innovation from the perspective of innovation output scale and quality, further enriching the literature on the economic consequences of bond financing.Furthermore, we analyze the spillover effect of direct debt financing (bond financing) on indirect financing (bank loans). Bond financing helps improve bank loan conditions, including loan cost and term structure, and thus promotes corporate innovation.We provide evidence of the underlying economic mechanisms through which bond financing improves corporate innovation.Finally, we reveal the conditions in which bond financing can improve corporate innovation. We find that the effects of different types of bonds on corporate innovation are heterogeneous. Compared with corporate bonds and convertible bonds, short-term commercial paper and medium-term notes with greater financing convenience a have stronger promoting effect on corporate innovation. This finding has important implications for policy-making during bond market reform in China.

# Helping Hand or Punching Fist? How Stock Liquidity Affects Corporate Innovation in China

LIN Zhifan   DU Jinmin   LONG Xiaoxuan

(Institute of Advanced Studies in Humanities and Social Sciences, Beijing Normal University; School of Economics, Jinan University; Strategic Development Center, Zhuhai Huafa Group Co, Ltd)

Innovation is crucial to economic development and provides strategic support for the construction of a modern economic system. The capital market plays a key role in promoting corporate innovation and driving economic growth. The Chinese stock market has been developing for nearly 30 years. Market liquidity is increasing with the vigorous development of a multi-level capital market. In this context, this paper explores how stock liquidity affects the innovation strategies of listed companies.

The theoretical literature observes that stock liquidity may have two opposing effects on enterprise innovation. One stream of the literature asserts that stock liquidity stimulates corporate innovation because higher stock liquidity lowers the transaction cost of voting with one's feet. This lower transaction cost is conducive to the entry and exit of large shareholders and institutional investors. Such shareholders and investors are usually active in collecting private information and monitoring managers and thus effective in alleviating the principal-agent problem. Managers therefore pay more attention to corporate governance and devote more resources to R&D activities that enhance company value. This account can be termed the "incentivizing mechanism" of stock liquidity on innovation.

Another stream of literature points out that stock liquidity may instead inhibit corporate innovation.This can be termed the "pressure mechanism". The inhibition of innovation occurs for several reasons. First, the volatility of stock prices caused by large-scale trading is smaller with higher liquidity. This makes it easier for malicious buyers to cover up large purchases in the secondary market. Managers need to spend more time and energy monitoring stock market transactions when facing such threats. Second, managers need to boost financial performance and maintain high stock prices to raise the costs of malicious purchases. This often requires the reduction of R&D activities. Finally, higher stock liquidity may attract more short-term speculators and passive institutional investors who neither care about corporate fundamentals nor have the incentive to supervise managerial decision-making.This effect often leads to myopic managerial behavior, which may also reduce innovation.

These theoretical controversies suggest that the problem of how stock liquidity affects innovation is essentially empirical. It is worth noting that the Chinese government has made innovation a national policy in recent years and the capital market pays special attention to the innovativeness of listed companies. Under capital market pressure, companies may resort to increasing marginal invention applications and filing many utility models and design patents so that they may appear to have good development prospects.

Our findings are as follows, empirically based on detailed patent data from Chinese listed companies.First, higher stock liquidity leads to significantly more invention applications but does not lead to more grants that are able to pass substantial review. This signals a decline in application quality. Second, higher stock liquidity leads to a significant increase in low quality utility models and designs in the Chinese patent system. These low-quality patents are shown to have negative effects on profitability, and companies less willing to maintain their legal validity. This finding implies that companies only innovate strategically under capital market pressure.Sub-sample regressions reveal that strategic patenting is particularly pronounced among non-state-owned companies, companies in traditional industries, and companies with low long-term institutional investor holdings.

We do not advocate suppressing market liquidity as a solution to the patent bubble problem. Market supervisors should instead persuade investors to base their investment decisions on listed companies' substantive innovative capabilities so that irrational speculative trading can be reduced. The government could also gradually introduce investors with long-term investment visions and value orientations into the capital market, such as social security pension funds. This would help to stabilize entrepreneurs' expectations and encourage innovation.

# Financial Expansion and Chinese Local Enterprises Innovation: An Inverted U-shaped Relationship

ZHANG Jie　WU Shufeng　JIN Yue

(Institute of China's Economic Reform & Development, Renmin University of China; School of Economics, Renmin University of China)

In the current phase of China's economic development, scholars and policy makers are becoming increasingly concerned about the financial capital that is now either "shifting from the real economy to the virtual economy" or self-circulating in the financial system. As a matter of fact, this is part of a trend in which large amounts of financial capital, even the operating funds of the real economy, are entering the virtual economy through various channels.

The most objective method of judging the role of these phenomena in the rapid expansion of the financial value added component of China's GDP is to test whether the expansion of China's financial sector or the extension of its financial industry chain to the shadow banking system have either effectively matched or supported local enterprises' ability to independently innovate or have instead diverted resources from the sustainable development of the real economy, which is dominated by the manufacturing industry. While the continuous expansion of financial value added in GDP is a periodic condition in the economic development of developing countries like China, it can have both positive or negative implications. On the one hand, it is an expected component of economic development, but on the other hand, it may indicate the presence of deep-seated risk factors that may slow financial development and the transformation of the financial structure.

Accordingly, using detailed micro data on innovation in enterprises, this study summarizes the characteristics of the rapid expansion of China's financial value added in GDP. Then, by taking advantage of the policy impacts of the Chinese government's deregulation of banking business in 2005, and referring to Stevenson (2010) and Ahern and Dittmar (2012), this study constructs a variety of unique instrumental variables and uses them to empirically explore the impact of financial expansion on the innovation activities of local enterprises in China and the mechanism that drives this process. We find that the relationship between the continuous expansion of the added value of GDP in the financial industry and the innovation investment of local enterprises has a stable inverted U-shaped, which verifies the basic fact that the financial expansion of China's provinces and regions has a dual effect on the innovation activities of micro enterprises. The results show that reasonable financial expansion is conducive to the innovation activities of China's local enterprises, but rapid expansion may have a significant inhibitory effect, particularly on the innovation activities of private enterprises. In an analysis of the impacts on internal and external innovation, we find that the inhibitory effect is stronger on the internal innovation activities of private owned enterprises and the external innovation activities of private enterprises.

More precisely, we find that the inhibitory effect is concentrated in 31.55% of the local enterprises and 45.98% of the privately owned enterprises in our sample. The analysis of internal and external innovation shows that the financial expansion of China's provinces has a significant inhibitory effect on the internal innovation activities of 31.38% of local enterprises and 55.66% of private enterprises. The inhibitory effects on external innovation activities are strongest in enterprises with independent legal personalities and private owned enterprises.

These empirical findings not only provide a unique perspective for understanding the theoretical relationship between financial development and innovation in developing countries like China, they also clearly highlight the occurrence and spread of the phenomenon of "shifting from the real economy to the vitual economy" in the financial system and the internal circulation of financial funds in China. They also show the impact of overly rapid financial expansion on the innovation activities of local enterprises. These insights have important policy implications for China as it seeks to accelerate the reform of its financial system through the development of financial services in the real economy and to build a modern industrial system that coordinates the development of the real economy, scientific and technological innovation, and modern finance.

# Research on Digital Finance and Regional Technology Innovation

NIE Xiuhua   JIANG Ping   ZHENG Xiaojia   WU Qing

(School of International Trade and Economics, University of International Business and Economics)

This paper examines the relationship between digital finance and regional technology innovation by analyzing province-level panel data from 2011-2018 in a two-step system generalized method of moments model and a dynamic threshold regression model. First, we construct a benchmark linear regression model to verify the influence of digital finance and its sub-indices on regional technology innovation.Second, we use the dynamic threshold panel model to further explore the potential non-linear relationships. The factors include the perfection level of digital finance, the quality of the institutional environment, and the internal absorptive capacity of technology. We also explore two possible mechanisms for digital finance to promote regional technology innovation:the easing of financing constraints and the upgrading of industrial structure. Finally, we explore the potentially differing roles of digital finance in promoting technology innovation in the spatial and temporal dimensions.

There are three main findings. First, digital finance exerts a significantly positive effect on the level of regional technological innovation by easing financing constraints and upgrading industrial structure. Second, the positive effect of digital finance on regional technological innovation is stronger in regions that have better developed digital finance, better institution quality, or a higher level of human capital. Third, we find significant heterogeneity in the spatial and temporal dimensions regarding the role of digital finance in promoting technology innovation.Specifically, the positive effect of digital finance on regional technology innovation is more pronounced in eastern regions and following reforms that promote the development of digital finance.

We propose the following policy implications based on our empirical findings. First, we should promote the deployment of digital finance in China and the digital reform of traditional financial institutions using financial technology under proper governance to improve digital finance in new technology scenarios. At the same time, we must adhere to the unity of marketization, legalization, and internationalization principles, stabilize the pace of development, fully incorporate financial activities into supervision, ensure the safety and stability of the financial system, and optimize the function and efficiency of financial services in the economy. Second, we should improve the institutional environmental quality, local human capital, and other key supporting factors to promote the role of digital finance. On the one hand, we need to refine the existing intellectual property protection laws and regulatory systems, improve law enforcement efficiency, and establish a multi-level legal publicity system. On the other hand, we should build a diversified talent training model and strengthen the construction of technology innovation teams, and formulate appropriate incentive measures and institutional arrangements based on the development status of different regions to maximize the positive effect of digital finance on regional technology innovation. Finally, we should accelerate the transformation of innovation models, improve the level of regional innovation quality review and the construction of innovation evaluation systems, cautiously prevent the appearance of "false" or "strategic" innovation behaviors, and strengthen the effectiveness of financial support and industrial policies that promote the improvement of regional technology innovation.

Our paper also contributes to the literature in several ways. First, we explore the effect of financial development on regional innovation in a new and extensive digital finance model, and validate two possible mechanisms for how digital finance affects the local innovation.To the best of our knowledge, this is the first paper to test the non-linear effect of financial development on technology innovation, thus providing an important supplement to the literature on financial functions.Second, this paper adopts a comprehensive variety of methods, including a dynamic panel model, instrumental variable method, and dynamic threshold panel model, to explore the linear and non-linear relationships between digital finance and the level of technology innovation; it thereby enriches the literature in terms of research methods in the field of innovation, and fully guarantees the robustness of the results.Third, this paper uses the market value of granted patents as a proxy variable, which effectively measures the level and quality of regional technology innovation, to comprehensively examine the impact of digital financial development on regional technology innovation. Therefore, this paper provides new insights on innovation measures and expands the literature on innovation.

# Do Local Government Talent Introduction Policies Promote Regional Innovation? Evidence from a Quasi-Natural Experiment

ZHONG Teng  LUO Jigang  WANG Changyun

(School of Banking and Finance, University of International Business and Economics; School of Economics, Fudan University; China Financial Policy Research Center, Renmin University of China)

The importance of highly skilled human capital in China's economic transformation is self-evident. Since 2008, China's central government and local governments have implemented a large number of talent introduction policies, making competition for talent increasingly fierce across regions. However, whether talent introduction policies, especially at the local level, promote innovation is still a controversial issue. On the one hand, such policies can introduce advanced concepts and technologies to a region and accelerate local innovative upgrades and industrial transformations. Furthermore, the policy subsidies can increase firm profits and productivity, thereby promoting regional innovation. On the other hand, some local governments may enact talent policies for the purpose of maintaining demographic dividends and performance projects. The introduction and implementation of policies are often accompanied by problems such as inefficient investment and fiscal waste, which may have a negative effect on regional innovation. Therefore, this study uses data on local governments' talent policies to conduct a systematic empirical study of whether the policies significantly improve regional innovation and whether there are incentive distortions. It also explores the underlying mechanisms and provides guidelines for optimizing local talent introduction policies so that they better achieve innovative development.

We take the local talent introduction policies enacted in 39 cities between 2009 and 2012 as a quasi-natural experiment and use the multi-period difference-in-differences (DID) method to explore the impact of local government talent introduction policies on regional innovation. First, using the "Guidelines for the Introduction of Overseas Technological and Innovative Talents in China's Provinces and Cities" compiled by the Department of International Cooperation of the Ministry of Science and Technology in 2013, we determine the time at which each city implemented its talent introduction policy. We consider this an appropriate setting for a quasi-natural experiment. To simplify our inter-city comparisons, we adopt the propensity score matching method (PSM). Applying one-to-one nearest neighbor matching to the cities' characteristic variables, we construct a control group of cities that are similar to those in the experimental group. Through the above process, we obtain a sample with 39 cities in the experimental group and 39 cities in the control group for the period 2006-2015. Second, we use two indicators to reflect a city's innovation level. One is the number of valid patent applications in a city over the sample period, collected from the Soopat database. This indicator measures regional innovation capabilities from the perspective of patent quantity. The other indicator is a city's score on the China City Innovation Index, issued by the Industrial Development Research Center of Fudan University, which measures regional innovation capabilities on the basis of patent value.

Based on the above specifications, we implement a multiple-period DID regression to investigate whether there are significant differences in the innovation capabilities of the experimental and control cities before and after the enactment of talent introduction policies. We draw the following conclusions. Local government talent introduction policies increase both the quantity and value of patents in the region. Specifically, the policies increase innovation by expanding the scale of R&D investments rather than by enhancing innovation efficiency.In regions with poorer business environments and less protection of intellectual property rights the main effect of the policies is an increase in the quantity of patents, but in regions with better business environments and more protections the policies improve the value of patents.Furthermore, we find that the policies are more effective in regions with lower fiscal investment in science and education than in regions with higher investment.

This study makes three contributions. First, previous research focuses on the role of talent policies at the national level and concentrates on qualitative analysis. In contrast, this study focuses on city-level talent polices. Through rigorous empirical analysis, we explore the impact of talent introduction policies on innovation at the local level.Second, we not only examine the direct effects of the policies but also discuss the underlying mechanisms, thus providing a more comprehensive and in-depth description of how the policies function. Third, China is currently facing a reduction in labor force and a slowdown in economic growth. Talent has become a new driving force that is urgently needed for local economic development. Hence, our conclusions have important policy implications for local governments seeking to optimize talent incentive policies and implement innovation-driven development strategies.

# Development Zone and Firm Innovation: Excitation or Extrusion? Evidence from National and Provincial Development Zones

CAI Qingfeng   CHEN Yihui   LIN Haihan

(School of Economics, Xiamen University; College of Finance and Statistics, Hunan University)

The development zone is a typical feature of the reform and opening up process that China has undertaken over the last 40 years. Development zones play a critical role in promoting system innovation and assembling production factors. China's development zones are divided into national and provincial development zones. The two types of zone are superficially different in their approval organizations.They differ more significantly in scale, facilities, policy support, and management systems. Accordingly, their impact on enterprises in the region may also differ. Compared with national development zones, provincial development zones are more susceptible to economic and industrial competition between regions.However, few studies address the heterogeneity in the influence on firms of national development zones and provincial development zones.

Innovation activities are an important factor enabling enterprises to gain market competitiveness and achieve sustainable development. They are a driving force for regions to achieve high-quality development. It is therefore important to clarify what effects development zones have on innovation behavior at the micro-enterprise level.

We construct a multi- time differences-in-differences model to conduct the research. We use non-financial listed companies from 2007 to 2018 as a sample, combined with the manual collection and collation of enterprise information in various development zones. Our results show that national development zones can significantly promote innovation in enterprises within the domain, while provincial development zones inhibit enterprise innovation. Mechanism research shows that national development zones encourage enterprises to increase innovation through policy effects and aggregation effects. Provincial development zones, however, are vulnerable to short-term behaviors such as GDP tournaments. They therefore inhibit corporate innovation activities. Our paper also finds that the impact of development zones on corporate innovation activities is heterogeneous in the areas of market environment and property rights. The promotion effect of national development zones on enterprise innovation is more obvious in regions with a higher degree of marketization.This reflects the complementary effects of the visible hand of the government and the invisible hand of the market in national development zones.Regarding ownership heterogeneity, the promotion effect of national development zones on enterprise innovation activities is more obvious in central state-owned enterprises than in non-state-owned enterprises. The extrusion effect of provincial-level development zones on enterprise innovation is also more obvious in state-owned enterprises, especially local state-owned enterprises.

This paper's contributions are as follows. First, we advance the literature on enterprise innovation by examining the effects of different types of development zone on enterprise behavior. Most existing studies focus only on regional-level evidence. Our paper addresses the impact of development zones on the innovation activities of enterprises in the region and reveals the mechanism of this impact.Second, we offer in-depth and extensive insights into development zone construction based on a comparative study of national development zones and provincial development zones. Previous research largely focuses on national development zones.No relevant empirical evidence has been provided regarding the differential impact of national and provincial development zones or the reasons for such differences. Our comparative study of national and provincial development zones also sheds light on aspects of regional GDP competition. Finally, our research expands the literature on government intervention and enterprise innovation from the perspective of development zones.

The paper's main policy implications are as follows. China should highlight the exemplary role of national development zones when constructing development zones. They should also promote the management and institutional mechanisms of provincial development zones to bring them on a par with the mechanisms of national development zones. In particular, the government should speed up the optimization and upgrading provincial development zones.Some should be given stronger foundations and developed into national development zones. Upgrading provincial development zones will enhance regional innovation by providing a more reasonable business environment and management system.

## 05  Financial Markets

## Textual Information of Central Bank Monetary Policy Report Macroeconomy and Stock Market Performance

JIANG Fuwei　HU Yichi　HUANG Nan

(School of Finance, Central University of Finance and Economics; School of Economics, Peking University; Harvest Fund Management Co., Ltd)

Since the 1990s, central bank communication has become a hot issue in macroeconomics and finance. Many scholars have conducted meaningful research on the issues such as the measurement of central bank communication, central bank communication and inflation expectations, and central bank communication and financial markets.Among them, the influence of central bank communication on financial markets and asset prices has received wide attention. A large number of empirical studies have shown that central bank communication has a significant impact on the stock market, the bond market and the foreign exchange market.As the People's Bank of China (PBC) has paid increasing attention to policy communication in recent years, many Chinese scholars have conducted research on the impact of PBC's communication on China's financial markets. However, there are two major shortcomings in the existing studies. First, they only focus on monetary policy tendency of PBC's communication and ignore other information contained in the communication.Second, most scholars construct quantitative indicators by manual reading and scoring, making the results highly subjective.

This paper uses text analysis techniques to analyze 71 Monetary Policy Implementation Reports (hereinafter referred to as "the reports") of PBC, calculates the text sentiment (tone), the similarity and readability and other text indicators of the reports, and explores the relationship between these text indicators and the macro economy and the stock market. Based on the Chinese financial sentiment dictionary developed by Jiang et al. (2020), this paper uses the sentiment unit method to calculate the tone of the reports. In addition, this paper uses TF-IDF weighted cosine similarity to characterize the similarity of the reports, and uses average sentence length to characterize the readability of the reports. The paper then uses correlation analysis to examine the relationship between the tone of the reports and macroeconomic indicators such as economic growth, inflation, and interest rates. With reference to Ehrmann and Fratzscher (2009), Zhang and Hu (2014), this paper adds tone, similarity and readability to the EGARCH model to explore whether textual indicators of the reports affect stock market returns and the volatility on the trading day after the release. Furthermore, this paper decomposes the content of the reports into two parts: economic and financial fundamentals and central bank policy guidelines, calculates the tone of the two parts and examines their impacts on the stock market respectively.

The empirical results show that the tone of the reports is significantly correlated with macroeconomic indicators such as economic growth, inflation, and employment levels, and higher value of tone indicates better economic situation. After controlling for variables such as economic growth and monetary policy, the tone of the report has a significant positive impact on stock market return after the report is released. The similarity of the report has a significantly negative impact on stock market volatility, whereas the readability of the report does not have a significant impact on stock market volatility. Further research shows that it is the part reflecting the central bank's policy guidelines rather than the part reflecting macroeconomic and financial fundamentals that has a significant impact on stock market returns.

This paper fills a number of gaps in the field of central bank communication and text analysis. First, this paper is the first to use cutting-edge text analysis techniques to conduct a comprehensive analysis of the monetary policy reports of PBC. Second, this paper fills the gap in quantitative analysis of the sentiment of central bank communication in China's academia.Third, this paper conducts an empirical study on the mechanism of PBC's communication affecting the stock market, and proves that the report's tone affects the stock market only through the policy guidance channel.

The findings of this paper are of great significance to strengthening financial supervision and promoting macro-prudential management in China. The results show that PBC communication can significantly affect the stock market, which fully affirms the effectiveness of PBC's commumication. Through adequate communication with the market, PBC can influence asset prices, thereby achieving the purpose of monetary policy regulation and maintaining financial stability. In addition, this paper points out that the part of PBC's reports that affects the market is the part that reflects central bank's predictions of the future economic situation and its policy guidance. Therefore, PBC should use its authority and influence to manage market expectations more effectively through timely announcements and clear explanations of economic and financial situation predictions and monetary policy guidance.

# Multiple Credit Rating and Bond Financing Cost: Evidence from Chinese Bond Market

CHEN Guanting    LIAN Lishuai    ZHU Song

(School of Economics and Management, Tsinghua University; Faculty of Economics and Management, East China Normal University)

Since China resumed treasury bond issuance in 1981, there has been a rapid growth in both the market size and the variety of bond types. At the November of 2020, the Chinese bond market had a capitalization of about 115.7 trillion RMB and has become the world second largest bond market. The bond market plays an increasingly important role in the reform and opening-up of the finance system. A sound and healthy bond market requires active investors, while the moral hazard problem of the issuers and the information asymmetry between issuers and investors stand in the way.

Bond rating is an important mechanism in mitigating the information asymmetry between issuers and investors and protecting the rights of investors, and therefore plays an important role in investors' decision making. While most issuers in the Chinese bond market disclose rating from only one rating agency nowadays, some issuers choose to have multiple ratings (MR) from more than one rating agency, and publicly disclose these ratings in the statement of bond issuance.

There are three explanations for the existence of MR, such as informational production, rating shopping, and certification. Kronlund (2019) suggests that compared to single rating, MR is less likely to be the results of rating shopping, and the evidence shows that rating shopping is more likely to exist when issuers disclose single rating. This paper tries to provide evidence for the other two explanations, informational production and certification, while excluding the rating shopping explanation.

Using a sample of ratings from 2004 to 2018 in the Chinese bond market, this paper finds that MR is associated with lower financing cost, indicating that MR provides incremental information, and reduces the information asymmetry between investors and bond issuers, and this effect is more pronounced for issuers with consistent ratings or using investor-paid mode. In addition, when multiple ratings are inconsistent to each other, the average rating is more informative than the single rating. Further analyses show that the effect of MR in reducing financing cost is more pronounced for private issuers or those obtaining ratings from agencies with better reputation.

We conduct several robustness checks for our results by using PSM method, two-stage Heckman model, alternative samples and variables, and we use the exogenous event of double rating system implemented by Chinese regulatory authorities in 2012 to test the causal relationship between multiple ratings and bond financing cost. All test results support our major conclusions.

We make three distinctive contributions in this paper. First, the existing studies on China's bond market mainly focus on single credit rating. We contribute to this line of literature by examining the relationship between multiple credit ratings and bond financing cost, which allows us to explore the implications of credit rating from a quantitative perspective.Second, the available mechanisms of multiple ratings in the literature are inconsistent with the empirical evidence, and most of these studies focus on the United States or other developed economies. Our focal point is on Chinese bond market system, and we reveal how the investors in the emerging market interpret the multiple ratings and the key mechanism of multiple ratings. Moreover, we provide a better theoretical explanation for the phenomenon of multiple ratings. Third, we evaluate the effect of different payment modes under multiple ratings on the cost of bond financing, which enable us to provide verification results under multiple rating system on the controversial question that whether "issuer payment" mode is better than "investor payment" mode.

Our findings have several implications for regulators, issuers and bond rating agencies. For regulatory institutions, our paper suggests that it is necessary to gradually implement the mandatory multiple rating system and promote the multiple rating model embedded in the investor-paid rating agencies. For bond issuers, our findings imply that the market can extract more accurate information through multiple credit ratings when confronting with different ratings from multiple rating agencies, which helps reduce their cost of bond financing.For credit rating agencies, we provide evidence that reputation is a valuable asset.

# Private Information, Rating Distortion, and Market Reputation of Credit Rating Agencies in China

KOU Zonglai  QIAN Qianqian

(China Center for Econonmic Studies, Fudan University; School of Economics and Finance, Xi' an Jiaotong University)

Credit rating agencies (CRAs) play an important role in the capital market. In theory, they provide reliable decision-making information for investors and mitigate information asymmetry in the capital market.However, the increasing number of debt defaults has led some investors to have serious doubts about CRAs.They suspect that CRAs do not play the role of gatekeeper in the capital market and may even collude with issuers to transfer risk to innocent investors.

This paper studies whether Chinese CRAs have lost their market reputation. Measuring their market reputation is difficult because it involves a paradox: on the one hand, to build their market reputation, CRAs must provide reliable information to investors; on the other hand, CRAs with a good market reputation can milk investors by providing misleading information. Indeed, if a CRA manipulates a credit rating but has no significant impact on investors or on the debt issuance cost, the rating will be a "rubber stamp"; that is, the CRA actually has no market reputation.This paper studies the market reputation of Chinese CRAs in two steps: (i) measuring the rating distortion of CRAs; and (ii) examining whether and how rating distortion and CRA characteristics affect the debt issuance cost.

To measure rating distortion, this paper makes two salient contributions to the literature.

First, We separate rating distortion from CRAs' private information. In the literature, it is common practice to regress a credit rating with respect to public information and use the residual to measure rating distortion. However, considering that the de facto observable ratings are only given by those CRAs that ultimately win the rating competition, this approach may pool the rating distortion and favorable private information observed by the winning CRA. To extract real rating distortion from the residual, we follow Tian (2011) and introduce the distances between CRAs and issuers to control private information. However, to address selection bias, we not only introduce the average distance between the issuer and all CRAs to capture the monitoring effect but also the variance of the distance to capture the effect of private information on rating competition. Intuitively, credit ratings should decrease in average distance because monitoring becomes more difficult over a greater distance; however, the "observed" credit rating should increase in distance variance, because with a mean-preserving transformation, the debt issuer will choose a CRA's rating only when the CRA moves closer to the issuer, finds favorable information, and gives a higher rating.

Second, we use the propensity score matching (PSM) method to mitigate possible endogeneity. Because we can only observe the actual rating for each bond, the regression prediction value based on the full sample will result in serious measurement errors if there is great heterogeneity among different bonds. Therefore, correctly measuring rating distortion entails constructing a reasonable benchmark rating for each bond. Our solution is as follows: for each bond, we use PSM based on our public information and distance variables to find similar bonds as a control group. The bonds in the control group should be rated by other CRAs; thus the treatment effect between two groups is a more accurate measurement of rating distortion.

The main data, taken from the Wind database, cover information on corporate bonds and enterprise bonds from January 2009 to October 2017. After excluding bonds without ratings, there are 6073 observations.Our findings are as follows.First, credit ratings decrease in average distance between debt issuers and the CRAs, in accordance with the monitoring mechanism. Second, credit ratings increase in distance variance, in accordance with the private information channel. Third, on average, CRAs in China still have a good market reputation because upward rating distortion significantly reduces the cost of issuing bonds. Fourth, there is significant heterogeneity among CRAs. Fifth, we perform a DID analysis using high-speed railway openings as a quasi-natural experiment to tackle possible endogeneity problems due to the agglomeration effect in the locations of CRAs and issuers. We find that all of the main results are robust.

# Can Opening the Capital Market Improve the Quality of Corporate Information Disclosure? An Analysis Based on the Shanghai-Hong Kong Stock Connect and Annual Report Texts

RUAN Rui    SUN Yuchen    TANG Yue    NIE Huihua

(Center for China Fiscal Development, Central University of Finance and Economics; School of Banking and Finance, University of International Business and Economics; Research Institute of Economics and Management, Southwestern University of Finance and Economics; School of Economics, Renmin University of China)

The Shanghai-Hong Kong stock market exchange mechanism (hereafter referred to as the Shanghai-Hong Kong Stock Connect) was implemented on November 17, 2014. Investors in Hong Kong have been able to buy and sell stocks on Shanghai Stock Exchange within a specified range since the implementation of the Shanghai-Hong Kong Stock Connect mechanism. Mainland investors, conversely, are now able to buy and sell Hong Kong Stock Exchange stocks within a specified range. We take this capital market opening policy as a quasi-natural experiment. We use data from A-share listed companies from 2010 to 2019 to study the impact of capital market opening on the quality of public information disclosure by listed companies.

Referring to the literature, we calculate two readability indicators to measure the quality of companies' public information disclosure. These indicators are the proportion of commonly used words and the degree of text certainty. We take companies affected by the Shanghai-Hong Kong Stock Connect as the experimental group, and the remaining companies as the control group.We use difference-in-differences (DID) estimation, propensity score matching (PSM), and the synthetic control method to identify the causal effect of this capital market opening on the quality of companies' public information disclosure. We source companies' annual report texts from the Juchao Information Network. The financial data come from the CSMAR database.

We find that the capital market opening has improved the readability of relevant companies' annual report texts and significantly improved the quality of public information disclosure. This result is robust to various processing methods, including the addition of corporate governance and information environment control variables, consideration of the Shenzhen-Hong Kong Stock Connect, and the adoption of time-varying DID estimation.Further heterogeneity analysis shows that the improvement of text readability is more pronounced in companies with greater earnings manipulation and less stock price information.This indicates that the capital market opening effect is more significant in companies with weaker governance and lower information disclosure quality.

The main contributions of our research are as follows.

First, we shift the research perspective from the amount of information disclosure by listed companies to information disclosure quality given the exogenous impact of capital market opening.Our findings indicate that capital market opening is an effective way to improve the market's overall information quality.

Second, we exploit text mining technology to construct text readability indicators, thereby enriching related research on information disclosure quality. We provide a more intuitive and less dependent method of measuring the quality of information disclosure by mining and analyzing listed companies' annual report texts. We thereby enhance understanding of the impact of capital market opening on the quality of information disclosure.

Third, we provide new empirical evidence of the impact of capital market opening on corporate behavior and performance. We find that capital market opening improves the quality of corporate public information disclosure. Our empirical evidence helps us to understand the important role of capital market opening in promoting the maturity of financial markets. It also provides theoretical support for the Chinese capital market opening policy.

Our study's policy implications for capital market opening and capital market system construction are as follows. First, China could open its capital market further to the global financial market, expand the market's capacity, make full use of the resources of both domestic and international markets, and guide enterprises to improve their governance. Second, the expansion of financial market opening leads to more stringent requirements for the quality of supervision. Supervisory departments should increase their emphasis on the quality of information disclosure and actively guide enterprises to improve their information disclosure quality, especially regarding public information. Third, supervisors should also pay attention to the difficulty of understanding disclosure texts and to minimizing false and ambiguous statements that may mislead investors. This will guide companies to improve the quality of their information disclosure in annual reports. For example, supervisors could ask companies to clarify unclear words in their annual reports to urge them to enhance their information disclosure.

# Does Short Selling Restrain Insider Selling? Evidence from Margin Trading Mechanism

MA Yunbiao    WU Yanping    SHI Beibei

(School of Accountancy, Central University of Finance and Economics; School of International Trade and Economics, University of International Business and Economics)

Insider selling has recently become a common feature of the Chinese stock market. The economic consequences of insider selling for listed firms and the capital market as a whole has attracted much attention from practitioners and academics. Insiders such as large shareholders, directors, senior executives, and supervisors often use their information and valuation advantages to inflate stock prices by manipulating information disclosure, engaging in capital operations, and paying large stock dividends. Thus, their holdings are likely to be overvalued by external investors, allowing insiders to gain abnormal trading profits through selling them. These opportunistic self-serving insider sales exhibit strong negative externalities, which not only harm the interests of external investors but can also have negative real effects. Insider selling can then attract the attention of regulators, and authorities will attempt to restrain it by issuing stricter laws and regulations.However, insiders may still attempt to sell their holdings and cash out, and some may deliberately seek loopholes in the trading rules. Thus, a market mechanism in addition to government supervision is required to restrain insider selling.

The implementation of a margin trading mechanism represents a major innovation in China's stock market, and opens the door to short selling. The price discovery function of short selling can increase the efficiency of stock pricing, thus reducing the likelihood of stock price overvaluation.Can short selling restrain insider selling by reducing stock price overvaluation?This question has not been previously addressed. We propose that if the main purpose of insider selling is to obtain excess returns, the incentives of insiders to sell their holdings will be weaker after the deregulation of short selling, as the market pricing efficiency increases and the degree of stock price overvaluation and the excess trading return of insider selling decrease.

In this study, we explore the effect of short-selling on insider selling in the context of China's implementation of the margin trading mechanism, using a sample of A-share listed firms from 2006 to 2016.Our findings are as follows. (i) Short selling can restrain insider selling. (ii) The restraining effect of short selling on insider selling is realized by alleviating the degree of stock price overvaluation. (iii) Short selling can restrain the share selling of large shareholders, directors, and management, but has no effect on that of supervisors. (iv) Short selling can reduce the excess profit of insider selling. (v) The effect of short selling on insider selling is stronger when insiders have a greater incentive to sell their holdings. (vi) Short selling improves stock price efficiency by restraining inside selling. (vii) Short selling also decreases insider buying.

Our study makes three main contributions to the literature. First, studies of insider selling mainly focus on the motivations behind it and its economic consequences, rather than how to restrain it through market mechanisms. We contribute to the literature by examining the effect of short selling on insider selling.Second, we provide new empirical evidence of the economic consequences of the margin trading mechanism and short selling. The effects of this trading mechanism after its implementation have been extensively examined. Its effectiveness has been confirmed, and short selling has been found to improve market price efficiency, reduce stock price volatility, and potentially contribute to the stability and healthy development of the stock market.However, another strand of literature suggests that the deregulation of short selling can increase the stock crash risk. Thus, the economic consequences of the margin trading mechanism remain unclear. In this study, we examine the governance effect of the margin trading mechanism from the perspective of insider selling, thus providing new empirical evidence of the economic consequences of margin selling and short selling. Third, Our findings also have implications for policymakers. Methods of restraining insider selling have been considered by regulators, but insiders with strong incentives to cash out will attempt to find loopholes in the trading rules and get around the ban to sell their holdings. Thus, restraining insider selling requires not only government supervision but also a market mechanism. We find that short selling can restrain insider selling by improving stock price efficiency, thus providing policy implications for securities regulatory authorities in further improving the construction of China's capital markets and protecting the interests of small and medium-level investors.

# A Study of the Time-Varying Characteristics of Herding Effects in China's Stock Market Based on a Regime-Switching Model

ZHENG Tingguo   GE Houyi

(School of Economics, Xiamen University)

Since 1990, the sharp rise and fall of asset prices has been a major issue in China's stock market. Ren et al. (2019) point out that one important reason for the drastic fluctuation of China's stock market is an investor structure dominated by individual investors. Due to limited information and insufficient rationality in investment decision-making, individual investors blindly follow stock market trends, which aggravates the fluctuation. Some scholars have argued that market information asymmetry and the herding effect caused by stock market participants' irrational activity lead to speculative froth in the stock market. For example, Liu et al. (2014) have found that under severe herding conditions, large irrational fluctuations in stock prices can lead to serious bubbles and financial crises. Tao (2017) finds that the synchronicity of Chinese stock prices is much higher than that of developed stock markets in Western countries, and herding behavior causes stock prices to rise or fall together. Therefore, identifying and analyzing the characteristics of herding behavior in China has practical significance for monitoring the stock market and providing early warning of risk.

Domestic studies mainly use a static model, neglecting the time-varying characteristic of herding behavior. A few studies have discussed the dynamic characteristics of herding behavior in the U.S. market (Bohl et al., 2016), but these conclusions may not be applicable to the Chinese stock market, given its differences from Western stock markets in terms of system and development level. Furthermore, China's stock market has a complex structure, comprising the Shanghai, Shenzhen, Hong Kong, and Taiwan markets.Herding behavior may vary due to the different systems and market environments of different sub-markets. To solve these problems, we use a Markov-Switching CCK model to analyze dynamic herding behavior and cross-herding behavior in China's segmented stock markets within a regime-changing environment.

Our sample was drawn from all of China's segmented stock markets during the 1997-2019 period. The data were collected from the Wind, CSMAR, and DataStream databases. The following findings were obtained based on empirical analysis. The cycle of Chinese stock markets can be divided into two regimes characterized by high volatility and low volatility respectively, and the intensity of the herding effect varies with the transition between regimes. For the Shanghai and Shenzhen stock markets, the herding effect is relatively brief and intense in the high-volatility regime, while in the low-volatility regime, the herding effect is longer but relatively mild. For the Taiwan stock market, the herding effect is found only in the high-volatility regime, and lasts for a short time. For the Hong Kong stock market, the herding effect does not exist in either the low-volatility or high-volatility regime. In addition, the A-share markets herd around the US and Hong Kong markets during the low-volatility regime.

The contributions of this paper are as follows. First, considering the special structure of China's stock market, we discuss the herding effect under different systems and market environments, which provides complementary evidence for the time-varying herding effect of China's segmented stock markets under different regimes. Moreover, we contribute to the literature on financial risk contagion. Based on the perspective of cross- border financial linkage, we extend the basic CCK model to the cross-border financial context.By examining the time-varying characteristics of cross-herding, this paper highlights the herding path of risk contagion between stock markets, thus deepening the understanding of financial risk contagion and financial risk management in an open environment.Second, to obtain more rigorous conclusions, we perform necessary parametric tests in the empirical analysis.This can be regarded as a valid method for performing an availability analysis of a Markov switching CCK model, which provides valuable guidance for scholars to conduct more comprehensive, more scientific and more effective research on such a model.

# Information Asymmetry, Overconfidence, and Stock Price Changes

GONG Rukai

(Glorious Sun School of Business and Management, Donghua University)

Both the non-synchronization of information transmission and investors' sentiments are typical characteristics of financial markets. The former creates information asymmetry, and the latter can lead to the overconfidence of investors. However, few studies consider how information asymmetry can arise from the process of information transmission or how the processing and updating of new information may trigger overconfidence of investors. Both these processes can affect stock prices and the explanatory power of existing models. Incorporating these sources of information asymmetry and investors' overconfidence into the traditional financial analytical framework has important theoretical and practical implications and deepens our understanding of the internal logic of stock price changes.

This study incorporates information asymmetry and investors' overconfidence into the traditional analytical framework and examines how the process of information transmission in real markets affects stock prices. Following Easley and Hara (2004), we model the transmission process of information as a gradual flow of information, which endogenously generates information asymmetry between investors. We then introduce one of the typical psychological characteristics of investors—overconfidence—and establish a two-stage dynamic sequential pricing model to explore whether stock prices are driven by the dual factors of information asymmetry and investors' overconfidence.

The main results show that first when investors are presented with new information, adjustments in their expectations of stock returns are positively correlated with the equilibrium price of stocks, that is, increasing investors' expectations of stock returns increases the equilibrium price of stocks, and vice versa. Second, when presented with good news, the proportion of investors who are overconfident tends to increase, the equilibrium prices of stocks increase, and stock returns decline. When presented with bad news, the proportion of investors who are overconfident tends to increase, and both the equilibrium price of stocks and investment loss decline.Third, as the proportion of overconfident investors and the degree of overconfidence increase, the market risk premium decreases. Fourth, investor groups diverge during the process of information transmission, forming heterogeneous beliefs; specifically, investors who have not obtained information and who have not become overconfident think that the stock price is overvalued, whereas investors who have obtained information and who are overconfident think that the price is undervalued, which triggers changes in market volume and stock prices.Fifth, both the proportion of overconfident investors and the increase in overconfidence have a positive impact on market efficiency but a negative effect on market depth. Finally, we use the theoretical results of this study to explain typical volatility characteristics such as asymmetric effects and volatility persistence in real markets.

This study extends the literature in three ways.First, it examines how the gradual flow of information into the stock markets creates potential information asymmetry among investors, which affects the formation of equilibrium stock prices. This is a useful supplement to research on information transmission in the stock markets. Second, based on the self-attribution bias theory, we incorporate a typical behavioral bias of investor—overconfidence—into our model of the information transmission process, which allows us to consider more realistic market environments. We then explore how stock price formation and changes are driven by the dual factors of information asymmetry and investors' overconfidence, expanding the research on stock pricing and price changes. Third, we use our theoretical results to analyze market price fluctuations, and find that we can explain typical features such as asymmetry and persistence. This enhances the understanding of the logic of stock price changes in real markets.

# Can Fund Networks Improve Investment Performance?

CHEN Shenglan    LI Jing

(School of Economics, Zhejiang University of Technology; School of Economics and Management, Inner Mongolia University)

Institutional investors managing public funds are rapidly becoming a crucial part of financial markets. Accordingly, there is widespread interest in how these fund managers make investment decisions. Recent studies show that due to the complementarity of information structures, social networks play an important role in fund managers' asset allocation and diversification decisions. We focus on how an important social network-enabled interaction between funds—the fund holdings network—affects the investment performance of funds.

There are different theoretical perspectives on how a fund's co-ownership network affects investment performance. On the one hand, such networks produce information diffusion effects, and fund managers at the center of a fund network will receive signals earlier and obtain more valuable information than fund managers at the periphery of the network. Furthermore, the information held by fund managers at the center of the network will be more accurate, which will have a positive impact on the investment performance of their funds. On the other hand, a fund network can induce the "free riding on friends" effect. Compared with fund managers at the periphery of the network, fund managers at the center of the network support more "free riders". Under this condition, the fund network may have a negative impact on their fund performance.

We use data on China's capital market stock funds from January 2005 to September 2018 to examine the impact of fund networks on investment performance.The results show that the centrality of a fund's position in a fund network has a significant positive impact on its investment performance. The results have obvious economic significance: we find that an increase of one standard deviation in the degree, closeness, or eigenvector measures of a fund's position in the network increases investment performance by an average of 54.43%, 51.15%, and 50.93% respectively.

We also examine the channels though which network position affects performance. Specially, we examine fund stock selection skills, asset allocation skills, and fund management skills. First, institutional investors located at the center of a network receive rich, accurate, and timely information about stock pricing. This information can promote fund managers' analyses and mastery of stock fundamentals, thereby improving their stock selection skills. Second, the transmission of information between funds is an important factor that affects managers' asset allocation strategy. Fund managers located at the center of a network have more accurate information and can use their information to allocate assets independently and effectively, that is, they have improved asset allocation skills. Third, social networks can promote the dissemination of information, thereby improving managers' fund management skills.

Finally, we examine the influence of fund networks on fund shares, which we define as a fund's market share.A fund network provides channels for the dissemination and exchange of information.Fund managers at the center of a network receive faster and more valuable information, which allows them to implement high-quality portfolio management and product differentiation strategies. High-quality portfolio management and product differentiation are effective strategies for gaining market share. This study shows that fund networks have a significant positive impact on funds' market share.

This research makes two major contributions.

First, we contribute to the literature on the interactions between institutional investors' shareholdings. Most studies have assumed that institutional investors are homogeneous, and there is a lack of research on the heterogeneity of institutional investors and their interactions. We expand this field by constructing a model of a dynamic co-ownership fund network. The fund network allows for the exchange of information between co-ownership funds, reflects the interactions between institutional investors, and distinguishes institutional investors' holdings on the basis of their network location. Using a series of centrality measurement methods, we examine the effects of network location on a fund's ability to obtain information and take actions.

Second, we contribute to the research on the impact of social relationships on investment performance by examining the impact of social networks on performance from the perspective of dynamic institutional investor interactions. We build a model of fund networks to illustrate dynamic institutional investor shareholding interaction, and examine its impact on fund investment performance. We find that in a fund network based on co-ownership, positive information diffusion effects dominate, which leads to better investment performance for funds with more relationships. In addition, the social interaction between funds in a network improve the managers' stock selection skills, asset allocation skills, and management skills, which ultimately improve the funds' investment performance.

# Nominal Price Illusion: Evidence from Security Analysts' Price Targets

HE Guihua　CUI Chenyu　GAO Hao　QU Yuanyu

(School of Accounting, Zhongnan University of Economics and Law; Business School, University of International Business Economics; PBC School of Finance, Tsinghua University; School of Banking and Finance, University of International Business Economics)

Investors suffering from the nominal price illusion tend to believe that low (high)-price stocks have more (less) upside potential (Birru and Wang 2016). A number of studies have examined the relationship between the nominal price illusion and corporate financial policies and asset prices in China's A-share stock market (He and Chen, 2003; Li et al., 2014; Yu et al., 2014; Xie et al., 2016; Luo et al., 2017). For example, Li et al. (2014) and Yu et al. (2014) find that unsophisticated retail investor are the net buyers after announcements of stock splits and mutual fund shares splits, indicating that retail investors prefer low-priced assets.

However, in the above studies, whether investors have biased beliefs about nominal share prices is unobservable, and thus the findings are likely to be contaminated by alternative rational explanations. In China, stocks are traded in lots of 100 shares. Therefore, retail investors with binding budget constraints cannot afford stocks with extremely high prices. Furthermore, retail investors who want highly diversified portfolios will also trade stocks with relatively low nominal prices, because such stocks give them more capital allocation flexibility. In other words, retail investors' revealed preference for low nominal price stocks is very likely to be the result of rational considerations, and not the result of the nominal price illusion.

This study uses analysts' price targets to directly test the nominal price illusion hypothesis. It looks at the associations between stock return expectations and nominal share prices. An advantage of our research design is that our setting is unlikely to be affected by the budget constraint. Although budget constraints inevitably impose trading restrictions in investors' portfolio formation, they should not have any real impact on investors' expectations of individual stocks.

We find that analysts' future return forecasts for low nominal price stocks are significantly higher than their forecasts for high nominal price stocks, even after controlling fundamental information, beta, and other characteristics of stock returns. Moreover, the above finding is stronger for hard-to-value stocks, as represented by small size, short listing years, high return volatility, low financial reporting transparency, and more intangible assets. We also use stock split events as exogenous shocks to conduct a difference-in-differences (DID) test, and document that analysts' post-split return forecasts become more favorable after a mechanical drop in a nominal share price, which strongly supports our hypothesis.

In addition, we conduct several further analysis to confirm that analysts' optimism about low nominal price stocks is the outcome of biased belief, rather than two alternative explanations: (i) that low nominal price stocks could earn higher ex-post future returns than high nominal price stocks; (ii) analysts with self-serving motivations strategically release favorable target prices for low nominal price stocks to cater to the preferences of investors.

Our paper makes two contributions to the literature. First, by using a large sample of analysts' price target forecasts, we directly identify the impact of the nominal price illusion, Our study documents how and why the nominal price illusion affects investor trading behaviors, corporate financial policies, and market anomalies. Therefore, our study not only confirms previous findings on the nominal price illusion but also provides micro-foundations for the literature (He and Chen, 2003; Li et al., 2014; Yu et al., 2014; Xie et al., 2016; Luo et al., 2017). Second, our study adds to the analyst literature. Previous studies focus on earnings forecasts and stock recommendations, whereas our study examines whether the nominal price illusion biases analysts' price targets. The findings enrich our understandings of how financial analysts are affected by behavioral biases (Hilary and Menzly, 2006; Hribar and McInnis, 2012; Cen et al., 2013; Pouget et al., 2017; Hirshleifer et al., 2019).

Our study also has policy implications. As professionals such as financial analysts are still vulnerable to the nominal price illusion, retail investors with limited knowledge and skills should be more aware of this illusion when trading stocks. As retail investors are the main participants in China's A-share market, we also suggest that regulators pay attention to self-dealing corporate behaviors that take advantage of unsophisticated retail investors by means such as initiating stock splits to boost the stock price.

## 06   International Economics & International Trade

## Measurement and Analysis of the Real Effective Exchange Rate Elasticity of Global Value Chains of Bilateral Exports

PENG Hongfeng    LIU Haiying

(School of Finance, Shandong University of Finance and Economics)

The RMB exchange rate has shown continuous appreciation since June 2020 due to China's effective COVID-19 prevention and control measures and stable economic recovery. However, exports have also shown rapid growth. The traditional macroeconomic hypothesis that exchange rate appreciation inhibits exports has therefore been challenged. The weak correlation between exchange rates and exports has attracted widespread attention in recent years (Yang, 2013; Ahmed et al., 2015). The main reason for this phenomenon is that, against the background of global value chains, countries have supply side relations through the intermediate goods trade. The traditional real effective exchange rate, based on Armington's demand theory, considers only demand-side relations between countries. This exchange rate can no longer accurately reflect the relationship between a country's price competitiveness and its exports: it is misleading in both direction and quantity (Bems and Johnson, 2012).

Bems and Johnson (2012, 2015, 2017) build a new model that measures the real effective exchange rate based on the input-output relationship in the global value chains. Ni (2018) extends this model to bilateral exports. This method provides an accurate measure of the changes in the competitiveness of bilateral export prices. We further apply this indicator to make a theoretical measurement and provide a structural decomposition of the real effective exchange rate elasticity of global value chains of bilateral exports. By introducing a third country's exchange rate effect and supply-side linkages, we can correct the quantitative and directional errors that ensue when the traditional exchange rate is used as a measure of relative price competitiveness to explain the relationship with exports.

This paper provides two main contributions. First, the research shifts from the revision of traditional exchange rate indicators to the exchange rate elasticity of bilateral exports.This is based on the models of Bems and Johnson (2012, 2015, 2017), Patel et al. (2014), and Ni (2018). It fully considers the supply-side linkages and exchange rate effects of a third country under global value chains. From the perspective of model construction, we measure and analyze the real effective exchange rate elasticity of global value chains of bilateral exports. We do this to explain key phenomena described by recent research, such as the irrelevance of exports and exchange rates, the weakening influence of exchange rate on exports, and even cases in which depreciation reduces exports. Second, we decompose the real effective exchange rate elasticity of global value chains of bilateral exports into three components. The three components caused by relative price changes are as follows: changes in the final product structure, changes in the structure of intermediate products, and changes in the structure of intermediate inputs and value-added substitution. This decomposition aids understanding of the structural factors behind the change in elasticity.

We use World Input-Output table data from 2000 to 2014 provided by the WIOD database for calculation. Our conclusions are as follows. First, the absolute value of the real effective exchange rate elasticity of the global value chains of China's exports to major trading partners is between 0.729 and 0.883. The role of exchange rates in weakening exports is less serious than that of traditional exchange rates, and there is no evidence that depreciation reduces exports. The traditional exchange rate does have large error: in both direction and quantity when describing changes in bilateral relative price competitiveness and export relations.Second, the further decomposition of the real effective exchange rate elasticity of global value chains of bilateral exports shows that the contribution of intermediate product structure changes caused by relative price changes to the total elasticity of China's exports to major trading partners has continuously increased. This has occurred alongside China's increasing participation and status in global value chains. We also find in the decomposition that the structural contributions of some countries and regions, such as Japan and the US, display similar values and changes.

It is therefore necessary to measure the real effective exchange rate elasticity of global value chains of bilateral exports to accurately assess the export trade situation, enhance the efficiency of export trade policy formulation, and correct errors in the traditional exchange rate elasticity measurement. We should pay attention to the changes in the structure of intermediate products for China's exports. In the short term, trade can be transferred by looking for alternative trading partners to calm export fluctuation when a shock occurs. In the long term, the issue still needs to be solved through structural adjustment and policy communication.

# Antidumping and Multiproduct Firm Export Activity: Evidence from Chinese Manufacturing Firms

XU Jiayun  ZHANG Junmei  LIU Zhuqing

(APEC Study Center, Nankai University; School of Economics, Nankai University; School of Economics, Fujian Normal University)

Since the reform and opening up, foreign trade in China has experienced an unprecedented level of rapid development. China has ranked first in the world in terms of trade scale and volume for many consecutive years and has long benefited from economic globalization. However, in the context of a new round of trade protectionism, China faces increasingly serious trade barriers in overseas markets. Certainly, enhancing the competitiveness of export enterprises and their ability to respond to foreign antidumping investigations can help achieve the orderly development of high-quality export trade and "external circulation". This paper attempts to answer the following related questions: What effect do antidumping measures have on the export activity and productivity of Chinese firms? By what mechanism are these effects realized?

Theoretically, antidumping measures have a multifaceted effect on export enterprises. Encountering antidumping measures increases production costs, weakens the price advantage and reduces profits, and thus negatively affects exports. As antidumping measures threaten the survival of export enterprises and intensify the competitive pressure they face, antidumping measures force enterprises to change their transformation and upgrade strategies to improve efficiency and product quality, fundamentally enhancing the competitiveness of their products. Therefore, the effect of antidumping measures on China's export enterprises represents an empirical problem. By answering the questions posed above, we can evaluate the operating conditions of China's export enterprises and deepen our understanding of the mechanism by which antidumping measures affect export enterprises. The answers to these questions also have strong practical significance for China's transformation of its economic development mode, the innovation-driven manufacturing industry and enhanced international competitiveness against the background of the global value chain.

The results show that for Chinese multiproduct firms, encountering antidumping measures has a positive effect on export prices, the concentration of export products and export market diversification but a negative effect on export volume and scope (i.e., number and variety of export products). These effects are limited by the firm's downstream and upstream participation in the global value chain. Heterogeneity tests show that the effects of encountering antidumping measures on export activity differ significantly among multiproduct firms depending on characteristics such as the type of ownership and mode of trade.Finally, by constructing a firm-level product competitiveness index, we find that Chinese multiproduct exporting firms tend to export a broader product mix, giving such firms a competitive edge and raising their productivity. This effect increases gradually as procedures for responding to antidumping measures are promoted. These conclusions indicate that encountering antidumping measures leads firms to focus on exporting core products and thus promotes the efficiency of Chinese export firms in the long run.

This paper makes the following innovative contributions. First, it combines the heterogeneous trade theory of manufacturers and products with micro data from Chinese multiproduct export firms to explore the effects of antidumping measures on the export behavior of these firms from the perspective of the internal export product structure. In contrast to most of the literature, this paper not only examines the effects of encountering antidumping measures on the scale of the quantity and types of export products but also examines the effects on export prices, the concentration of export products and the diversification of the export market. Thus, this paper not only enriches the literature on the effect of antidumping measures on exports but also deepens our understanding of how antidumping measures affect a firm's export behavior. Second, in addition to using the propensity score matching-difference-in-differences (PSM-DID) method to investigate the average effect of antidumping measures on firms' export behavior, this paper incorporates the global value chain into its analytical framework. By measuring upstream embeddedness, downstream embeddedness and global value chain status, this paper investigates the role of global value chain status in the effect of antidumping measures on firms' export behavior. Few studies address the role of the global value chain in the effect of antidumping measures on trade. Third, this paper further explores the effect of antidumping measures on the productivity of multiproduct firms from the perspective of intra-firm export product reallocation, and thus it enriches the literature on the effect of antidumping measures on exports.

# How Does Financial Structure Affect the Choice of Foreign Direct Investment Entry Mode?

JING Guangzheng    SHENG Bin

(School of Economics, Nankai University)

Foreign capital can enter the market of a host country through two main channels: greenfield investment and cross-border mergers and acquisitions. As the choice of foreign capital entry mode is one of the core decisions made by multinational corporations when they enter the market of a host country, it is not only directly related to the success or failure of the enterprise's own transnational operation, but also has a significant impact on the economy of the host country. Financial systems are the core of modern economies. Whether a host country can use a sound financial system to attract foreign investment, which can lead to the diffusion of cutting-edge technology and the promotion of the host's global value chain, has become a topic of interest in academic circles. At the same time, the host country's business environment, including current and expected policies and the institutional and behavioral environment, not only directly affects the returns and risks of transnational investment, but also indirectly affects the returns of foreign direct investment by affecting the allocation efficiency of financial resources under the condition of incomplete contracts (Antras and Helpman, 2004). A few studies have discussed the relationship between financial development and foreign investment entry, but very few have examined how the different business environments of different countries affect the relationship between financial structure and the choice of foreign investment entry mode.

Following Levine (2002), we construct a cross-country index of financial structures and then investigate the influence of different financial structures on foreign investment mode selection. We consider how the choice of financial structure affects the mechanism of foreign investment, and comprehensively investigate the relationship between the business environment and the choice of foreign investment mode. Our findings suggests that to promote financial supply side structural reform, China should improve its business environment and improve the quality of foreign capital introduction.The study uses transnational panel data on 65 countries from 2003 to 2017. The data are mainly from the databases of international organizations such as the United Nations and the World Bank.

This study draws the following conclusions. First, compared to a bank-dominated financial structure, a market-oriented financial structure makes it easier for foreign investment to enter through cross-border mergers and acquisitions, and the promotional effect of such a financial market is clearly stronger in developed countries than in developing countries. Second, the analysis of the transmission mechanism finds that technological innovation and national risk control are the important channels through which financial structure influences the choice of foreign capital entry mode; more generally, we find that the choice of financial structure is more strongly associated with economic risk, and has limited association with political risk. Third, improving the business environment not only directly promotes the entry of foreign capital, but also indirectly regulates the role of the financial market in improving the structure optimization of foreign capital entry. The role of the business environment is significantly greater in developed countries than in developing countries.

The findings of this study have clear policy implications. First, China should continue to extend the structural reform of its financial supply side by effectively promoting financial marketization, liberalization, and internationalization and reducing the entry and operation costs of foreign enterprises. Furthermore, China needs to adjust its policies for attracting foreign investment by improving the system for managing the pre-establishment of national treatment and negative list for foreign investment. It should consider policies that promote greenfield investment and cross-border mergers and acquisitions, which would improve the structure and quality of foreign investment.Second, the Chinese government should further strengthen technological innovation and guard against national risks. Its innovation incentive policies should promote the transformation from "quantity" to "quality", enhance the ability of financial services to support the real economy, and adopt an innovation performance evaluation system that realizes the flexible nature of scientific research.Furthermore, in the context of increasing global economic uncertainty, China needs to improve its financial risk prevention mechanisms so that it can effectively control and defuse the systemic and non-systemic risks faced by domestic and foreign enterprises. Third, China's investment policies should be committed to improving the business environment, following the principle of competitive neutrality for domestic and foreign firms, establishing and perfecting a foreign investment promotion mechanism, and creating a stable, transparent, predictable, and fair competitive market.

# The Exchange Rate Uncertainty and Cross-border Mergers and Acquisitions

MENG Wei    JIANG Guohua    ZHANG Yongji

(Guanghua School of Management, Peking University; School of Management and Economics, Beijing Institute of Technology)

In the context of an increasingly uncertain international situation and the market-oriented reform of the RMB exchange rate, exchange rate fluctuations among countries have become the norm. The potential financial risks and the operational risks for micro firms associated with these increasingly unpredictable exchange rate fluctuations will have a profound impact on the sustainable development of China's economy. The international environment is becoming increasingly complex, characterized by growing uncertainty and instability. Firms engaged in cross-border mergers and acquisitions (M&As) face three additional uncertainties: (i) uncertainties caused by anti-globalization, trade disputes and protectionism, and geopolitical conflicts; (ii) uncertainty in the relationship between the acquirer's and the target's countries; and (iii) uncertainties in the economic, political, security, legal, and other spheres of the target country. Unexpected exchange rate fluctuations are related to these three uncertainties.

Based on the China's aim to achieve a high-quality opening up, we define Exchange Rate Uncertainty as the condition of being unable to accurately predict the direction, range, or distribution probability of future exchange rate fluctuations. In this condition, exchange rate fluctuations cannot be predicted based on historical trends and existing information. In general, Chinese firms join international markets through cross-border M&As. This study suggests two mechanisms through which fluctuations in exchange rates affect this process. (i) Real Option Effect. Exchange rate uncertainty constrains firms' cross-border M&A decisions by increasing transaction costs and earnings uncertainty and by aggregating external financing difficulties. (ii) Risk: Hedging Effect. Exchange rate uncertainty encourages firms to increase their market share and hedge exchange rate risks by engaging in cross-border M&As that enhance their market competition. Using a sample of cross-border M&As announced by A-share firms in the 2000 to 2019 period, we find that uncertainty in the nominal exchange rate of the RMB against the US dollar reduces the likelihood of cross-border M&As, indicating the dominance of the real option effect; while uncertainty in the nominal effective exchange rate of RMB has a positive impact on the number of M&As, which reflects the risk hedging effect. Further cross-sectional analysis shows that the negative effect of NUTR uncertainty is more significant among firms with higher trading and translation risks and tighter financing constraints. In addition, firms in industries with intense competition and firms that face higher economic risk from exchange rate fluctuations are more likely to conduct cross-border M&As when NEER uncertainty intensifies. Tests of the mediating effects of financial friction and corporate risk further prove that both NUTR and NEER uncertainty affect firms' decisions to engage in cross-border M&As via the real option mechanism and risk hedging effect, respectively. Finally, the financial performance of cross-border M&As is better during periods when the exchange rate is uncertain.Cross-border M&As reduce the sensitivity of firm stock prices to changes in effective exchange rates (NEER); that is, they reduce the economic risks of exchange rates, but have no significant mitigation effect on the risk exposure created by bilateral exchange rates.

 This study distinguishes the role of bilateral and effective exchange rate uncertainty and expands our understanding by considering the economic consequences of exchange rate fluctuations and uncertainty. At the same time, this study also supplements the literature on the factors that influence cross-border M&As. It provides a theoretical basis for regulators' guidelines for firms seeking active international economic cooperation.These guidelines could help firms to improve their core competitiveness and to participate in the reform of the global economic governance system. In particular, to obtain stability in an uncertain environment, firms must pay attention to exchange rate risk and improve the efficiency of cross-border M&As. This study explores the spillover effect of exchange rate uncertainty from the perspective of the stock market and provides a basis for the market-oriented reform of the RMB exchange rate system under the Dual Circulation development pattern.

# 07  Fiscal, Taxation & Local Government

## Housing Price Control, Local Government Debt and Macroeconomic Fluctuations

MEI Dongzhou    WEN Xingchun    WANG Siqing

(School of International Trade and Economics, Central University of Finance and Economics; School of Banking and Finance, University of International Business and Economics; School of Economics and Management, Tsinghua University)

Since the Housing System Reform in 1998, China has experienced a sharp rise in house prices. Although rising house prices have brought a large amount of social funds and bank loans to the real estate sector, they have also prompted local governments to use land reserves to borrow large-scale loans from banks, resulting in a high level of local government debt. As house prices are strongly correlated with land prices, which are also strongly connected to the solvency of local governments, inadequate regulation of house prices is likely to trigger debt risk for local governments (Mao and Cao, 2019). This leads to two questions: can house price regulation direct funds to the manufacturing sector? What is the link between house price regulation and local government debt risk?

By identifying the stylized facts of China's macroeconomy, we find that under the current financing mode of local governments, local government revenue depends heavily on "land finance". Controlling house prices will reduce land prices, which in turn will affect the solvency of local governments. When local governments are unable to repay their debt or when the central government is unwilling to bail them out, local governments may default, which will have a serious negative impact on the economy through the financial system. Based on these facts, this paper builds a multi-sector DSGE model. To characterize the relationship among house prices, land finance, and local government debt, we incorporate local governments and their land finance behavior into the model. In addition, to characterize the impact of local government borrowing behavior on the financial sector, following Iacoviello (2015) and Bernanke et al. (1999), we introduce financial frictions.

The results of numerical simulations show that controlling house prices leads to a decline in land prices, which directly affects the ability of local governments to repay their debt. If the decline in land prices does not trigger local government debt default, it will have two effects:first, the decline in land prices will lead to a decline in local government revenue, which will affect local government expenditures, resulting in a decline in output in the infrastructure sector and in total output; second, the decline in local governments' mortgage lending caused by the decrease in land prices will lead to a decline in the deposit and loan premiums of the financial sector and a reduction in the cost of other sectors to obtain loans from the financial sector. This will be further amplified through the financial accelerator effect, leading to increased investment and output expansion in non-infrastructure sectors. However, if the decline in land prices triggers local government debt default, that is, local governments are unable to repay loans obtained from the financial sector and the central government is unwilling to bail them out, then default will result in a loss of assets in the financial sector. This will lead financial intermediaries to reduce loans and sharply increase their deposit and loan premiums, resulting in a sharp increase in the cost of all sectors of the economy to obtain funds, amplified by financial accelerators, and ultimately resulting in a sharp drop in investment and output in all sectors of the economy.

Further counterfactual policy analysis shows that to avoid local government default, we should use fiscal funds to supplement bank capital or reduce bank reserve ratios to reduce the deposit and loan premiums of financial intermediaries. In this way, we can avoid local government default and reduce the cost of financing in the whole economy, which will ultimately minimize the negative economic impact of house price regulation.

Compared with previous research, this article makes the following contributions. First, the problem of local government debt has always been a major concern in house price regulation. However, existing studies are mostly qualitative and not systemic. In this regard, this article builds a multi-sectoral DSGE model to describe how house prices affect local government debt and examines the key factors that determine the relationship between the two.Second, most studies of the effect of house price regulation on economic fluctuations are primarily qualitative. This article is the first to construct a multi-sector DSGE model to identify the channels through which house price regulation affects economic fluctuations from a general equilibrium perspective, and examines the role of various factors in this relationship. Third, the question of how to stabilize house prices and direct funds to the manufacturing sector without triggering local government debt default remains unclear.By clarifying relevant ideas through model analysis, this article attempts to answer this question and offers relevant policy suggestions.

# Tax-Fee Substitution: VAT Tax Reduction, Non-tax Revenue Management and Corporate Investment

ZHAO Renjie    FAN Ziying

(School of Economics and Management, Northwest University; School of Public Economics and Administration, Shanghai University of Finance and Economics)

Tax competition has in recent years resulted in lower tax rates worldwide. Promoting corporate investment and economic development has been the key target of the large-scale tax cuts in China's tax reform policies.The reduction of value-added tax and inclusive tax cuts for small enterprises are expected to reduce the tax burden and promote investment. However, the effectiveness of the tax reduction policy has been debated and the responses of some firms do no reflect the reduction in tax. Private investment has not increased significantly since the implementation of the tax reduction policy. Does the tax reduction policy then reduce the burden on firms? How do such policies affect corporate investment?What factors restrict the effectiveness of tax reduction policies? By addressing these questions we can better understand the actual effects of tax reduction policies, and thus tax reduction reforms can be further improved.

The tax reduction policies of China's central government often result in fiscal reductions for local governments under the tax sharing system. The financial stress faced by local governments from the implementation of tax reduction policies prompts us to investigate how they can strategically respond to tax reduction shocks. Non-tax fiscal revenue is essential for local governments, which they have the autonomy to collect and manage. However, the tax reduction policies implemented by the central government can reduce local tax revenues.

To ensure a fiscal balance, local governments can better enforce the collection of non-tax revenues, which leads to an increase in the non-tax burden of enterprises, and the effect of "tax-fee substitution" in local fiscal revenues and corporate expenses, which eventually hinders the effectiveness of tax reduction policies.

Value-added tax is the main type of shared tax in China. When first established, value-added tax could not be deducted from the fixed assets purchased before tax, which significantly increases a firm's financial burden. In 2004, China began to pilot value-added tax transformation in its northeastern regions. This policy allows firms to deduct value-added tax from fixed assets purchased by enterprises before taxation, thus reducing the tax burden. We investigate the effect of the value-added tax reform implemented nationwide in 2009 based on prefectural city-level panel data from 2008 to 2011. The main findings are as follows. (i) The reform has greater and more adverse effects on regions that rely more on value-added taxes. (ii) These regions increase non-tax revenues relative to others, and thus the value-added tax reform leads to fee-tax substitution.

In addition, based on 2008-2011 firm-level data from the national tax survey database, we use a difference-in-differences (DID) method to evaluate the impact of VAT transformation on firms' non-tax burden. We find that although the reform reduces tax burdens, it significantly increases corporate non-tax burdens. The effects of the reform on the reduction in tax for firms are not significantly different. However, the effects on the non-tax burden differ with the types and sizes of firms. Raising the non-tax burden mainly affects small, very small, and private firms. it has no significant effect on large and medium-sized firms and non-private firms. Thus, the tax and fee substitution are asymmetric. The fiscal pressure caused by tax cuts for local governments is mainly transferred to small businesses and private firms through an increase in the non-tax burden.

Tax and fee substitution will affect government fiscal revenue quality and corporate fixed asset investment behavior. Compared with taxation, local governments have greater autonomy in terms of non-tax items, and the resulting non-tax burden is much more uncertain for firms. The substitution effect of tax and fees resulting from the tax reduction policy increases the uncertainty of tax and fees for firms, prompting them to adopt more cautious investment strategies.

In the context of recent global tax cuts, we emphasize that the central government should fully consider the financial pressure that the reduction of the shared tax policy places on local governments.The fees they incur should also be reduced in the policy, along with taxes for small and very small firms. Regulating local governments' non-tax revenue collection from small and very small firms and gradually creating a central government tax and fee management process are both necessary to prevent tax reductions.Local governments have increased the non-tax collection from small and very small firms and its management, thus leading to increased uncertainty in the tax burden of small and micro enterprises, which ultimately adversely affects their development.

# The Price and Welfare Effects of Tax Cuts and Fee Reduction Policies: An Analysis Based on an Input-Output Model with a Cost Transmission Rate

NI Hongfu　YAN Bingqian

(Institute of Economics, Chinese Academy of Social Sciences; National Academy of Economic Strategy, Chinese Academy of Social Sciences)

Tax reduction and fee reduction are key parts of fiscal policy that play important roles in stimulating economic vitality. The effect of tax reduction on firms' costs is closely related to the cost transmission rate. From the macro perspective, the producer price will drop if the cost of taxes and fees is partially transmitted. This will further reduce production cost and thus increase firms' profits. However, producer prices are also affected by many other factors, such as strong market demand. When demand is greater than supply, producer prices may rise. This leads to our research question: what is the price effect of the tax and fee reduction policy implemented in China (especially in 2019) and how does this policy influence consumers' welfare? This paper evaluates the effects by constructing an input-output price model with a cost transmission rate. Indirect taxes and fees such as VAT, social security fees, and other production taxes are embedded in the input-output model. The paper focuses on the price and welfare effects of tax and fee reduction. It analyzes the advantages and disadvantages of different tax and fee reduction policies by designing different structural tax reduction scenarios.

Our results show that tax cuts and fee reductions decrease product price and production cost in all industries. The price reduction in the service sector is the highest. The higher the cost transmission rate, the larger the price reduction. When the cost transmission rate is 1/3, the estimated degree of reduction of PPI is the closest to the actual PPI change. Regarding the welfare effect, tax cuts and fee reductions decrease the consumer price and thus improve household welfare. The welfare improvement of a urban household is greater than that of a rural household. The welfare improvement discrepancy between urban households and rural households increases with the increasing cost transmission rate.

This paper's main marginal contributions are as follows. First, by introducing the cost transmission mechanism, this paper constructs an input-output price model with incomplete cost transmission of taxes and fees-Value-added tax, social security fees, and other indirect taxes.The traditional input-output price model assumes that price is completely forward transitive. In fact, most cases are imperfect competition markets.Second, this paper analyzes the impact of China's actual tax and fee reduction policy on PPI and welfare under different cost transitive scenarios. Based on the actual tax reduction rate data of various industries obtained from the tax bureau, the paper estimates tax collection and management ability and then simulates and analyzes the price and welfare effects of the actual tax reduction.Third, this paper constructs three scenarios of structural tax and fee reduction and their impacts on price and welfare. It follows the principles of tax rate simplification and tax rate reform to promote the effective allocation of resources. The paper therefore provides a reference point for further promoting tax system reform and macro policy-making.

We obtain the following policy implications from our research conclusions. First, tax reduction can effectively reduce the producer price index, reduce the cost burden of enterprises, and improve consumer welfare. China still faces many risks and challenges in its post-pandemic economic development.It is crucial to implement a tax and fee reduction policy and reduce the burden on enterprises. The state must put into place preferential policies for preventing and controlling the COVID-19 pandemic, resuming work and production, stabilizing foreign trade, and expanding domestic demand.Second, the design of tax and fee reduction policies should take into account that the industry sector's partial cost transmission rate might weaken the effect of policy implementation. We should estimate the industry sector's cost transmission rate, design the range and size of tax and fee reduction, and truly reduce enterprises' burden. Third, structural tax and fee reduction policies are conducive to better policy effects. Fourth, this paper contains some shortcomings which are worthy of further investigation. For instance, the paper gives the same value to the cost transmission rate for all industries, due to the limited availability of data. The cost transmission rate of course differs between industries, so we can further explore how to estimate different industries' cost transmission rates. This will improve our input-output price model with a cost transmission rate. This paper can also be extended to the general equilibrium model with an input-output structure.

# Intergovernmental Revenue Sharing and Fiscal Budget Revenue Deviation

LYU Bingyang    CHEN Zhigang

(School of Finance, Renmin University; College of Economics, Shenzhen University)

Budget deviation is defined as the difference between the government's budgeted and final Account values. Since the reform of the national tax sharing system, the Chinese government has experienced large budget deviations. Although greater budget deviations are generally seen in low-income countries compared with high-income countries, China's provinces reported average budget deviations as high as 9.38% from 2000 to 2014. This rate is not only much higher than those in developed countries but also much higher than the rates reported in many developing countries. As a budget is a plan for revenues and expenditures, a gap between the budgeted values and final accounts is expected. However, if the gap is too large, it causes a series of problems. If excessive budget deviations persist, government budgets may be considered unreliable and nonauthoritative, and modern budget and fiscal systems could be challenged. These negative outcomes could greatly alter the effects of fiscal regulation on the economy. Therefore, it is important to understand the causes of revenue budget deviation and develop targeted measures to establish a modern budget system, improve the performance of fiscal management activities and even promote the modernization of national governance.

Although the literature discusses the causes of budget deviations from the aspects of technology, economy and system, few studies focus on the impact of intergovernmental fiscal relations. Accordingly, this paper systematically analyzes the impact of intergovernmental revenue sharing on revenue budget deviation. First, it analyzes the institutional background of revenue sharing and budget management. On this basis, a simple static model is constructed and analyzed, revealing that against the background of the sharing method used widely by China's intergovernmental revenue division, a change in intergovernmental revenue sharing would have two opposite effects on budget deviation: fiscal pressure and fiscal expansion. The fiscal pressure mechanism means that the local government will face increased fiscal pressure as the ratio of shared fiscal revenue decreases. To alleviate this fiscal pressure, the local government must strengthen tax collection and management or vigorously develop its economy to increase its final revenue. This eventually leads to an increase in revenue budget deviation. The fiscal expansion mechanism means that the degree of tax effort decreases as the share of fiscal revenue decreases, resulting in a decrease in the final fiscal revenue. This eventually leads to a decrease in revenue budget deviation.

Using the manually collected budget reports of provinces at the People's Congress, this paper collates the budgetary and final account data of 30 Chinese provinces from 2000 to 2013. Specifically, this paper considers the subprovincial governments as a whole and empirically analyzes the impact of revenue sharing on revenue budget deviation using a two-way fixed effect model. The results support the fiscal pressure mechanism: as the ratio of fiscal revenue sharing decreases by 1 percentage point, the revenue budget deviation increases by 0.3 percentage points. Further analysis shows that the impact of revenue sharing on budget deviation is not significant at the provincial level and decreases as the economic development level increases. This result holds through a full battery of robustness checks, which include changing the method of measuring revenue budget deviation and considering the effects of transfer payment and endogeneity, the influence of budget deviation in the previous period and the spatial influences of variables.

This paper makes several main contributions. First, research on budget deviation is limited by the available data.Previous studies suffer from a lack of in-depth data or inadequate data acquisition.This paper uses subprovincial budget deviation data collected from the budget report of the Provincial People's Congress.Second, the literature mainly discusses the influences on budget deviation at a theoretical level and therefore lacks in-depth analysis of specific factors and corresponding empirical testing. This paper systematically explores and tests both the theoretical and empirical aspects of the influence of fiscal revenue sharing on revenue budget deviation.Third, most studies have explored either fiscal pressure or fiscal expansion as the outcome effect of a change of fiscal revenue sharing on local government behavior. This paper considers both effects, which oppose each other, on budget deviation.

# Local Public Debt and Return on Capital: Evidence from New Debt Data and the Triple Mechanism Test

JI Yunyang    MAO Jie    WEN Xueting

(School of Economics and Trade, Hunan University; School of International Business and Economics, University of International Business and Economics; Taikang Asset Management Co., Ltd.)

For China, preventing systemic economic risks while achieving high-quality economic development has become a general objective. Debt-financed investment by local governments is one popular tool for stabilizing economic growth and supply-side structural reform. Local government debt has been expanding on a massive scale since the 2008 financial crisis. By the end of 2019, local public debt had risen to 21.3 trillion yuan, more than double the amount in 2013. At the same time, macro returns on capital have been falling. According to the calculations of Bai Chong' en and Zhang Qiong (2014), since 1993, China's return on capital has been on a downward trend, especially since 2008. Compared with the beginning of reform and opening up, return on capital dropped by 11.3 percentage points in 2013. To explain this, we empirically test the effect of local public debt expansion on return on capital and regional heterogeneity by using matching data on local public debt and return on capital at the prefecture-level city level, and examine the three mechanisms of the effect.

In the past decade, when promoting economic development, local governments have increasingly relied on debt-based investment and financing. The resulting huge public debt greatly loosens local governments' budget constraints, but at the same time it occupies a large amount of credit capital, which will inevitably lead to capital misallocation if investment efficiency is low or other more productive types of investment are crowded out. From the perspective of the local public debt operating process (i. e., financing-investment-repayment), First, in the financing stage, large-scale borrowing by local governments may crowd out the credit resources of banks, thus raising the cost of credit capital of enterprises within the jurisdiction, leading to a crowding out effect. Second, in the investment stage, local government debt funds are mainly used for infrastructure construction. If infrastructure investment has low efficiency, this also indirectly indicates the low efficiency of local government debt fund expenditure. Third, in the repayment stage, the widespread phenomenon of using land sales to pay off debts and land financing will encourage local governments to push up house prices and develop real estate; however, when capital is excessively concentrated in real estate, this will aggravate the economic structural imbalance and capital mismatch between industries. To put it simply, local public debt has an effect on capital mismatch through the crowding out of micro-enterprise investment and financing, the efficiency of infrastructure investment, and the capital concentration of real estate, and thus affects the return on capital.

This paper makes three contributions to the literature.First, in terms of data, it uses matching data of the new calibre of public debt and return on capital at the prefecture level to conduct regression analysis, and provides more representative basic data for empirical analysis. Second, in terms of content, although the literature discusses various factors that affect China's return on capital, it does not consider the effect of China's expansion of local public debt on the influence of return on capital. This article makes up for this research gap and enriches the literature by identifying the influencing factors of return on capital.Third, in terms of mechanism, this paper takes capital mismatch as a logical starting point and comprehensively analyzes the intermediary mechanism of local public debt affecting the return on capital from three perspectives: the efficiency of infrastructure investment, the proportion of investment in real estate, and the crowding out effect of enterprise investment. It provides new evidence to understand the internal correlation between local public debt and return on capital.

The main conclusions of this paper are as follows. First, the expansion of local public debt significantly reduces the return on capital. Second, the negative impact of local public debt on return on capital is mainly realized through three mechanisms: reducing the efficiency of infrastructure investment, increasing the proportion of real estate investment, and squeezing out corporate investment. In short, the expansion of local public debt leads to a decline in the efficiency of capital allocation. Third, the negative impact of local public debt on return on capital is more obvious in non-urban agglomerations, non-large and non-medium-sized cities, and cities with greater dependence on land financing. These conclusions are of great significance for understanding China's economic growth model, and provide policy reference for deepening the reform of the investment and financing system of local governments. In the future, we should pay greater attention to the performance management and efficiency of debt funds to promote high-quality economic development.

# Have Public Finance Policies Induced Financial Institutions to Support Agricultural Development? An Evaluation of the Effects of the Reward Policy On Incremental Agricultural Loans in China

XING Weibo　ZHANG Simin

(School of International Trade and Economics, University of International Business and Economics)

Every year, the issue of "agriculture, countryside, and farmers" is noted as a priority in the Chinese Central Government's Policy Document No.1 Agriculture in China is currently in a critical transition period. The mode of agricultural production is shifting from labor-intensive to a mode that is both capital-and technology-intensive, which means that funds must be efficiently invested to promote agricultural development.However, there has been a widespread lack of funding in rural areas, and asymmetrical access to information and the failure of rural financial markets are also serious problems. Agricultural loans, including agricultural credits, are the main policy tools for poverty alleviation in rural areas.

Over the years, the central government has promulgated a large number of fiscal and financial policies to support rural loans and the agricultural economy. Recently, a series of government decisions indicate that China is trying to use fiscal policies to guide the allocation of financial resources to rural areas. To encourage financial institutions to increase agricultural loans, the Ministry of Finance has since 2009 overseen a pilot reward policy for institutions making incremental agricultural loans. lt is an important measure to integrate fiscal policy and financial policy.

Drawing on theories of rural finance and agricultural economic growth, this study assesses the impacts of the Reward Policy for Incremental Agricultural Loans on agricultural economic development in China. In addition, this study explores the mechanism through which the policy affects agricultural economic development.As 25 provinces successively entered the reward policy pilot program over the 2009 to 2014 period, this study establishes a time-varying difference-in-differences model to evaluate the effect of this exogenous incentive policy on the development of the local agricultural economy. The model uses relevant agricultural economic data from 31 provinces from the 2006 to 2018 period as the research sample. First, we construct an empirical model that uses grain output and farmers' income as the explanatory variables, and policy interaction terms as the core explanatory variables. Then we add control variables such as climatic conditions, input factors, fiscal expenditure on agriculture, local financial development, and agricultural industrialization. Second, to ensure the reliability of the empirical results, we conduct a robustness test.Third, to assess whether the incentive policy has heterogeneous impacts across provinces, we add the interaction terms of geographic location and policy variables to the model and then conduct a heterogeneity test. Fourth, we identify the channels through which the incentive policy affects the agricultural economy by examining the impacts of the policy on the agricultural loan balance, power of agricultural machinery, fixed assets investment of rural households, transportation, and water conservation infrastructure construction.The data are from the China Statistical Yearbooks, Wind database, and CSMAR database.

The empirical results show that the Reward Policy for Incremental Agricultural Loans has significantly promoted the growth of grain output and farmers' income. This conclusion remains valid in the robustness tests. Furthermore, the impacts of the policy on the agricultural economy of provinces in different geographical locations is obviously heterogeneous, i. e., the central and western provinces have been more affected. This may be due to the lower proportion of primary industry and relatively mature financial market in the eastern region. Finally, the analyses of the mechanisms show that the policy mainly promotes local agricultural economies by promoting local agricultural loans, which in turn improve the level of agricultural mechanization and optimize rural infrastructure in areas such as transportation and water conservation.

Based on the empirical evidence, we put forward the following policy recommendations. At present, we should continue to encourage financial institutions to support agriculture. The coordination and cooperation of fiscal policies and monetary policy tools achieves a win-win situation for financial institutions and farmers.Differentiated fiscal policies (including targeted fee subsidies and tax incentives for loans) could also be used to encourage financial institutions to focus on the countryside and increase agricultural investment.

# 08 Inclusive Finance, Regional Finance & Social Development

## The Impact of Housing Wealth on Urban Household Consumption in China

YIN Zhichao    QIU Hua    PAN Xuefeng

(School of Finance, Capital University of Economics and Business; School of Finance, University of International Business and Economics)

China is embracing opportunities and challenges as it heads toward a new era of economic upgrading and transformation. China has proposed a plan to build a domestic circle in which economic growth relies on domestic markets more than on international markets. A critical aim of the domestic circle is to boost consumption and increase its contribution to the economy. Household income in China has displayed fast and steady growth over the last few decades. This has increased the demand for housing. As a result, housing now represents the biggest share of household worth in China. An increase in house prices can add to a household's net worth and thus household consumption. Fast-growing house prices also increase mortgage burdens and therefore restrain consumption. The effects of housing wealth on consumption are thus theoretically ambiguous. This is confirmed in the literature. It is therefore interesting in policy and academic terms to explore how changes in housing wealth affect consumption in China.

We examine the effect of changes in housing wealth on household consumption and the channels of this effect by utilizing China Household Finance Survey (CHFS) data spanning 2013-2019. The CHFS is a biennial national representative survey, launched in 2011, that records information on household finance positions in 29 of the 34 provinces in China. The survey records details of income, consumption, financial assets, housing wealth, debt, jobs, and demographic characteristics, among many variables. Each round of the survey revisits a set of households that were interviewed in the previous round. We trace a set of households that were surveyed in all the survey rounds from 2013-2019 and build a balanced panel of 13, 328 households.

When examining the link between housing wealth and consumption in a baseline model, we impose household fixed effects to account for idiosyncratic and time-invariant omitted variables (e.g., beliefs). It is furthermore possible that consumption also affects housing wealth, because consumption is driven by income, which also contributes to housing demand and house prices. We use a province's average house price in the year prior to each round of the survey (i.e., in 2012, 2014, 2016, and 2018) as the instrumental variable (IV) for the housing wealth of the households in that province. This alleviates the two-way causality. We then re-examine the effect of housing wealth on consumption using the two-stage least squares and fixed effects methods.

The results show that an increase in housing wealth raises household consumption, with a marginal propensity to consume out of housing wealth (house-price MPC) averaging at 2%. Increases in housing wealth furthermore reduce the share of life necessities in consumption and raise that of hedonic goods, thus increasing household consumption. Additional investigations show that housing wealth influences household consumption via a collateral channel that relaxes borrowing constraints and finances consumption growth as house prices rise. As home equity loans are not available in China, part of the credit for the consumption growth is from credit cards. We find evidence that as house prices increase, credit card limits and balances both go up. This implies that credit cards provide funding for the housing wealth effect. Finally, we find that the housing wealth effect on consumption is stronger for households with a second home and for households in central and western China.

We make two main contributions. First, we identify a house-price MPC of 2% and provide evidence of the housing wealth effect on consumption by combining the fixed effects and TV methods to fix endogeneity issues.Second, we find that credit cards fund consumption growth as house prices increase when home equity loans are not available. This proves the universality of a collateral channel regardless of financial institutions.

The implication of our findings is that policy makers should utilize the housing wealth effect to boost and upgrade household consumption when risks and leverage are under control.

Future studies could explore administration data from banks to confirm the link between credit card credits and the housing wealth effect. Other funding sources that are popular in China (e.g., private lending) and their impacts on the housing wealth effect could also be an interesting topic.

# Housing Provident Fund and Households' Investment in Risky Financial Assets: Evidence from China's Household Finance Survey of 2013

CHEN Xuanjuan    LIN Hongmei

(School of Finance, Shanghai University of Finance and Economics)

Limited participation in stock markets is a widespread and puzzling phenomenon, but it is a particularly serious problem in China. We need to understand the factors that affect households' decisions to make risky financial investments. Previous studies indicate that house purchase price is a crucial factor in explaining the level of stockholdings. From 2000 to 2015, China's house purchase price grew rapidly, with a growth rate exceeding the rates in developed countries. In the same period, Chinese households show very high enthusiasm for housing investment. Housing investment requires substantial funds and may reduce households' exposure to risky financial assets.

Following the example of Singapore's Central Provident Fund, in 1994, China implemented the housing provident fund (HPF) to improve housing affordability. The HPF scheme affects the disposable income of households in two ways. On the one hand, according to the tax law, there is no need to pay personal income tax on payments to or withdrawals from the HPF. Therefore, the HPF increases households' future disposable income and lifetime wealth. On the other hand, payment to the HPF enhances a household's current liquidity constraints and the interest rates for HPF deposits are low. Furthermore, unlike endowment insurance, the impact of the HPF is different on households with and without housing.Households without housing cannot use withdrawals from the HPF as a down payment or to repay housing loans. Although households can withdraw funds from the HPF to pay rent, the amount that can be withdrawn for this purpose is limited.

Accordingly, this study addresses three main problems. First, does the HPF significantly influence households' investment in risky financial assets? Second, what is the mechanism through which the HPF affects households' investment in risky financial assets? Third, we discuss the heterogeneity of the impact of the HPF on different types of households.

We use data from the 2013 China Household Finance Survey (CHFS). The CHFS database includes detailed information on household assets, liabilities, financial wealth, income, and insurance. This survey of 28151 sample households covers 29 provinces (autonomous regions and municipalities) and 262 counties (districts and cities). As the majority of people with an HPF are urban, we delete rural households. After data pre- processing, our sample contains 11093 urban households.

We use a Probit model to test the impact of the HPF on the possibility that a household will make risky financial investments. Then, we use a Tobit model to test the impact of the HPF on the proportion of risky financial investments made by households. Finally, we examine the mediating factors to determine the mechanism driving this relationship. To address endogeneity concerns, we use an instrumental variable. We also use the Heckman two-step model and panel fixed effects model as robustness tests.

The empirical results show that the HPF can significantly increase the possibility and proportion of risky financial investments made by households with houses. However, the HPF has no significant impact on households that do not own the place in which they live. The analyses of the mechanism show that the HPF significantly increases households' disposable incomes and improves their risk preference levels, and thus increases the possibility and proportion of investments in risky financial assets. These findings suggest that it is necessary to strengthen the support function of the HPF for households without houses. For example, by relaxing the conditions under which households can make withdrawals from the HPF. In addition, it is very important to increase the interest rate of HPF deposit, to reduce the opportunity cost of the mandate deposit of HPF.

The contributions of this study are as follows. First, this study is the first to link the HPF to risky financial investments and confirms that the HPF can significantly affect households' investment in risky financial assets. We put forward new evidence to explain individuals' limited participation in the stock market, expand the research on the HPF, and provide new topics for follow-up research. Second, the results indicate that the HPF not only improves housing affordability, but also regulates households' investment in risky financial assets. This conclusion provides insights into ways to increase households' property income and to promote the development of a multi-level capital market. Third, the heterogeneity analysis shows that the HPF has no significant impact on investment in risky financial assets by households that do not own housing. This suggests that the government needs to pay attention to the implementation of the HPF system.

# Do Traditional Family Values Restrain Participation in Commercial Pension Plans Among the Urban Population? A Study Based on the Perspectives of Financial Trust and Financial Literacy

ZHENG Lu    XU Minxia

(School of Social Sciences, Tsinghua University)

In China, accelerating population aging is increasing the national eldercare burden. To address this problem, China has implemented a proactive national strategy that includes a multi-pillar pension system. In addition to the state-run first pillar and employment-based second pillar, the third pillar comprises personal retirement products. However, the rate of participation in commercial pension plans is far lower in China than in developed economies. The studies on this limited participation phenomenon focus on various factors, such as institutional setups and policies, financial market development and individual and household characteristics. these studies are based on the "economic man" assumption while largely ignoring crucial cultural factors.

Culture has important effects on individual financial behaviors. It not only affects the formal and informal institutional arrangements in which personal financial activities are embedded but also influences individuals' preferences for risk, liquidity and consumption. All of which shape individuals' financial decision-making. Chinese traditional values are centered on family and strongly emphasize raising children for old age and filial piety, which profoundly influence individual participation in commercial pension plans. Individual trust in financial institutions and individual financial literacy are other important cultural factors that affect the likelihood of participation in commercial pension plans.

Drawing on the CHFS 2015 dataset, this study examines how traditional Chinese family values shape financial trust and financial literacy, which in turn influence individual participation in commercial pension plans. The CHFS, a biennial national survey, was first conducted in 2011. It covers a large sample of households from 29 of the 34 Chinese provinces and records detailed information on many variables, such as household income, consumption, financial assets, housing, debt and demographic characteristics. This study's sample consists of 15659 urban residents who participated in the CHFS 2015 and provided complete information on the variables of interest.

Methodologically, we first construct an index of traditional family values using factor analysis. We then use ordinary least squares and logistic regressions to examine the effects of traditional family values, financial literacy and financial trust on participation in commercial pension plans. The Sobel, KHB and bootstrap tests are used to verify the mediating effects of financial trust and financial literacy on the relationship between traditional family values and participation in commercial pension plans. Instrumental variable estimation is also used to address endogeneity concerns. Additionally, we assess robustness by changing the samples and the measurements of the variables. Finally, we examine the effects on subgroups divided by region, educational level and occupation.

The empirical results show that traditional family values inhibit Chinese urban residents from purchasing commercial pensions. The finding remains valid after accounting for endogeneity. Further analysis indicates that financial trust and financial literacy mediate the relationship between traditional family values and participation in commercial pension plans. Specifically, traditional family values reduce individual trust in financial institutions and divert attention from financial information, thus inhibiting participation in commercial pension plans. Meanwhile, traditional family values are also associated with a lower level of financial literacy, which tends to decrease the likelihood of purchasing a commercial pension.Our analysis also reveals that the negative effects of traditional family values are more prominent in underdeveloped regions and among less educated people.

In contrast to the rational economic perspective, this study offers a cultural perspective and thus sheds new light on individuals financial behaviors and financial market development. It not only enriches our understanding of these topics but also has important practical implications. First, Chinese elderly people, who are deeply influenced by traditional family values, prefer to rely on their children and families and thus require innovative family-based elderly care policies and solutions to meet their needs. Second, China should provide more information channels to improve individual financial literacy and financial market regulation and boost public trust in financial institutions. Last but not least, people living in inland provinces and those without a college education would be better served by a more inclusive financial system. In conclusion, China's elderly care pension market has great potential. All market participants should take the available opportunities and meet its challenges to develop the market in an equitable, balanced and high-quality manner.

# When can I Go Home? School Provisioning and the Decision to Immigrate

LI Ming    ZHENG Liming

(School of International Trade and Economics, University of International Business and Economics)

In recent years, the existing population of China has begun to relocate among different cities. This is exemplified by a new trend among China's massive migrant population of returning to their hometowns. With the relaxation of the Hukou system, it is worth considering how to promote the reasonable and orderly flow of labor and improve the efficiency of human resource allocation. Many factors influence migration. Tiebout proposed that residents flow into the region that best matches their preferences, after considering the public goods and tax levels of each location. Studies of developed countries suggest that this mechanism exists (Bayoh et al., 2006; Kleven et al., 2013; Dustmann and Okatenko, 2014; Akcigit et al., 2016; Moretti and Wilson, 2017).However, due to the uniform tax system and Hukou system in China, the effectiveness of the Tiebout model is debated, especially in the context of populations returning to their hometowns.

We empirically investigate the causal effect of public goods supply on a migrants' decisions to return to their hometowns.We obtain data on residential address and "usual place of residence five years ago" from the 2005 National Sample Survey to construct a dynamic variable denoting whether migrants return to their hometowns. We also construct a proxy variable for change in the number of schools at the city level according to the extended implementation of the "School Consolidation" policy in China. This is a public policy promoted in China since 2001 that aims to improve the quality of education by eliminating many smaller schools and merging them into larger institutions. Using a quasi-natural experimental approach, we divide the sample into treat and control groups based on the presence of children aged 6-10 years in the family (a child was 10 years old in 2005 when the data was collected, given that he/ she started primary school at 6 years of age in 2001) and build a difference-in-differences model.

Our findings are as follows. First, a decrease in the number of schools significantly hinders the return of the migrant population. Furthermore, the greater the decrease in the number of schools, the greater the negative impact on the return of the migrant population. This result still holds when considering endogeneity and other factors. Second, the results of our heterogeneity analysis show that the impact above is valid for both rural and urban areas and is more obvious among smaller families and families with boys. Third, the impact is not only on parents but also on their school-age children, meaning that the availability of educational public goods affects the migration decisions of two generations.

Beyond confirming the Tiebout model, this paper contributes to the literature in at least in two additional ways. First, we demonstrate the impact of public goods on migrants returning home and enrich the literature in this field. Most existing studies exploring the impact of public services on migration are based on an outflow perspective, and little attention has been paid to returning inflows. Further, due to limited data, the available studies are more theoretical in nature. Second, our identification setup is new. We attempt to explore the dynamics of migration based on cross-sectional census data at the household level, which may inform future studies.

The conclusions of this paper are informative in the context of policy decisions. In developing countries, improving the efficiency of public resource distribution and optimizing the provision of public goods such as education could help break down barriers to labor mobility and thus further promote economic growth and quality of life.For cities trying to attract talent, enhancing the provisioning of public goods could help to stimulate further population inflows. In this paper, we focus on the impact of changes in the number of schools.Future studies could assess the impacts of public education quality or other public goods (e.g., health care) to explore the effect of public goods supply on population mobility to a broader and deeper extent.

# Land-renting, Farmers' Agricultural Credit Demands and Credit Constraints: An Analysis of CHFS Data

LU Xiaomeng  WU Yu

(Survey and Research Center for China Household Finance, Southwestern University of Finance and Economics)

According to China's 14th Five-Year Plan, it is necessary to consolidate and improve the basic rural management system to ensure the separation of rural contracted land ownership, contracting rights, and management rights. Land-renting is an important component of both the deactivation of management rights and the optimal allocation of rural land resources. The three-rights separation reform of agricultural land not only promotes the exchange of land management rights but also releases the value of the land and enables its full potential to be realized.

The financing problems faced by farmers are crucial in the land-renting process. Issues such as the scale of land-renting, the choice of transfer method, and the speed of transfer largely depend on the resolution of financing issues. Research on the issue of land-renting by rural households focuses on the factors affecting land transfer and its performance. The studies on credit provided to farmers mostly focus on credit behavior and the importance of credit to farming households. To address a gap in the research, this paper focuses on the relationship between land-renting and the credit behavior of farmers.

Using large-scale micro survey data from the nationwide China Household Finance Survey (CHFS) in 2015 and 2017, this paper conducts an in-depth study of the credit needs, credit constraints, and credit satisfaction of rural households from the perspective of land-renting. The findings are as follows: (i) Compared with farmers who have not transferred land, those who have transferred land express a stronger demand for agricultural credit, which is not accompanied by a significant increase in demand for non-agricultural credit. (ii) Both the proportion of agricultural credit awarded to farmers who have transferred land and the proportion of farmers facing credit constraints have increased significantly. Further research on farmers who have obtained agricultural credit reveals that those who rent land have low credit satisfaction and identifies a relatively large gap in credit constraints. By analyzing the scale of farmers' land transfers, this paper finds that this phenomenon is more obvious in farmers who undertake larger-scale land transfers. The results suggest that during the process of land-renting, farmers face greater agricultural credit constraints; therefore, financial support for land transfer should be increased.

This paper makes the following academic contributions: (i) It enriches the literature on land transfer and farmers' credit behavior. The literature on credit among farmers mainly focuses on their credit behavior and the importance of credit to farming households. Research on land-renting also mainly focuses on the influencing factors and performance of land transfer. This paper studies the credit behavior of farming households during the process of land-renting and thus provides a powerful supplement to the literature. (ii) The studies on the credit behavior of farmers mostly focus on their credit constraints and credit needs. This paper is the first to explore the credit satisfaction of farmers and thus extends the scope of research. (iii) This paper uses nationwide sample survey data to study the credit behavior of farmers. Therefore, its conclusions are more representative of the general population.

This paper has two significant policy implications.

First, the conclusions provide direction for the new-era government to promote reforms in agriculture and rural areas, increase the flow of more factors to the countryside, and enhance the vitality of agricultural and rural development.

The construction of a land circulation system would not only be conducive to the deregulation of management rights but would also promote the optimal allocation of rural land resources. Although the state has recently introduced many rural financial policies, such as the microfinance policy for farmers, the findings in this paper show that credit remains a major problem for farmers who have transferred land. The conclusions in this paper can help the government and relevant departments understand the credit constraints faced by farmers during the process of land-renting and thus promote healthy development of the land transfer market.

Second, the conclusions can also help consolidate and expand the association between poverty alleviation and rural revitalization. Overall, our country has achieved victory in the decisive battle against poverty.Consolidating and upgrading the results of poverty alleviation is a primary task set forth in the 14th Five-Year Plan.The role of finance in this process cannot be ignored. This study finds that farmers face more serious credit constraints during the process of transferring land. The government should continue to increase the credit support provided to farmers who are transferring land to alleviate their credit constraints.It should also establish a stable system to help farmers invigorate rural development.Finally, it should consolidate and expand the long- term mechanism of poverty alleviation to further revitalize rural areas.

# Can Compulsory Education Law Improve Intergenerational Mobility?

CHEN Binkai    ZHANG Shujuan    SHEN Guangjun

(School of Economics, Central University of Finance and Economics; Government Big Data Lab, Shenzhen Research Institute of Big Data; Lingnan (University) College, Sun Yat-sen University)

Social mobility affects national stability and long-term growth. Equality of opportunity is crucial to the stable development of society. Since the reform and opening up began, China's economy has experienced rapid growth, leading to significant improvement in people's living standards. This has led to the realization of the concept stated as "some people get better off earlier" and an increasingly insurmountable gap in social class. Additionally, the correlation coefficient of intergenerational education and income in China has continued to rise over the past 30 years, indicating a decline in intergenerational mobility.

Although research focuses extensively on measuring and describing intergenerational mobility, relatively few studies examine the ability of public policy to increase social mobility. Drawing on data from the Chinese Household Income Project Survey 2013 and National Population Survey 2005, this paper uses temporal and geographical variations in the implementation of the Compulsory Education Law (CEL) as an exogenous shock to identify how education policy impacts intergenerational mobility. We find that the CEL has a significant beneficial effect on intergenerational education mobility, as the greatest benefits are incurred by children whose parents have low levels of education and employment and earn fewer benefits.

This paper makes four major novel contributions to the literature. First, this study of intergenerational mobility is focused on the factors that influence educational mobility; therefore, this paper fills a gap in the literature, which is focused mainly on income or occupational mobility. Second, this paper examines the mechanism underlying the effect of compulsory education on intergenerational mobility, whereas the literature focuses on the measurement and definition of intergenerational mobility but fails to explore what influences it. Third, this paper identifies the impact of public policies on social mobility, using the CEL as an exogenous shock; thus, it addresses the identification of cause and effect, which is the main challenge encountered in studying the factors influencing mobility. Fourth, the literature contains many discussions on the effects of compulsory education policy on the rates of return and health. This paper extends these discussions from the influence of compulsory education policy in China to intergenerational mobility. It thus complements the literature and provides a reference for adjusting compulsory education policy.

The findings also have important policy implications. For example, a policy of compulsory nine-year education is shown to have a positive impact on the promotion of educational mobility because it significantly promotes the education of children of lower socioeconomic status by mitigating family constraints. Therefore, this policy effectively promoted the accumulation of human capital in the early stages of the reform and opening up and laid a good foundation for subsequent economic and social development. However, some recent changes emphasize the need to extend the duration of compulsory education. On the one hand, rapid economic and social development have increased the demand for high-quality labor; on the other hand, the trend of overall social mobility in China remains negative. Extending the number of years of compulsory education can simultaneously alleviate both of these socioeconomic issues, thus enabling China to achieve educational equity and, importantly, to improve the overall national quality. The ability of public policy to improve intergenerational mobility should be further exploited to promote social equity and justice by equalizing educational opportunities.

# Does Targeted Poverty Alleviation Affect Corporate Risk?

ZHEN Hongxian   WANG Sanfa

(School of Accounting/ China Internal Control Research Center, Dongbei University of Finance and Economics)

Targeted poverty alleviation is a national strategy and an innovative form of poverty alleviation proposed according to China's special national conditions. Enterprises' participation in targeted poverty alleviation can not only give full play to the inherent advantages of industrial poverty alleviation and implement "blood-creating" poverty alleviation, but also obtain, a larger platform for creating value. Therefore, the targeted poverty alleviation by corporate is an important part of winning the battle against poverty, and also becomes a new form for corporate to fulfill their social responsibility. Then, does the capital market pay attention to the targeted poverty alleviation actions of listed companies? Does the participation of corporate in targeted poverty alleviation affect corporate risk?

The research on the relationship between corporate social responsibility and corporate risk has formed two competing views: the risk reduction hypothesis and the risk increase hypothesis. Regarding the hypothesis of increased risk, neoclassical economics believes that corporate social responsibility has deviated from the goal of maximizing shareholder value. Under the condition of limited corporate cash flow, overtaking of social responsibilities will occupy corporate resources, which may result in companies having to reduce strategic investments such as R&D investment and long-term investment, weakening corporate competitiveness, reducing corporate value, and increasing corporate risk. According to principal-agent theory, managers tend to be opportunistic, and their active fulfillment of social responsibilities may be social activities that have nothing to do with the development of enterprises in order to improve their personal reputation and social influence. Wasting the limited resources of an enterprise on social activities unrelated to the creation of shareholder value will weaken the competitiveness of the enterprise and increase its risk. For self-interested motives, managers may use social responsibility tools to divert negative news and cover up the problems in the business performance of enterprises, so that enterprises perform social responsibility only has "tool characteristics" rather than "value-creating characteristics". Therefore, it is ultimately an empirical question that this study aims to address.

In order to answer these questions, this paper downloaded from the CSMAR database the non-financial listed companies that participated in targeted poverty alleviation in China's A-share market in 2016-2018 as a sample to empirically study the impact of targeted poverty alleviation on corporate risk. The empirical research conclusions of this paper mainly include the following points. First, the targeted poverty alleviation action is significantly negatively correlated with the equity market risk. Second, the lower the corporate information transparency, the stronger the effect of targeted poverty alleviation on the risk reduction of the stock market, indicating that the lower the transparency of corporate information, the stronger the "information communication" role of the targeted poverty alleviation actions of enterprises. Third, in regions where the institutional environment is weaker, the targeted poverty alleviation behavior of companies has a stronger effect on reducing equity market risk. This shows that in areas where the institutional environment is relatively weak, the government allocates a greater proportion of economic resources.

The main contributions of this paper are as follows: First, this paper studies the impact of corporate social responsibility on corporate risk from the perspective of targeted poverty alleviation, enriching the research scope of corporate social responsibility and corporate risk. Second, based on the perspective of equity market risk, this article finds that investors pay attention to the targeted poverty alleviation behavior of enterprises and can identify the strategic significance of targeted poverty alleviation by enterprises. Third, the conclusions of this article have important policy significance. This article explores the mechanism of the enterprise's targeted poverty alleviation affecting enterprise risk from the perspectives of reputation effect, resource effect and information effect.

# Do Green Investors Play a Role? Empirical Research on Firms' Participation in Green Governance

JIANG Guangsheng   LU Jianci   LI Weian

(Business School/China Academy of Corporate Governance, Tianjin University of Finance and Economics)

  With the rapid development of industrialization and urbanization in China, ecological environment problems become more prominent, seriously hindering the inclusive growth of humans and nature. In recent years, China's green finance policies have led to a group of particular institutional investors-green investors. As the main body of social responsibility investment, they aim to choose the investment responsibility for the society, guide the enterprises to carry out the green concept into the social behaviors such as clean operation and promote the enterprises to pursue economic benefits and pay more attention to social responsibility and public interests. Whether and how green investors affect the participation of enterprises in green governance have become the critical issue of our research. To this end, our study first examines the impact of green investors on firms' participation in green governance, and then explores heterogeneity on the pollution level, the nature of property rights, and regional environmental awareness. Finally, we investigate the social and economic benefits of firms' participation in green governance.

  Using a sample of A-share listed firms from 2006 to 2016, we explore the impact of green investors on firms' participation in green governance. Our findings suggest that green investors play an active role in the promotion of corporate green governance. Further investigation indicates that the promotion effect of green investors on green action is more substantial in enterprises with weak environmental awareness, the impact on green expenditure is more substantial in heavy polluting enterprises and state-owned enterprises, and the effect on green governance performance is more substantial in non-heavy polluting enterprises and state-owned enterprises and enterprises in weak environmental awareness. Finally, we find that the enterprises with more green governance participation are more likely to be recognized by green investors; although the green expenditure reduces the performance (Roa), the green action and green governance performance increase the performance (Roa).

The contributions of this paper are as follows: First, we explore the influencing factors of green governance from the enterprise level, which provides a new perspective for the research on corporate green governance. Second, starting from the investment purpose and green concept of green investors, considering the influence ways of "voting with hands" and "voting with feet", we explore the influence mechanism of green investors on firm's participation in green governance, which is a useful supplement to the existing research.

Our findings also have important policy implications. First, China should not only actively guide the investment of green investors and play an effective role in the implementation of sustainable development strategy, but also establish a sound green financial system, create an excellent external financing environment for corporate green governance.Second, from the perspective of its long-term sustainable development, enterprises should fully realize the scientific nature of incorporating green investors, corporate green governance, and long-term business performance into the framework of enterprise performance management, actively cooperate with and strive to practice the investment intention of green investors, establish a good corporate image to build a relationship network worthy of investors' trust. Moreover, enterprises should also strive to identify the cognitive requirements and expectations of social participants for the sustainable development of enterprises to obtain more green financing.

## 09  Corporate Governance & Corporate Finance

## Employee Salary Competitiveness and the Adoption of Employee Stock Ownership Plan

ZHANG Huili    ZHAO Jianyu    LU Zhengfei

(Business School, Beijing Normal University; School of Accountancy, Central University of Finance and Economics; Guanghua School of Management, Peking University)

Rank-and-file employees are important to the development of firms, because their engagement determines how a firm's strategy is finally executed. The incentives of non-executive employees are a major concern in both academia and practice, as non-executive employees are recognized as essential motivators of the maximization of corporate value. Thus, aligning the interests of employees with shareholders and improving their relationships have become key areas of focus in China. In June 2014, the China Securities Regulatory Commission issued its "Guiding Opinions on the Pilot Program of Employee Stock Ownership Plans for Listed Companies," which sets out policies for supporting the pilot implementation of employee stock ownership plans (ESOPs) for listed companies. ESOPs have since become increasingly popular. However, little evidence of firms' actual motivations for adopting ESOPs has been provided.

Proposing the concept of ESOPs, Kelso and Adler (1958) argue that they can ease internal conflicts and align the interests of employees with those of shareholders, thus supporting the long-term interests of capitalism. According to social comparison theory, employee-shareholder conflict is often caused by salary competitiveness, in which employees compare their salaries with those of their counterparts outside the company. A lower level of salary competitiveness may be related to a more passive working attitude and a higher employee turnover rate, which can hinder the efficiency of a firm's productivity. Thus, is salary competitiveness a main concern in terms of employee stock ownership? Addressing this question is important for regulators and can also enrich the ESOP-related literature.

We investigate this question using a sample of Chinese listed A-shares firms from 2006 to 2017. We control for the effects of corporate finance and corporate governance characteristics. Following studies such as those of Bova et al. (2014, 2015), we include firms adopting employee stock ownership plans or stock options/restricted stocks for non-executive employees as our observations. We collect data from the China Stock Market & Accounting Research (CSMAR) and Wind Databases, exclude financial firms and missing values, and winsorize all the continuous data at the 1% and 99% levels. To calculate the salary competitiveness index, at least three observations are required in the same industry.

Our empirical evidence indicates that the weaker a firm's level of employee salary competitiveness is, the more likely it will be that the firm adopts ESOPs. Our conclusions remain unchanged after conducting a series of robustness tests and considering any potential endogenous problems. We also find that the less competitive employee salary is, the more attention will be paid to maintaining the stability of the ESOPs, including demanding a longer locking period, covering more non-executive employees, and offering more shares to rank- and-file employees. We further document that the negative relation between employee salary competitiveness and the adoption of ESOPs is only significant in firms with more employee turnover pressure, higher human resource costs, and more severe financial constraints. In general, we find that adopting ESOPs is the most realistic choice for Chinese firms, as it makes up for less competitive salaries when facing the challenges of external labor mobility and internal human resource costs and capital constraints.

This study makes several contributions. First, our research provides new insights into why ESOPs are adopted, from the perspective of employee salary competitiveness. Our results show that firms use ESOPs to make up for less competitive employee salaries, and thus support regulators' original aims of promoting ESOPs.Second, our empirical evidence can bring some enlightment to the relevant regulatory authorities about improving the design of ESOPs to help protect employee interests.Our conclusions also provide regulators with methods of optimizing the ESOP policy environment and can help firms to create harmonious environments for their internal employees.Third, we enrich the literature related to ESOPs, employee salaries, and income distribution.

# Increased Holdings of Controlling Shareholders Under Equity Pledge: Value Signal or Behavioral Signal?

XU Longbing  WANG Bin

(School of Finance, Shanghai University of Finance and Economics)

In recent years, controlling shareholders have increased their holdings of the company's stocks. Most controlling shareholders claim that they increased their shares because they are confident in the company's trajectory and optimistic about its future prospects. However, studies have found that many controlling shareholders increased their holdings following an equity pledge. Why are controlling shareholders keen to increase their holdings after an equity pledge? Do holdings under different backgrounds send different signals ?How does the market interpret the signals?

Traditional signal theory claims that an increase in the controlling shareholders' holdings transmits signals about the company's fundamentals and future development. Rational investors will use the signal to judge the company's value. They will believe that the current stock price deviates from the intrinsic value, which is considered the signal transmission effect. According to behavioral finance studies, investors have bounded rationality: their decision-making process has reference point dependence and representative deviation. A traditional signal transmission becomes a behavioral signal when the investor habituates the traditional signal.The behavioral signal is essentially a signal, but it does not reflect the company's fundamentals. Rather, it influences the investor's decision-making through their judgment of behavioral habits, resulting in the signal transmission effect. This paper argues that the increase in holdings under equity pledge is a behavioral signal, and the controlling shareholders have a motive to use the behavioral signal effect from an increase in holdings to stabilize the stock price, thus mitigating the risk of the equity pledge.

This study empirically tests a sample of A-share listed companies from 2008 to 2017 and finds that controlling shareholders are more inclined to increase shareholdings under an equity pledge. Their inclination strengthens with the increase in pledge rate, indicating that the controlling shareholder's increase in holdings is an attempt to alleviate liquidation pressure and prevent the transfer of control. In the short term, there is no significant difference in the degree of positive market reaction between the non-pledged group and the pledged group. In the long run, the long-term stock price and the pledged group's operating performance after the increase in holdings are weaker than the control group. The non-pledged group is better than the control group, indicating that the increase in holdings under the pledge of equity is not a value signal but a behavioral signal. Further analysis reveals that the positive effect of the equity pledge on the increase in holdings is more pronounced in companies with high liquidation pressure, low-quality companies, and underdeveloped areas with loose regulatory environments. This finding proves that controlling shareholders increase their holdings under an equity pledge to alleviate liquidation pressure. Expansion tests show that a controlling shareholder under an equity pledge is more inclined to net increase in holdings after considering the impact of a reduction in shareholding. It also shows that management and other major shareholders cater to the controlling shareholder's increase in holdings. Finally, this article excludes the hypothesis of value underestimation, the hypothesis of political motivation, the hypothesis of enhanced control, and the hypothesis of overconfidence as alternative explanations.

This study makes three main contributions to the literature. First, this article deepens the research in the field of equity pledge. It connects the equity pledge with controlling shareholders and insider transactions and finds that the controlling shareholder under the equity pledge is motivated to alleviate the risk of a control transfer by increasing their holding. It also expands the perspective of equity pledge research.Second, this article provides new evidence from China for behavioral corporate finance research. From the perspective of behavioral signals, this article finds that the controlling shareholder's behavior is an attempt to leverage the representative deviation of investor psychology. By sending behavioral signals, the stock price will rise in the short term, alleviating the risk of control transfer. Third, this article's conclusions have some policy implications.For the regulatory authorities, it is necessary to further improve the shareholder increase system and the equity pledge information disclosure system, and strengthen the supervision of controlling shareholder increases under equity pledges.

# Internal Governance and Capital Structure Adjustment: Evidence from the Perspective of Non-CEO Executives' Independence

ZHANG Bo    HAN Yadong    LI Guangzhong

(School of Business, Renmin University of China; School of Business, Sun Yat-sen University)

Decisions regarding capital structure directly affect long-term corporate performance and value. Morellec, Nikolov, and Schurhoff (2012) emphasize the role of agency conflicts in corporate financing decisions and develop a tradeoff model to investigate the importance of manager-shareholder conflicts in capital structure choice. Following Morellec et al. (2012), other studies investigate the roles of various corporate governance mechanisms, such as external governance mechanisms, board oversight, and executive compensation contracts, in alleviating the problem of sub-optimal capital structures caused by the conflicts between shareholders and managers.

However, most studies focus on individual CEOs as the representatives of the top management team, the roles of non-CEO executives in corporate decision-making have not been fully examined. Non-CEO executives have a significant influence on corporate decision-making as they are the implementers of business decisions, and thus monitor and constrain the self-interested behavior of CEOs. The internal monitoring that takes place from the bottom up within a top management team (TMT) is known as TMT internal governance.

The effectiveness of internal governance within a TMT requires non-CEO executives to be independent from the CEO. In China, a CEO has the right to propose the appointment or dismissal of non-CEO executives. The CEO may prefer to select non-CEO executives who share similar values, and these executives may also be grateful to the CEO who hired them, thus diminishing their monitoring role. In this study, we use the proportion of the top four highest-paid non-CEO executives appointed before a current CEO's arrival to measure TMT internal governance. The larger this proportion, the greater the independence of non-CEO executives and the stronger the TMT internal governance.

Using a sample of Chinese listed companies from 2001 to 2017, we investigate the effect of TMT internal governance on capital structure decisions. We find that TMT internal governance significantly increases a firm's leverage when its actual leverage is lower than the target leverage ratio, particularly for non-state-owned enterprises (non-SOEs). In addition, the effect of TMT internal governance is greater for firms with more severe agency problems and those with non-CEO executives who have stronger incentives to monitor the CEO. Our analysis of the mechanism reveals that TMT internal governance reduces the degree of deviation from the target leverage ratio by reducing the agency costs.

Our study contributes to the literature on corporate governance and capital structure and has important policy implications for the further development of the corporate governance of Chinese listed companies. Our study contributes to the literature focusing on the impact of corporate governance on capital structure decisions by taking the perspective of TMT internal governance, which has previously been neglected. Our study also provides policy implications for improving corporate governance and optimizing capital structures.

# Building a Cooperative Customer Relationship: Empirical Evidence from Credit Provision to Major Customers

JIANG Wei    DI Lulu    LIU Chengda

(School of Business, Renmin University of China; School of Accounting, Southwestern University of Finance and Economics; Management School, Zhejiang University of Technology)

It is critical for managers to make appropriate decisions in dealing with supply chain risks (McKinsey, 2010). The literature suggests that, if a supplier firm and its customers can build a cooperative rather than an arm's length relationship, the communication and cooperation between them will not only mitigate the hold-up problem and operating risk induced by major customers (Bensaou, 1999), but also enhance firm performance and value (Kalwani and Narayandas, 1995; Patatoukas, 2012; Irvine et al., 2016). However, few studies in the accounting and finance literature have explored how to build and maintain a cooperative relationship with customers, especially major customers (Anderson and Dekker, 2009). Several scholars have provided limited empirical evidence on cooperative relationship building from the perspectives of capital structure, accounting policies, and earnings management (Banerjee et al., 2007; Kale and Shahru, 2008; Raman and Shahrur, 2008; Dou et al., 2013).

In the literature on trade credit, most studies have focused on the role of accounts receivable as financing (Love et al, 2007; Giannetti et al., 2011), neglecting its role as a product quality warranty when the supplier firm and its customers are attempting to build a cooperative relationship (Smith, 1987). Because it is challenging to obtain large-sample information on specific products and terms of trade credit, the empirical evidence on the role of accounts receivable as a product quality warranty is not only limited, but also indirect (Long et al., 1993; Klapper et al., 2012; Dass et al., 2015). Considering the potential hold-up problem and operating risk induced by major customers, there is a lack of direct empirical evidence on whether and how supplier firms use accounts receivable as a product quality warranty when building and maintaining a cooperative relationship with major customers. Empirical evidence on this topic would provide insight into integrating supply chains and improving supply chain finance, thus enhancing a country's global economic competitiveness.

Our initial sample consists of all firms listed on China's Shenzhen and Shanghai Stock Exchanges from 2005 to 2015. Our sample period starts in 2005 because this is the first year in which a sizable portion of listed firms started disclosing information about their top five customers. In addition, before 2005, to enhance their transparency in response to investors' demands, publicly listed firms in China began to disclose the names of their top five debtors and the corresponding amounts and age of their accounts receivable. We therefore manually collect the location of each top five customer and each top five debtor and the amount and percentage of sales to them for all listed firms between 2005 and 2015. All financial data, the names of the top five debtors, and the corresponding amounts and age of accounts receivable are from China Stock Market and Accounting Research (CSMAR) and China Center for Economic Research (CCER).

Our results show that, when customer concentration is high, credit terms are more lenient; that is, a larger amount of accounts receivable with a longer maturity is provided to major customers. Further evidence shows that, when the geographic proximity between a supplier firm and its major customers is distant, when the supplier firm is in a competitive industry, and when the supplier firm is located in a region with high level of business environment, the positive relation between customer concentration and lenient credit terms strengthens. Lastly, we find that the more credit that is provided to major customers, the better the supplier firm's performance.

This paper makes two contributions to the literature. First, we contribute to the accounting and finance literature on how to build a cooperative relationship with major customers, because there is limited empirical evidence in the literature from the perspectives of capital structure, accounting policies, and earnings management.Second, using the unique data from disclosed information on Chinese listed firms' top five debtors and top five customers, we provide relatively direct empirical evidence on the role of accounts receivable as a product quality warranty when the supplier firm and its major customers are building and maintaining a cooperative relationship. Because it is challenging to obtain large-sample information on specific products and terms of trade credit, the empirical evidence on the role of accounts receivable as a product quality warranty is not only very limited, but also indirect.

# Rehired Independent Directors and Corporate Misconduct: Learning Effect or Relationship Effect?

DU Xingqiang    ZHANG Ying

(Center for Accounting Studies/School of Management, Xiamen University)

In August 2001, the China Securities Regulatory Commission statutorily required that the longest tenure of each independent director of a Chinese listed firm must be less than six years. Due to this limitation, a number of independent directors left after their term expired. However, they can be rehired by their former firm after a cooling-off period. Scholars and practitioners have expressed concern about the economic consequences of independent directors. Nevertheless, whether rehired independent directors improve corporate governance is a pending question.

Rehired independent directors are those who leave a firm at the end of their second term (i. e., the sixth year) but are then rehired as independent directors by the same firm after a cooling-off period. Given the non-scarcity of independent directors in China, why some Chinese listed firms rehire former independent directors is an open question. On the one hand, the learning effect suggests that rehired independent directors are different from other independent directors because they have accumulated knowledge and potentially formed relationships, allowing them access to internal information. Thus, rehired independent directors can better perform supervisory and consultative roles. On the other hand, the relationship effect suggests that the close relationship between a rehired independent director and the firm may impair the independence of the director.

We assess a sample of Chinese listed firms from the 2003-2016 period to examine the effect of rehired independent directors on corporate misconduct, and then distinguish the learning effect from the relationship effect. First, the findings show that for firms with rehired independent directors, the number of reported corporate misconduct issues is significantly lower in the rehired period than that in the cooling-off period (vertical comparison). Second, compared with the cooling-off period, the number of instances of corporate misconduct is significantly lower in the first-term period (vertical comparison). Third, the number of corporate misconduct issues is significant lower in firms with more rehired independent directors than in firms with no or fewer rehired independent directors (horizontal comparison). These results suggest that the presence of rehired independent directors mitigates corporate misconduct, validating the learning effect, and it is unlikely that firms rehire independent directors to circumvent regulations. These conclusions stand after a variety of sensitivity tests and correction of the endogeneity effect.

The present study makes several contributions to the existing literature. First, given the inconsistent results of previous studies, we focus on rehired independent directors to examine the influence of rehired independent directors on corporate misconduct, supplementing the literature on the relationship between independent directors and corporate governance. In addition, we vertically compare the number of corporate misconduct issues during the first-hired period, the cooling-off period, and the rehired period to mitigate the endogeneity problem (i. e., the selection of independent directors may be influenced by corporate governance structure, corporate performance, and other factors). Second, existing studies do not examine why independent directors are rehired or the economic consequences of rehiring. This paper fills this gap in the literature. Third, we attempt to determine whether former independent directors should be rehired after a cooling-off period. Previous studies find that it is appropriate to extend an independent director's tenure, but do not mention the specific service term. We find that rehired independent directors play a more important role in improving corporate governance than other independent directors.

This study has several practical implications. First, we explore the economic consequences and motivations of rehired independent directors, thereby contributing to the improvement of the independent director system. The findings will also help governments to better monitor independent directors.Second, the results will help investors to understand the phenomenon of "rehired independent director". The conclusions provide empirical guidance for the selection of future independent directors by Chinese listed firms and document a practical approach to mitigating corporate misconduct.

# Large Shareholders' share Pledging and Capital Operations of Listed Companies

LU Rong    LAN Yuan

(School of Finance, Shanghai University of Finance and Economics; Shanghai Institute of International Finance and Economic)

In recent years, it has become common in China's capital market for large shareholders to use stock pledging for financing purposes. However, due to market turbulence, large shareholders are facing a pledge crisis, which has become a hot topic in the capital market and has raised concerns about systemic risk. Stock pledging seems to be a financing behavior of shareholders that is unrelated to their companies. However, because shareholders occupy a special position, once the risk of the pledged stocks is high, it will have a significant impact on the company's control, stock price, operating performance, and information disclosure, among other effects. Therefore, in the face of risk, large shareholders are strongly motivated to take measures to stabilize the company's stock price.

Some scholars have studied the measures adopted by large shareholders, such as information disclosure manipulation or tax evasion. However, these studies have ignored one important aspect: capital operations. In fact, listed companies have often stabilized their share prices through capital operations. Capital operation refers to the process of adding value to a company through the use of capital market instruments and financial instruments by skillfully operating capital. Capital operations mainly include asset acquisition, equity transfers, asset divestiture, absorption and mergers, debt restructuring, asset replacement, and tender offers.

Capital operations are often used by companies, and may be a way for large shareholders to alleviate equity pledge risk. First, in reality, many listed companies suspend trading for long periods due to capital operation uncertainty in attempts to avoid a further decline in their stock price.Second, some studies have shown that capital operations are an effective method for listed companies to increase their excess return.Therefore, we try to answer the following question: when the proportion of large shareholders pledging stocks is high or when the stock price reaches the closing line, will listed companies use capital operations to survive potential risk? If the answer is yes, how does this affect their capital operations? Furthermore, what is the mechanism behind large shareholders' use of capital operations to avoid pledge risk?

Based on these questions, we investigate the relationship between stock pledging by large shareholders and capital operations using Chinese A-share listed companies over the 2007-2018 period. The results show that (i) the higher the proportion of stocks pledged, the greater the possibility of capital operations in companies; this relationship is more significant in margin calls and in private listed companies. (ii) The mechanism test shows that when the pledge ratio increases, the suspension time after capital operations increases; from the perspective of the effect of stock price promotion, capital operations can improve the stock price and alleviate pledge risk in the short term, but the effect is not significant in the long term. (iii) The main types of capital operations in listed companies are equity transfers, asset acquisition, and asset divestiture.Further analysis shows that large shareholders mainly use asset acquisition and asset divestiture to increase the suspension time and use equity transfers to increase the stock price.

We contribute to the literature in the following ways. (i) From the perspective of capital operations, we find new evidence that large shareholders influence the behavior of companies. In addition, one of the main contributions of this study is to identify the mechanism of capital operations to alleviate equity pledge risk, that is, large shareholders can alleviate the pledge crisis by influencing the market reaction and the suspension time of capital operations. (ii) We expand relevant research on the suspension of listed companies. So far, the literature has mainly analyzed the economic consequences of suspension. Based on the motivation for the suspension of listed companies, we find that shareholders may use this suspension to realize their own interests. (iii) Previous research has mainly focused on the measures taken by companies when faced with stock pledge risk, but there is little discussion of whether these measures can actually address this risk. We provide an answer to this question and find that improving stock prices through capital operations can resolve stock pledge risk in the short term, but the effect is not significant in the long term.

# Identification and Estimation of Earnings Management to Avoid Delisting and Satisfy SPO Conditions: Evidence from a Bunching Design Study

ZHANG Hong   WANG Xiaoquan

(Institute of Industrial Economics, Jinan University; Faculty of Economics and Management, East China Normal University)

In 2001, the China Securities Regulatory Commission (CSRC) officially cancelled the Particular Transfer (PT) of stocks and announced that listed companies reporting losses for three consecutive years will have their listings suspended within 10 days of the announcement of the third annual report. In the same year, the CSRC required listed companies that want to issue new stocks to meet the requirement that the average of the weighted average return on equity (ROE) of the previous three fiscal years must not be less than 6%. Given these regulations, listed firms are likely to attempt to manage their earnings to avoid delisting or to satisfy secondary public offering (SPO) conditions. In this paper, we use a bunching design method to estimate the earnings management frequency (how many companies manage their earnings) and the earnings management magnitude (how many companies' earnings are manipulated) from the distribution of weighted average ROE of listed companies for the 2002-2017 period using two thresholds; 0 (delisting policy) and 6% (SPO conditions). The results shed light on whether the scale of earnings management is economically significant.

Although many papers focus on the estimation of earnings management, they do not solve the problems associated with estimations in the case of multiple thresholds.Furthermore, the estimation models used have too many assumptions. Domestic research on the estimation of the earnings management of listed companies has stagnated over the last 10 years. However, many policy changes have taken place during this period, such as allowing listed companies to conduct non-public secondary issuance and the strengthening of financial supervision. Therefore, we use a new methodology—bunching design—to determine whether the previous findings still hold after such policy changes and to simultaneously estimate the frequency of earnings management at two thresholds.

In contrast to existing studies, which assume the specific form of the ROE density function, we use a polynomial function and other control variables to approximate the ROE density function beyond the threshold intervals.Estimated parameters in the approximation are used to estimate counterfactual ROE density within the threshold intervals. The difference between the counterfactual ROE density and the real ROE density yields an estimation of earnings management that represents how many firms manipulate their ROE from the left side of the threshold to the right side.

Using a bunching design, our estimations of the frequency and magnitude of earnings management show that about 3.184% of listed companies managed their earnings to avoid reporting losses, accounting for 59.25% of firms with losses if no earnings management was conducted. The counterfactual estimations suggest that about 93% of firms with an ROE within-1.5~0 engaged in earnings management. The firms that conducted earnings management increased their ROE by 2.115 percentage points on average.Although only 0.28% of listed companies managed their earnings to satisfy SPO conditions, these firms account for 58.13% of all successful SPOs. The counterfactual estimations suggest that firms with an ROE within 5~6% were most likely to engage in earnings management.

We also analyze the heterogeneity of earnings management. First, we estimate the frequency and magnitude of earnings management year-by-year.

During the 2002-2015 period, the earnings management incentives for listed companies to avoid delisting were relatively stable, but our estimations are not significant after 2016 as the CSRC strengthened its financial supervision. The proportion of companies that managed their earnings to satisfy SPO conditions was the highest in the 2002-2004 period and has fallen sharply since then, which may be attributable to the deregulation of non-public secondary issuance.Second, the frequency of earnings management for special treated (ST) companies is 3.62 times that of non-ST companies. High-leverage companies have stronger earnings management incentives to avoid delisting and satisfy SPO conditions. Finally, industry analysis suggests that the manufacturing industry has a high incidence of earnings management to avoid delisting, and that the agriculture industry has the largest magnitude of earnings management at the 0 threshold.

The conclusions of this paper have practical implications.From the macro perspective, the intention of using accounting indicators as a hard constraint to supervise listed companies is to eliminate poor-performing firms from the stock market and enable strong-performing companies to refinance. However, this policy has unintentionally strengthened firms' incentives to manage earnings to avoid delisting or having to issue additional shares. If the regulatory agency requires accounting indicators as a hard constraint of supervision, strict earnings management supervision should be supplemented to achieve the desired effect. From the micro perspective, we estimate the aspect of earnings that is most likely to be falsely reported.Regulators should focus their review and supervision efforts on these listed companies.

## Does Managerial Macro-cognition Have "Imprinting"? Evidence from the Effect of Management Style

LUO Yonggen    RAO Pingui    CHEN Can

[Institute of Capital Market and Audit Governance Studies for the Greater Bay Area (Guangdong, Hong Kong, Macau) /School of Accounting, Guangdong University of Finance & Economics; Management School, Jinan University; Faculty of Business Administration, University of Macau]

Due to the complexity of the business and economic environment, managers are faced with a large amount of complex and vague information, leading to a serious problem of information overload. However, managers have bounded rationality, which makes them unable to fully process and interpret environmental information. Managerial Macro-Cognition (MMC) refers to the managerial macro cognitive structure and cognitive process used by managers to process, interpret and apply macro environmental information in decision-making processes. Although they face the same changes in the macro environment, different managers make highly personalized interpretations and judgments, affecting their corporate policy choices and decisions. As a result, managers' perception of macro environmental information is affected by their personal experience, personality, thinking and values, thereby reflecting clear personal management styles.

This study investigates whether MMC involves a management style and its mechanism. Taking all Chinese listed firms as our sample, we use natural language processing technology to extract their macroeconomic vocabularies from the Management Discussion and Analysis (MD&A) section of their annual reports and construct an MMC measurement index to test whether MMC has a management style. The results show a clear form of individual "imprinting", that is, a management style, in MMC. Furthermore, this management style is significantly affected by the personal characteristics of managers. We find that managers' academic qualifications and overseas experience are positively correlated with the effect of management style and that the government background of managers is significantly negatively correlated with the effect of management style. Moreover, their managerial ability is significantly positively correlated with the effect of management style in MMC.

Our study contributes to the literature in several ways.

First, previous studies identify a firm's management style in its investment decisions, risk preference, tax avoidance, earnings performance and information quality.This study demonstrates that MMC also has a management style, indicating the differences in the effect of management style between different companies. This finding enriches the literature on the impacts of management style on the decision-making of Chinese enterprises. In addition, this study provides a new research perspective on managers' personal characteristics and related attributes. It provides an important reference for companies to choose suitable managers and offers empirical evidence to better understand the decision-making process of Chinese companies.

Second, previous studies have measured managerial ability in terms of individual education level, test scores, etc. (Borghans et al., 2008; Almlund et al., 2011). Firm-level research traditionally uses managers' personal experience to construct a managerial ability index, which quantifies the level of executive capability in terms of general purpose skills or professional skills (Custódio et al., 2013; Mishra, 2014; Zhao Ziye et al., 2018). From the new perspective of managers' ability to interpret and respond to changes in the macro environment, our study uses the macro environmental information contained in the MD&A section to construct the MMC index, which enables us to examine the specific reasons for the formation of managers' macro cognitive abilities.

Third, this study expands related research on managerial cognition. Prior studies have mainly focused on managers' cognitive abilities from the perspective of individual demographic characteristics. In contrast, this study measures managers' cognition of macro environmental information from the perspective of the macro environment, enriching research on managers' cognition.

Fourth, this study has practical significance. In a complex and changing economic environment, managers with higher MMC benefit their firms by allocating limited resources to more profitable projects. At the same time, giving the information asymmetry in the labor market, companies can screen senior managers based on their personal characteristics and hire managers with high MMC to improve the efficiency of enterprise decision- making.

# Does the Front-stage Behavior of Entrepreneurs Affect Firm Value? Evidence from Sina Microblogs

SUN Tong    XUE Shuang    CUI Qinghui

(School of Business, Zhejiang Wanli University; Institute of Accounting and Finance/School of Accounting, Shanghai University of Finance and Economics; College of Business, Shanghai University of Finance and Economics)

Entrepreneurs who serve as board directors or CEOs play an important role in the development of enterprises. Traditionally, they influence enterprise value mainly through back-stage behaviors, such as mapping the firm's strategy, making financing and investing decisions, or conducting operational management. With the development of information transmission in the Internet era, a revolution is occurring in business models and the management of enterprises. Increasingly, entrepreneurs are moving from the back stage to the front stage and actively interacting with the public.

With the rapid development of the Internet, the influence of we-media has increased dramatically. We-media is becoming a powerful method for transmitting information. Sina microblogs is an example of we-media that has been popular since 2010. Some entrepreneurs have registered their own Sina microblog account and use it to post news or express their viewpoints. Microblogs offer a rapid, comprehensive, and low-cost channel through which to engage with the public. However, it is a significant time investment for entrepreneurs to write or maintain a blog. Entrepreneurs are busy, and the time cost is higher for an entrepreneur than for a regular employee. There is also a reputation risk for an entrepreneur writing a blog. Considering the benefits and costs of microblogs for entrepreneurs, is it beneficial for entrepreneurs to disclose or share information or viewpoints on a microblog? There is no clear answer to this question in the literature.

Some studies focus on firms' official microblogs and find that they can effectively promote communication between enterprises and investors. Although a few papers investigate the behavior of entrepreneurs on we-media platforms and attempt to explain the effect of this behavior from the perspective of the entrepreneur's image or spirit, the impact of an entrepreneur's personal microblog on his/her firm's valuation remains unknown.

Based on the theory of information transmission, we investigate the impact of the release and content of entrepreneurs' microblogs on their firms' valuation. We use a Python script to search and process entrepreneur's microblog data from the Sina microblog platform. Other data come from the China Stock Market and Accounting Research Database. The empirical results reveal the following. (i) The front-stage behavior of an entrepreneur, which is defined as the release of a microblog, has a positive impact on the firm's value in terms of operating cash flow and reduced systematic risk. (ii) Text analysis of entrepreneurs' microblogs reveals that enterprise value is increased when the proportion of a microblog's content that is personal, frequency of the use of "@," and proportion of text with a positive tone are higher. (iii) The higher the degree of information asymmetry, the more likely the entrepreneur will be to choose to open a microblog account.

The findings in this paper fill a gap in the literature and have important implications for entrepreneurs deciding how to behave when facing the public. This paper makes four main contributions. First, we analyze the front-stage behavior of entrepreneurs through an information asymmetry framework and clarify the channels through which entrepreneurs' front-stage behavior impacts firm value.This not only enriches the literature on the economic consequences of entrepreneurs' front-stage behavior, but also expands the literature on we-media from the perspective of information disclosure and information transmission. Second, in the Internet era, the internal and external information environment of enterprises has changed in important ways. The modes of information collection and transmission must also change to match this evolving environment. Entrepreneurs need to re-examine the modes and channels of information disclosure. The findings of this study have important implications for entrepreneurs hoping to understand whether and how to make use of we-media. Third, the present literature on the impact of we-media on enterprises mainly focuses on enterprises' official microblogs. In contrast, we address entrepreneurs' personal microblogs, which is a more interesting perspective as they contain more diverse information about entrepreneur. Understanding entrepreneurs' characteristics, viewpoints, and outlooks on life and the world is critical for helping investors to interpret or predict their strategies or decisions. Fourth, This study finds that entrepreneurs can directly or indirectly transmit information related to enterprise value via their personal microblogs, which is an efficient, fair, low-cost, and sustainable method that is also in line with the development concept of modern China.